DATE DUE

Presidential Swing States

Presidential Swing States

Why Only Ten Matter

Edited by
Stacey Hunter Hecht and David Schultz

ROWMAN & LITTLEFIELD
Lanham • Boulder • New York • London

Published by Rowman & Littlefield
A wholly owned subsidary of The Rowman & Littlefield Publishing Group, Inc.
4501 Forbes Boulevard, Suite 200, Lanham, Maryland 20706
www.rowman.com

Unit A, Whitacre Mews, 26-34 Stannary Street, London SE11 4AB

British Library Cataloguing in Publication Information Available

Library of Congress Cataloging-in-Publication Data

Presidential swing states : why only ten matter / edited by David Schultz and Stacey
Hunter Hecht.
     pages cm
  Includes bibliographical references and index.
  ISBN 978-0-7391-9524-6 (cloth : alk. paper) — ISBN 978-0-7391-9525-3 (electronic)
1. Presidents—United States—Election. 2. Political culture—United States—States.
3. Voting—United States—States. I. Schultz, David A. (David Andrew), 1958- editor
of compilation. II. Hecht, Stacey Hunter.
  JK528.P76 2015
  324.973—dc23

                                                                    2015029858

∞™ The paper used in this publication meets the minimum requirements of
American National Standard for Information Sciences—Permanence of Paper
for Printed Library Materials, ANSI/NISO Z39.48-1992.

Printed in the United States of America

Contents

Acknowledgments and Dedication

To Steve and Rosie. I'd like to acknowledge my TAs Kali Schwartz and Zoe Vermeer who helped with bibliographical research, and Virginia Gray, who taught me nearly all of what I know about state politics.

Stacey

To Helene. And to all my terrific political science professors over the years who taught me well.

David

Introduction

Swing States and Presidential Elections

Stacey Hunter Hecht and David Schultz

The 2016 presidential race is arguably already over in approximately 40 states and the District of Columbia. If recent presidential election trends are any indication of what will happen in 2016, Democrats in Texas and Republicans in New York, for example, might as well stay home on election day because their votes will matter little in the presidential race. The same might be said for some partisan voters in 38 other states too. Conversely, for voters in Ohio, Florida, Iowa, and a handful of other states, their votes matter and their states will be battered with a barrage of presidential candidate visits, commercials, and political spending. Understanding the presidential race in terms of a competitive event where either one of the two major parties realistically can win a particular state is the subject of the book. The question is to explain the phenomena of swing states in presidential politics.

Although presidential elections are national affairs, they are lost or won in the states. The lessons of the 2000 presidential election remind us that in monitoring a presidential race we focus too closely on the national popular vote at our own peril. In the 2000 presidential contest that pitted Vice President Al Gore against Texas governor George Bush, pre-election polls predicted an easy victory for the former (Frankovic & McDermott 2001; Pomper 2001: 140). Even on election night exit polls forecasted that Gore would win Florida, only to find that the prediction had to be retracted (Pomper 2001: 126). What then ensued was a complicated, contentious, and litigious battle in the courts and in the media over who would eventually would win the Florida popular vote, its electoral votes, and then ultimately the presidency. The Florida 2000 controversy culminated in the Supreme Court's *Bush v. Florida* decision that invalidated the recount procedures in four counties on Equal Protection grounds and, more importantly, declared a controversial halt to any recounts, effectively then declaring George Bush the winner of the state's popular vote by 327 votes, enough to give him the 271 electoral votes to win the presidency (Greene 2001).

Florida 2000 offers many lessons about presidential campaigns. Some ask what impact the presence of third-party candidates such as Ralph Nader and Pat Buchanan had on the election. Other critics expressed concern about ballot design, voter fraud, or voter suppression (Gillman 2001). All of these are valid and important items when it comes to understanding presidential elections, at least when it came to Florida 2000. But the election also spoke to several other issues. First, this was the fourth presidential election in American history where the winner of the popular vote did not win the election. The other three were the election of John Quincy Adams in 1824 (Andrew Jackson was the popular vote winner), 1876 when Bill Tilden won the popular but lost to Rutherford Hayes, and in 1888 when Grover Cleveland won the popular vote but lost the Electoral College to Benjamin Harrison. The split between the winner of the national popular vote and the electoral vote is a reminder that presidential elections are won or lost at the state level. Essentially, there is really no national presidential election; it takes place in 50 individual states plus the District of Columbia.

Underscoring the fact that the presidential election is not really national but a state-by-state contest is the fact that rules for voter eligibility too are mainly set by the individual states. For the most part, who can vote, how, and where are issues states decide. There is no national electorate for the presidency—each state defines who its electorate is, subject to some parameters set by the US Constitution and federal legislation. The fact, for example, that voter identification laws or felon disenfranchisement regulations differ across the 50 states again speaks to the more local or state-based nature of presidential elections.

But if presidential elections are 51 separate contests (50 states plus the District of Columbia) one would think there actually would be 51 Floridas. By that, there would be 51 closely contested state races where the major candidates compete vigorously for votes, as evidenced by the number of visits or money spent in those states. By the reality is that Florida or Floridas are outliers. The vast majority of states—approximately 40 states or 80%—are hardly competitive at all. These are states where comparatively speaking, presidential candidates seldom visit or spend money and where, often to the relief of voters, there are few political commercials. It is in these 40 states one can say that one knows in advance who will win that state.

The main reason or reasons why 80% of the presidential contests are uncontested or predictable has to do with several factors. One is party identification. Party identification remains a powerful predictor of voting (Campbell 1964; Verba and Nie 1972; Miller and Shanks 1996; Lewis-Beck 2011;

Pomper 1975). In many states one party or another has sufficient dominance that it is unlikely to lose a presidential race. Second, in some states one party might be sufficiently well organized or better organized and mobilized than another and that gives it a competitive advantage. Third, the policy preferences of the state, or even its ideological orientations vis-a-vis the rest of the nation, may make it more liberal or conservative than the rest of the country as a whole, thereby pushing the presidential race or electorate more firmly in the direction of one party as opposed to another (Erikson, Wright, and McIver 1993).

Thus, states such as New York or California seem firmly in the camp of the Democratic Party for now, while Texas, Oklahoma, and Wyoming are certain winners for Republican presidential candidates. This means perhaps that voters of the minority party might effectively have little incentive to even vote, or that some voters will choose not to vote because they do not think it will matter (Nivola 2005). Of course this is not completely true. If no one voted or if voters stayed home thinking casting a ballot was futile or unnecessary, such action, replicated on a larger scale, might change election outcomes and make uncompetitive states competitive. Further, states that may be non-competitive at the presidential level may nonetheless be competitive for other races or offices down the ballot (although increasingly there is evidence, although mixed, of the nationalization of local politics and a polarization in voting that carries further down the ballot) (Keeter 2014).

But beyond the 40 reliable states and the District of Columbia that vote consistently and predictably for one party, there is a small core that do not. These are the states such as Florida 2000 where the outcome is not certain in advance and where their allegiance to either the Democrats or Republicans is in doubt. These are states in which candidates travel, parties spend money, and where the balance of power and the winner of the presidential election is really determined. These are the swing-states.

THE CONCEPT OF A SWING STATE

The phenomena of a state being labeled a swing state is largely a product of the media and recent campaign invention. The idea of a swing state goes far back into American presidential campaign history. As will be discussed more fully below, the swing-state phenomena is a construct of the current way states apportion electoral votes. But back in the nineteenth and early twentieth centuries there were always states that were the focus of presidential campaigns because they were perceived to be close. In the 1888 presidential race, New York, Ohio, Connecticut, and Indiana, for example, were perceived as decisive to Benjamin Harrison's victory over Grover Cleveland, even though the latter received more popular votes than the former (Baumgarden 1984). In 1896 the race between William McKinley and William Jennings Bryan saw Ohio and Indiana as closely contested races, but others such as Oregon, California, and Kentucky were fiercely challenged too (Fite 2001). In 1948 Harry Truman actually defeated Thomas Dewey, newspaper headlines to the contrary, with the winner of Ohio, California, Indiana, Illinois, and New York decided by less than one percent of the popular vote (Gullan 1998). And in the close 1960 race between Richard Nixon and John Kennedy, ten states, including Missouri, New Mexico, and Texas were won by less than two percent (six by less than one percent) (White 1980). In each of the races candidates concentrated their resources campaigning in a finite number of states, largely assuming that the others were safely on their side. These were the main battleground states for presidential elections.

Conversely, journalists love predictions and horse races. The same may be true of political pundits. They are constantly in search of oracles or signs of what is to come–sort of looking to ghosts of Christmas present to give them insights into the ghosts of Christmas future. Much of political reporting often focuses on a particular race, such as the 1991 special US Senate election in Pennsylvania where Harris Wofford defeated Richard Thornburgh, running on the issue of health care (Starr 1991). His election was deemed by some to set the theme of health care reform that Bill Clinton successfully trumpeted in his victory in 1992. Thus, political operatives and journalists often search for narratives, signs, or test cases to offer predictions for what will happen in the future. For campaigns, this is searching for data on strategy, for journalists this is the essence of political reporting much in the same way that surveys and polls have become mainstays of news.

Maine was seen as a nineteenth-century bellwether state. From 1832 to 1932 Maine went with the winning candidate 19 out of 26 races (73%). Its status spawned the well-quoted phrase "[as] Maine goes so goes the nation," only to have it derisively ended when in 1936 Alf Landon won Maine and Vermont, but otherwise was routed by Franklin Roosevelt. "As Maine goes, so goes Vermont" was the sarcastic conclusion of some after that election, thereby ending the state's reputation as a bellwether. New Mexico from the 1912 until and including the 1972 election cast its electoral votes with the candidate who won the presidency (100%).

But in presidential politics perhaps the most famous bellwether state is Missouri. From 1904 to 2004 (with the notable exception of 1956 when Adlai Stevenson defeated Dwight Eisenhower) Missouri voted with the winner of the presidential election 25 of 26 races or 96%. Reasons for its bellwether status, as will be discussed in the chapter on it in this book, range from it being the geographic center of the United States to its demographic profile being identical to the rest of the US in terms of urban versus rural, ethnicity, and party alignments. But its status as a bellwether ended with the 2008 presidential election when John McCain won the state (but only by less than 4,000 votes or 0.13 % of the vote) despite losing to Barack Obama. Missouri again went with the losing candidate in 2012 voting for Mitt Romney over Barack Obama. Missouri is now 0–2, but still has a better record than Maine had as a bellwether over a 100 year period; thus this may not spell an end to its special predictive status in presidential elections.

Yet the terms battleground and bellwether states are closely related to but are a phenomena often confused with and perhaps conceptually different from that of being a swing state. Frequent use of the term swing state is a relatively recent phenomena among journalists, even though as Scott McLean points out in chapter 1 that the first use of the term dates back to 1936 and the *New York Times*. For example, using the EBSCO host Advanced Academic Search Premier data base, the first instance of the use of the term "swing state" appears in a 2000 *New York Times* article by Richard Perez-Pena. Perez-Pena opens his article by stating: "Making his campaign premiere in the Rocky Mountain states, Senator Joseph I. Lieberman of Connecticut said today that the Democrats now see Colorado, long dominated by Republicans, as a swing state, and they plan to contest it vigorously." Lieberman is not quoted as directly using the term swing state, but Perez-Pena attributes such a sentiment or description to him in terms of how he described that state..

The next day another *New York Times* piece by R.W. Apple describes the shifting of several swing states toward Al Gore and away from George Bush during the presidential election. A few weeks later, again in the *New York Times*, James Dao's article headlined "Democrats Ask Nader to Back Gore in Swing States" (Dao 2000). Then again Richard Perez-Pena on November 6, 2000 (A24) in the *New York Times* headlines an article with "Lieberman Races to Energize Democrats in Swing States." Thus the *New York Times*, Perez-Pena and Dao, or perhaps Senator Lieberman, seem to be the inventors of the term in reference to a state that was once leaning one way politically in the presidential race but now potentially moving in a different direction. Yet once more in the 2000 election cycle the term swing states is used. It is in a post-election piece by Eleanor Clift (2000) in *Newsweek* entitled "Calling All Swing States."

In the 2004 election cycle, the Advanced Academic database produced 24 journalistic articles using the term "swing state." It is really in this election that the term came into popular usage. By 2008 a similar search produced only eight references to swing states. Perhaps that drop was indicative of an election that really was not close and where polls from early on suggested that

Obama would easily defeat John McCain (Pomper 2010: 56-58). But then in 2012 there were 90 references to swing-states in the Advanced Academic Search Premier data base. By then swing-states had become a term of art, at least among journalists. For comparison, a "swing states" keyword search of the on-line *New York Times* database or archive of their articles produced 139 references in 2000, 321 in 2004, 231 in 2008, and 581 in 2012. According to Ostermeier (2012) in a study of journalistic terminology from January to July 2012 found that swing state was the preferred term of art overall, narrowly edging out battleground state. He found that during this time period swing state was used in 1,154 broadcast reports, slightly ahead of battleground with 1,092 usages. Swing state was preferred by CBS, FOX, MSNBC, NBC, and NPR, whereas ABC and CNN preferred battleground. Ostermeier also contended that the use of swing state goes back at least to 1986 when ABC used it, although neither its frequency or whether swing state was the preferred term is clear.

But how was the term swing state deployed? In "It's All About the Swing States" (Newman 2012), swing state is defined as a toss-up state, one of eight (at the time of this article) that were deemed possibilities that either Obama or Romney could win in 2012. These states included New Hampshire, Virginia, Florida, Ohio, Iowa, Wisconsin, Colorado, and Nevada. Page (2012) defines swing states as those "that typically decide the outcome of presidential elections." Arguing that "In 12 swing states, they're starting from scratch," Page uses swing states interchangeably with battleground states. The same is true according to Feldman: "Obama leads in three key swing states, but Romney can still sway voters" (Feldman 2012). The *Almanac of American Politics 2014* e-book edition refers to swing states in three places (Barone 2013: 16050, 21985, 88704), using the term in reference to states which were battleground or competitive, such as Florida and Wisconsin. Zelenkauskaite, Gao, and Rich (2012: 90, 99) note how beginning around 2000 journalists such as Tim Russert began using the term "swing state" interchangeably with battleground and "purple" states. Purple referred to states neither liberal or conservative, left/right, or Democrat or Republican.

Other print or digital media usages of the term that appeared in the Advanced Academic Search Premier data base used swing state interchangeably with battleground states, bellwethers, or in reference to states where polls suggested competitive elections. Yet not surprisingly, swing-states as a concept is not well defined or consistently given a meaning beyond being used as a substitute term for the others noted above.

Why the increased use of the term since the 2000 presidential elections? There are several possible reasons. One is simply a new chosen word or phrase that can be used in lieu of battleground, competitive, or bellwether state. Thus, it is simply a rhetorical construct. Second, it is a term first used by happenstance either by senator and then vice-presidential candidate Joseph Lieberman in 2000, or at least a term a *New York Times* reporter attributed to him or his description of Colorado in terms of its status in the presidential race. This use of the term too is simply a rhetorical choice of words.

But another possibility is that swing state describes the emergence of a real and emerging phenomena in American presidential politics. For example, political scientists have noted the declining competitiveness of many races across the country—in David Mayhew's (1974) terms, declining marginals, at least when it come to congressional races. A similar phenomena may be occurring at the state level, especially when it comes to presidential campaigns. The roots of this may have something to do with the polarization of American politics and the changes in the political composition of the two major parties. This polarization may be part of a long-term realignment of the parties, especially with the transformation of the once solid Democrat south turning Republican (Benen 2014). There is also the argument that people are increasingly making political-geographic choices–the big sort according to Bill Bishop (2009). All of this is producing what journalists and pop culture refer to as the creation of red and blue states, with the former representing states solidly Republican and the latter Democrat. These changes are producing a new and real phenomena–a decline in the real number of states that are competitive where either one of the major party candidates has a real chance of winning. Rob Richie and Fairvote effectively make this claim (Koza et al. 2013). Thus, swing states may be a real phenomena, but if the term simply refers to competitiveness, then there have always been swing states and the concept is not new but simply describes a something that has always been around.

How is swing state to be understood then? While scholars may not like Wikipedia, its popular usage and impact is significant. Wikipedia's definition of the term is: "In presidential politics of the United States, a swing state (also, battleground state or purple state (in reference to red states and blue states) is a state in which no single candidate or party has overwhelming support in securing that state's electoral college votes" (Wikipedia 2015). In one of the first journalistic pieces seeking to describe swing states, reporter Meghann Cuniff (2004) of the *Oregon Daily Emerald* defined a swing state as "a state where political affiliations are not distinctly cemented—they can swing from one candidate to another." In this article she quoted political scientist Joel Bloom as declaring that campaigning in swing states is different from campaigning nationally. Because of the Electoral College "it makes no sense at all for a candidate to spend time in a state that's not a swing state." Dictionary.com (2015) defines swing state as "a state of the U.S. in which the Democratic and Republican candidates both have a good chance of winning." Dictionary.com also lists swing states as referred to as battleground or purple states.

Oxford Dictionary on line pronounces that a swing state is a "US state where the two major political parties have similar levels of support among voters, viewed as important in determining the overall result of a presidential election." About Politics (2015) offers two definitions: " A swing state in American politics is one that has a high probability of tipping the balance in presidential elections in favor of one candidate," and a "swing state can also be one in which voters alternately support Democrats and Republicans in presidential elections. These states are also referred to as battleground states." Al Jazeera offers a more nuanced definition of swing states, indicating that they are "states that have voted for presidential candidates from both major parties since 2000, and that are also expected to be close this year" (Haddad and Bollier 2012). This definition or usage of the term swing state indicates a state that has demonstrated its capacity to flip from support for a Democratic or Republican presidential candidate over three recent elections. Using its methodology, it calculated eight states, Maine, Virginia, North Carolina, Florida, Ohio, Iowa, Colorado, and Nevada, as swing.

The *Dictionary of American Government and Politics* (2010) offers a definition of swing states.

> Swing states are states in which no single party dominates, resulting in intense competition for victory in presidential and other elections. States such as New Jersey are liable to switch from one party to another and therefore have a significant role in determining the outcome of contests. When those states have a large population, they carry sizeable weight in the Electoral College. They are therefore the focus of strong campaigning for parties and their candidates, with heavy financial and personnel resources being devoted to them.

Overall, it is clear from these few definitions, as well as the others provided by journalists and pop culture references, the concept swing state is not precisely defined.

SWING STATES AND POLITICAL SCIENCE

Political scientists have generally not studied or examined the concept of swing states as a distinct presidential election phenomena, except in terms of analyzing it either in ways similar to journalists, or describing them as competitive states.

A keyword search of Political Research Online on February 22, 2015 encompassing papers from APSA conventions 2002–2005 yielded no results for swing states. Similarly a review of the Social Science Research Network (SSRN) on the same date produced only six responses for "swing states," none of which yielded a significant discussion of the topic at all, let alone in terms of understanding or explaining why some states are bellwether, battlegrounds, or competitive. Among the introduction to American politics textbooks, William Bianco and David T. Canon's *American Politics Today* (2015), use the term twice (314, 342), in reference to a discussion of the Electoral College. They note how in 2012 Romney and Obama concentrated their campaign strategies on nine states, identifying them as states where "neither candidate was significantly ahead" (342). In fact, there was little discussion explaining why these states were even competitive. Ken Kollman's *The American Political System* uses swing states in reference to Ohio and Florida to refer to states which were "key" and decided by small margins (473). In John Geer et al. (2014), the third edition of their book *Gateways to Democracy: An Introduction to American Government* on page 332 has a subsection titled swing states and here the authors distinguish battleground from swing states, with the latter discussed in the context of presidential elections. Based on this limited sample of three books, there is no clear sense in terms of how "swing-state" is used or what it means. An examination of other introductory texts found many did not use the term or used concepts such as purple states, competitive, or battleground states.

Examination of recent books on presidential elections yields no or little discussion of swing states. The classic election series first edited by Gerald Pomper that covers elections from 1980 to 2000 produces no references to the use of the term swing states. Nor does Pomper refer to that term in his 1975 *Voters Choice: Varieties of Electoral Behavior*. In his *The Election of 2000* Pomper does reference or use the term "critical states" or "close states" to explain some of the campaign activity of Bush and Gore (134, 139), and one of the chapters in this anthology by Kathleen Frankovic and Monika McDermott uses the term swing voters (74). Michael Nelson took over from Pomper the editing of this series and in *The Elections of 2004* (Nelson 2005), in his chapter Pomper for the first time uses the term swing state in reference to Ohio (59) but otherwise uses the term competitive to refer to some states. In *The Elections of 2008* (Nelson 2009) Pomper again refers to swing voters but not swing states (52). And in Michael Nelson's *The Elections of 2012* (2013) Marc Hetherington's discussion of the presidential contest uses the term "battleground states" (66–7).

Elsewhere, in Michael Nelson's *The Elections of 2000* (2001) his chapter on the presidential contest discusses swing voters but not swing states (67-8). Mary Stuckey in Robert Denton's *The 2004 Presidential Campaign: A Communication Perspective* (2005) talks about both Bush and Kerry mostly campaigning in swing states and seeking to "swing the vote" (58-9). In the tenth edition of Nelson Polsby and Aaron Wildavsky's classic *Presidential Elections* (2000) they argue that the Electoral College creates an incentive to campaign for the big-state votes (most populous) (53) and how voter turnout seems to favor Republicans (189), but there is no discussion of swing states. Additionally, Kathleen Hall Jamieson's *Electing the President, 2012: An Insiders' View* (2013) references swing voters but no discussion of swing states. To the extent that states are viewed as competitive it is because of the existence of swing voters.

Political scientists use "competitive state" (Johnson 2005) to refer to a similar phenomena. In the political science literature "competitive" or "tight" states have usually been defined as those where Democratic and Republican popular vote totals fall within five percentage points of one another (James and Lawson 1999; Johnson 2005). This concept of competitiveness, as Mayhew applied it as noted above when it comes to Congress, is about declining marginals. For Congress, this is the general decrease in the number of competitive seats and the rise of more safe ones. Some estimates such as by Congressman Steve Israel are that congressionally there are only 60 to 75 truly competitive seats as of 2015, with the vast majority being solidly Democrat or Republican (Leonhardt 2015). Nate Silver in 2012 estimated only about 35 (Silver 2012).

Applied to presidential contests, one could see a phenomena where over time there are fewer and fewer states that are competitive, i.e., with the winning candidate capturing the state by less than five percent of the vote. In 2012 for example, only four states–Florida, North Carolina, Ohio, and Virginia could have been classified as competitive. In 2008 it was seven states, in 2004 it was 11, and in 2000 it was 12. Evidence of declining marginal or competitive states may be seen just in these four elections. But taking a broader perspective, since 1960 there have been 14 presidential elections. During that time there has been a total of 149 competitive state races, averaging out to 10.64 competitive races per election cycle. This longer cycle does not necessarily reveal a longer-term pattern of declining competitiveness; in 1964, 1972, and 1984, there were fewer competitive presidential state races than in the last four elections. Instead, there may be periods of declining or increasing competitiveness across states attributable to many factors such as changing demographics and policy preferences of electorates or the political positions of presidential candidates or national parties. Or it could be something as simple as the quality of candidates in particular races.

**Table X.I. Number of Competitive
Presidential States per Election: 1960-2012**

Year	Number of Competitive States
1960	20
1964	3
1968	13
1972	0
1976	20
1980	16
1984	3
1988	12
1992	17
1996	11
2000	12
2004	11
2008	7
2012	4

Perhaps the origin of thinking about competitiveness in presidential elections begins with V.O. Key. His *Southern Politics in State and Nation* (1949) offered a critical examination of southern politics, noting, especially in the case of presidential elections (but also further down the ticket) how the Democrats had a firm control on elected offices in this region. Part of this solid south was a legacy of slavery, the Civil War, and Reconstruction politics. But the point was that the south was solidly Democrat, giving them a fair share of electoral votes that they did not have to contest. For all intents and purposes, the South was not a battleground and there was little evidence that states here were either bellwethers or harbingers of what would happen in the presidential election overall.

Yet the solid South broke up and in many ways has flipped. Beginning first with Barry Goldwater's 1964 campaign and more so with Richard Nixon in 1968, they appealed to Southern conservative whites upset with the Democrats support for civil rights. Indeed, President Johnson with his signing of the 1964 Civil Rights Act is purported to have said that this legislation meant that Democrats would lose the south for the rest of the century. Writers such as Thomas Edsell (Edsell and Edsell 1991) and Marie Gottschalk (2015: 148) essentially agreed with this sentiment that the Southern strategy helped flip the South. Over a period of perhaps 20 if not 30 years the South has changed from solidly Democrat to solidly Republican. In the process these states—mostly constituting what was once the Confederacy—have become uncompetitive and certainly no bellwethers. The two exceptions are Virginia and to some extent North Carolina, which in the last three presidential election cycles have been both competitive and in the case of North Carolina, flipped from Republican to Democrat and back to Republican again.

A simple answer explaining this shift in competitiveness may be located in the concept of political culture. Daniel Elazar's *A View from the States* (1966) distinguishes three basic political cultures in the United States–moralistic, individualistic, and traditional–and he describes the origin and spread across the country as a result of forces such as original settlement and immigration patterns. These political cultures bring with them patterns of political orientation and policy preference. Presumably, then, as state political cultures change, as a result of immigration and demographic shifts, states might become more or less competitive, perhaps even flipping from support for one party or another at the presidential level. While political culture analyses provide an interesting answer, they leave many questions unaddressed. They assume politics or policy preferences flow simply from demographics (Erikson, Wright, and McIver 1993), or that somehow cultural values are distinct from people themselves, or that attitudes are not affected by political institutions. The field of comparative politics, for example, offers a rich debate on the merits of political culture as an explanatory value, noting strengths and weaknesses (Lim 2010; Bill and Hardgrave 1973). In many ways, referencing political culture as a reason for why states are competitive is a description without an explanation.

Another possible way political scientists could potentially explain the concept of swing states is via voting studies and behavior. Dating back to the 1950s political scientists have examined the determinants of voting behavior and voter choice. In the original *American Voter* (Campbell, Converse, Miller, and Stokes 1966) the authors articulate the concept of the "normal vote." Voting preference and turnout are strongly correlated with partisan identification. Specifically, the more strongly partisan one, is the more likely one is to vote in general and also to cast ballots in a straight party line fashion. One of the early paradoxes of voting studies sought to explain voting behavior among Democrats. More individuals identified as Democrats yet they seemed to be less likely to turn out in some elections, especially in non-presidential years. This led political scientists to consider other factors, such as social demographic variables that include race, class, and gender, as additional factors that impact voter turnout (Lewis-Beck et al, 2011; Miller and Shanks 1996). While voting studies since the publication of the *American Voter* have articulated many reasons to explain why some people do not vote, the core thesis that there is a connection between voting decisions and the depth of partisan attachment remains consistent and valid.

Voting studies thus can provide valuable insights into perhaps why some states are more competitive than others. For example, there is significant evidence that party identification has declined over the last 30 or 40 years. While at one point in the 1950s only 6–9% of those surveyed indicated that they were not a member of the two major parties (Lewis-Beck et al, 2011: 114), more recent studies suggest a hollowing out of partisan identification. According to the 2012 presidential exit polls, 38% of the American public identified as Democrat, 32% Republican, and 29% as independent or something else (*Washington Post* 2012). Some political scientists question whether nearly 30% of the public is really independent, contending instead that many of these voters actually do lean or vote for one party or another. The suggestion is that perhaps less than 10% of the voters are truly independent (Lewis-Beck et al. 2011: 115).

Yet whether the number is 29% or something significantly less, these independent voters may be critical to explaining why some states are competitive or swing. First, these voters have weaker attachments to the major parties than other voters. This weaker attachment might explain why some vote at all and if they do vote, why they might demonstrate patterns of switching from one party to another when casting ballots. Thus, with potentially up to 30% of the voters in play or even the more conservative 10%, one might explain competitiveness as a situation where in some states there are greater concentrations of independent voters than others, and their decision if and how to vote could affect the outcome of presidential elections. This is especially the case in states where no one party commands a 50%+1 support among its electorate but which votes in high percentages for its candidates.

This discussion of the rise of independent voters has produced some analysis of what some refer to as swing voters. Linda Killian's *The Swing Voter: The Untapped Power of Independents* (2011) identifies the swing voter as

> . . . not reliably conservative or liberal. Many of them never registered with a party and have been Independent voters their entire lives. Others are former Republicans and Democrats who became disaffected with their parties because of social or economic policies. Many Independents say they have been driven from the two parties by their extremism and a failure to focus on the nation's most important issues. Independent voters think the parties care more about winning elections than about solving the nation's problems, and they have largely lost faith in the two-party system. Nearly two-thirds of these voters say they believe both parties care more about special interests than about average Americans (Killian 17).

Killian goes on to note how these voters swing back and forth in terms of the parties they are voting for. These voters are geographically disbursed across the country, but are especially concentrated in swing states such as New Hampshire, Colorado, Ohio, Virginia, Florida, and Pennsylvania (17).

She sees these voters as often determining the outcome of elections, especially in Florida 2000.

In constructing the profile of swing voters Killian as a journalist relies not on statistical analysis of aggregate data but instead on interviews. She finds the swing voters to be socially moderate and fiscally conservative, comprising what once used to be the Rockefeller Republicans (Killian 19). They moved away from the party especially during the George W. Bush years, presumably because of his stance on the war in Iraq and because of a shifting of the overall Republican party to the right. The other group of swing voters she identifies are voters who used to be called Reagan Democrats—largely male, working-class voters in the Midwest and rust belt. They stand for what Killian calls an "American first" policy of protectionism and policies to benefit this country first. They are socially conservative too (20).

A third constituency among the swing voters are those under 35—members of the Gen X and Millennial generations. These are voters enamored by Obama's promise of a post-partisan politics, and they are distrustful of traditional party labels, seeing them as not adequately capturing their social libertarianism and fiscal conservatism (Killian 21). Other studies similarly support the decreased party attached among Millennials (Pew Research Center 2011). The final and largest group of swing voters for Killian are the suburban and exurban moms and dads. They are socially moderate and are concerned about education and national security issues (Killian 21–22). While Killian calls them the Starbucks moms and dads, they might be the proverbial soccer moms and dads.

The focus of Killian's book is a chapter-by-chapter profile of these four groups, describing them through the eyes of interviews with particular individuals. For each of her four swing voter profiles she connects them to particular states, New Hampshire (Rockefeller Republicans), Colorado (Gen Xers and Millennials), Virginia (her Starbucks moms and dads), and Ohio (the home of the Reagan Democrats). Killian especially describes Ohio as the ultimate swing state. The final focus of her book is in her assertion that these new swing voters want to fix the political system and she muses on their ability to bring what she calls sanity to Congress and the polarization facing the country.

Killian's journalistic account is backed up by some research that supports her profiles. For example, a Pew 2011 study found evidence that Millennials, even though leaning Democrat, also were more skeptical of traditional party politics and less likely to align with a party than previous generations. But the strength of the book is in its connection between examining swing voters and how they produce swing states or competitive states.

There are few political science books on swing voters, with William G. Mayer's *The Swing Voter in American Politics* (2008) perhaps being the most detailed. This brief edited volume questions first whether swing voters really do swing (Clymer and Winneg 2008), and how independent they really are. Despite self-description as independent, they may nonetheless still vote more for one party than another. However, Mayer defines a swing voter as

> . . . a voter who could go either way: a voter who is not so solidly committed to one candidate or the other as to make all efforts at persuasion futile. . . . Put another way, swing voters are ambivalent, or to use a term with a somewhat better political science linage, cross-pressured. (Mayer 2)

Swing voters express cross-pressures to vote in different ways. They are effectively the Seymour Martin Lipset political man (1960); voters with multiple social cleavages or allegiances that leave them neither fully supportive of the two major parties (Mayer 3). Mayer operationalizes his definition of the swing voter, using American National Election Studies (ANES) data. Using the ANES feeling thermometer questions about the two parties that asks for a rating on a scale of 0-100 (with 100 being a strong positive feeling), Meyer contends that voters who rate the two parties are no more than a -15 or +15 difference between them would be classified as swing voters (Mayer 9). Comparing data from the 1972 to the 2004 presidential elections, he finds an average of 23% of the voters qualify as swing voters, with the high point being 1975 (34%) and the low 2004 (13%) (Mayer 9). His analysis does not show any historical pattern in a rise in the number of swing voters.

But Mayer extends his analysis, asking about how people identify themselves for partisan reasons and how they actually vote in presidential elections. He does this by recognizing that some partisans do not vote straight party line whereas self-identified independents might tend to vote in a specific direction. He takes ANES data on this and crosstabulates it with his data on swing voters, finding only about 13% of independents are swingers (Mayer 12). Mayer also examines other categories of voters, such as party switchers and undecideds, finding they do not fully explain or account for all the individuals who constitute swing voters. Mayer then connects his efforts to identify swing voters to earlier research on the topic, specifically Stanley Kelley's *Interpreting Elections* (1983), which Mayer describes as the only other political science scholarship offering a sustained examination of this voter. Kelley too employed ANES to identify what he called "marginal voters," yet he drew upon open-ended questions which asked respondents questions about the two major parties. In then end, Mayer sees parallels between the voters he labels as swing and those whom Kelley labeled as marginal.

Why is this discussion of swing voters significant? Mayer contends that it is the swing voter who controls the balance of power in elections. Elections are won or lost based on how well the two major parties mobilize their bases and then sway swing voters to their side (Mayer 20). For example, in the 2004 presidential election he contends that the base Democrat vote constituted 42% of the voters, with 96% of them voting for Kerry. The Republican base constituted 45% of the voters, and 98% voted for Bush. That then left 13% of those who voted as swing voters and 53% went for Kerry. However, Bush won both because the GOP had a larger base and because more of them voted for him. Dating back to 1972, presidential elections are won or lost based on the size of candidate's party base, the percentage that vote for him, and the percentage of swing voters also voting for him. Mayer also contends that dating back to 1972 and through the 2004 election, the percentage of voters whom he classifies as swing has fallen to 13%; down from a high of 27% in 1980.

Compared to non-swing voters, swings are less partisan and slightly more moderate in their political views (Mayer 23). They are also less involved and less informed about politics compared to non-swing voters (Mayer 25). Finally, swing voters are demographically diverse, with Catholics as the only overrepresented subgroup. Other authors in Mayer's book reach slightly different conclusions and measurements regarding who the swing voter is (Shaw 2008; Dimock, Clark, and Horowitz 2008), but they do not fundamentally contest his core findings. Moreover, Lori Wright's *Swing Voters? Catholic Voting Behavior in U.S. Presidential Elections From 1992 to 2004* and Philip D. Dalton's *Swing Voters: Understanding Late-deciders in Late Modernity* parallel many of the arguments made in the Mayer book. Catholics seem to be the voters most in flux or swinging, at least during the time period studied by Wright, and the swing voter for Dalton is generally less well informed and partisan than non-swing voters.

If Mayer is correct in his analysis of the size and profile of the swing voter it is somewhat easy to connect this discussion to swing states in presidential elections. Swing states presumably would be those which have a greater percentage of swing voters or, more particularly, states where the relative bases of the two major parties are equal and the swings are of sufficient number to affect the outcome of elections. Thus, it would be simple to argue that swing states are those with a percentage of swing voters sufficiently numerous and where the bases for the two parties are sufficiently at parity compared to non-swing states.

Mayer's book does suggests that demographics are the key to understanding whether a particular state is a swing state. Demographic shifts are critical to many explanations for political behavior in American politics. Journalist Bill Bishop's *The Big Sort* (2009) contends that there is a political geographic overlay in the US, with individuals increasingly choosing where to live based on the political affiliations of their neighbors—we like to live near others who share our political views. Some argue that such a political sorting is exaggerated (Glaeser and Ward 2005). This tendency explains a political clumping of Democrats and Republicans in some neighborhoods or areas. At the congressional level such a phenomena, if accurate, explains the difficulty in apportioning districts to make them competitive and it might also explain the declining number of marginal districts. Applied to presidential elections, the sorting or clumping of voters across states might explain why some states are more solidly devoted to one party or another. It, along with long-term political or critical realignment trends, may explain the gravitation of some voters, such as pro-life Catholics or southern whites who are hostile to the Democrat Party's embrace of civil rights, to the Republican Party (Edsell and Edsell 1991).

Changing demographics is central to one of the few books examining the swing state phenomena—Ruy Teixeira's *America's New Swing Region: Changing Politics and Demographics in the Mountain West* (2012). This edited anthology focuses in on six states, Idaho, Nevada, Utah, Colorado, New Mexico, and Arizona, contending that because of changing demographics these states have a potential to become more supportive of Democrats in the future. This is especially the case for Arizona and Colorado. For the various authors in this book, increases in the Hispanic population, an exodus of Californians to these states, urbanization, and a rising Millennial generation of voters less attached to the current two parties is creating a demographic mixture that is transforming these states from once solid Republican to more swing if not future Democrat voting majorities.

While there is much to praise in the Teixeira book, it suffers from two deficiencies. First, it is not a systematic attempt to define or identify swing states. It is more isolated to exploring six states in the Mountain West. Second, the book automatically assumes that changing demographics is enough to account for transforming a state's politics or rendering it a swing state. While there may be correlations between demographics and voting, one needs to be careful not to over argue this point.

Robert Erikson, Gerald Wright, and John McIver make this point in their *Statehouse Democracy* (1993). They contend that simple appeals to demographics are insufficient explanations to why some states are liberal or conservative, or why they legislate specific policies. Instead, they assert that one needs to connect demographics to ideology which then informs policy outcomes (182). Applying their argument to presidential elections, Erikson, Wright, and McIver declare:

> The patterns of ideology and partisanship we find in the states are not simple reflections of the demographics of the states. We find that the states have distinct ideological centers of gravity and patterns of partisan attachment that are not attributable simply to the social and economic characteristics of our respondents. The importance of this finding is that it demonstrates that states, as political communities, do have values and traditions that can be measured with survey research and are explainable in terms of a shared common political culture. State publics are, in a sense, more than the sum of their demographic parts. (244–5)

According to the authors, state socioeconomic variables do not drive ideology, they reflect them. Applying their findings to presidential politics they argue that one needs to understand how a state's overall ideology and partisanship stand in relationship to national partisanship. By that, if the state's ideology moves its parties to the left or right vis-à-vis the national parties and candidates, that will impact how the state votes in a presidential race. According to the authors:

> The dependence is revealed by the way state partisanship correlates with state-level voting for president, for which the relevant party positions are nationally fixed rather than variable by state. Where state partisanship is skewed Republican by overly liberal parties, presidential voting is more Democratic than one would expect; where state partisanship is skewed Democratic by overly conservative parties, presidential voting is more Republican than one would expect. (246)

One needs to understand where the median voter is in a specific state compared to that nationally for a particular party. Using their analysis, non-swing states are those where there is a correlation between median voters in a state and the presidential candidates of a party. Conversely, swing states are those where the median voter is somewhere between that of the position of the two national parties, and where neither of the two state parties have a sufficient number of supporters to be able to amass a majority on their own. Swing states have more centrist median voters compared to the national parties, thereby creating a scenario where there are enough voters who are not attached to straight party line voting.

In addition to Teixeira's book on swing states, examination of the phenomena is generally thin. For example, Tova Wang, Samuel Oliker-Friedland, Melissa Reiss, and Kristen Oshyn published a 2008 report "Voting in 2008:

Ten Swing States," in cooperation with Common Cause and the Century Foundation (Wang 2008). Its focus was not on explaining swing states but on looking at voting laws in what they describe as seven battleground states: Florida, Georgia, Michigan, Missouri, Ohio, Pennsylvania, and Wisconsin, plus three others they consider to be close in 2008, Colorado, New Mexico, and Virginia (3). There is no methodological explanation as to how these states were selected and since the focus was on voting laws, there is no reason to think that the report should have addressed this issue.

Another major study that at least indirectly examines the swing-state phenomena is John Koza, John R. Barry Fadem, Mark Grueskin, Michael S. Mandel, Robert Richie, and Joseph F. Zimmerman's *Every Vote Equal: A State-Based Plan for Electing the President* (2013). This is an advocacy book prepared by a coalition favoring a reform of presidential elections and the Electoral College. They advocate for what is called the national popular vote, an interstate state compact which would require states to allocate their electoral votes according to the outcome of the national popular vote.

In making their case for this alternative schema for selecting the president they make two arguments. First, the use of the Electoral College is anti-democratic or at least out-of-date and it produces perverse effects, as evidenced by George W. Bush's victory over the popular vote winner Al Gore in 2000. Second, this coalition points outs that increasingly presidential candidates are making campaign visits to fewer and fewer states. In the 2012 presidential election, only 12 states received post-convention campaign visits or events, with four of these states—Ohio, Florida, Virginia, and Iowa—the recipient of two-thirds of these events. This pattern, they assert, is a consequence of the winner-take-all allocation of electoral votes in 48 states.

The National Popular Vote coalition further contends that this candidate pattern of concentrating campaign activity in a few states has accelerated–by that, we are seeing over time fewer and fewer states with visits. In effect, the perversities of the Electoral College are making it less necessary to visit all 50 states. The reason is that so few of them are swing states. The book quotes John Hudak as defining swing states as those "which were decided by 10% or less (of the popular vote) in the previous election" (44). Koza use swing state interchangeably with battleground and competitive states.

The strength of *Every Vote Equal* is in its revelation of how few states really have presidential campaign activity and its potentially powerful critique of the Electoral College. Still two questions remain. First, though this book asserts a trend of fewer and fewer competitive states, as pointed out earlier in this introduction, there seems to be no clear long-term pattern in terms of the decreased number of competitive states in presidential races. Second, the book ascribes lack of competitiveness to the Electoral College when in fact it may be only one cause. Yes, because of the Electoral College states such as New York at present do not appear competitive in the sense that either of the two major party presidential candidates can win the state (or have an equal chance to do so), they therefore do not garner much campaign activity. Yes perhaps the National Popular Vote may change that campaign activity pattern. But nonetheless the advocates for this plan still do not offer an explanation for why the 12 states they identity are so close, competitive, or are swing.

Finally, Sean Trende, senior columnist for political scientist Larry Sabbato's "Sabbato's Crystal Ball" also attempts to define swing state. He does so by comparing the partisan vote index of specific states to those of the national average since the 1984 election. For Trende, he defines a swing state as those with a partisan vote index "that are within one point of the national average."

Overall, unlike journalists, political scientists seem to have largely stayed away from using the term swing state. They prefer to use the term competitive, but even then, little analysis is given to why some are competitive or not, generally referring to demographic factors that explain this trend.

DEFINING SWING STATES

So is the concept of a swing state simply an artifact of journalism or campaign strategy, serving as a substitute word for competitive, battleground, bellwether, or purple state? No; the thesis of this book is that in fact all of these terms have distinct meanings and that in fact swing state in an independent political phenomena worth examining. It is worth examining both because of its frequent media use and a need for political scientists to subject the concept to more vigorous empirical analysis, and because it at present appears to be the preferred term used by journalists when discussing presidential elections and therefore is a term that is part of popular or public usage in the United States. In sum, this book examines the concept of swing state, choosing to use the term as a way to bridge the gap between popular and scholarly usage, with the goal being to work toward conceptual clarity with a term that is already in widespread use, and testing the concept to see if it holds merit.

A bellwether state is a state such what Maine once was, or Missouri was for a century, or even how some classify Ohio. Such a state is one whose popular vote and therefore allocation of electoral votes mirrors that of the United States. More simply stated, if a candidate wins a specific state then he or she will win enough electoral votes to win the presidency. A near perfect bellwether would be like a state such as Missouri was for a century where the candidate who won that state also won the presidency. The correlation was nearly 1.0. Maine's bellwether status during the nineteenth and early twentieth centuries was not as good, only 73%. Bellwethers are effectively statistical state samples of the broader population of the presidential contest in terms of who wins the electoral votes.

A competitive state is one as political scientists have defined it. It is a state where in the last presidential contest the margin of victory for the winner was less than 10% of the popular vote. Ohio and Florida in the last three presidential election cycles are examples of competitive states.

A battleground state is one where presidential candidates choose to campaign. It is a state that may be competitive, although not always, or one which candidates hope to make competitive, or where candidates travel for the purposes of forcing the opposing candidate to spend resources to defend. It may also be a bellwether. At one time Missouri was a battleground state because it was competitive. That also made it a bellwether. A great example of a battleground state we will argue is Pennsylvania. Pennsylvania may not really be as competitive as some candidates think given the margins of victory in the last three presidential election cycles, but it is a battleground state. In 2012 Mitt Romney directed some late campaign resources to the state, perhaps he thought he could make it competitive, that he could win it, or simply to force Obama to commit resources to it and thereby draw resources away from another state that Romney thought he could really win. This now brings us to defining a swing state.

A swing state is more than a state that is competitive or a battleground state. It is a state with a proven track record of actually having flipped back and forth in terms of going for a Democrat or a Republican candidate in recent presidential elections. It is not necessarily a bellwether; it is a state that we define as having four characteristics, from the time period of 1988 through the 2012 elections. This time period covers the last seven presidential elections, beginning with the first post-Reagan contest. There are several reasons for starting with 1988. First, the 1984 election was highly unusual in terms of the magnitude of Reagan's victory. Second, there are many reasons to think that the electorate of 30 years plus ago is very different from that of today. Demographics, voting patterns, and simple policy preferences of 30 years ago are different from today. Third, one might argue that the 1984 election was the culmination of some type of electoral realignment in American politics and that 1988 represents the first in a new alignment which we are still experiencing (Busch 2005). Finally, one can argue that a survey of seven election cycles over a 28-year period gives one sufficient data to study when it comes to presidential contests.

In seeking to determine what a swing state is, this book began with an initial hypothesis regarding which states might qualify for the study. This working list consisted of 14 states: Arizona, Colorado, Florida, Indiana, Iowa,

Missouri, Nevada, New Hampshire, New Mexico, North Carolina, Ohio, Pennsylvania, Virginia, and Wisconsin. These states were selected because both the political science literature, media accounts, and campaign activity by the candidates suggested these are states that might meet the criteria for swing states.

In examining presidential races from 1988 to 2012, there were three primary criteria used to define a swing state. First, it is a competitive state in the political science meaning of the term. Other scholars have suggested a 10 percentage point margin or less in the last election as competitive (Glaeser and Ward). Instead, this book employs a five percentage point standard as a first decisional criteria. That is, a state had to have been won by five percent or less difference in the popular vote between the winner and second place finisher in the last presidential election (2012). We looked to how many elections from 1988 to 2012 (seven total) a state had a winning margin by five percentage points or less.

Second, in a nod to the "bellwether" designation in the media, this book assesses whether a state has sided with the winner in presidential elections through the period. By that, over the last seven elections, how many times has a state's popular vote (which candidate received the most popular votes and therefore was awarded its electoral votes) matched that of the final result in the presidential election. Did that state "vote" with the national winner in that presidential election.

The third criteria for being a swing state is the incidence of flipping during the past seven presidential contests. This really speaks to the "swing" in the label swing state—that is how often does the state change with regard to its vote for president? This is assessed through a simple count of the number of times the state flips from Democrat to Republican and vice versa in awarding its electoral votes.

Finally, using data from Koza et al., this book examined the number of post-convention campaign events there were in 2012. This criteria speaks to the sense that a state is a battleground. Koza lists all of the states that had post-convention activities, with there being only 12 states with events. Notably excluded from events were Arizona and New Mexico.

Appropriately, we looked to states which demonstrated a majority of seven elections where they displayed competitiveness, bellwether, flips, and battleground criteria. As Table X.2 shows in part, some interesting patterns emerged. Five states have had four or more presidential elections where their popular vote could be labeled competitive (Florida, Nevada, North Carolina, Ohio, and Wisconsin). All the states were bellwethers to a degree in that all of them followed the national electoral votes winner in at least four elections. All of the states on the original 13 except for Wisconsin have flipped

Table X.2. Swing-States: 1988-2012

State	Competitive: Number of Elections Vote Within 5% Margin	Bellwether: Number of Elections State Popular Vote Predicts National Electoral College Winner	Flips: Number of Elections Popular Vote Flips Party Direction
Colorado	3	6	3; RDRRRDD
Florida	4	6	3; RRDRRDD
Indiana	1	4	2; RRRRRDR
Iowa	1	5	2; DDDDRDD
Missouri	3	5	2; RDDRRRR
Nevada	4	7	3; RDDRRDD
New Hampshire	3	6	3; RDDRDDD
New Mexico	3	6	3; RDDDRDD
North Carolina	4	4	2; RRRRRDR
Ohio	5	7	3; RDDRRDD
Wisconsin	4	4	0; DDDDDDD
Virginia	3	5	1; RRRRRDD

at least once. Finally, using the Koza data to assess battleground states, all but Arizona, Indiana, and New Mexico appear as places where campaigns did campaign events. In general, states that demonstrated more as opposed to less of these criteria became the basis for inclusion as swing states.

Table X.3. 2012 Post-Convention Campaign Events

State	Number of 2012 Post-Convention Campaign Events
Ohio	73
Florida	40
Virginia	36
Iowa	27
Colorado	23
Wisconsin	18
New Hampshire	13
Nevada	13
Pennsylvania	5
North Carolina	3
Michigan	1
Minnesota	1

Given our criteria, ten states qualify as swing states: Colorado, Florida, Iowa, Ohio, Nevada, New Hampshire, New Mexico, North Carolina, Virginia, and Wisconsin. These are states that really do swing in the sense they seem genuinely in play and subject, as in the last seven presidential elections, of being won by either of the two major parties. Some states are better swingers than others. At the top of the list are states such as Colorado, Florida, Ohio, Nevada, New Hampshire, New Mexico, and Virginia. These would be the top-tier swing states with Iowa, North Carolina, and Wisconsin constituting a second tier. Examining why these states are swingers—why of the 50 states these are basically the ten in play for 2016—is the subject of this book.

In addition to these 10 states, two other states are the subject of this book–Missouri and Indiana. Missouri is included because of its historic status as a bellwether, competitive, battleground, and campaign state. Its status as a predictor for presidential elections (and its supply of electoral votes) made it at one time a critical state for any candidate seeking a road to the White House. Yet, as the chapter on Missouri will tell, it may no longer be a swing state. Understanding why it has slipped from this rank offers critical insights into what it means to be a swing state and the forces that might maintain swing state status. Indiana is also included. Only once in 2008 did the state swing Democrat and generally is not a battleground or competitive state. Understanding why not, and why once it did swing, and how it might do so in the future, is the reason why Indiana is included.

Indiana's inclusion is important because it also perhaps offers insight into other states which may become swing states in the future. For example, Democrats increasingly believe that Texas is poised to become a swing state (Smith 2012). They point to the fact that most major cities in that state have voted Democrat or have become two-party competitive. Or they point to the shifting demographics and an increasing Latino or Hispanic population as a harbinger of a future Democrat state. In fact, the 2014 gubernatorial election that showcased Democrat Wendy Davis was supposed to be a sign of a more competitive Texas. Democrats point to 2016, or more likely 2020, as an election where a tipping point will be reached and the state will be competitive again. Others point perhaps to Georgia and thought the 2014 candidacy of Michelle Nunn would show the impact of changing demographics (McCrary 2013). But, as this election revealed, demographic changes may create the possibilities for political change but do not guarantee it. Real turnout is still important and some groups, such as Hispanics, while growing in numbers and generally favoring Democrats, do not always vote in high percentages (Pew 2014). Indiana may thus offer some useful thoughts on where demographics fit into a discussion of swing state status.

This book also excludes Pennsylvania. Some would argue that it is either already a swing state or poised to be one (Shrader 2011). There is no question that it is a battleground state, among the few that both Romney and Obama visited in 2012. But it is certainly not a bellwether and it has not demonstrated that it is either competitive or that it is flipping back and forth between the two major parties from 1988 on. In fact if anything its recent history suggests it is moving more firmly into the Democrat safe camp as opposed to being Republican or more swing than a generation ago. Pennsylvania attracts lots of attention because of its large number of electoral votes. Presidential candidates may think the state is a swing state and therefore treat it as a battleground state. Or as in the case of 2012, Romney campaigned there at the last minute either in the hope of flipping it or perhaps to force Obama to defend it and therefore divert resources from other really competitive states, such as Iowa or Wisconsin.

The point in including or excluding Indiana, Missouri, and Pennsylvania speaks perhaps to analyzing trends and making some guesses about where states have been, where they seem to be trending in terms of being swing states, or simply their curiosity in terms of what they tell us about recent presidential campaign activity. The same is true when it comes to Wisconsin. So far it is not a state that has yet flipped from Democrat to Republican, but it remains a competitive, weak bellwether, and a competitive state. Given that its state elections are trending Republican, Wisconsin merits discussion as one that might become a real swing state.

SWING STATES AND THE ELECTORAL COLLEGE

The swing state phenomena arguably is a product of the Electoral College. As Gary Bugh (2010: 10) points out, as early as 1947 Senator Henry Cabot Lodge, Jr. sought to change the Electoral College system because it created a "pivotal state evil" whereby some states such as Illinois, Ohio, and Pennsylvania would have enormous impact on presidential races. Duquette and Schultz (2006) have pointed to how the Electoral College distorts state influence and gives some voters more influence than others, thereby perhaps giving swing voters in swing states disproportionate voting strength. Thus, as a state-based system for electing the president, the Electoral College creates specific campaign incentives that give rise to the swing state phenomena.

The Electoral College was a product of political compromise at the Constitutional Convention. It was proposed as one of many compromises between the less and more populous states. It has been defended vigorously by Martin Diamond (1959) and others as an electoral mechanism that was supposed to overcome regional and sectionalism in presidential politics, and it was also supposed to represent a way to ensure the best qualified candidates were selected. Other critiques contend that the Electoral College was an elitist institution meant to limit the ability of the common person to select the president. In effect, the Electoral College is an anti-democratic feature of the American political system whose usefulness—if ever it was useful—has long since passed (Dahl 2003).

The Constitution entrusts to the states the power to select the president. Each state is allocated a number of electoral votes equivalent to the size of the congressional delegation. State legislatures were given the authority regarding how to select the electors or individuals who would cast these electoral votes. As originally designed and practiced state legislators determined the electors but commencing in the early nineteenth century states gradually let voters select the electors who then cast the electoral votes. By the middle of the nineteenth century, all states used popular elections to determine the composition of the Electoral College. In order to be elected president, a candidate must receive a majority of the electoral votes cast by all the states. Today that includes all 50 states and the District of Columbia. There are 538 total electoral votes, meaning that 270 is the winning number. If no candidate secures 270 then the Constitution outlines a procedure for how the House and Senate select the president and the vice president.

This brief outline of the Electoral College process makes it clear that the selection of the president while in theory a national affair, it is really 51 individual elections, with each state setting its own rules for voter eligibility and allocation of electoral votes (Schultz 2014: 84; Miller 2012). It is a battle to win electoral votes in each of the states and it is not necessarily who wins the most popular vote across the country. As pointed out earlier, in several instances in American history the popular vote and Electoral College winners were not the same person, creating controversy, confusion, and call to abolish the Electoral College. The Electoral College thus makes the presidential selection process a state-by-state adventure (Powell 2004).

What adds complexity to the Electoral College is the process of how states actually allocate their electoral votes. Or more technically speaking, how it determines who its electors are. Contrary to common misunderstanding, the Constitution does not mandate specifically how a state will allocate its electoral votes, so a state can exercise a variety of options. It could simply allocate its electoral votes in proportion to the popular vote in its state. It could allocate the electoral votes based on who wins specific congressional districts. This is what Nebraska and Maine do. Or it could do what 48 states practice, by awarding all of the electoral votes to the presidential candidate who receives the most popular votes in its presidential election. A presidential popular vote in 48 of the states plus the District of Columbia is a winner-take-all affair. The candidate who receives the plurality of the popular vote is allowed to seat his or her electors who will presumably cast their votes accordingly. Yet occasionally there are "faithless" electors who do not cast their votes as they promise. Most recently this occurred in 2000 when Barbara Lett-Simmons refused to cast her Washington, D.C., electoral vote for Al Gore. However, faithless electors are rarities.

The swing-state phenomena is arguably related to the winner-take-all electoral vote allocation mechanism. Because the presidential election is not really a national popular vote and because it is a state election process where it is winner-take-all for the electoral vote, some states are politically safe for one candidate or party. By that, if one party has a clear electoral advantage in terms of party registration and mobilization, then there is little chance that the opposition party candidate will win or even campaign in that state. Thus, at present, New York and Massachusetts seem like safe Democrat states, whereas Texas and Oklahoma seem safe for the Republicans. Total up the number of safe seats between the two parties and the estimate is that it reaches 40. In essence, there are 40 safe states (41 including the District of Columbia) and only ten states where there is a serious chance that one or the other party can win. The balance of presidential power resides in these ten swing states because among the other 41, no one party commands enough safe electoral votes to have a lock on the presidency. These ten states account for 115 electoral votes, or 42.5% of the 270 needed to win the presidency.

The criticism then of the Electoral College is that it distorts presidential campaigns. As the 2012 campaign revealed, presidential campaign visits or events are confined to only a handful of states. But as some have pointed out, even beyond the campaign there is evidence that electoral considerations affect presidential first-term travel and visits (Doherty 2010). First-term presidents may only travel to certain states, disproportionally favoring those which are perceived as swing. It is also possible that these states receive a disproportionate reward in terms of presidential policy initiatives and largess.

Among those criticizing the Electoral College along these lines are those who are supporters of the National Popular Vote campaign. They would use state compacts to bypass constitutional amendments to eliminate the Electoral College. They call for states to allocate their electoral votes according to the national popular vote for the president. Whether such a proposal is a good or bad idea is not an issue for discussion here. Yet the question is whether adopting that proposal would change campaign strategies or alter the swing versus safe state phenomena is debatable. It might encourage candidates to campaign in more states, new ones, or the same. Some states might still be battlegrounds now for popular votes instead of electoral votes. Again, this is not an issue to be resolved here. States might still lean in one or another direction and depending on their population and allocation rules may or may not create incentives for presidential candidates to visit there and campaign. But candidates might still make allocative or resource decisions as to where to campaign and therefore might change some battleground strategies or affect how a state might be viewed as a bellwether but from a point of view of what it presently means to be a swing state it will change.

Overall, the point is that the Electoral College has helped create the conditions that make swing states a real phenomena because presidential elections are state-based. There is no indication that in the foreseeable future the Electoral College is going away and even if it does, there might still be incentives that make some states more competitive, thereby contributing to the criteria that define what a swing state is.

OVERVIEW OF BOOK

Since the Electoral College is likely to remain a feature of American politics for the foreseeable future, this volume looks at the factors that cause swing states to swing. Our authors arrive at differing conclusions that point to the significance of both national- and state-level factors in affecting the state's status as a swing state, and given the rich and varied political histories of the states, this result is not at all surprising. Each chapter further substantiates the individual state's status as a swing state, reviews the state's political history, discusses factors that make the state swing, and concludes with predictions for 2016 and beyond.

We begin with an introduction to the state level strategies of presidential campaigns, which places the states in national context. Scott McLean reviews presidential campaign strategies in states with large populations of swing voters. McLean begins his chapter by providing an overview of the changing landscape of presidential elections. He describes how the number and identity of competitive and uncompetitive states has changed over time, and he also describes the evolution of the winner-take-all rule in the Electoral College for almost all of the states. But much of his chapter offers a detailed analysis of campaign activity and media communications in presidential races, describing the various factors that go into determining whether states are battlegrounds or actually swingable. McLean additionally provides a discussion of voter turnout, partisanship, and the role of independent voters in the swing states. Overall, McLean argues that campaigns target particular categories of voters in swing states, rather than swing voters as a whole, crafting a narrative that removes some obstacles to participation for independent and less likely voters in these states.

Following McLean's national-level analysis, we turn our attention to state-by-state analysis of each swing state to uncover the factors that explain the phenomenon. We begin with Warren and Jacob's consideration of what had been the classic swing state, Missouri. These authors conclude that national factors, an increase in the number of Republican voters along with their enhanced mobilization, a rise in a politicized evangelical religious base, and race-based tactics and effects have removed Missouri from the roll call of swing states. They also point out that the selection of recent presidential candidates that the Democrats have offered seems out of step with a large proportion of the Missouri electorate. In effect, the national Democratic Party has selected presidential candidates who are more liberal than the median Missouri voter, thereby pushing the state away from its more bellwether and centrist position. Missouri has moved more into the Republican camp because the median national Democratic party member is selecting presidential candidates further to the left than where the median Missouri voter is. At one time both the national Republican and Democratic Parties picked candidates closer to where the median Missouri voter was, but that is no longer the case. The national Republican Party presidential candidates may now be closer to where the median Missouri voter is now.

Missouri's replacement as the nation's quintessential swing state may well be Ohio. The Buckeye state's role in presidential elections seems oversized according to the authors, generally drawing unusual amounts of attention from the presidential candidates. It is a state that seems to follow national popular vote trends well in terms of mirroring close elections, but even when it is not close in Ohio it still draws significant presidential candidate attention. It is both a bellwether and swing state. In Ohio, Hendriks and Van Doorn see a diverse state composed of five major regions. These regions have distinct cultural, economic, and political forces that drive them, mirroring national trends in terms of diversity. But the authors also note that the partisan demographics of Ohio seem to align with national partisan profiles. They suggest that the closeness of the 2000 and 2004 presidential elections in Ohio have reinforced its image as a battleground state. Overall, Hendriks and Van Doorn argue that national political factors, that is, the shift in political ideologies of the national parties, along with the demographic reality of "5 Ohios," have caused Ohio's rise to prominence as a swing state. Significantly, many of the factors that have moved Missouri out of the swing state column have solidified Ohio's position as one. The experiences of Missouri and Ohio also structure the discussions of other states, serving as examples or case studies of the forces causing states to be swingers.

Perhaps standing next in Ohio in terms of its recent importance to presidential elections is Florida. Sean Foreman describes several factors transforming Florida into a competitive swing state. He argues that the national shift in political parties over the last generation or so which has also led to a realignment of the Republican Party across the south, including Florida. Foreman also describes a Republican Party benefitting from demographic changes ranging from northern retirees and Cubans, all located in different parts of the state. Thus, similar to Ohio's five regions, Florida too has several political areas that have produced more competitive state elections. It is three states with ten media markets. These competitive state elections, along with a highly energized Republican Party, especially during and since the 2000 *Bush v. Gore* contest, have pushed the GOP into a competitive battle with the Democrats, despite the latter's overall lead in party registration. The multiple regions of the state, along with unstable political alliances and shifting demographics among many groups, and, with that, shifting public opinion have made Florida a swing state that will continue into the near future.

Unstable partisan divisions that favor "flipping" are perhaps the most obvious factors that make states swing. In North Carolina, Cooper and Knotts first review the history of the state, one that is normally thought of as part of the once solid south. But that image was always a simplification, with sizeable numbers of Republicans elected at the state level. They too point to a legacy of a state with many regions and a partisan ideology similar to the average voter across the country. Cooper and Knotts suggest that the state ideological "push-pull" with conservative policy dominating activity in the state legislature serves to stimulate liberal activism and voting. It is, as they conclude, the bluest red state in the country, attributable to shifting party allegiances, regional competition, and broader political movement found across the south in general and specifically driven by North Carolina's unique political demography and history.

Wisconsin is a political oddity. Known for many years as a liberal enclave perhaps because of the location of its capital in Madison and the state university there, or perhaps because of the progressive politics in Milwaukee, the state is increasingly trending Republican. At the state level Republicans have dominated the governorship since Tommy Thompson (except with Jim Doyle's two terms), and the state legislature is similarly dominated by Republicans. In the last few years Wisconsin has demonstrated close presidential races. Why? Kraus and Weinschenk demonstrate that Wisconsin's voters almost perfectly match national numbers in terms of how they identify ideologically. With 40% of their voters describing themselves as moderates, a large portion of the Wisconsin electorate is up for grabs and can swing from supporting liberals such as Senator Tammy Baldwin to conservatives such as Governor Scott Walker. Many voters are thus willing to cast their ballots for candidates with strikingly different party affiliations and ideologies. Exactly why this pattern of split voting has emerged may be due to a variety of factors, including a shift away from strong partisan attachments for an increasing percentage of the electorate.

New Mexico is a paradox. With only five electoral votes one would not think that it would be a state many candidates would care about, especially when compared to the weight of Florida, Ohio, and North Carolina. Yet being a swing state is not so much about the electoral weight as it is about the winability of it by either the Democrats or Republicans. At least this is the argument of Donald Beachler. New Mexico has flipped three times, being a bellwether six times, and won by less than 5% three times in the last seven presidential elections. It has been a swing state. Certain states seem particularly susceptible to "swinging" based upon the state's particular demographics. Donald Beachler suggests that New Mexico's precarious swing state status is largely the result of the state's big demographic shifts. Specifically, it is a state with the largest Native American and Mexican population percentages in the country, but historically these groups did not vote, leaving the state's politics to be dominated by whites. But as the percentages of these populations have increased, this demographic change has changed the electorate. It is an electorate and a state divided into three distinct regions, thereby making for competitive elections at the state level in ways similar to Ohio and Florida. These competitive state elections across the three regions go a long way in explaining New Mexico's recent swing status. But as the demographics further tilt and also include younger and better educated whites, Beachler sees a state perhaps leaving the swing state club. Evidence of that perhaps was in 2012 where New Mexico did not receive a single post-convention visit from the two major presidential candidates.

Demographic changes along with a high percentage of young people or independent voters are important themes to an understanding of how swing states persist or come or go out of existence when it comes to Colorado and Nevada.

Preuhs, Provizer, and Thangasamy point to demographics in Colorado, specifically a change in partisan affiliation in the state. Over the last three presidential election cycles (starting in 2004) Republicans have gone from a plus seven in terms of party affiliation to where by 2008 those considering themselves a member of that party, as Democrats, or independent was essentially even. This parity in terms of party registration occurred in part because of a rise of new young voters with less firmly grounded partisan attachments. But Colorado has also experienced a growth in urbanization and in the Latino populations, both of which the authors note have also worked to the advantage of Democrats, and the state has a higher than national average when it comes to median incomes and college-educated citizens. All these demographics are important as they are linked regional patterns in the state that divide the front range and urban areas of Denver and Boulder from the rest of the state. Combine all this with policy preferences, turnout, and partisanship in Colorado voting and Preuhs, Provizer, and Thangasamy see a state that is unclear how it will vote in 2016.

Similarly Damore and Gill suggest that population growth and demographic change affect party divisions in Nevada. Nevada, they argue, has an oversized influence in national electoral politics, including recent presidential contests or the 2010 Senate contest involving Harry Reid. Damore and Gill contend that Nevada is a case study in "how population growth, increased urbanization, and ethnic and racial diversification are reshaping the geography of partisan composition." The state's powerful population growth has also led to an increase in its electoral vote totals, increasing its presidential importance. The authors chart a history of Nevada that shows it to be historically a reliable bellwether state. But they also point out how weak parties and the strength of personal political organizations have characterized Nevada, with many politicians having withstood national political storms due to their ability to create their own operations. Part of the key to understanding Nevada is how personal political organizations, such as most recently Harry Reid's, are able to take control of parties and use them effectively both for themselves and for either the Republicans or Democrats. Often these organizations buck national political trends and instead align more closely with the policy preferences of state voters. Finally, they also describe the three political regions of Nevada and how they split along partisan and demographic cleavages as important factors to understand why Nevada will continue as a swing state into the future.

Like Nevada, New Hampshire has an unusually large role in presidential elections. Part of that arises from it being the first primary in the nation, but its influence extends beyond it to the general election, despite its three electoral votes. At one time New Hampshire was a reliable Republican stronghold, home to the *Manchester Union Leader* and William Loeb. Yet New Hampshire, Niall Palmer contends, has seen a transformation in its political culture as a result of three factors. The first is that the population changes "in and around New Hampshire" have driven its partisan loyalties and political culture. The exodus of many from Boston, Massachusetts, as commuters has had one impact on liberalizing the state as young professional and aging Baby Boomers moved to New Hampshire. Over the last few years Democrats have nearly caught up to Republicans in terms of self-identification, with a large percentage of the population—more than 40%—self-reporting as independents. The second change is the increased voter turnout, partly driven by the demographic change. This too has worked to the Democrats' advantage. The third factor has to do with the nature of the Republicanism in New Hampshire. This is not a religious or social values Republican state. The Republicans and the independents are more business-orientated or secular libertarian, at odds with the trends in the national Republican party which appears more captured by southern and religious values. This then puts this state's Republicans perhaps to the left or left out from the mainline trends of the national party. As a result both state elections have become more competitive and swing, bringing with it a presidential election climate that has recently favored Democrats but which is clearly capable of swinging.

Although demographics exert a considerable effect in many of these states, clearly demographics alone are not a sufficient explanation for all of the states under consideration. Demographic changes lead to changes in public opinion, policy, party strength, and voting behavior as these chapters reveal. John McGlennon makes these connections clear, noting that in Virginia demographic change, occurring alongside the emergence of "previously quiescent voting blocs" along with a partisan realignment, causes the state to swing. To a large extent urbanization of Virginia, demographic changes in the suburbs outside of Washington, D.C., and economic forces have changed the state. Barack Obama was successful in seeing these changes and in appealing to, and creating a coalition that took advantage of these trends that were producing a more moderate and to some extent Democratic state, as evidenced by the election of several recent moderate Democratic governors and senators. The challenge for 2016 is the ability of the next Democratic nominee to hold together the coalition that Obama created.

In some states unique structural factors, including Iowa and New Hampshire's first-in-the-nation caucus and primary, respectively, are amongst the reasons that the state "swings." Donna Hoffman and Christopher Larimer suggest that the Iowa caucuses have created competitive and highly organized party structures which do an excellent job mobilizing voters. These caucuses bring significant candidate and media attention to the state, providing incentives and the information to encourage voter mobilization. But other state-level factors additionally contribute to making Iowa a true swing state, as evidenced by how it has actually switched parties in recent presidential elections. Factors such as non-partisan redistricting which has created competitive congressional elections, along with the ability of voters to easily change party affiliation also facilitate a competitive political environment. What one sees in Iowa are party registrations where the Republicans and Democrats are close and the number of independents is more than a third of the electorate. There are also geographic overlays to party strengthen, rural and western Iowa for the Republicans, urban and the eastern part for the Democrats. These factors have created a competitive state politics that translates over into competitive presidential contests that will continue into the future.

In the final state-specific chapter Matthew Bergbower writes that in Indiana that down-state ballot results, state public opinion, and Democratic campaign strategy contribute to a climate where the state may be poised to swing in the future. Although Indiana has long been perceived as largely a "safe" Republican state, its vote for Obama in 2008 demonstrated that under the right conditions the state could swing and move more into a Democrat camp. Bergbower argues that conditions may be favorable for a change in its status. To understand why Indiana may swing in the future this chapter looks to why Obama won the state in 2008 but not in 2012. Part of the answer lies in how Obama targeted Indiana in 2008 but McCain did not, but also part of the story is about the mobilization of African Americans and the Democrats and the way state public opinion stands on a variety of national issues. This chapter suggests that reading the "tea leaves" of both state-level and national-level factors may allow for a clearer sense of whether, and which, states will swing in 2016 and beyond. In some sense, looking to whether and how Indiana may become a swinger brings us back to Missouri, looking to understand the factors that once made it swing, why it does not now, and whether it might do so in the future.

After consideration of the work of these scholars in assessing their states individually, we conclude this volume with a summary of findings and our assessment of which states will continue to swing and why in 2016 and beyond. The varied and particular story of the twelve states considered yields patterns worthy of consideration in national elections where only a few citizens in a few states seem to matter. We turn our attention to them now.

BIBLIOGRAPHY

About Politics. 2015. "Swing State." Located at http://uspolitics.about.com/od/glossary/a/What-Is-A-Swing-State.htm. Site last visited on March 10, 2015.

Anon. 2010. "Swing States." *Dictionary of American Politics*, on-line edition. Located at http://ezproxy.hamline.edu:4984/content/entry/eupamgov/swing_states/0. Site last visited on March 10, 2015.

Anon. 2011. *The Generation Gap and the 2012 Election: Angry Silents, Disengaged Millennials*. Washington, D.C.: Pew Research Center.

Anon. 2012. "Exit polls 2012: How the vote has shifted." *Washington Post* (November 6). Located at http://www.washingtonpost.com/wp-srv/special/politics/2012-exit-polls/table.html. Site last visited on March 10, 2015.

Apple, R.W. 2000. "Bucking the Swing-State Trend, Ohio Holding Steady, Polls Show," *New York Times*, September 19, A1.

Barone, Michael, et al. 2013. The *Almanac of American Politics 2014* e-book edition. Chicago: University of Chicago Press.

Baumgarden, James L. 1984. "The 1888 Presidential Election: How Corrupt?" *Presidential Studies Quarterly* 14: 416–27.

Benen, Steve. 2014. "GOP domination of the South is now complete." MSNBC (December 8). Located at http://www.msnbc.com/rachel-maddow-show/gop-domination-the-south-now-complete (Site last viewed on March 14, 2015).

Bianco, William, and David T. Canon. 2015. *American Politics Today*. New York: W.W. Norton.

Bill, James A., and Robert L. Hardgrave, Jr. 1973. *Comparative Politics: The Quest for Theory*. Columbus, Ohio: Charles E. Merrill Publishing Company.

Bishop, Bill. 2009. *The Big Sort: Why the Clustering of Like-Minded Americans is Tearing Us Apart*. New York: Mariner Books.

Bugh, Gary E. 2010. *Electoral College Reform: Challenges and Possibilities*. Burlington, VT: Ashgate Publishing.

Bugh, Gary E. 2010. "Introduction: Approaching Electoral College Reform." In Bugh, Gary E., ed., *Electoral College Reform: Challenges and Possibilities*. Burlington, VT: Ashgate Publishing.

Busch, Andrew E. 2005. *The Presidential Election of 1980 and the Rise of the Right*. Lawrence, KS: University Press of Kansas.

Bush v. Gore. 2000. 531 U.S. 98.

Campbell, Angus, et al. 1964. *The American Voter*. New York: John Wiley & Sons.

Clift, Eleanor. 2000. "Calling All Swing States." *Newsweek*, November 20, 2000, p 10.

Cuniff, Meghann. 2004. "Portrait of a Swing State. *Oregon Daily Emerald* (October 4). Located at http://dailyemerald.com/2004/10/04/portrait-of-a-swing-state/. Site last visited on March 10, 2015.

Dahl, Robert. A. 2003. *How Democratic is the U.S. Constitution?* New Haven: Yale University Press.

Dalton, Philip D. 2006. *Swing Voters: Understanding Late-deciders in Late Modernity*. Cresskill, N.J.: Hampton Press.

Dao, James. 2000. "Democrats Ask Nader to Back Gore in Swing States," *New York Times*, October 31, A 20.

Diamond, Martin. 1959. "Democracy and The Federalist: A Reconsideration of the Framers' Intent." *American Political Science Review* (March), pp. 52-68.

Dictionary.com. 2015. "Swing State." Located at http://dictionary.reference.com/browse/swing+state. Site last viewed on March 10, 2015.

Dimock, Michael, April Clark, and Juliana Menasce Horowitz. 2008. "Campaign Dynamics and the Swing Vote in the 2004 Election." In Mayer, William G., ed., *The Swing Voter in American Politics*. Washington, DC: Brookings Institution Press, pp. 58–74.

Doherty, Brendan J. 2010. "Electoral College Incentives and Presidential Actions: A Case for Reform?" In Bugh, Gary E., ed., *Electoral College Reform: Challenges and Possibilities*. Burlington, VT: Ashgate Publishing, pp. 175–186.

Duquette, Christopher, and David Schultz. 2006. "One Person, One Vote and the Constitutionality of the Winner-Take-All Allocation of Electoral College Votes." *Tennessee Journal of Law and Policy*, v: 2:3 pp. 453–485.

Edsell, Thomas Byrne, and Mary D. Edsell. 1991. *Chain Reaction: The Impact of Race, Rights, and Taxes on American Politics.* New York: W.W. Norton.

Elazar, Daniel. 1966. *A View from the States.* New York: Cambridge University Press.

Erikson, Robert S., Gerald C. Wright, and John P. McIver. 1993. *Statehouse Democracy: Public Opinion and Policy in the American States.* New York: Cambridge University Press.

Feldmann, Linda. 2012. "Obama leads in three key swing states, but Romney can still sway voters." *Christian Science Monitor* (August 1) 1.

Fite, Gilbert C. 2001. "The Election of 1896." In Arthur Schlesinger, Jr., ed., *History of American Presidential Elections,* vol. 2.

Frankovic, Kathleen A. and Monika L. McDermott. 2010. "Public Opinion in the 2000 Election: The Ambivalent Electorate." In Pomper, Gerald M., ed., *The Election of 1984.* Chatham, NJ: Chatham House Publishers, Inc., pp. 73–91.

Geer, John, et al. 2014. *Gateways to Democracy: An Introduction to American Government.* Independence, KY: Cengage.

Gillman, Howard. 2001. *The Votes That Counted: How the Court Decided the 2000 Presidential Election.* Chicago: University of Chicago Press.

Glaeser, Edward L. and Bryce Ward, 2005. "Myths and Realities of American Political Geography," NBER Working Paper, December 2005.

Gottschalk, Marie. 2015. *Caught: The Prison State and the Lockdown of American Politics.* Princeton: Princeton University Press.

Greene, Abner. 2001. *Understanding the 2000 Election: A Guide to the Legal Battles That Decided the Presidency.* New York: NYU Press Press.

Gullan, Harold I. 1998. *The Upset That Wasn't: Harry S. Truman and the Crucial Election of 1948.* Chicago: Ivan R. Dee.

Haddad, Mohammed, and Sam Bollier. 2012. "Charting 'swing states' in US 2012 election" (November 6). Located at http://www.aljazeera.com/indepth/interactive/2012/09/201291763829868734.html. Site last visited on March 10, 2015.

Hetherington, Marc J. 2013. "The Election: How the Campaign Mattered." In Nelson, Michael, ed., *The Elections of 2012.* New York: CQ Press, pp. 47–72.

James, Scott C. and Brian L. Lawson, 1999. "The Political Economy of Voting Rights Enforcement in America's Gilded Age: Electoral College Competition, Partisan Commitment, and the Federal Election Law." *American Political Science Review* 93(1): 115.

Jamieson, Kathleen Hall. 2013. *Electing the President, 2012: An Insiders' View.* Philadelphia: University of Pennsylvania Press.

Johnson, Bonnie J. 2005. "Identities of Competitive States in U.S. Presidential Elections: Electoral College Bias or Candidate Centered Politics?" *Publius: The Journal of Federalism* 35(2): 337–355.

Keeter, Scott. 2014. *Political Polarization in Action: Insights into the 2014 Election From the American Trends Panel.* Washington, D.C.: Pew Research Center.

Kelley, Stanley. *Interpreting Elections.* 1983. Princeton: Princeton University Press.

Key, V.O. 1949. *Southern Politics in State and Nation.* Knoxville, TN: University of Tennessee Press.

Killian, Linda. 2012. *The Swing Vote: The Untapped Power of Independents.* St. Martins' Press.

Kollman, Ken. 2015. *The American Political System.* New York: W.W. Norton.

Koza, John R., Barry Fadem, Mark Grueskin, Michael S. Mandell, Robert Richie, and Joseph F. Zimmerman. 2013. *Every Vote Equal*, 4th edition. National Popular Vote Press.

Leonhardt, David. 2015. "Democrats Are Seeing A Field of One for 2016." *New York Times* (March 12), A1.

Lewis-Beck, Michael S., et al. 2011. *The American Voter Revisited.* Ann Arbor: University of Michigan Press.

Lim, Timothy C. 2010. *Doing Comparative Politics: An Introduction to Approaches & Issues.* Boulder, CO: Lynne Rienner Publishers.

Lipset, Seymour Martin. 1960. *Political Man: The Social Bases of Politics.* New York: Doubleday & Company.

Mayer, William G. 2008. *The Swing Voter in American Politics.* Washington, DC: Brookings Institution Press.

Mayhew, David. "Congressional Elections: The Case of the Vanishing Marginals." *Polity.* Vol. 6, No. 3 (Spring), pp. 295–317.

McCrary, Zac. 2013. "Sweet Georgia Blue: Why Democrats Should Be Bullish on the Peach State." *Huffington Post* (June 4). Located at http://www.huffingtonpost.com/zac-mccrary/sweet-georgia-blue_b_3385459.html (Site last visited on March 14, 2015).

Miller, Derek T. 2012. "Invisible Federalism and the Electoral College," *Arizona State Law Review*, vol. 44, pp. 1238–1292.

Miller, Warren E., and J. Merrill Shanks. 1996. *The New American Voter.* Cambridge: Harvard University Press.

Nelson, Michael. 2001. *The Elections of 2000.* New York: CQ Press.

Nelson, Michael. 2001. "The Election: Ordinary Politics, Extraordinary Outcome." In Nelson, Michael, ed., *The Elections of 2000.* New York: CQ Press, pp. 55–92.

Nelson, Michael. 2005. *The Elections of 2004.* New York: CQ Press.

Nelson, Michael. 2010. *The Elections of 2008.* New York: CQ Press.

Nelson, Michael. 2013. *The Elections of 2012.* New York: CQ Press.

Newman, Rick. 2012. "It's All About the Swing States," *U.S. News Digital Weekly* (September 7), Vol. 4, Issue 36.

Nivola, Pietro S. 2005. *Thinking About Political Polarization.* Washington, DC: The Brookings Institution. Policy Brief 139. January 2005.

Ostermeier, Eric. 2012. "Swing States, Battleground States, or Purple States?" *Smart Politics Blog.* Located at http://blog.lib.umn.edu/cspg/smartpolitics/2012/08/swing_states_battleground_stat.php (Last viewed on March 9, 2015).

Oxford Dictionary. 2015. "Swing State." Located at http://www.oxforddictionaries.com/us/definition/american_english/swing-state. Site last visited on March 10, 2015.

Page, Susan. 2012. "In 12 swing states, they're starting from scratch." *USA Today*, (May 7), A1.

Page, Susan. 2012. "Swing State Primaries—A Difficult Balance," *USA Today*, (January 9), A1.

Perez-Pena, Richard. 2000. "Lieberman Races to Energize Democrats in Swing States." *New York Times*, November 6, 2000, A24.

Perez-Pena, Richard. 2000. "Lieberman Sees Colorado As Swing State." *New York Times*, September 18, A17.

Pew Research Center. 2014. "Hispanic Voters in the 2014 election." Located at http://www.pewhispanic.org/topics/hispaniclatino-vote/ (October 29). (Site last viewed on March 16, 2015).

Polsby, Nelson W., and Aaron Wildavsky. 2000. *Presidential Elections: Strategies and Structures of American Politics*. New York: Seven Bridges Press.

Pomper, Gerald M. 2010. "The Presidential Election: Change Comes to America." In Nelson, Michael, ed. *The Elections of 2008*. New York: CQ Press, pp. 45–73.

Pomper, Gerald M. 1985. *The Election of 1984: Reports and Interpretations*. Chatham, NJ: Chatham House Publishers, Inc.

Pomper, Gerald M. 2005. "The Presidential Election: The Ills of American Politics After 9/11." In Nelson, Michael, ed., *The Elections of 2004*. New York: CQ Press, pp. 42–68.

Pomper, Gerald M. 1989. *The Election of 1988: Reports and Interpretations*. Chatham, NJ: Chatham House Publishers, Inc.

Pomper, Gerald M. 2001. "The Presidential Election." In Pomper, Gerald M., ed., *The Election of 1984*. Chatham, NJ: Chatham House Publishers, Inc., pp. 125–154.

Pomper, Gerald M. 1981. *The Election of 1980: Reports and Interpretations*. Chatham, NJ: Chatham House Publishers, Inc.

Pomper, Gerald M. 1993. *The Election of 1992*. Chatham, NJ: Chatham House Publishers, Inc.

Pomper, Gerald M. 1987. *The Election of 1996*. Chatham, NJ: Chatham House Publishers, Inc.

Pomper, Gerald M. 1985. "The Presidential Election." In Pomper, Gerald M., ed., *The Election of 1984: Reports and Interpretations*. Chatham, NJ: Chatham House Publishers, Inc., pp. 60–91.

Pomper, Gerald M. 2001. *The Election of 2000*. Chatham, NJ: Chatham House Publishers, Inc.

Pomper, Gerald M. 1975. *Voters Choice: Varieties of American Electoral Behavior*. New York: Harper & Row.

Powell, Richard. 2004. "The Strategic Importance of State-Level Factors in Presidential Elections." *Publius: The Journal of Federalism* 34:3(Summer 2004) 115–130.

Schultz, David. 2014. *Election Law and Democratic Theory*. Burlington, VT: Ashgate.

Shaw, Daron R. 2008. "Swing Voting and U.S. Presidential Elections." In Mayer, William G., ed. *The Swing Voter in American Politics*. Washington, DC: Brookings Institution Press, pp. 75–101.

Shrader, Nathan R. 2011. "A Swing State in Transition: Assessing Pennsylvania's Democratic Party Statewide Performance 1970-2010 (or, What's the Matter with

Pennsylvania?).” Paper presented at the 2011 New England Political Science Association.

Silver, Nate. 2012. “As Swing Districts Dwindle, Can a Divided House Stand?” *New York Times* (December 27), located at http://fivethirtyeight.blogs.nytimes.com/2012/12/27/as-swing-districts-dwindle-can-a-divided-house-stand/?_r=0 (site last viewed on March 12, 2015).

Smith, Sonia. 2012. Will Texas be a Swing State by 2016? *Texas Monthly* (November 1). Located at http://www.texasmonthly.com/story/will-texas-be-swing-state-2016 (Site last visited on March 14, 2015).

Starr, Paul. 2011. *Remedy and Reaction: The Peculiar American Struggle Over Health Care Reform*. New Haven: Yale University Press.

Stuckey, Mary E. 2005. “Swinging the Vote in the 2004 Presidential Election.” In *The 2004 Presidential Campaign: A Communication Perspective*. Lanham, MD: Rowman & Littlefield Publishers, pp. 153–166.

Teixeira, Ruy A. 2012. *America’s New Swing Region: Changing Politics and Demographics in the Mountain West* Washington, DC: Brookings Institution Press.

Trende, Sean. 2014. “Is the Republican Presidential Vote Inefficiently Distributed?” Located at http://www.centerforpolitics.org/crystalball/articles/is-the-republican-presidential-vote-inefficiently-distributed/ (Site lasted visited on March 12, 2015).

Verba, Sidney and Norman H. Nie. 1972. *Participation in America: Political Democracy and Social Equality*. Chicago: University of Chicago Press.

Wang, Tova, et al. 2008. “Voting in 2008: Ten Swing States.” Washington, D.C.: Common Cause.

Washington Post. 2012. “Exit polls 2012: How the vote has shifted.” http://www.washingtonpost.com/wp-srv/special/politics/2012-exit-polls/table.html (November 6). (Site last visited on March 14, 2015).

White, Theodore H. 1980. *The Making of the President, 1960*. New York: Atheneum.

Wikipedia. 2015. “Swing State.” Located at http://en.wikipedia.org/wiki/Swing_state. Site last viewed on March 10, 2015.

Wright, Lori. 2008. *Swing Voters? Catholic Voting Behavior in U.S. Presidential Elections From 1992 to 2004*. Saarbrücken, Germany: VDM Verlag.

Zelenkauskaite, Asta; Ya Gao; Powell, Rich. 2012. “Content Analysis Shows ‘Red States’ Used More Than ‘Blue States.’” *Newspaper Research Journal*, Vol. 33, Issue 3, p. 89–100.

Chapter One

Purple Battlegrounds

Presidential Campaign Strategies and Swing State Voters

Scott L. McLean

In 1936, *The New York Times* for the first time dubbed competitive presidential election states "swing states" or "battleground states." But the terms appeared in only four articles that year, and then only appeared sporadically for the next five decades (Goux 2010). This lack of media interest in swing states is understandable because swing states were more common and less consequential, until the 1990s. In presidential elections between 1924 and 1960, there were only ten consistently uncompetitive states: Arizona, Arkansas, Georgia, Kansas, Louisiana, Nebraska, Oklahoma, Utah, Vermont and Virginia. Most states were in play during that time (Johnson 2005). In 1988, though conventional wisdom expected a close race, only fourteen states were projected to be competitive, the lowest number of close states since 1968 (FairVote 2011). With that, between 1988 and 1996, the *Times* increased the mentions of "swing states" or "battleground states" by 200% (Goux 2010). As the media increasingly framed each successive election in simple terms of a "culture war" between red states and blue states, it also turned its focus to these battleground "purple states." Eventually with the rise of 24-hour cable news networks, swing states were covered more extensively than ever. Eric Ostermeier's (2012) analysis of ABC, NBC, CBS, FOX, CNN, MSNBC, FOX Cable News, and NPR in the 2012 campaign found that the term "swing state" appeared in 1,154 news reports, while "battleground state" was used in 1,092 reports (Ostermeier 2012).

This profound shift in media focus on swing states since the 1990s is a reflection of an equally profound shift in modern campaigns. Increasingly vast campaign resources are being concentrated on an ever-shrinking number of swing states that decide who wins the presidency. The 2012 election is a case in point. On its face, the presidential election of 2012 was a blowout win for the Democrats. In President Obama's 332 electoral vote reelection, there were 35 states in which the winning margin was over 10 percent—the largest number of blowout states in history. Yet 2012 was one of the closest elections in modern history, with four states decided by less than 5 percentage points (Florida, Ohio, Virginia, and North Carolina). This was the smallest number of close states in modern election history. In the 27 presidential elections since 1904, only nine have involved five or fewer states decided by less than five percentage points. But each of those elections—except 2012—was a landslide. Since 1960, the number of uncompetitive states in presidential elections has expanded, while the list of close states has become extremely short. The shrinking number of competitive states defies conventional wisdom; about a third of the states had been considered competitive at the start of the 2012 campaign, and less than one-fifth ended up close (Wayne 2012). Georgia, written off at first as a clear red state, was more competitive than five states that the media initially designated as battlegrounds (Arizona, New Mexico, Michigan, Missouri, and Wisconsin), but which turned out to be decided by margins larger than 5 percent.

Table 1.1 illustrates perhaps the most remarkable trend in U.S. politics since 2000: Presidential elections have become more competitive nationally, but the campaign battles occur in a shrinking number of close swing states. Meanwhile an increasing majority of states are uncompetitive spectators.

The 2012 election was an anomaly, but was it also a harbinger of things to come? The purpose of this chapter is to explore this narrowing of American politics down to a few swing states, and the ways campaigns capitalize, yet create and sustain this state of affairs. Other chapters have told us in detail how each swing state has its own particular story, or if you wish, its own character. As important as it is to understand swing states individually and in detail, we should not overlook the national trend since 1960: The rising number of "landslide states," and the decreasing number of very close swing states. One perspective on this trend is that changing demographics are creating a divided nation. Is it demographics only? The question in this chapter is

Table 1.1.   Elections Since World War II Decided by Less than Five Percentage Points

Election	National winner's national margin of victory	States with Margin of Victory 5% or Less	States with Margin of Victory 10% or More
1960	0.2 %	20	16
1968	0.7 %	13	22
1976	2.1 %	20	19
2000	–0.5 %	12	28
2004	2.4 %	11	29
2012	3.9 %	4	35

Source: Federal Election Commission (2012).

not so much "what causes a state to swing?" but rather "why are there so few swing states, and so many more landslide states?" Could it be that the intense focus on swing states—with all the news media coverage, campaign ads, phonebanking, and door-knocking focused on just a few states—are in some ways maintaining the exclusiveness of the "swing club?" Party loyalties are eroding across the nation, but do they erode differently in swing states, and do the operations of campaigns affect these processes? Finally, are there broader implications for the way parties and campaigns have functioned historically to connect citizens in the states to the national government? When the focus on national politics centers on a list of perennial swing states electoral cycle after electoral cycle, and that list seems to be shrinking, how does it effect on the way most citizens engage in the national election?

THE ELECTORAL COLLEGE AND THE
EVOLUTION OF PRESIDENTIAL CAMPAIGNS

The winner-take-all aspect of the Electoral College makes it necessary for presidential campaigns to devise battleground strategies which will maximize their Electoral College vote count. Well before the election, campaigns must decide on a list of states where victory is possible yet uncertain, and which state will receive more targeted appeals, television ads, candidate visits, and grassroots canvassing efforts than other states. Some of these battlegrounds are swing states, though not all. Even though campaigns are more able to raise record-breaking sums that might expand the campaign into more states, it is still a finite amount of money, and they must spend the vast majority of it in battleground states. These modern strategic imperatives are built into the system at its origin in 1787.

The Electoral College was based on an afterthought. The framers imagined the Union as a community of distinct republics, whose divergent interests would be harmonized under a Federal Constitution. But the election of the president did not fit neatly into this theoretical blueprint, despite the post hoc rationalizations of Hamilton in *Federalist* Number 68. At the Philadelphia Constitutional Convention in 1787, seven proposals for electing the presi dent were made and rejected, so the matter was postponed and referred to the Brearley Committee (Roche 2000). There seemed to be no satisfactory compromise: Should the Executive be directly elected by the people? By the state legislatures? By Governors? By Congress? Once the delegates worked out the difficult (if cynical) trade-offs over Congressional representation, the Electoral College seemed to be a perfect compromise. State legislatures would control the mode choosing Electors, small states were guaranteed three electoral votes, and large states had proportional weight in the choice. The president would be elected indirectly, but state legislators had the option of direct election of their Electors.

The framers accepted the Electoral College proposal as if it was too good to be true. And it was too good to be true. The fundamental fact about the Electoral College is that it is the only Constitutional institution that has never operated as originally conceived. Washington was the consensus choice to be the first President, but he would have been elected under any system the framers might have devised. By the divisive election of 1800 it was clear the system needed reform. It has been changing ever since, albeit informally, through legislation at the state level, and through changes in the way presidential campaigning is conducted. First the emergence of mass political parties and expansion of suffrage transformed the Electoral College system. In the first presidential election, six states had direct election of Electors. By 1824, a majority of the states had direct election. By 1832, states widely accepted the winner-take-all "unit rule" whereby each party put forward whole slates of Elector candidates. By 1836, all the states but one adopted the unit rule.

Observing elections during his visit to America in 1832, Alexis de Tocqueville (1945) remarked that the national election unleashed majoritarian passion as parties pushed for popularly elected Electors in the states:

> As the election draws near, the activity of intrigue and the agitation of the populace increase; the citizens are divided into hostile camps, each of which assumes the name of its favorite candidate; the whole nation glows with feverish excitement; the election is the daily theme of the public papers, the subject of private conversation, the end of every thought and every action, the sole interest of the present. (Tocqueville 1945)

Yet Tocqueville found it remarkable that the Electoral College system confines the storm to the most competitive states and reduces tumult across the entire nation. "As a calmer season returns, the current of the State, which had nearly broken its banks, sinks to its usual level: but who can refrain from astonishment at the causes of the storm" (Tocqueville 1945)? Political passion and participation remained tied to locality, and place of residence was established as the foundation of representation in the nineteenth century. Partisan turmoil was particularistic first, and national secondarily. What Tocqueville surveyed was a country where presidential campaigns were beginning to be carried out by the state parties which built coalitions in support of a presidential party nominee across many states. After the 1840s, parties became more centrally organized statewide. In such a world, more states were competitive and thus likely to swing.

After the Civil War, elections started to become ever more nationalized and candidate-centered and a wide array of states swung between competitiveness and solid partisanship. In the thirteen presidential elections between 1896 and 1944, there were 15 states that were competitive in most of those elections. It was during this same period that presidential candidates and their personal campaign visits began to displace the activities of state and local party organizations engaging voters. In 1880 it was considered unorthodox at best when James Garfield actually received delegations of visitors at his Ohio home during the campaign. In 1896, William Jennings Bryan was really the first presidential candidate to leave his home state to address party rallies in other states. Bryan travelled 18,000 miles and gave over 600 speeches, and nearly collapsed from exhaustion at the end of the campaign (Wayne 2012). As time passed, campaigns had to find ways to preserve the candidate's time and energy, not to mention the campaign's treasury. Still, presidential candidates made many visits to strategically important states. A case in point is Franklin Roosevelt's use of the "whistle-stop" campaign in 1932. Roosevelt rode a train which would stop at railroad stations along his route to Chicago where he was headed to receive the Democratic Convention's nomination. Roosevelt travelled 13,000 miles and visited 36 states (Wayne 2012). In 1948, Harry Truman initiated his famous comeback against Thomas Dewey by taking a whistle-stop tour of 22,000 miles in eight weeks, speaking to an estimated six million people as he stopped in 30 states from Ohio to California (Schwab 2008).

The rise of television in the 1950s changed the way candidates traveled when they engaged voters, and changed the relationship between the states, the parties, and the candidates. This was the dawn of the modern candidate-centered campaign system. In 1952, both the Stevenson and Eisenhower campaigns spent millions of dollars on TV advertising. Candidates could make direct appeals to voters without the kind of exhausting travel schedule Truman maintained, yet create the illusion of a personal encounter with the candidate on the street. At first this was done awkwardly, as we can see in President Eisenhower's series of campaign ads where actors playing common folk would ask Ike a question, and he would give a scripted answer. In 1960, in order to make good on his pledge to visit every state in the Union during the campaign, Richard Nixon spent the final weekend of his campaign in Alaska with its three electoral votes, while John Kennedy barnstormed in vote-rich Illinois, New Jersey, and New York (Tartar and Benson 2012). Nixon was the first candidate to win the majority of state contests, yet lose in the Electoral College count. Nixon's pledge to visit every state in 1960 ultimately had a very high political cost, and it explains why he was the last presidential candidate to make an attempt to visit every state in the Union (Johnson 2005).

My account of the shift from party-centered campaigns to candidate-centered campaigns is intended to demonstrate how modern campaigns and swing states influence one another. We can hardly think of a state swinging between the parties over a span of time, without also imagining that each successive pair of major party presidential campaigns will invest themselves in a battle to win that state. Campaigns think of swing states in terms of their overall "battleground strategy." Although a state's ability to be swung is necessary for it to be designated a battleground state, there are many other factors that presidential campaigns take into account. Moreover, while media reports tend to envision a political geography of red and blue states with a few purple swing states and spectator states, campaigns in fact divide up the country differently. They establish their formulas for achieving 270 electoral votes by envisioning a complex landscape of base states, strong, leaning, toss-ups, and must-win states (Jamieson 2006). Campaigns do not consider exclusively partisan competitiveness as a reason to invest heavily into a state. Presidential campaigns do not necessarily select their battlefields according to swing state status. For example, presidential campaigns need to focus on the magnitude of the swing vote, more than they need to consider the number of times a state switches between the parties. As Daron Shaw's (2006) research on presidential campaign strategies in from 1988 to 2004 shows, Republican and Democratic candidates alike create a list of battleground states that is normally longer than the list of tight swing states. Campaigns make strategic decisions based on their estimations of which states are likely to be most competitive and "swingable," but they also consider other factors as well. The electoral track record of statewide elected officials from the same party as the presidential candidate matters. Whether the candidate enjoys a lead in statewide polls that is at or slightly above the candidate's national poll numbers matters too. Whether the campaign can count on the most popular statewide elected leaders to support the campaign is also a factor. Native son effects come into consideration when a state is in a region close to the presidential candidate's home state. The cost of advertising is also a consideration. One reason why New Jersey is sometimes bypassed as a battleground is that advertising must be purchased in the high-priced Philadelphia and New York media markets. Exploiting financial advantages also plays into the decision, as is evidenced by the fundraising superiority of the Obama campaign in 2008 and 2012. Consider the 2008 Obama campaign's decision to make Indiana, Georgia, and North Carolina into battlefields, despite outside criticism of the decision. In his post-election defense of this decision, Obama campaign strategist David Plouffe said, "If [McCain's campaign] ended up spending more money in Indiana and North Carolina, that was a great benefit. But we went in there because we thought we could win. . . . In Indiana, we got 13 percent of the Republican vote. It was our highest Republican share of any battleground state" (Jamieson 2011).

Most importantly, presidential campaigns are interested in choosing battlegrounds in states with large numbers of electoral votes (Goux 2011). Pennsylvania is the best example of this. Pennsylvania has consistently voted Democratic in every presidential election since 1992, and seven times out of the last ten presidential elections. With the exception of a close victory for the Democrats in 2004, Pennsylvania's final vote margin has been larger than 5 percent every election since 1992—yet it has remained a perennial battleground for many election cycles. A state can be a battleground without being a swing state.

CAMPAIGN COMMUNICATIONS

With the rise of the 24-hour news cycle, candidate travel had a new rationale. Where the candidates go, the media follows, and increasingly the candidates are campaigning in the swing states. In 2008, 98 percent of candidate visits and presidential advertising occurred in only 15 states. In 2012, it became even more focused. After the conclusion of the final 2012 party nominating conventions, the major party presidential and vice presidential candidates visited 12 battleground states a total of 253 times. The other 39 states were

Table 1.2.   Where Candidates Held Events From Democratic National Convention Until Election Day

State	President Obama	Vice President Biden	Governor Romney	Congressman Ryan	Total
Colorado	5	3	6	9	23
Florida	9	8	15	8	40
Iowa	5	6	7	9	27
Michigan	0	0	0	1	1
Minnesota	0	0	0	1	1
Nevada	4	2	3	4	13
New Hampshire	4	4	3	2	13
North Carolina	0	2	1	0	3
Ohio	15	13	27	18	73
Pennsylvania	0	0	3	2	5
Virginia	6	4	17	9	36
Wisconsin	5	6	1	6	18
The 39 Other States	**0**	**0**	**0**	**0**	**0**
Total	53	48	83	69	253

Source: Fair Vote (2014)

visited zero times (FairVote 2014). As Table 1.2 shows, in 2012 after the Democratic Convention, the major party tickets only visited eleven states, with Ohio, Florida, and Virginia having the most candidate visits.

The media has also become more adept at tracking where the campaigns are spending their advertising dollars. Tables 1.3 and 1.4 show where advertising dollars went in 2012. Obama spent $20 in ads per voter in swing states, but only $7 nationwide. Romney spent $10 in ads per vote in the swing states, and $4 per vote in the country as a whole. Again, Florida, Ohio, and Virginia were major targets. It is important to note that the amount of money spent in a state does not necessarily reflect the concentration of advertising in that state. Table 1.3 shows New Hampshire received the second least amount of advertising dollars from the Obama campaign (after Wisconsin), but was the costliest state for the campaign in terms of number of votes received per advertising dollar spent.

The Wesleyan Media Project notes that 2012 saw the heaviest volume of TV spots in presidential election history with over 900,000 ads aired, and most of it targeted to swing states (Wesleyan Media Project 2012). The highest concentration of ads from the Obama campaign were in Denver (9,950 ads), Orlando (3,283 ads), and Tampa (3,905 ads). For Romney's campaign, the greatest concentration of TV spots were in Norfolk (1,692 ads), Cleveland (1,626 ads), and Denver (1,677 ads). This of course does not include all the ads produced and paid for by the parties, SuperPACs, and other kinds of advocacy groups, which are mostly negative ads (Wesleyan Media Project).

As Karl Rove learned in 2004, it is possible to win an election, not by trying futilely to persuade voters who have mainly made up their minds, but by

Table 1.3. Obama 2012 Advertising Expenditures per Vote Received

State	Obama $ spent for ads (millions)	$ spent per vote received
FL	$67.9	$16
VA	$57.8	$29
OH	$58.3	$21
NC	$36.7	$17
CO	$25.9	$20
IA	$23.4	$28
NV	$21.9	$41
WI	$10.3	$6
NH	$17.2	$47
Swing state Total ad expenditure	**$319.4**	**$20**
national total media expenditure	**$483.3**	**$7**

Sources: OpenSecrets.org (2015a), Federal Election Commission (2013) and Washington Post (2012)

Table 1.4.   Romney 2012 Advertising Expenditures per Vote Received

State	Romney $ spent for ads (millions)	$ spent per vote received
FL	$33.8	$8
VA	$31.0	$17
OH	$27.2	$10
NC	$21.8	$10
CO	$13.5	$11
NV	$8.7	$19
WI	$4.4	$3
NH	$3.4	$10
Swing state total ad expend	**$154.8**	**$10**
National total media expenditure	**$240.4**	**$4**

Sources: OpenSecrets.org (2015b), Federal Election Commission (2013) and Washington Post (2012)

"microtargeting" and mobilizing small segments of the nonvoting population who tilt in your party's direction on key issues (Penn 2007). Microtargeting is far more complicated than portrayed in the media myth of Democratic leaning independents driving their Volvos between Starbucks and Whole Foods, and of Republicans driving their Chevys between Cracker Barrel and Chick-Fil-A (Tierney 2005). But the idea that consumer preferences correlate with political leanings is becoming more and more important as campaigns seek to find new voters in tight swing states. Modern digital technology has taken this process to the next stage. Campaigns have become far more adept at using survey and marketing data to identify and target swing voters in states where a shift of a few percentage points could mean the difference between victory or defeat. Campaigns have learned to hire contractors who collect data from web browser histories to generate correlations between consumer preferences and implicit political preferences of millions of voters and nonvoters (Brennan 2012). In fact, this search for new voters may be part of the explanation of why swing states have higher turnout than other states, on average.

VOTER TURNOUT IN SWING STATES

Competitive elections generally tend to lead to higher voter turnout. As the gap between competitive swing states and uncompetitive swing states widens, there is also a turnout gap between swing states and the country at large. Do swing states have higher turnout because of campaign effects or because of demographic changes in the population? Table 1.5 shows that since 2000,

Table 1.5.   Voter Turnout in Swing States*

State	2012	2008	2004	2000
Florida	62.8	66.1	64.4	55.9
Ohio	64.5	66.9	66.8	56.7
North Carolina	64.9	65.5	57.8	50.7
Virginia	66.1	67.0	60.6	54.0
Wisconsin	72.9	72.4	74.8	67.6
Colorado	69.9	71.0	66.7	57.5
Iowa	70.3	69.4	69.9	63.2
Nevada	56.4	57.0	55.3	45.2
New Mexico	54.6	60.9	59.0	48.5
New Hampshire	70.2	71.1	70.9	63.9
Average	**65.3**	**66.7**	**64.6**	**56.3**
National turnout	**58.6**	**62.2**	**60.7**	**55.3**

*Turnout Figures are based on the Voting Eligible population.

Source: McDonald (2014)

the gap between swing state voter turnout and national turnout has been expanding from 1% difference in 2000 to 5.7% difference in 2012. The four states won by the closest margins in 2012 (Florida, Ohio, Virginia, and North Carolina) averaged a voter turnout of 64.6 percent. The voter turnout of the four least competitive states of 2012 (Utah, Hawaii, Wyoming, and Vermont) averaged at 54.8 percent (McDonald 2014).

In the standard account, voters in a competitive electoral environment receive more information about the issues and candidates, as well as hearing that the state is competitive, which in turn generates more interest in voting. However, as Keena Lipsitz (2009) has demonstrated, it is not voter awareness of a tight race that promotes higher voter turnout in swing states. Voter awareness and interest in the campaign are not much greater in the non-swing states. Rather, swing states have higher turnout because the campaigns in swing states are more effective at identifying voters, outreach, and mobilizing them for action (Lipsitz 2009). In his study of campaign effects in battleground states, Costas Panagopoulos (2009) found that aggregate voter preferences tend to shift more in battlegrounds than in non-battlegrounds, which shows that campaigns in the swing states are having an effect. Battleground campaigns and parties are generally more effective, of identifying likely voters and turning them out to vote on election day (Panagopoulos, 2009). According to Gimpel, Kaufman, and Pearson-Merkowitz, this campaign activity raises voter turnout among low-income voters, because it reduces the costs of participation that low-income voters in non-battleground states usually have to surmount (Gimpel et al. 2007).

PARTISAN VOTE BALANCE

Another feature of swing states is that they tend to be more evenly balanced between the two major political parties. There are a variety of methods for measuring partisan balance. Nate Silver defines a swing state in terms of its "closeness to the national average in partisan orientation" (Silver 2012). Partisanship scores in one election provide a rather accurate prediction of how parties will do in the next election. It also can provide glimpse into long-term changes. For example, FairVote's measure defines a swing state as a state where the presidential vote totals are between 47% and 53% of the candidate's national percentage of the vote (FairVote 2012). By that measure, Colorado, Florida, Minnesota, Iowa, Nevada, New Hampshire, North Carolina, Pennsylvania, Virginia, and Wisconsin have the most competitive partisanship ratings. The most detailed partisanship analysis is by Charlie Cook (2014). The "Cook Partisan Vote Score" focuses on the average partisan lean at the congressional district level for two elections, compared to the party's national vote percentage.

Whatever the measure used, analyzing the partisan vote, rather than party identification, gives us clues about which states will become more competitive or less competitive in the future (Cook 2014). As Table 1.6 shows, Cook's PVI score can be useful in predicting emerging swing states. Cook's

Table 1.6.　Most Balanced Partisan States, 2014

State	Partisan Voter Index 2014	Partisan Voter Index 2002	Trending Toward:
Colorado	D+1	R+5	DEMOCRATS +6
Florida	R+2	R+1	REPUBLICANS +1
Iowa	D+1	EVEN	DEMOCRATS +1
Michigan	D+4	D+2	DEMOCRATS +2
Minnesota	D+2	D+3	REPUBLICANS +1
Missouri	R+5	R+2	REPUBLICANS +3
Nevada	D+2	R+3	DEMOCRATS +5
New Hampshire	D+2	EVEN	DEMOCRATS +2
New Mexico	D+4	EVEN	DEMOCRATS +4
North Carolina	R+3	R+7	DEMOCRATS +4
Ohio	R+1	R+2	DEMOCRATS+1
Oregon	D+5	EVEN	DEMOCRATS +5
Pennsylvania	D+1	D+1	EVEN
Virginia	EVEN	R+5	DEMOCRATS +5
Washington	D+5	D+3	DEMOCRATS +2

Source: Cook (2014).

ratings suggest that Michigan, Minnesota, Missouri, New Mexico, Oregon, Pennsylvania, and Washington are possible future swing states. Moreover, competitive states that have been trending most strongly since 2002 toward the Democrats are western states Colorado, Nevada, New Mexico, and Oregon, along with North Carolina and Virginia.

One of the swing states criteria we use in this book is the frequency that a state swings from one party to the other across several elections. But an additional related factor is the magnitude of the swing vote—how widely a state's margin of victory can vary from election to election. The swing vote is estimated by examining several recent elections and taking the highest percentage of the vote won by one party and subtracting the lowest percentage of the vote won by the same party. The states with the largest swing are considered to have the highest number of persuadable voters, and thus are likely choices as battlefields. Table 1.7 shows the swing states examined in our volume and estimates their swing vote potential. Looking at more recent history from 2000 to 2012, the states with the largest swing vote are Colorado, Virginia, Nevada and New Mexico. We might estimate a decreasing swing vote for some current swing states by comparing the swing vote in the last four elections (2000 to 2012) with the previous four elections (1988 to 2000). The results show that several of the swing states had much larger vote swings before 2000, especially in Florida, Nevada, and New Hampshire.

BATTLEGROUND SELECTION

Campaigns do focus their get-out-the-vote efforts on strong partisans, but they focus their efforts at communication and persuasion on unaffiliated independent voters. Swing voters are persuadable, and are more likely to hold the key to understanding how campaigns play a role in the states that swing. Some states swing because they are "elastic" and shift back and forth between the parties in the midst of a campaign, in reaction to events. For example, if presidential job approval ratings should change by 5 percent nationally, an elastic state would also shift by 5 percent or even more (Silver 2012). Elastic swing states have a high percentage of independents who do not lean toward either party, and they tend to respond to shifts in media coverage or changes in who is leading in national horserace polls. New Hampshire is a typical elastic state that swung from being a Republican state to being a swing state tilting toward the Democrats. New Hampshire has the highest percentage of independents among the swing states and its swing voters are largely white, non-evangelical Christians who only lean weakly toward the Republicans. Other elastic swing states are Colorado, Iowa, New Mexico, and Wisconsin

Table 1.7. Swing Vote and Swing States, 1988–2000

Swing State	Electoral Votes	Victory Percentage and Winning Party						% Swing 2000–2012	% Swing 1988–2000
		2008	2004	2000	1996	1992	1988		
Florida	29	3 D	5 R	0 R	6 D	2R	22 R	8	28
Ohio	18	5 D	3 R	3 R	6 D	2 D	11 R	8	17
North Carolina	15	1 D	12 R	13 R	5 R	1 R	16 R	14	15
Virginia	13	7 D	8 R	9 R	2 R	4 R	21 R	16	19
Wisconsin	10	14 D	1 D	0 D	10 D	4 D	3 D	14	7
Colorado	9	9 D	5 R	9 R	2 R	4 D	8 R	18	13
Iowa	6	10 D	1 R	1 D	10 D	3 D	10 D	11	7
Nevada	6	12 D	3 R	4 R	2 D	2 D	21 R	16	23
New Mexico	5	15 D	1 R	0 D	7 D	9 D	5 R	16	14
New Hampshire	4	9 D	1 D	1 R	10 D	1 D	26 R	10	27

Source: Federal Election Commission (2013)

(Silver 2012). Silver goes on to characterize "inelastic swing states" as states that do not shift between parties very quickly or easily. Their independent voters are more firmly rooted in party preferences. For example, North Carolina is an inelastic state, because its high percentage of black voters will reliably vote Democratic, and its large white evangelical population will tend to vote for Republicans. That does not leave very many persuadable independents who might change their votes because of events happening in the campaign. Inelastic states swing very slowly—sometimes over two or three election cycles. Joining North Carolina as an inelastic swing state is Virginia (Silver 2012). In the elastic swing states, campaigns can have a great deal more influence on the direction a state may swing. But in the inelastic states, campaigns can make much less difference. Using the elasticity concept, we next turn to independent voters in the swing states, to get a better idea of which way they are swinging and how likely it is that campaign messages and tactics might help the swinging along.

HIGH PERCENTAGE OF INDEPENDENTS

We turn, then, to the independent voters in swing states. Are "swing states" distinguished by a higher than average percentage of swing voters? This is not an easy question to answer. It is first important to distinguish independent voters from swing voters. Mayer's (2008) study defines a swing voter as "a voter who is not so solidly committed to one candidate or the other as to make all efforts at persuasion futile" (Mayer 2007). In short, swing voters are individuals who have a strong likelihood of voting, yet are persuadable in ways that voters with strong party identification are not. When we refer to independents, we either mean voters who are not registered with any political party, or voters who on surveys state that they do not identify with the Democrats or Republicans. There is certainly some overlap between independent voters and swing voters, but they are by no means identical. Many independents will "lean" toward a party and keep a fairly consistent partisan voting pattern. True swing voters are much less predictable in the party they will support. The relationship between swing voters and the swing states is also quite complex. Like swing voters, swing states are states that cannot be firmly counted upon to vote for one candidate or another. But this analogy is quite limited. When we think of swing voters "changing their minds" we think of an individual making a decision, from election to election. Swing states certainly may have a sizeable percentage of swing voters, but swing states do not "change their minds." Some swing state voters may be persuadable to change their support from election to election, but it seems clear that what a swing state is changing is not individual minds, but changing demographics. Swing states do swing, but only partly because voters have changed their mind. Theoretically it is possible for a state to swing from one party to the other, without a single voter from the previous election changing his/her mind. How? Demographic change. Indeed, all states experience change in their populations due to birth, mortality, and migration. Swing states are states where population shifts between elections bring into the electorate new proportions of key groups that can shift the electoral balance.

There is another important distinction between swing voters and swing states. Swing states are far easier to target than swing voters. Even if there were sufficient numbers of swing voters to swing a non-competitive state, it would be nearly impossible to effectively target them with persuasion. But campaigns can target swing states and insure that their messages are being received by thin slices of the swing voters that might deliver the victory. Finally, campaigns have a better idea of how to target independent voters than they do elusive swing voters. Some swing states, like New Hampshire, have a higher percentage of independent voters than other swing states—but those independents seem to be tilting more toward Democrats in the past several election cycles.

The Gallup organization frequently ranks states according to partisan lean by comparing the percentage of Democratic identifiers to the percentage of Republican identifiers in each state, including independents who lean toward a party (Saad 2014). For 2013, Gallup found that Pennsylvania, Nevada, Kentucky, West Virginia, Wisconsin, and Ohio had a slight (3% or less) Democratic lean. North Carolina, Arizona, Virginia, Louisiana, Iowa, and Georgia leaned slightly to the Republican side. Nevertheless, as Jay Cost points out, the problem is that Gallup's rankings of partisan competitiveness does not correspond very well with swing state status (Cost 2010). For example, Gallup counts such red states as Kentucky and West Virginia as leaning Democratic. And swing states Florida, Colorado, New Hampshire, and Iowa are deemed uncompetitive in terms of party identification. There may be plausible reason to believe some of Gallup's red states may eventually become more competitive in non-presidential elections, but they simply do not qualify as presidential swing states. Another difficulty with the Gallup approach is that it tends to define "competitive" states in terms of the smallness of the percentage of independent voters. In fact, most swing states have a higher-than-average percentage of independents.

I propose a different approach. Recognizing these previously mentioned caveats, if we are trying to get a general idea of the percentage of swing voters residing in the swing states, the best place to look is among independent voters in the swing states, and then to gauge how much they swing. We can compare the election with the lowest percentage of the independent vote received by each party, with the election showing the highest percentage of support for a party. That way, we can estimate the "swing" in the independent vote: the gap between the highest and lowest percentages of support from independent voters.

Among the swing states, which ones have the greatest amount of swing in the independents, and how important is this in explaining the overall amount of swing in a swing state? Instead of looking at the balance of party identification (with leaners) as Gallup does, it is wiser to consider the percentage of independent voters, and how they swing from election to election. Pre-election polls can provide some clues about independent voters, but different polling organizations often survey different swing states at varying stages of the campaign. By tracking exit poll data instead, we can get a sense of how much independent voters are swinging from one party to the other, and where the trends are headed. Table 1.8 illustrates some important features shared by the swing states we have identified for this book. Independents in Colorado, Nevada, New Mexico, and Ohio are swinging slightly closer to the Republicans, while New Hampshire and Wisconsin's independents are swinging slightly toward the Democrats.

Table 1.8 shows there is a great deal of variation in the independent swing for different states. North Carolina, Virginia, Colorado, and Iowa showed independents swinging at or a little below the average national independent swing. Florida, Ohio, Wisconsin, Nevada, and New Mexico were more than the national average for independent swing. The amount of swing from one party to another over time matters more than the raw percentage of independents. Presidential campaign staffs seeking to identify their battleground states analyze the independent swings with greater precision and detail than

Table 1.8.   Swing State Independent Vote 2004-2012

State	Margin 2012	Margin 2008	Margin 2004	% Independent Swing 2004–2012
Florida	D+3	D+7	D+16	23
Ohio	R+10	D+8	D+19	29
North Carolina	R+15	R+21	R+15	6
Virginia	R+11	D+1	R+10	12
Wisconsin	D+2	D+19	R+12	31
Colorado	R+4	D+10	D+7	14
Iowa	D+4	D+15	D+8	11
Nevada	R+7	D+13	D+12	20
New Mexico	R+7	D+15	D+7	22
New Hampshire	D+7	D+20	D+14	13
AVERAGE	**R+3.8**	**D+8.7**	**D+4.6**	**5**
NATIONAL EXIT POLL	**R+5**	**D+8**	**D+1**	**13**

Source: Exit Polls 2004-2012, National Voter Pool (2012)

is necessary for this chapter, but Table 1.8 shows the independent swing in our selected swing states. Every one of the ten swing states is swinging toward the Democrats except Iowa, though Iowa maintains a tilt toward the Democrats. New Hampshire, Nevada, Virginia, and Florida have swung the farthest toward the Democrats. All four went Republican in 1984 and 1988, and all four went Democratic in 2008 and 2012.

In fact, as Table 1.9 shows, swing states have a greater percentage of independent voters on election day than the national average. The swing states have an average of 32.9 percent independents in 2012, compared to 29% nationally. In other words, the independent vote in swing states is growing, and the independent vote in uncompetitive states is shrinking. In the least competitive states identified by Gallup, we see even fewer independents. The average percentage of independents in "heavy blue" 2012 states Connecticut, Maryland, and New York is 22.7 percent, and the average for the 2012 "heavy red" states Kansas, Alabama, and Montana is 29.7 percent. This trend is consistent over several presidential election cycles. The average percentage

Table 1.9. 2012 Independent Vote in Swing States and Highly Uncompetitive States (Includes D & R Leaners)

Swing States	% independent voters	Obama ind. vote	Romney ind. vote	Difference
Florida	33	50	47	3
Ohio	31	43	53	−10
North Carolina	29	42	57	−15
Virginia	29	43	54	−11
Wisconsin	31	49	47	2
Colorado	37	45	49	−4
Iowa	34	55	51	4
Nevada	34	43	50	−7
New Mexico	28	41	48	−7
New Hampshire	43	52	45	7
Highly Uncompetitive States				
Maryland	23	53	41	12
New York	23	49	45	4
Connecticut	22	51	46	5
Kansas	24	43	51	−8
Alabama	24	23	75	−52
Montana	41	40	53	−13
SWING STATE AVERAGE	**32.9**	**46.3**	**50.1**	**−3.8**
UNCOMPETITIVE STATE AVERAGE	**26.2**	**43.2**	**51.8**	**−8.7**
NATIONAL EXIT POLL	**29**	**45**	**50**	**−5**

Source: 2012 Exit Poll, National Voter Pool.

of independents in the swing states increased from 28.2 percent in 2004, to 31.9 percent in 2008, to 32.9 percent in 2012.

Another key swing state feature is that independents make up a larger proportion of the electorate in swing states than they do nationwide. When comparing the proportion of independent voters in swing states to the proportions in the most uncompetitive states (both strongly Republican and strongly Democratic states), the uncompetitive states have significantly smaller percentages of independents. In one sense, this is not surprising: Certainly part of the explanation is that swing state voters are exposed to more campaign news, candidate appearances, television ads and campaign phone calls than voters in uncompetitive states. And as we have already discussed, voter turnout is higher in swing states than the national average. Swing state independents are more informed and more connected to campaigns, so they are more likely to turn out than independents elsewhere.

In fact, there is a more complex process occurring. Table 1.10 shows the proportions of independents are rising in the swing states since 2008, while independent percentages are holding steady in uncompetitive states and nationally. Most public polls determine whether an independent "leans" toward one of the major parties, and adds these leaners to the estimate of Democratic and Republican identifiers. As Table 1.11 demonstrates, if party leaners are excluded from what counts as an "independent," the resulting percentage of independent voters in swing states is then consistently lower than the percentage of independent voters nationally. Two important, yet apparently contradictory facts about swing states emerges from this data. First, the proportion of independent voters in swing states is increasing at a much faster rate than nationally or in spectator states. Second, the percentage of "pure" independents is declining in swing states, much more rapidly than in spectator states or in the nation at large. What this suggests is that even though swing states appear to have more independent swing voters, in fact the percentage of true independents is smaller in swing states. Contrary to conventional thinking, states begin to swing when the percentage of swing voters actually begins to decline below the national state average.

As an illustration, Table 1.12 shows how, for Florida and Ohio at least, voters who say they are independents are more likely to lean toward a party, especially in a presidential election year. Kenneth Winneg and his colleagues (2014) found a similar pattern in their comparison of independents in battleground states versus non-battlegrounds in presidential elections from 2000 to 2012. They found that during the course of these campaigns, independents in battlegrounds gravitated toward identifying with a party (more toward the Democrats than the Republicans), while non-battleground independents held more steady throughout the campaign. Presidential campaign activities in Florida and Ohio may be turning voters who would otherwise be independents into quasi-partisans (Winneg et al. 2014).

Table 1.10.   Independent Vote in Swing States and Selected Uncompetitive States 2004–2012 (Includes D & R Leaners)

	Independent Vote (%)		
SWING STATE	*2012*	*2008*	*2004*
Florida	33	29	23
Ohio	31	30	25
North Carolina	29	27	21
Virginia	29	27	26
Wisconsin	31	29	27
Colorado	37	39	33
Iowa	34	33	30
Nevada	34	32	26
New Mexico	28	28	27
New Hampshire	43	45	44
SELECT TOP UNCOMPETITIVE STATES			
Maryland	23	21	22
New York	23	25	26
Connecticut	22	31	33
Kansas	51	44	52
Alabama	75	64	66
Montana	53	53	46
UNCOMPETITIVE STATE AVERAGE	**41.2**	**39.7**	**40.8**
SWING STATE AVERAGE	**32.9**	**39.7**	**28.2**
NATIONAL EXIT POLL	**29**	**27**	**26**

Source: Exit Polls 2004-2014, National Voter Pool (2012)

* 2014 Exit Poll data not available for least competitive states

Table 1.11.   Independents as a Percentage of Likely Voters: Selected Swing States and Uncompetitive Democratic States (Excludes D & R Leaners)

State	2014	2012	2010	2008	% Change 2008–2014
Pennsylvania	23%	27%	42%	43%	20%
Florida	23%	29%	36%	41%	18%
Ohio	33%	30%	43%	43%	10%
National	*35%**	*38%*	*44%**	*43%*	*7%*
New Jersey	36%	34%	46%	47%	–9%
New York	29%	48%	39%	35%	–10%
Connecticut	35%	40%	42%	50%	–15%

Source: Quinnipiac University Polling Institute (2012), Swing State Poll of likely independent voters "Election Eve" Surveys, 2008-2014

* survey of registered voters

Table 1.12.   **Estimated Party Lean of Independents in Florida and Ohio, 2008–2014***

	2014	2012	2010	2008
Florida	–10%	–3%	–7%	–2%
Ohio	–9%	–2%	–8%	–1%
National	0%	0%	+2%	–3%

*Based on differences between National Exit Poll to "Closest To Election Day" Quinnipiac University Polls of independents, excluding leaners.

One possible explanation is found in research on how independents display "implicit preferences" for Democrats or Republicans, regardless of how strongly they insist they are independent. By measuring the reaction time between words representing "Democrats" and "Republicans" and words representing "self" and "other," social psychologists have found evidence that undecided voters who connect one party faster with "self" and the other party faster with "other" have an "implicit preference" that would be impossible to detect in election surveys (Hawkins 2012). If presidential campaigns are bombarding independent voters in swing states with media information, campaign visits, phone calls and advertising, it is reasonable to consider that voters in those states will have a stronger partisan lean than in states where voters are reminded frequently of the insignificance of their preferences on the nightly news.

In sum, what national party polarization means for voters in the spectator states is a widening of the gap between Democratic and Republican identifiers, thereby adding to the number of uncompetitive states with every passing election cycle. But in swing states, polarization appears to operate differently. Polarization in swing states is more the result of polarized national presidential campaigns operating in swing states. The more that the presidential campaigns concentrate their vast resources on voters in a vanishingly small number of swing states, the more we see the percentage of party-leaning independents increase in those states. At the same time, the campaigns help independents lean to Democrats or Republicans. Swing states do tend to have larger proportions of independent voters than other states. But, on the other hand, independents are more likely than independents in other states to lean back toward the Republicans and Democrats—at least part of the way. To put it another way, in swing states, "true swing voters" are more numerous among the likely voters than they are in spectator states.

REFLEX/UNRELIABLE INDEPENDENTS

Certain groups of voters are unlikely to turn out for non-presidential elections, but become engaged when a presidential campaign year arrives. This is especially true when these "peripheral voters" perceive a tight contest. Core voters or "reflex voters" turn out to vote reliably in statewide elections, like a reflex. This "surge and decline" model (Campbell 1960) is distinct from the elasticity concept discussed above. Peripheral voters are not necessarily "swing" voters or independents. They can have strong party identification, yet not turn out reliably in both nonpresidential elections. Young voters tend to be peripheral and tilt strongly toward the Democrats, but over half of them skip the midterm elections. Older voters, though, are more reflexive and turn out in high numbers in presidential and non-presidential elections (Issenberg 2014).

Since the 2000 election, swing states have "swung" because even though both peripheral and the core voters have tended more and more to align themselves with parties, a greater number of peripheral voters tend to lean to the Democratic candidates. Democratic peripheral voters include the young, Hispanics, and lower-status voters. Yet those partisan leanings are not always stable and can be affected by campaign activities and news. Reflex voters increasingly lean toward Republican candidates, and include more white, upper income, older voters (Issenberg 2014). Therefore the reason that Republicans have been more successful in off-year elections for Congress and Governor since 2010 is the increasing Republican cast of the reflex voters and the Democratic leanings of peripheral voters.

What about independent voters? Are they more reflexive than independents in other states? Table 1.13 focuses on exit polls in the elections of 2008, 2010, 2012, and 2014 for Pennsylvania, Florida, and Ohio in comparison to national exit polls. It shows that not only is the percentage of independents among likely voters declining between presidential election years and congressional election years, but the percentage tends also to decline overall. In other words, for Florida, Pennsylvania, and Ohio, independent voters tend

Table 1.13. Independent Reflex Between Presidential and Congressional Elections in Key Swing States, as a Percentage of Likely Voters Selected Swing States and Uncompetitive Democratic States (Excludes D & R Leaners)

STATE	2014	2012	2010	2008	Average Independent REFLEX
Pennsylvania	23%	27%	42%	43%	−2.5%
Florida	23%	29%	36%	41%	−6.0%
Ohio	33%	30%	43%	43%	3.3%
National	*35%**	*38%*	*44%**	*43%*	*3.3%*

Source: Quinnipiac University Swing State Poll (2014) "Election Eve" Surveys, 2008-2014

* survey of registered voters—all others results are of likely voters.

to be more reflexive than voters nationally. Nationally, the proportion of independent voters on election day has held steady since 2004 at an average of 28 percent. It is astounding that since 2004 the proportion of independent voters has steadily climbed from an average of 28% in 2004, to an average of nearly 33% in 2012.

CONCLUSION

As the case studies found in other chapters show, each swing state has its own story, its own peculiar set of ingredients which keeps it swinging. My purpose here was to point out how presidential campaign strategies are part of those stories. Campaigns do not simply react to states that swing—they undertake strategies in hope of causing them to swing in their candidate's favor. Campaigns devise electoral strategies to pinpoint persuasive messages at key groups of voters within a set of battleground states, and although swing states are not the only states targeted as battlegrounds, they are the most important ones. Rather than simply target swing states as units, campaigns identify groups of voters within swing states that are receptive to their appeals, and who might become mobilized or shifted during the election season. Voters in the swing states receive more targeted appeals, more personal communications from parties and campaigns, and hear frequently in the news how important their state is for the future of the country. Even though there is only mixed evidence that independent voters are better informed in swing states than elsewhere, it is clear that the greater resources and attention given to voters in swing states makes a difference in lowering several of the obstacles to voting that independents and peripheral voters experience. Voter turnout is on average, higher in swing states, and independents are pulled more strongly toward political partisanship in swing states. Which specific obstacles to voting are lowered, how, and for which groups, is a question answered by more detailed research on key groups and specific localities in swing states.

Despite the great demographic changes occurring within the swing states and elsewhere, there appears to be fewer and fewer highly competitive states in recent presidential elections, which compels presidential campaigns to focus their increasing stockpiles of resources on this narrowing collection of states. Should we blame campaigns for not spreading their resources and not trying as hard to appeal to independents in uncompetitive states? No. Campaigns are after all trying to win the current election, not a future one, and they cannot afford the luxury of playing the game too many moves ahead. Besides, it is difficult to precisely spot the right signs that an uncompetitive state is about to become a swing state. Until that kind of prophecy is achieved, campaigns will have to heed Churchill's warning that the chain of destiny can only be forged one link at a time.

Do these insights about independent voters in swing states support the idea of reforming or eliminating the Electoral College? Although we can lament the fact that the Electoral College leads to a situation of unequal influence for some voters in battleground states, a thoroughgoing critique of the Electoral College system is beyond the scope of this chapter. Nevertheless, we should be cautious about presuming that a major reform of the Electoral College would lead automatically to higher levels of voter engagement and participation nationally. For example, the most promising reform is the model National Popular Vote Bill, now supported by ten states plus the District of Columbia. This is a pledge by states to require their Electors to cast their votes for the winner of the popular vote, and would take effect when enacted by the number of states representing a majority of the Electoral College vote (National Popular Vote, 2015). Assuming that it would survive a Supreme Court challenge, this reform would indeed change the strategies of presidential campaigns and would make swing states less relevant in achieving an electoral majority. Making every vote count equally is an attractive ideal. But in practice a national popular vote will not lead campaigns to give equal attention to every voter or even every state, nor will it reduce the relentless pursuit of campaign dollars. Without an Electoral College, campaigns would focus less on states, but more on large regions. I have argued in this chapter that, as long as presidential campaigns have finite resources, and must devote those resources where it is most likely to produce a victory, key voter blocs will receive disproportionate amounts of persuasion and grassroots mobilization focus from the national campaigns. They would begin to focus the most densely populated areas, or on regions where they find high percentages of hardcore partisans as well as persuadable independents that can be mobilized on election day. In any case the implications are almost impossible to fully calculate. Simply put, advocates of a national popular vote scheme should be careful what they wish for.

FOR FURTHER READING

Campbell, J. E. (1987). "The Revised Theory of Surge and Decline." *American Journal of Political Science* 31.4: 965–979.

Cook C. (2014). "Partisan Voter Index by State, 1994–2014." *Cook Political Report.* Retrieved from http://cookpolitical.com/file/filename.pdf.

Jamieson, K. H. (ed.) (2013). *Electing the President, 2012: The Insiders' View.* Philadelphia: University of Pennsylvania Press.

Mayer, W. G. (ed.) (2008). *The Swing Voter in American Politics*. Washington, DC: Brookings Institution.

Panagopoulos, C. (2009). "Campaign Dynamics in Battleground and Nonbattleground States." *The Public Opinion Quarterly* 73.1: 119–129.

Paulson, A. (2007). *Electoral Realignment and the Outlook for American Democracy. Boston: Northeastern University Press.*

Penn, M. (2009). *Microtrends: Small Forces behind Tomorrow's Big Changes*. New York: Hachette.

Quinnipiac University Polling Institute (2015). http://www.quinnipiac.edu/news-and-events/quinnipiac-university-poll/.

Shaw, D. R. (2006). The Race to 270: The Electoral College and the Campaign Strategies of 2000 and 2004. Chicago: University of Chicago Press.

de Tocqueville, A. (1945). *Democracy in America* (volumes 1–2). Edited by P. Bradley, H. Reeve, and F. Bowen. New York: A. A. Knopf.

Wayne, S. J. (2012). *The Road to the White House: The Politics of Presidential Elections (9th edition). Boston: Wadsworth.*

Winneg, K., K. H. Jamieson, and B. Hardy (2014). "Party Identification in the 2012 Election." *Presidential Studies Quarterly* 44.1: 143–156.

BIBLIOGRAPHY

Brennan, A. (November 5, 2012). "Microtargeting: How Campaigns Know You Better Than You Know Yourself." *CNN.com. Retrieved from* http://www.cnn.com/2012/11/05/politics/voters-microtargeting/index.html.

Campbell, A. (1960). "Surge and Decline: A Study of Electoral Change." *Public Opinion Quarterly* 24.3: 397–418.

Campbell, J. E. (1987). "The Revised Theory of Surge and Decline." *American Journal of Political Science* 31.4: 965–979.

Cebula, R. J., and C. M. Duquette (2013). "Battleground States and Voter Participation in U.S. Presidential Elections: An Empirical Test." *Applied Economics* 45.25/27: 3795–3799.

Cheng, H., and D. Riffe (2008). "Attention, Perception, and Perceived Effects: Negative Political Advertising in a Battleground State of the 2004 Presidential Election." *Mass Communication and Society* 11.2: 177–196.

Cook C. (2014). "Partisan Voter Index by State, 1994–2014." *Cook Political Report.* Retrieved from http://cookpolitical.com/file/filename.pdf.

Cook, R. (October 5, 2012). "When the Whole Map Was in Play." *Rasmussen Reports.* Retrieved from http://www.rasmussenreports.com/public_content/political_commentary/commentary_by_rhodes_cook/when_the_whole_map_was_in_play.

Cost, J. (July 26, 2010). "A Note on Gallup's Party Identification Map." *RealClearPolitics HorseRace Blog.* Retrieved from http://www.realclearpolitics.com/horseraceblog/2010/07/note_on_gallups_party_id_map.html.

FairVote (2012). Presidential tracker. Retrieved from. http://www.fairvote.org/research-and-analysis/presidential-elections/presidential-tracker/#.USZbjWdyTj4

FairVote (June 2011). "Not Your Parents' Presidential Elections: The Decline of Swing States, 1960–2008." *Center for Voting and Democracy. Retrieved from* http://www.fairvote.org/research-reports/not-your-parents-presidential-elections/.

Federal Election Commission (2013). *Federal Elections 2012: Results.* Retrieved from http://www.fec.gov/pubrec/fe2012/federalelections2012.pdf.

Gimpel, J. G., K. M. Kaufmann, and S. Pearson-Merkowitz (2007). "Battleground States versus Blackout States: The Behavioral Implications of Modern Presidential Campaigns." *The Journal of Politics* 69.3: 786–797.

Glaeser, E. L., and B. A. Ward (2006). "Myths and Realities of American Political Geography." *The Journal of Economic Perspectives* 20.2: 119–144.

Gopoian, J. D., and S. Hadjiharalambous (1994). "Late-Deciding Voters in Presidential Elections." *Political Behavior* 16.11: 55–78.

Goux, D. (2010). *The Battleground State: Conceptualizing Geographic Contestation in American Presidential Elections, 1960–2004 (doctoral dissertation). Retrieved from* http://escholarship.org/uc/item/8dp32778.

Hawkins, C. B. (2012). "The Independent Voter: Not So Middle-of-the-Road." *Society of Personality and Social Psychology Connections. Retrieved from* https://spsptalks.wordpress.com/2012/12/08/the-independent-voter-not-so-middle-of-the-road-after-all/.

Hill, J. S., E. Rodriquez, and A. E. Wooden (2010). "Stump Speeches and Road Trips: The Impact of State Campaign Appearances in Presidential Elections." *PS: Political Science and Politics* 43.2: 243–254.

Issenberg, S. (April 27, 2014). "How the Democrats Can Avoid Going Down this November: The New Science of Democratic Survival." *The New Republic.* Retrieved from http://www.newrepublic.com/article/117520/how-democrats-can-avoid-going-down-2014-midterm-election.

Jamieson, K. H. (ed.) (2013). *Electing the President, 2012: The Insiders' View.* Philadelphia: University of Pennsylvania Press.

Jamieson, K. H. (ed.) (2011). *Electing the President, 2008: The Insiders' View.* Philadelphia: University of Pennsylvania Press.

Jamieson, K. H. (ed.) (2006). *Electing the President, 2004: The Insider's View.* Philadelphia: University of Pennsylvania Press.

Johnson, B. J. (2005). "Identities of Competitive States in U.S. Presidential Elections: Electoral College Bias or Candidate Centered Politics?" *Publius: The Journal of Federalism 35, no. 2 (2005): 337–355.*

Lipsitz, K. (2009). "The Consequences of Battleground and 'Spectator' State Residency for Political Participation." *Political Behavior* 31.2: 187–209.

Mackelprang, A. J., B. Grofman, and N. K. Thomas (1975). "Electoral Change and Stability: Some New Perspectives." *American Politics Research* 3.3: 315–339.

Mayer, W. G. (ed.) (2008). *The Swing Voter in American Politics.* Washington, DC: Brookings Institution.

McDonald, M. (2014). *United States Election Project.* Retrieved from http://www.electproject.org/home/voter-turnout/voter-turnout-data.

McKee, S. C., and J. M. Teigen (2009). "Probing the Reds and Blues: Sectionalism and Voter Location in the 2000 and 2004 U. S. Presidential Elections." *Political Geography* 28.8: 484–495.

National Popular Vote (2015). Retrieved from http://www.nationalpopularvote.com/pages/explanation.php.

National Voter Pool (2012). "Exit Polls." Retrieved from http://elections.nbcnews.com/ns/politics/2012/all/president/#exitPoll.

OpenSecrets.org (2015). "Barack Obama." Retrieved from https://www.opensecrets.org/pres12/candidate.php?id=N00009638.

OpenSecrets.org (2015b). "Mitt Romney." Retrieved from https://www.opensecrets.org/pres12/candidate.php?id=N00000286.

Ostermeier, E. (August 2, 2012). "Swing States, Battleground States, or Purple States?" *University of Minnesota Smart Politics Blog, August 2, 2012. Web. Accessed November 1, 2014.* http://blog.lib.umn.edu/cspg/smartpolitics/2012/08/swing_states_battleground_stat.php.

Ostermeier, E. (November 19, 2012). "Death of the Battlegrounds? The 2012 Election in History." *University of Minnesota Smart Politics Blog. Retrieved from* http://blog.lib.umn.edu/cspg/smartpolitics/2012/11/death_of_the_battlegrounds_the.php.

Panagopoulos, C. (2012). "Campaign Context and Preference Dynamics in U.S. Presidential Elections." *Journal of Elections, Public Opinion and Parties* 22.2: 123–137.

Panagopoulos, C. (2009). "Campaign Dynamics in Battleground and Nonbattleground States." *The Public Opinion Quarterly* 73.1: 119–129.

Paulson, A. (2007). *Electoral Realignment and the Outlook for American Democracy. Boston: Northeastern University Press.*

Penn, M. (2009). *Microtrends: Small Forces behind Tomorrow's Big Changes.* New York: Hachette.

Quinnipiac University Polling Institute (2014). "Election Eve Surveys, 2008–2014." Retrieved from http://www.quinnipiac.edu/news-and-events/quinnipiac-university-poll/.

Raskin, J. B. (2008). "Neither the Red States nor the Blue States but the United States: The National Popular Vote and American Political Democracy." *Election Law Journal* 7.3: 188–195.

Richie, R., and A. Levien (2013). "The Contemporary Presidency: How the 2012 Presidential Election Has Strengthened the Movement for the National Popular Vote Plan." *Presidential Studies Quarterly* 43.2: 353–376.

Roche, J. P. (2000). "Constitutional Convention of 1787." In L.W. Levy and K. L. Karst (eds.), *Encyclopedia of the American Constitution*, 2nd ed. (vol. 2), 517–523. Detroit: Macmillan Reference USA.

Schwab, N. (January 17, 2008). "Dewey Defeats Truman? No Way. Truman 'Gave 'Em Hell' on His Whistlestop Tour of 1948." *U.S. News & World Report*. Retrieved from http://www.usnews.com/news/articles/2008/01/17/when-harry-gave-em-hell.

Shaw, D. R. (1999). "The Effect of TV Ads and Candidate Appearances on Statewide Presidential Votes, 1988–96." *The American Political Science Review* 93.2: 345–361.

Shaw, D. R. (2006). The Race to 270: The Electoral College and the Campaign Strategies of 2000 and 2004. Chicago: University of Chicago Press.

Silver, N. (May 21, 2012). "Swing Voters and Elastic States." New York Times Online. Retrieved from http://fivethirtyeight.blogs.nytimes.com/2012/05/21/swing-voters-and-elastic-states/.

Tartar, A., and E. Benson (October 14, 2012). "The Forever Campaign." *New York Magazine*. Retrieved from http://nymag.com/news/politics/elections-2012/election-timeline.html.

de Tocqueville, A. (1945). *Democracy in America* (volumes 1–2). Edited by P. Bradley, H. Reeve, and F. Bowen. New York: A. A. Knopf.

Washington Post (2012). "Mad money." *Washington Post Web*. Retrieved from http://www.washingtonpost.com/wp-srv/special/politics/track-presidential-campaign-ads-2012/.

Wayne, S. J. (2012). *The Road to the White House: The Politics of Presidential Elections (9th edition). Boston: Wadsworth.*

Wesleyan Media Project (October 24, 2012). "2012 Shatters 2004 and 2008 Records for Total Ads Aired." Retrieved from http://mediaproject.wesleyan.edu/releases/2012-shatters-2004-and-2008-records-for-total-ads-aired/.

Winneg, K., K. H. Jamieson, and B. Hardy (2014). "Party Identification in the 2012 Election." *Presidential Studies Quarterly* 44.1: 143–156.

Wolak, J. (2006). "The Consequences of Presidential Battleground Strategies for Citizen Engagement." *Political Research Quarterly (Formerly WPQ)* 59.3: 353–361.

Chapter Two

The One That Got Away

Missouri's Break from Ultimate Swing State Status

Kenneth F. Warren and Rafael Jacob

No more focus by national political pundits. No more calls from foreign journalists asking about what's happening in Missouri. The Show-Me State might show them no more. Missouri's claim to being a bellwether, a political microcosm that reflects the mood of the country, is likely over.

—Terry Ganey, *Columbia Tribune*

The most extraordinary thing about Missouri may be how ordinary it is. For the past century or so one would be hard pressed to find another state more reflective of the nation as a whole than Missouri in terms of its urban and rural mix, its Catholic/Protestant and white/black ratios, its size and population, and its location in the middle of America's heartland. Yes, until recently the "Show-Me State" acted as the undisputed perennial electoral bellwether[1]—the ultimate swing state. If there ever was a state that served as a microcosm for the country, Missouri was it.

Indeed, from 1904 to 2004, Missouri sided with the presidential election winner in every single instance but one—in 1956, when Democratic nominee Adlai Stevenson carried the state by less than a quarter of a percentage point as incumbent President Dwight D. Eisenhower was cruising to reelection. When looking at the popular vote, the only split other than 1956 over this timeline occurred in 2000, when Democratic nominee Al Gore won both Missouri and the national popular vote but narrowly lost in the Electoral College to the Republican nominee, George W. Bush. This means that over the course of 26 consecutive elections Missouri cast its lot the same way as the country an unparalleled 24 times. Missouri, in short, was second-to-none when it came to picking presidential winners (Table 2.1).

But then something happened. In 2008, even as he was claiming the national popular vote by over seven percentage points and the Electoral College by almost 200 electoral votes, Democratic nominee Barack Obama lost Missouri to Republican nominee John McCain by less than a percentage point. Four years later an even more remarkable break occurred—Republican nominee Mitt Romney won the state by close to ten percentage points, while losing the national popular vote to Obama by close to four. This was not merely the second consecutive time Missouri had supported the losing national candidate—an occurrence not seen since the multiple candidacies of William Jennings Bryan around the dawn of the previous century—but also the biggest discrepancy of the sort observed since the presidential contest of 1880 when Winfield Hancock beat national winner James Garfield in the Show-Me-State by just shy of fourteen points.

The split with the popular will of the electorate nationwide that occurred in 2008 and grew even wider in 2012 goes beyond Missourians simply backing the "wrong horse"—it is also remarkable in terms of actual vote shares. In the 12 presidential contests from 1960 to 2004, the Democratic nominee's share of the Missouri vote fell, on average, 1.5% from his national share—a stunning degree of proximity. Over almost half a century, simply looking at the vote in Missouri did not merely provide a perfect harbinger of which candidate won the presidency, but it also offered an extraordinarily close approximation of the candidate's national vote share. In 2008, this 1.5% gap between Missouri and the nation as a whole more than doubled, as Obama underperformed in the Show-Me State, in relation to the country, by 3.7%. In 2012, the gap more than *quadrupled*: Obama's share of the vote was 6.8% lower in Missouri than at the national level. Graph 2.1 below illustrates the extent to which the last two elections constitute outliers.

It is clear that the change over the last decade in Missouri politics—at least at the presidential level—has been dramatic. What remains perplexing for many is *why*. However, close scrutiny of these recent electoral trends in Missouri politics seems to provide very credible explanations for why Missouri has taken at least a momentary hiatus from its swing state status.

DEMOCRATIC PRESIDENTIAL CANDIDATES, 1992–2012: A BRIEF OVERVIEW OF THEIR "FITNESS" FOR MISSOURI VOTERS

One place to start is with the candidates themselves. The most recent presidential nominees put forward by the Democratic Party have for ideological,

Table 2.1. National and Missouri Presidential Popular Vote Winners and the Difference between the Winning Vote Percentage Nationally and in Missouri, 1904-2012*

Year	National Vote Winner	Missouri Vote Winner	National Winning Vote %	Missouri Winning Vote %	Difference in Winning %	% Difference Between Nat'l Winning Margin and Missouri's Winning Margin**
2012	Barack Obama	Mitt Romney	51.0%	53.6%	6.7%	(13.2%)
2008	Barack Obama	John McCain	52.9%	49.4%	3.7%	(7.4%)
2004	George W. Bush	George W. Bush	50.7%	53.3%	2.6%	4.8%
2000	Al Gore	George W. Bush	48.4%	50.4%	1.4%	(3.9%)
1996	Bill Clinton	Bill Clinton	49.2%	47.5%	1.7%	2.1%
1992	Bill Clinton	Bill Clinton	43.0%	44.1%	1.1%	4.7%
1988	G.H.W. Bush	G.H.W. Bush	53.4%	51.8%	1.6%	3.9%
1984	Ronald Reagan	Ronald Reagan	58.8%	60.0%	1.2%	1.8%
1980	Ronald Reagan	Ronald Reagan	50.7%	51.2%	.5%	2.8%
1976	Jimmy Carter	Jimmy Carter	50.1%	51.1%	1.0%	1.5%
1972	Richard Nixon	Richard Nixon	60.7%	62.3%	1.6%	1.4%
1968	Richard Nixon	Richard Nixon	43.4%	44.9%	1.5%	.5%
1964	Lyndon Johnson	Lyndon Johnson	61.0%	64.0%	3.0%	5.6%
1960	J. F. Kennedy	J. F. Kennedy	49.7%	50.3%	.6%	.5%
1956	D. Eisenhower	Adlai Stevenson	57.4%	50.1%	7.3%	(15.6%)
1952	D. Eisenhower	D. Eisenhower	55.2%	50.7%	4.5%	9.3%
1948	Harry Truman	Harry Truman	49.6%	58.1%	8.5%	12.1%
1944	F. D. Roosevelt	F. D. Roosevelt	53.4%	51.4%	2.0%	4.5%
1940	F. D. Roosevelt	F. D. Roosevelt	54.7%	52.3%	2.4%	5.1%
1936	F. D. Roosevelt	F. D. Roosevelt	60.8%	60.8%	0%	2.0%
1932	F. D. Roosevelt	F. D. Roosevelt	57.4%	63.7%	6.3%	7.0%
1928	Herbert Hoover	Herbert Hoover	58.2%	55.6%	2.6%	5.6%
1924	Calvin Coolidge	Calvin Coolidge	54.0%	49.6%	4.4%	19.8%
1920	Warren Harding	Warren Harding	60.3%	54.6%	5.7%	14.7%
1916	W. Wilson	W. Wilson	49.2%	50.6%	1.4%	.6%
1912	W. Wilson	W. Wilson	41.8%	47.3%	5.5%	1.0%
1908	William H. Taft	William H. Taft	51.6%	48.5%	3.1%	8.5%
1904	T. Roosevelt	T. Roosevelt	56.4%	49.9%	6.5%	14.9%

* ( ) indicates that Missouri did not vote for the winning candidate in the popular vote. ** The marginal difference is calculated by subtracting the national loser's popular vote percentage from the winner's percentage; then subtracting the loser's popular vote percentage from the winner's popular vote percentage in Missouri; then calculating the marginal difference nationally and in Missouri. Note: Only the percentages for Democrats and Republicans are computed. Only in 1912 did a third-party candidate, Theodore Roosevelt, finish ahead of a Republican or Democratic candidate in the presidential elections in this Table.

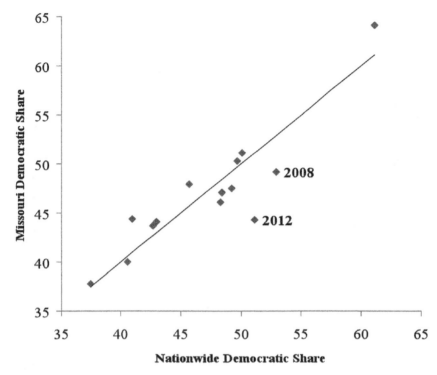

Graph 2.1. Democratic presidential nominee's share of the vote (%) nationwide and in Missouri, 1960–2012

cultural, geographical, and racial reasons proven to be a poor match for the Missouri electorate, causing many Missouri voters to shy away from supporting these candidates.

Bill Clinton Was a Comfortable Fit for Missouri Voters

Consider the evolution of presidential voting in Missouri's counties over the last two decades. In 1992 Democrats nominated William Jefferson Clinton, a southerner who had served as governor of neighboring Arkansas for over a decade. Clinton had not only extensively experienced small-town life himself, but for years had actively campaigned for—and won—the votes of people living in Arkansas' rural communities, many of them disdainful of big-city, coastal "elites."

Despite having been educated at Georgetown, Clinton was gifted at maintaining and highlighting his genuine, deeply-rooted connections to the heartland. As all Democratic presidential candidates in recent decades, Clinton, of course, did very well in Missouri's two major cities, St. Louis and Kansas City, but he also happened to do quite well in suburban, exurban, and even rural Missouri in both his 1992 and 1996 campaigns—something other Democratic presidential candidates since Clinton (Gore, Kerry, and Obama) have not come close to replicating, as Graph 2.2 makes clear. It is important to point out that the presence of Independent/Reform candidate Ross Perot in both elections does not suffice to explain Clinton's success in Missouri's 115 counties since Clinton not only twice won a plurality of the vote in a majority of the counties, but even an outright majority in many of them.

Perhaps unsurprisingly, except for the state's metropolitan areas, Clinton did best in those counties close to Arkansas—including Mississippi, New Madrid, Pemiscot, and Reynolds, where he won north of 55 percent of the vote—a remarkable achievement considering Perot's strength as the third-party candidate. But he also won a majority of the state's counties and swept most of northern Missouri, winning upwards of 50 percent in very lightly populated and geographically remote areas like Clark County in Northeastern Missouri. A similar scenario occurred four years later, with Clinton again posting commanding wins in dozens of rural counties, including double-digit majority victories over GOP nominee Robert Dole in Chariton, Linn, and Randolph counties in north central Missouri. He carried Clark County by over 20 percentage points.

Al Gore's D.C. Image Failed to Connect With Missourians, Especially in Rural Areas

In choosing a successor to Clinton for the 2000 presidential election, Democrats picked his heir apparent, Vice President Al Gore. Although originally also from the South, Gore was essentially a fixture of Washington, D.C. He had lived most of his adult life there, representing Tennessee in the U.S. Senate before serving in the White House for eight years. Complicating Gore's task was the balancing act he tried to perform, claiming credit for the incumbent administration's successes while distancing himself from his boss' personal shortcomings, most notably the Monica Lewinsky scandal. The contrast between Clinton's 1992 and 1996 performances and Gore's 2000 showing at the county level is nothing short of stunning. Whereas Clinton had twice carried upwards of 60 counties, Gore won only eleven of them, mostly because he did so poorly in virtually all of Missouri's rural counties. Gore lost the

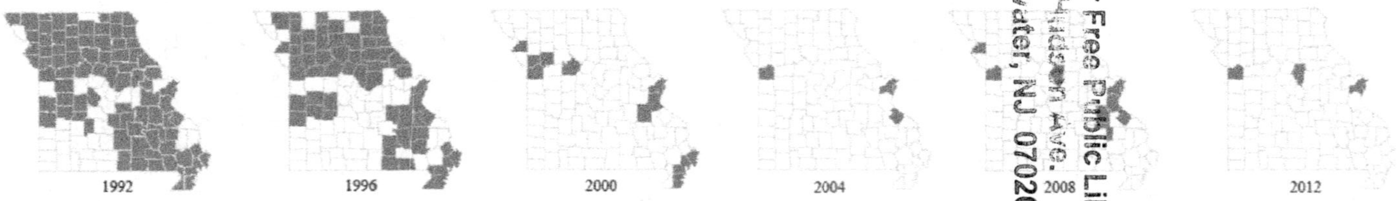

Graph 2.2.   Maps of Missouri Counties Carried by the Democratic Presidential Nominee, 1996-2012

state to Republican nominee George W. Bush, despite winning the national popular vote, becoming the first candidate since 1956 to do so. Missouri's status as a swing and bellwether state was beginning to crack.

John Kerry's Northeastern, Urban Liberalism
Turned Off Missouri Voters

In their effort to bring back Missouri into their column, Democrats did not do their party any favors four years later by nominating Senator John Kerry. Having represented Massachusetts in the upper chamber for close to two decades, Kerry had amassed a voting record ranked by *National Journal* as the most liberal of the entire U.S. Senate. (Harris 2004). Married into the wealthy Heinz family, he was often regarded as being more comfortable windsurfing off Nantucket Island than connecting with average voters in middle America, noted most infamously when talking about visiting "Lambert Field" while in Wisconsin (VandeHei 2004). These were features the Bush campaign made a point of highlighting and repeating. It launched its summer campaign bus tour entitled "Heart and Soul of America" in Springfield, Missouri with Bush exclaiming at the rally that "the heart and soul of America is found right here." This was an obvious attack on Kerry's roots and his campaign's alliance with liberal Hollywood financiers (Fox News 2004). With the "rally-around-the-flag" still strong less than three years after the September 11, 2001, terrorist attacks, the incumbent commander-in-chief additionally chastised Kerry for being too weak and prone to "flip flopping" on foreign policy. Any doubt about Missouri becoming a Republican-leaning state should have dissipated by that November. Kerry carried a meager three counties—Jackson, St. Louis, and St. Genevieve (a small exurban county south of St. Louis)—the only Democratic presidential nominee to perform this poorly in Missouri since George McGovern's historical 49-state landslide loss in 1972.

Barack Obama: Too Urban, Too Liberal, and Too Black For
Socially Conservative Voters

Rather than rebound in 2008 by nominating a candidate more attuned with Missouri voters (and "heartland" voters in general), Democrats picked Illinois Senator Barack Obama—a Chicago-machine politician who had followed in Kerry's footsteps by claiming the title of most liberal Senator during the previous year (CNN 2008) and infamously derided small-town Americans from the Midwest for bitterly "cling[ing] to their guns and religion" (Pilkington 2008). Despite his liberal track record, Obama still almost carried Missouri, losing by only .13%. However, this needs to be placed into perspective since Obama was running in a presidential election year that was destined to be bad for virtually any Republican presidential candidate. By 2008 the floundering Bush Administration was being blamed for the Iraq War that had become increasingly unpopular and the great financial collapse, as well as a host of scandals. Bush was leaving office with record-breaking disapproval ratings. Consequently, Obama was able to win rather handily the 2008 presidential election, yet he lost in Missouri. And he lost again in 2012 even though Obama easily won reelection nationally. Considerable attention is devoted later in this chapter to why Obama lost these elections in Missouri. Special attention is devoted to examining the claim that Obama lost in Missouri because of an elevated percentage of racist voting, even though Obama performed quite well in other swing states. Strong evidence presented in that section reasonably substantiates the claim that Obama's race likely caused him to lose in Missouri, especially in 2008. First, however, it is helpful to show just how much Missouri has supported Republican presidential candidates since 1996 before we offer more plausible explanations for why Missouri has so disproportionately favored the Republican Party's presidential candidates, as compared to the electorate nationally, in the past four presidential elections, causing the state to lose its reputation as a swing and bellwether state.

Swelling Turnout for Republican Presidential Candidates Helped Derail Missouri's Swing-State/Bellwether Status

What becomes very clear when examining Missouri voter turnout data since 1996 is that voter turnout statewide has increased enormously, but especially among voters voting for the Republican nominee for president. This reality goes far in explaining why Republicans have done so well in Missouri's presidential elections since 1996 and why Missouri has gone from a reliable swing state and most celebrated bellwether state to a red state in recent presidential elections. Let us look at these revealing turnout statistics.

It is important to stress that while voter turnout has increased dramatically in Missouri's presidential elections since 1996, Missouri's population has increased only slightly. In fact, Missouri's population increased at such a modest pace compared to many other states during the census decade from 2000–2010 that Missouri lost an electoral vote after the 2010 census. In 2000 Missouri's population was 5,595,211. According to the 2010 U.S. Census, Missouri's population had grown to only 5,988,923, constituting a population gain of just 393,712 or an increase of only 7%. The Census estimate for 2012 put Missouri at 6,024,522, for a gain of 7.7% since 2000. This compares to a national population increase of 11% between 2000 and 2012 (from approximately 281 million to 314 million).

These census figures are important to keep in mind when assessing Missouri's voter turnout numbers because voter turnout far outpaced the population increases, suggesting that Get-Out-the-Vote (GOTV) drives by both political parties must have been quite successful, but especially by the GOP. Of course, other factors could have accounted for the disproportionate increase by pro-Republican voters (e.g., more appealing Republican candidates; better issue appeal by the GOP candidates; disproportionate campaign time and money spent in Missouri by the Republican presidential candidates; a combination of all of these factors). Before examining the increased voter turnout rates by party preference, it is worthwhile to examine the overall voter turnout rate in the presidential contests in Missouri from 1996 through 2012. Table 2.2 shows the overall increase in presidential votes cast between 1996 and 2012. This table, when compared to Missouri's population growth figures, shows that the percent in voter turnout far exceeded the population growth in Missouri. In fact, while Missouri's population only increased by 7% between 2000 and 2010, Missouri's voter turnout increased by 24% between 2000 and 2008 (two fewer years) or 3.4 times faster.

However, although voter turnout increased significantly for both Democrats and Republicans since 1996, turnout for Republican presidential candidates outperformed turnout for Democratic presidential candidates by impressive margins. Table 2.3 shows votes for Republican presidential candidates in Missouri 1996–2012. Table 2.4 displays turnout statistics for Democratic presidential candidates during the same period. In 1996 President Bill Clinton won easy reelection nationwide and in Missouri, likely accounting for low turnout numbers in Missouri for Republicans in that election year. Once again, Missouri's bellwether status was upheld and Clinton's percent win over Republican candidate Robert Dole was close to Clinton's percent win over Dole nationally (49.2% to 40.7% nationally; 47.5% to 41.2% in Missouri). However, since 1996, the turnout statistics in Tables 2.3 and 2.4

Table 2.2. Presidential Votes Cast in Missouri, 1996-2012

Year	Total Votes Cast	% Increase Since 1996	% Increase Since 2000
1996	2,158,065	—	—
2000	2,359,892	+9.4%	—
2004	2,731,364	+26.6%	+15.7%
2008	2,925,205	+35.5%	+24.0%
2012	2,757,323	+27.8%	+16.8%

Table 2.3. **Votes for Republican Presidential Candidates in Missouri, 1996-2012**

Year	Total Votes Cast	% Increase Since 1996	% Increase Since 2000	% Change Since 2004
1996	890,016	—	—	—
2000	1,189,924	+33.4%	—	—
2004	1,455,713	+63.6%	+22.3%	—
2008	1,445,814	+62.4%	+21.5%	−0.7%
2012	1,482,440	+66.6%	+24.6%	+1.8%

convey in stark numbers that Republicans have been able to turn out a far greater number for their presidential candidates than the Democratic Party has for their presidential candidates. One can only speculate as to why Republicans have turned out in far greater numbers for their presidential candidates than Democrats for theirs. As suggested earlier, maybe issues in Missouri favored Republicans more.

For example, in 2000 the negative reaction to the scandalous baggage left over from the Clinton administration (for example, Whitewater; the Foster incident; the Monica-Lewinsky affair; Clinton's impeachment) may have hurt Gore's chances. In 2004, the 9/11 attacks and the war on terrorism likely favored President George W. Bush since polls usually favor Republicans more than Democrats in "handling foreign policy and defense." Foreign policy and defense issues would play particularly well in Missouri. In fact, President Bush in 2002 campaigned hard in Missouri to help fellow Republican Jim Talent get elected to the U.S. Senate, pushing his Republican administration's positions on foreign policy and the war on terrorism. The Bush campaign in 2004 continued to stress foreign policy and the war on terrorism issues. In addition, the Bush presidential campaign advanced traditional family value and religious issues; issues that also resonate well among more socially conservative Missourians, especially with Missouri's large bloc of evangelicals. Although the Iraq War was growing unpopular with Americans by 2008, even in Missouri, John McCain still benefited from his past military background and

Table 2.4. **Votes for Democratic Presidential Candidates in Missouri, 1996-2012**

Year	Total Votes Cast	% Increase Since 1996	% Increase Since 2000	% Change Since 2004
1996	1,025,935	—	—	—
2000	1,111,138	+8.3%	—	—
2004	1,259,171	+22.7%	+13.3%	—
2008	1,441,911	+40.5%	+29.8%	+14.5%
2012	1,223,796	+19.3%	+10.1%	−2.8%

especially from his super-patriot, heroic status as a former POW. In 2008 and 2012, while the usual socially conservative values continued to connect with Missourians, some measurable racism (discussed in next section) helped John McCain in 2008, as well as Mitt Romney in 2012, defeat Barack Obama. In 2012 Romney also benefited from the stiff opposition to Obamacare among the vast majority of Republican voters. Regardless of the actual impact of issues during the 2000–2012 presidential campaigns, turnout for Republican presidential candidates in Missouri has been very impressive since 1996 compared to turnout support for Democratic presidential candidates, helping Republicans defeat all four Democratic presidential candidates in Missouri in the twenty-first century, turning Missouri into an apparently solid red state and removing Missouri from the list of swing or battleground states.

Table 2.3 shows that in 1996 Missouri voters gave the Republican presidential candidate only 890,016 votes, compared to 1,025,935 for the Democratic presidential candidate. That is, the Democratic turnout was 15.3% higher, easily accounting for Clinton's comfortable victory over Dole in 1996. But votes for the Republican presidential candidate rose sharply in 2000 to 1,189,924 or 33.4% higher than it was just four years before. On the other hand, Table 2.4 shows that vote gains for the Democratic presidential aspirant were very modest, increasing by only 8.3% from 1996 to 2000 or to 1,111,138. In just four years Republicans in Missouri had eliminated their turnout deficiency, actually turning out more Republican votes for president than the Democrats for their presidential hopeful, allowing G.W. Bush to defeat Al Gore in Missouri's popular vote, 50.4% to 47.1%, even though Bush lost nationwide in the popular vote by over one-half million votes or by 48.4% to 47.8%. This means that Missouri deviated from the Gore's winning popular vote percentage by 3.9%. Since bellwether status is technically based on reflecting the nation's popular vote, not its electoral vote, after the 2000 presidential election suddenly some electoral behavior scholars started to view Missouri's bellwether status as suspect.

Nonetheless, political reporters tended to think that Missouri continued to keep its bellwether status in 2000 because Bush won Missouri and won the Electoral College nationwide, thus allowing him to win the presidency. Thus, when the 2004 presidential campaign started, political reporters still covered Missouri intensely as a bellwether, interviewing its citizens and its political analysts.[2] However, it is important to stress that technically a state's bellwether status is determined by how closely a state mirrors the popular vote of the nation as a whole, not the electoral vote since even a cursory examination of presidential election outcomes shows that the popular vote percentages for the presidential candidates may not be anywhere close to the electoral vote percentages. To reiterate, what made Missouri the best bellwether state in the nation from 1904 through 1996, excepting 1956, was Missouri's uncanny ability to reflect so closely the winning presidential candidate's popular vote percentage, allowing people to say, "as Missouri goes, so goes the nation."

Preference by Missouri voters for Republican presidential candidates over Democratic presidential candidates in succeeding presidential elections would only tend to improve, assuring Republican presidential candidates even more comfortable victories, causing Missouri's bellwether and swing-state status to become a distant memory. In the 2004 George W. Bush won the presidency by defeating John Kerry, 50.7% to 48.3% nationally or by a margin of 2.4%, although in Missouri Bush won by a much greater percentage, 53.3% to 46.1% or by a margin of 7.2%—exactly three times more than Bush's winning percentage nationwide. Missouri was quickly taking on the status of a red state, mostly because pro-Republican voters were now easily out-voting pro-Democratic voters in presidential elections.

In 2004, Bush's victory was assured because Missourians started to show a much stronger preference for the Republican presidential candidate over the Democratic challenger. Although in the 1996 presidential election Dole garnered only 890,016 votes in Missouri, in 2004 the turnout for G.W. Bush rose to 1,455,713, constituting an astounding 63.6% increase in turnout since 1996 for the Republican presidential candidate. Presidential votes in 2004 for the Democrats increased 22.7% since 1996 to 1,259,171, suggesting that Democratic GOTV efforts were moderately successful, yet still turnout for the Republican presidential candidate had outpaced turnout for the Democratic presidential candidate by a ratio of almost 3:1.

Nationally, 2008 promised to be a prosperous election year for Democrats. President Bush's job approval had plummeted to record lows, while the Republican Party's numbers were also in the tank. Across the nation Americans were in a mood to elect Democrats. Predictably, Democratic presidential candidate Barack Obama coasted to victory nationwide, winning over Republican presidential candidate, John McCain, by a margin of 7.3%, 52.9% to 45.6%. However, in Missouri the outcome was quite different. Obama actually lost in Missouri. Although Obama lost in Missouri by only a fraction of a percent (.13%), the point is that he lost when nationally voters were voting for Obama, even in some traditional Republican states such as Virginia and North Carolina.

Turnout in the presidential election in Missouri is again key in explaining McCain's victory and Missouri moving still further away from its bellwether/swing-state reputation. In 2008 Missouri was off by only 2.6% from Obama's winning national percentage, but Missouri was way off stride from the national winning margin of Obama over McCain, missing the mark by a wide margin of 7.39%, further off from mirroring the margin between the presidential winner and loser since 1956 (Table 2.1). Republicans were less enthusiastic for McCain than they were for Bush in 2004, but presidential turnout was still stronger for McCain than Democratic support for Obama. Turnout for Republicans dipped from 1,455,713 in 2004 to 1, 445,814 in 2008, a turnout decline of only .7%. Obama's almost "rock star" status in the 2008 campaign had energized Democrats nationwide and in Missouri as well. Democratic turnout in Missouri increased by 14.5% from 1,259,171 to 1,441,911. However, the Democratic gains, even in this banner year for Democrats nationwide, still was not enough in Missouri to overcome the vote strength for McCain.

It is worth noting that between 2004 and 2008 votes for the Republican presidential candidate declined nationwide from 62,039,073 to 59,934,814, a decrease of 3.4%, compared to Missouri's slight dip of just .7%. Missouri's decline was almost five times less. Meanwhile, the Democratic vote nationwide increased dramatically from 59,027,478 to 69,456,897, a vote increase of 17.7%, compared to Missouri's increase of 14.5%. McCain was able to win Missouri, despite the significant increase in Democratic voters for president during a peak year for Democrats, because the Republican base in Missouri had increased so dramatically since 1996. The very fact that Obama lost in Missouri, despite his comfortable national win, shows how much Missouri's voters had moved to the right in presidential elections since 1996. After the 2008 election no credible political pundit was arguing any longer that Missouri was a swing state. In 2012 the presidential candidate, President Obama, hardly paid any attention to Missouri, which is typical when a state is no longer a battleground state—no longer a competitive, swing state. Obama's campaign organization simply conceded Missouri to Romney.

The 2012 presidential election result in Missouri underscored how far Missouri had moved from its historic bellwether status of the twentieth century. Although nationwide President Obama easily won reelection, winning by about five million votes, 51% to 47.1%, Obama got trounced in Missouri, losing by almost double digits, 53.6% to 44.3% or by a margin of 9.3%. In clear contrast, in 2012 Democratic turnout in Missouri for Obama had dropped off sharply from its 2008 peak of 1,441,911 to 1,223,796, a decline of 15.1%. Republican votes for presidential candidate, Mitt Romney, actually increased from 1,445,814 to 1,482,440. Now looking back to 1996, we can see that Republican voters for president have increased from 890,016 in 1996 to 1,482,440 in 2012, for a total vote increase of 66.6%. In comparison, Democratic votes for president in Missouri have gone from 1,025,935 in 1996 to 1,223,796 in 2012 for an increase of just 19.3% in this sixteen-year period. This modest increase is more than three times less than for Republicans. Where have all these Republican voters come from?

Voter turnout analysis by county discloses that voter turnout since 1996 has increased proportionately more in Missouri's Republican counties than Democratic counties, greatly benefiting Republican presidential candidates in the past four presidential elections. Almost all of these Republican counties are rural with quite small voting populations, but significant voter turnout hikes in these hundred-plus rural counties have cumulatively accounted for major Republican gains at the polls.

A few examples of increases in Republican voter turnout in these rural counties, compared to rather stagnant or even declining turnout for Democrats in these same counties, convey a clear picture. Jasper County is a rural county in southwest Missouri near the Oklahoma border. In 1996, 18,361 voted for the Republican presidential candidate, Robert Dole. In 2012, the Republican presidential candidate, Mitt Romney, received 31,349 votes, representing an increase of 70.7% increase in Republican voter support. In contrast, in 1996 Democratic candidate Bill Clinton won 11,462 votes, while in 2012 President Obama captured 12,809 votes or only 11.75% more votes. Republican voters from Ozark County, near the Arkansas border, cast 1,882 votes for Dole in 1996, but 3,080 votes for Romney in 2012, a gain of 63.7%. However, Democratic votes for president actually declined in Ozark County from 1,445 in 1996 to 1,261 in 2012, for a decrease of 12.7%. Similar vote patterns can be seen in other rural counties between 1996 and 2012 (for example, Texas, + 87.4% increase for Republicans, -26.2% for Democrats; Pike, +107.2% increase for Republicans, -26.1% for Democrats; Shelby, +80.4% for Republicans, -31.5% for Democrats).

The two largest Republican counties in Missouri both showed very significant gains for Republican presidential candidates since 1996. One is Greene County in southwest Missouri. In 1996 Dole received 48,193 votes, but in 2012 Romney garnered 76,900 votes or 59.6% more votes than Dole. Clinton gathered 39,300 votes in Greene County in 1996, while Obama won 46,219 votes in 2012, up a more modest 17.6%. But maybe the biggest reason for Republican presidential candidate successes in Missouri since 1996 can be seen in St. Charles County. St. Charles County is a Republican stronghold just west of St. Louis. A few decades ago St. Charles County was half the size of St. Louis and did not have nearly the voter clout of St. Louis. In 1996 St. Charles's population was 254,332, while the St. Louis's population was 362,042, but by 2012 St. Charles's population had grown to 368,666, while St. Louis's population had dwindled to 318,172 (U.S. Census Bureau 2014). In 1996 St. Charles County cast 47,705 votes for Dole, accounting for 5.4% of the total votes cast statewide for Dole, but in 2012 Romney received 110,784 votes or well more than double Dole's votes and constituting 7.5% of the total votes cast statewide for Romney. St. Charles County has emerged as easily the most voluminous Republican county in presidential elections in Missouri, contributing significantly to Republican presidential wins in Missouri and simultaneously to Missouri's demise as a swing state.

While Republicans have counted on capturing a large percentage of the total votes from Missouri's 105 rural counties, as well as Greene and St. Charles counties, historically Democrats have relied on winning the presidency by securing lopsided vote majorities in St. Louis City and Kansas City, combined with St. Louis County in more recent decades. Dramatic population losses in St. Louis since 1950 have created a sad story for Democratic presidential hopefuls. In 1950 St. Louis was America's eighth largest city with a population of 856,796. As a Democratic stronghold, Democratic presidential candidates could count on St. Louis to cast a hefty percentage of Missouri's total Democratic votes for them. Truman, for example, as well as Adlai Stevenson, John Kennedy, and Lyndon Johnson, won Missouri in large part because they received significant vote totals from Saint Louisans. But by the time Barack Obama ran for reelection in 2012, St. Louis City's population was down to 318,172, losing 538,624 people or 62.9% of its 1950 population. During the last three decades of the twentieth century and into the twenty-first century Saint Louisans continued to cast lopsided votes for Democratic candidates, but St. Louis's percentage of the total state vote was becoming much smaller and thus much less important to Democratic presidential candidates.

A look at a few presidential elections in Missouri's distant past shows St. Louis's decline as a Democratic vote stronghold. In 1948 Democratic presidential candidate Harry Truman won 64.5% of the St. Louis vote, receiving 220,654 votes or 24.1% of Missouri's total Democratic presidential votes, allowing him to soundly trounce in Missouri his Republican challenger, Thomas Dewey. In 1956, the only time since 1904 that Missouri deviated from its bellwether status during the twentieth century, Stevenson won 60.9% of the St. Louis vote, receiving 202,210 votes or 22% of Stevenson's total votes in Missouri. In 1960 Democratic presidential candidate, John Kennedy, squeaked out a narrow victory in Missouri, reflecting his narrow victory nationally and returning Missouri to its former bellwether status which it would continue to hold until 2000. Kennedy's Missouri victory was helped by the 202,319 votes he won in St. Louis; 66.6% of the St. Louis vote and 20.8% of the total votes cast for Kennedy statewide.

As the presidential elections passed, it became more obvious that the St. Louis vote for Democrats was not nearly what it once was. In 1980, Democratic candidate Jimmy Carter won a typical lopsided victory for the Democratic presidential candidate in St. Louis, winning 69.5% of the vote. But by then the 113,697 votes Carter received in St. Louis only accounted for 12.2%

of Missouri's total Democratic presidential vote, a far cry from the 24.1% of the total statewide vote for the Democratic presidential candidate in 1948. By the 1992 presidential election St. Louis's percent of Missouri's total Democratic vote percentage dipped to 9.7%, although Democratic candidate Bill Clinton won an even greater lopsided percentage than previous Democratic presidential candidates, winning over George H.W. Bush, 80.1% to 19.9% (excluding third-party candidates in these percentages).

From the post–World War Two days to present, St. Louis City's enormous population losses were due largely to high crime, poor public schools, and deteriorating neighborhoods, causing significant "white flight," but in general the loss of the more affluent and Republican Saint Louisans, many of whom migrated to the surrounding suburbs (Jefferson County, but especially to St. Louis and St. Charles Counties). When Obama ran in 2008 St. Louis's demographics had changed dramatically since 1948. Saint Louisans were less affluent and less white (83% in 1950; 44% in 2010) with blacks now constituting the plurality of Saint Louisans (18% in 1950; 49% in 2010) (Campbell 2013). These demographics virtually guaranteed a very lopsided vote for Democratic presidential candidates in St. Louis, but a lopsided vote not weighty enough to help Democratic presidential candidates secure a win in Missouri. St. Louis's total vote in 2008 constituted only 4.5% of the statewide vote compared to 21.8% in 1948. Obama did win the highest Democratic percentage ever won by a Democratic candidate in St. Louis in 2008, 84.1%, due largely to an unusually high turnout among black voters who cast almost all of their votes for Obama, yet still this generated only 9.2% of the total Democratic vote statewide. With enthusiasm dipping for Obama, by 2012 Obama won only 118,780 votes in St. Louis, down from 132,925 in 2008. Obama won 83.8% of the St. Louis vote in 2012. St. Louis's Democratic percentage of the total state vote was actually up .5% from 2008 to 9.7% because overall total votes cast for the Democratic presidential candidate in Missouri had declined by 218,115 votes or 15.1% from the 2008 presidential election, allowing Romney to win in Missouri by 9.4%. Since Obama won nationally by a 3.7% margin, this means that Missouri deviated from Obama's national winning percentage by a whopping 13.1%, making political analysts wonder just how the "swing state" of Missouri could stray so far from its once renowned bellwether accuracy?

While St. Louis City, on Missouri's eastern border, had declined in importance for Democrats, Kansas City, on Missouri's western border, had also become less important to Democratic presidential hopefuls. Jackson County's more Republican suburbs have grown quite fast since 1950, benefiting Republican presidential candidates. Kansas City, the chief Democratic area within Jackson County, has hardly grown since 1950; growing from 456,662 in 1950 to 464,310 by the 2012 election or just 1.7%. Kansas City has experienced a sharp relative decline, going from the 20th largest city nationally in 1950 to the 37th largest city by 2012. These population trends within Jackson County have hurt Democratic presidential candidates. The Democratic vote for president in Kansas City did increase from 79,455 in 1996 to 105,670 in 2012 for a 33% increase. However, the Republican vote in Jackson County, excluding Kansas City, went from 56,906 in 1996 to 93,199 in 2012, for an increase of 63.8%.

While St. Louis City and Kansas City have declined in importance for Democratic presidential candidates, St. Louis County has emerged as their last bastion of hope. For most of its history, however, St. Louis County was not friendly territory for Democrats. Even in his home state, Truman actually lost St. Louis County to Dewey, 52.2% to 47%. As St. Louis County grew from 406,349 in 1950 to over one million by 2012 (U.S. Census, State and County QuickFacts 2014), mostly due to many St. Louisans migrating to St. Louis County, the County gradually became less Republican. Yet early migration patterns showed mostly more affluent white, Republican voters moving into St. Louis County, allowing St. Louis County to remain solidly Republican for decades to come.

Eventually, however, many African-Americans began to move from north St. Louis City into St. Louis County, especially into northeast St. Louis County, changing rapidly the balance of electoral power in favor of the Democrats. In 1950 St. Louis County's population was almost exclusively white with a minority population of only 4.2%; by 1970 only 5.2%; by 1980 12.5%; by 1990 15.8%; and by 2000 23.2% (U.S. Bureau of the Census in Laslo). By 2013, St. Louis County's population had dropped to 68% white, non-Hispanic/Latino with a black population alone of 23.7% (U.S. Census Bureau, State and County QuickFacts 2014). With this influx of minority voters into St. Louis County (voters who tend to vote overwhelmingly Democrat), Democrats finally started to win most elections on a regular basis in St. Louis County by the late 1980s. Although Ronald Reagan and George H.W. Bush won their presidential elections easily in St. Louis County in 1980, 1984, and 1988 respectively, 1988 would be the last time a Republican presidential candidate would win a presidential election in St. Louis County. In 1992 and 1996 Bill Clinton coasted to easy victories in St. Louis County. Gore, Kerry, and Obama did the same in succeeding elections. The widest winning margin was posted in 2008 when Obama beat McCain 333,123 (59.5%) to 221,705 (39.5%) or by 111,418 votes. The fact that St. Louis County is so large and can generate so many votes for Democrats is still the key to possible Democratic presidential victories in Missouri in future elections. St. Louis County's vote constitutes about 20% of Missouri's total vote, so a Democratic presidential candidate's formula for winning the presidential election in Missouri is to win St. Louis County, St. Louis City, and Kansas City by landslide vote percentages, pick up a few other winnable counties for Democrats, and then not get totally "blown away" in Missouri's rural counties.

In sum, the above is the best scenario for Democratic presidential hopefuls in Missouri in upcoming presidential elections. However, voter statistics presented in this section suggest that Democrats may have a hard time turning back the clock and making Missouri a swing state again. Republicans have simply outvoted Democrats in Missouri since 1996, particularly in the 2004 and 2012 presidential elections. However, these voting numbers only tell one side of the story. That is, Missouri voters in recent presidential elections have favored Republicans, but these numbers do not tell us why Missouri voters have suddenly preferred Republicans over Democrats. Earlier it was noted that Democratic presidential candidates since Clinton may not have been a "good fit" for Missouri voters because they could not relate to the majority of Missouri voters for various reasons. However, the next section scrutinizes the often-voiced contention that Missouri may have drifted away from the Democratic presidential candidate Barack Obama, not just because he may have been perceived as too liberal for Missourians, but because at least enough Missourians may have voted against him because of his "race alone."[3]

Did Racist Voting in 2008 and 2012 Help Move Missouri From its Swing-State Status?

There is little question that racist voting does not play the role it once did in American elections when presidential candidates such as Strom Thurman in 1948 and George Wallace in 1968 made blatant racial appeals in their campaigns. This point is displayed in Graph 2.3 by Nate Silver and Allison McCann in their article, "Are White Republicans More Racist than White Democrats?" (Silver and McCann 2014). However, it would be wrong to ignore the possible role that racist voting played in the 2008 and 2012 presidential elections nationwide, as well as in Missouri, especially since numerous electoral behavior studies have documented that racist voting still lingers in America and did play at least some role in these two elections (for example, Carmines and Stimson 1989; Sniderman and Carmines 1997, pp. 78–91; Piston 2010; Wagner and Flanigan 2014, pp. 148–54; Tesler 2013; Silver and McCann 2014; Pasek et al. 2014).

Of course, measuring racist attitudes/voting is challenging since few people normally admit that they voted against a candidate because of his race. Most often people will tell pollsters that they voted against an African American candidate for reasons other than the person's race. For instance, they may say that they did not like his/her stand on immigration, law and order, welfare,

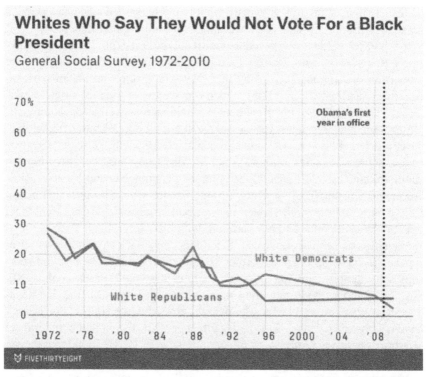

Whites Who Say They Would Not Vote For a Black President

General Social Survey, 1972-2010

Graph 2.3.   Whites Saying They Would Not Vote for A Black Presidential Candidate. Fivethirtyeight.com. Reprinted with the permission of Nate Silver and Allison McCann.

Obamacare, even though they are actually voting against the person because of his/her race. Some scholars refer to this as "implicit racism" or "symbolic racism" (Pasek et al. 2014). This kind of racism is very difficult to measure, as opposed to what scholars call explicit racism (Rabinowitz et al. 2012; Pasek et al. 2014) or what some scholars call "old fashioned racism" (Tesler 2013). In short, as Michael Wagner and William Flanigan conclude, "Interpreting racial attitudes can be tricky" (Wagner and Flanigan 2014, p. 149).

Many scholarly studies on racist voting conclude that racist voting does not have to play a significant role in a state's voting to alter the outcome of an election, especially in a swing state where the presidential contest is competitive. If just 3–6% of the state's electorate votes against a candidate because of his race, as most of these studies show (Davidowitz 2012; Tesler 2013; Pasek et al. 2014), then such racist voting could swing a state to the white candidate. Parenthetically, given that McCain won the presidential election in Missouri by just .13% in 2008, this is exactly what likely happened since easily racist voting in Missouri far exceeded McCain's .13 winning percentage.

In the Pasek study it was noted that most surveys on explicit racism (for example, CBS/*New Times*, Gallup, Stanford) have consistently found that "the proportion of Americans who say that they would not vote for an African-American candidate because of his race is currently in the mid-single digits" (Pasek et al. 2014). But electoral behavior scholars, as well as psychologists, present evidence to suggest that actual racist voting may be much higher than the expressed explicit racist voting percentages indicate because, as acknowledged, some voters responding to survey questions may be unwilling "to admit holding a socially sanctioned opinion" (Tourangeay and Ya 2007; Holbrook and Krosnick 2009). Thus, common sense would suggest that actual racist voting may be well hidden in "symbolic racism" answers, something scholars have attempted to measure, but with difficulty.

Nonetheless, scholars have concluded that "anti-African-American racism appears to have been an important component of the 2008 election, perhaps considerably reducing Obama's share of the vote" (Pasek et al. 2014). Spencer Piston's research led him to the same conclusion: "I find that negative stereotypes about blacks significantly eroded white support for Barack Obama" (Piston 2010, p. 431). Tesler offers another insight that could impact Missouri's possible return to swing-state status in 2016. He found that racism played a significant role in the 2008 presidential election, as well as in the 2010 midterm elections, and contends it will likely continue into 2012 and after since the Obama presidential election of 2008, as well as the Obama presidency, have activated racist tendencies dormant for decades. Tesler argues that Obama has activated both old-fashioned racism, rooted in the belief that blacks are socially and intellectually inferior and "new racism," grounded in the belief that "blacks violate such traditional American values as individualism and self-reliance, the work ethic, obedience and discipline." Racist voting against Obama, he explains, occurred because "Obama independently taps into both the classic symbolic racism theme that blacks have too much influence in politics, and old-fashioned racists' concerns about the leadership of a president from a racial group whom they consider to be intellectually and socially inferior" (Tesler 2013).

Establishing the role that racist voting played in Missouri in the 2008 and 2012 presidential elections is critical to our analysis, because if racist voting in Missouri only mirrored the average for other swing states, it could not be considered a causal factor for why Missouri moved away from its bellwether/swing state status—at least in 2008 and 2012. However, showing that racist voting against Obama in Missouri was above average for swing states, possibly well above average, tipping the elections to McCain and Romney, would help explain why Missouri has moved, at least momentarily, from being a swing state to a red state. Also, if it can be established that anti-Obama votes are partly rooted in racist sentiments, it is possible that Missouri's new red state status could become long-lived since, as Tesler maintains, a renewed alignment between partisan preference and racism may promote "polarized white partisanship" for the foreseeable future, as voters tend to cling to their partisanship and partisan beliefs for life (Tesler 2013).

In 2008 Barack Obama was the only black candidate running statewide in Missouri. This is the norm in socially conservative Missouri. The only other black candidate to ever run statewide in Missouri was former Democratic U.S. Congressman Alan Wheat in 1994, but he was beaten badly by Republican John Ashcroft by 24%. In reviewing all seventeen U.S. Senate races in Missouri between 1970 and 2012, only one other major party candidate received a vote percentage lower than Wheat and this was Democrat Jay Nixon when he ran against two term incumbent Republican U.S. Senator John Danforth in 1988, who outspent Nixon by an enormous margin. Wheat's percentage was only 3.95% higher statewide than Nixon's vote total in his 1988 U.S. Senate race, but this was because Wheat did considerably better than Nixon in St. Louis City (63.2% to 57.6%), St. Louis County (37.9% to 29%), and Jackson County (46.7% to 38.7%) where large blocs of African-Americans voted overwhelmingly for Wheat. Otherwise, Wheat did worse overall than Nixon in very white, rural Missouri. The fact that Wheat's losing percentage was 35.7%, but the average losing vote percentage in Missouri's U.S. Senate contests between 1970 and 2012 was 43.6%, legitimately raises questions about the willingness of white Missourians to vote for an African-American candidate in statewide elections. This unwillingness to vote for a black candidate was very likely a factor helping to derail Missouri from its swing-state status, but possibly for just the 2008 and 2012 presidential elections when a black candidate was on the presidential ballot.

While Obama did well nationally in 2008 with a winning popular vote percentage of 52.7% to 45.6% over Republican rival John McCain (by a 7.3% margin), Obama lost in Missouri by a very slim margin, 49.36% to 49.23%. This .13% gap represents 3,903 votes out of 2,925,205 votes cast. Nonetheless, Obama lost in Missouri during an election year that went very poorly for McCain nationwide. Meanwhile in 2008, all but one statewide Democratic candidate on the Missouri ballot, all white, won election victories, two by blowout numbers. Democrat Jay Nixon easily won the governorship, 58.4% to 39.5% over Republican Kenny Hulshof. Robin Carnahan won Secretary of State over Republican Mitchell Hubbard, 61.8% to 35.6%. Democrat Clint Zweifel beat Republican Brad Lager for State Treasurer, 50.5% to 47.1%, while Democrat Chris Koster defeated Republican Mike Gibbons, 52.9% to

47.1%. Only one Republican won statewide, Peter Kinder, over Democrat Sam Page, 49.9% to 47.3% in Missouri's closest statewide race, other than the presidential race.

This trend worsened in the 2012 presidential election, moving Missouri further away from being considered a swing state. While incumbent President Obama won comfortably nationwide, defeating Mitt Romney by 3.7%, he lost in Missouri by 9.37%, resulting in a spread of 13.1% between Obama's winning percentage nationally and his losing percentage in Missouri (Leip 2012). Yet, three white Democrats on the statewide ballot embarrassed their Republican opponents, winning by crushing margins. Democrat Claire Mc-Caskill won reelection to the U.S. Senate by 15.7% over Republican Todd Akin. Democrat Jay Nixon won reelection as governor by 12.3% over Republican David Spence. Democrat Chris Koster won reelection as Attorney General over Republican Ed Martin by 15.3%. Two other Democrats won by slimmer margins, Democrat Clint Zweifel over Republican Cole McNary by 5% and Democrat Jason Kander over Republican Shane Schoeller by 1.5%. Peter Kinder, running for reelection as Lt. Governor, was the only Republican to win statewide besides, of course, Mitt Romney. Kinder defeated Democrat Susan Montee by 3.8%.

This begs the question, why did Obama, who almost reached "rock star" status nationwide during the 2008 campaign, lose in Missouri, especially considering that in 2008 Obama even won in two traditional southern Republican states, North Carolina and Virginia? Obama seemed to have a picture perfect family and, as hard as the Republicans tried, their opposition research found him to be squeaky clean with no scandals. Obama also espoused policy positions that most Americans supported in 2008: ending the Iraq War and bringing home the troops, yet maintaining a strong defense and aggressively fighting terrorism; energy independence; rebuilding the broken economy; and fixing the cost-ineffective health care system. Perhaps most importantly, Obama did about everything he could to not campaign as a black man in sharp contrast to Jesse Jackson's presidential candidacies in 1984 and 1988.

The fact that Obama in 2012, as an incumbent president coasting to victory nationally, received literally hundreds of thousands votes less than some other Democratic candidates running below him on the ballot has to raise concern over whether Obama's skin color in fact did cause some Missouri voters to vote against him. The reality is this, as one Missouri political pundit wrote after the 2012 general election: "More than a quarter of a million voters in this state wouldn't elect a black man at the same moment they were giving landslide wins to white candidates in his own party" (Hartman 2012). Table 2.5 shows the glaring contrasts between the total votes cast for Obama versus

Table 2.5. Obama's Votes v. Votes for Other Democratic Candidates Running Statewide on the Missouri Ballot in 2008 and 2012

MO. Dem. Candidate/Office/Date	Votes For	Obama Votes	Vote Diff.	% More*
Nixon (Gov.) (2008)	1,680,611	1,441,911	+ 238,700	16.6%
Carnahan (Sec. of State) (2008)	1,749,152	1,441,911	+ 307,241	21.3%
Koster (Attorney General) (2008)	1,471,647	1,441,911	+29,736	2.1%
Zweifel (State Treasurer) (2008)	1,394,627	1,441,911	-47,284	(–3.3%)
Page (Lt. Gov.) (2008)	1,331,177	1,441,911	-110,734	(–7.7%)
McCaskill (U.S. Senate) (2012)	1,494,125	1,223,796	270,329	22.1%
Nixon (Gov.) (2012)	1,494,056	1,223,796	270,260	22.1%
Koster (Attorney General) (2012)	1,491,139	1,223,796	267,343	21.8%
Zweifel (State Treasurer) (2012)	1,332,876	1,223,796	109,080	8.9%
Kander (Sec. of State) (2012)	1,298,022	1,223,796	74,226	6.1%
Montee (Lt. Gov.) (2012)	1,219,457	1,223,796	4,339	(-.4%)

* Percent more for Democratic candidate than for Obama. A minus (-) indicates the percent less the Democratic candidate received versus Obama.

the votes captured by other Democrats in both 2008 and 2012, providing powerful circumstantial evidence to support the contention that some votes cast against Obama were rooted in racism since so many white Democratic candidates did so well, but the one black candidate did not. Table 2.5 shows that in 2008 1,441,911 Missourians voted for Obama, yet 238,700 more voted for Democrat Jay Nixon for Governor, while 307,241 more voted for Democrat Robin Carnahan for Secretary of State. The fact that Obama garnered more votes than Clint Zweifel and Sam Page means very little since these candidates were running for lesser offices down on the ballot where fewer votes are usually cast due to normal "drop-off" voting. In 2012 five Democrats running statewide received more votes than Obama. McCaskill, Nixon, and Koster dwarfed Obama's vote total, winning about 22% more votes than their party's standard-bearer.

These comparative statistics only support a circumstantial case for racist voting against Obama, although this evidence seems weighty. Naturally, there are many legitimate reasons to have voted against Obama that have nothing to do with race. For example, we would expect most Republicans to not vote for Obama simply because he is a Democrat. And we can imagine that many Missourians could have voted against him because they legitimately opposed his issue stands. However, textbook conclusions on determinants of vote choice make it clear that voting on the basis of issues comes in a dismal last compared to partisanship and candidate image. This is because few people

follow or know the issues very well, so issues do not serve as a major determinant of vote choice for most voters (Wagner and Flanigan 2014, chap. 5;
Ansolabehere and Jones 2010).

Furthermore, our focus is on the large number of voters, mostly Democrats, who voted against Obama at the top of the ballot, but then switched to
voting for the other Democrats on the ballot. It is common for this to happen,
but it is uncommon for the vote differential to be so large. For example, in the
1996, 2000, and 2004 presidential elections in Missouri, the Democratic vote
for president, compared to the Democratic vote for other Democrats running
statewide, were much more in line than in 2008 and 2012 when Obama was
on the ballot (Missouri Secretary of State 2014). Was racist voting against
Obama at least partly responsible for this? Again, circumstantial evidence
suggests "yes," but this supposition needs further explanation.

One factor that has changed Missouri's politics and may have contributed
to moving Missouri away from its swing-state status has been Missouri's
almost stagnant demographics. That is, while Missouri's population growth
has remained quite stable, it has also remained quite white. While many other
states have experienced noticeable increases in their minority populations,
especially among Hispanics and Latinos, Missouri has not. According to the
2013 U.S. Census estimates, Missouri's white population alone (not Hispanic or Latino) was 80.4%, while the country's was 62.6%. This is because
Missouri's white population (not Hispanic or Latino) had hardly changed
since 2000 where the white population (not Hispanic or Latino) was 82.8%.
Between 2000 and 2013 the Hispanic or Latino population had increased
in the U.S. from 12.5% to 17.1%, while in Missouri the Hispanic or Latino
population grew from 2.1% to 3.9%. The black population nationwide and in
Missouri remained fairly stable, increasing nationwide from 12.3% in 2000
to 13.2% in 2013, while in Missouri from 11.2% to 11.7%. During this same
period, the Asian population increased from 3.6% to 5.3% nationwide, but
only increased from 1.1% to 1.8% in Missouri. These demographical changes
are very different for the U.S. as a whole than for Missouri, explaining in part
why Missouri may not be voting as a swing state any longer. Electoral behavior studies tend to show that people vote for who they are most comfortable
with (for instance, blacks vote disproportionately for black candidates; Irish
for Irish candidates; Hispanics for Hispanic candidates; Mormons for Mormon candidates, and so forth). For example, CNN Exit Poll data show that
in the 2012 Republican Presidential Primary in Utah Romney, a Mormon,
received 93% of the vote in a state primarily Mormon (62.2% in 2012), while
Obama in 2008 in the General Election won over 95% of the black vote.
Thus, it would not be surprising to find white Missourians voting more for
white candidates than black candidates, especially in Missouri's rural counties where the black population, with few exceptions, is miniscule.

Acknowledging that voters tend to vote more for people "like themselves" may be a common finding by electoral behavior researchers, but it still does not mean that voting against a black candidate because of his skin color is not racist. Polling conducted nationally and in Missouri supports the hypothesis that Obama's race apparently undercut his ability to win by a greater margin nationally, but caused him to lose Missouri, especially in 2008 because Obama lost by only .13%. Exit poll data for the 2008 presidential election reported by CNN show that there was not much of a difference between the percent of whites voting for Obama nationally and in Missouri. While 43% of whites voted for Obama nationally, 42% of white Missourians did. However, if this 43% excluded the mostly non-battleground southern states, the gap between Missouri and other battleground states is more pronounced. For example, only 10% of whites in Alabama voted for Obama; 14% in Louisiana; 11% in Mississippi; 35% in North Carolina; 26% in South Carolina; 39% in Virginia; 41% in W. Virginia; 34% in Tennessee; 36% in Kentucky; 29% in Oklahoma; and 26% in Texas. Not any of these states historically have been considered swing states, although recently Virginia and North Carolina have been in play.

To determine whether racist voting, as least circumstantially, contributed to Missouri losing its swing state status during Obama's presidential bids in 2008 and 2012, it must be determined whether Missouri's white voters voted significantly less for Obama than white voters in other swing states. Table 2.6 shows the states that were designated as swing states entering the 2008 and/or the 2012 presidential elections by political news sources such as CNN, Associated Press, and RealClearPolitics. Missouri, since 2008, has not been considered a swing-state. Is it because Missouri's whites voted quite differently than whites in the other battleground states, causing Missouri to become the only battleground state in 2008 to vote for McCain and against the national tide for Obama? Possibly, because in 2008 only two other battleground states in Table 2.6 show a lower percentage of whites voting for Obama than Missouri, North Carolina (35%) and Virginia (39%), although New Mexico and Florida tie Missouri at 42%. However, the important difference is that the white percentage in Florida (71%), New Mexico (50%), North Carolina (72%), and Virginia (70%) are much lower than Missouri's 82%, helping greatly to minimize the impact of the white vote against Obama, as well as causing these states to remain battleground states. With only 43%% of Missouri's whites voting for Obama in 2008, constituting 82% of the state's vote, it can be understood why Missouri voted for McCain and why Missouri was knocked from its swing-state status, at least for the presidential elections involving the black candidate, Barack Obama.

Table 2.6 confirms that Missouri moved even further from its swing-state role in 2012, voting for Romney over Obama by almost a 10 point margin,

Table 2.6.   Percent of White Voters in Swing States Voting for Obama in 2008 and 2012

Swing States	% White Voting 2008	% White For Obama 2008	% Obama Win/Loss 2008	% White Voting 2012	% White For Obama 2012	% Obama Win/Loss 2012
Colorado	81%	50%	54-45% W	78%	44%	51-46% W
Florida	71%	42%	51-48% W	67%	37%	50-49% W
Iowa	91%	51%	54-44% W	93%	51%	52-46% W
Michigan	82%	51%	57-41% W	77%	44%	54-45% W
Missouri	**82%**	**42%**	**49-49% L**	**78%**	**32%**	**54-44% L**
Nevada	69%	45%	55-43% W	64%	43%	52-46% W
New Hampshire	94%	54%	54-45% W	93%	51%	52-46% W
New Mexico	50%	42%	57-42% W	51%	41%	53-43% W
North Carolina	72%	35%	50-49% W	70%	31%	50-48% L
Ohio	83%	46%	51-47% W	79%	41%	51-48% W
Pennsylvania	81%	48%	54-44% W	78%	42%	52-47% W
Virginia	70%	39%	53-46% W	70%	37%	51-47% W
Wisconsin	89%	54%	56-42% W	86%	48%	53-46% W

Sources: CNN Exit Poll 2008, http://www.cnn.com/ELECTION/2008/results/polls.main/
CNN Exit Poll 2012, http://www.cnn.com/election/2012/results/race/president
David Leip's Atlas of U.S. Presidential Elections, http://uselectionatlas.org/

while nationwide Obama won by 3.7%. Romney won comfortably in Missouri largely because only 32% of its white voters, constituting 78% the state's total vote, voted for Obama. Table 2.6 shows that only one other swing-state, North Carolina, was in the win column for Romney, but because of North Carolina's larger minority vote, Obama lost by only two percentage points, 50% to 48%. More importantly, North Carolina was the only state with a lower percentage of white voters voting for Obama than Missouri, but only by 1%. But even more importantly, the critical ratio between the percentage of white voters voting in the state and the percentage of white voters voting for Obama was worse in Missouri than for any other swing state, 78%: 32%, causing Missouri's popular vote percentage for Obama to be considerably lower than for all the other battleground states, even 8% lower than North Carolina's vote for Obama. Consequently, this caused Missouri to sway much further from Obama's nationwide winning percentage than any other swing state. Table 2.7 shows that Missouri deviated from Obama's 2012 winning percentage by 13.9%, while all other swing states were reasonably close to Obama's winning percentage, especially Colorado (+1.1%), Ohio (+.9%), and Virginia (+.1%).

Table 2.7. Percent Missouri Deviated From Obama's 2012 Winning Percentage Nationwide Compared to Other Swing States

Swing States	Obama's Win/ Loss % In Swing States 2012*	Obama's National Winning % 2012	% State Deviating From Obama's Winning %
Colorado	5%	3.9%	+1.1%
Florida	1%	3.9%	−2.9%
Iowa	6%	3.9%	+2.1%
Michigan	9%	3.9%	+5.1%
Missouri	**−10%**	**3.9%**	**−13.9%**
Nevada	6%	3.9%	+2.1%
New Hampshire	6%	3.9%	+2.1%
New Mexico	10%	3.9%	+6.1%
North Carolina	-2%	3.9%	−5.9%
Ohio	3%	3.9%	+.9%
Pennsylvania	5%	3.9%	+1.1%
Virginia	4%	3.9%	+.1%
Wisconsin	7%	3.9%	+3.1%

Sources: David Leip, "2012 Presidential General Election Results," http://uselectionatlas.org/RESULTS/national.php?year=2012&off=0&elect=0&f=0

* Percentages are rounded.

Regardless of why so many whites in Missouri voted against Obama in 2008 and 2012, the fact remains that they did. This suggests racism constituted a certain percentage of the white votes against Obama, certainly enough to cost Obama the election in Missouri in 2008. *The St. Louis Beacon* commissioned *The Warren Poll* to conduct an exit poll for the 2008 presidential race in the St. Louis metropolitan area, including St. Louis City, and the counties of Jefferson, St. Louis, and St. Charles. This represented 34.6% of Missouri's total voters. The *Beacon* was particularly interested in measuring the extent explicit racism played in the election contest, so *The Warren Poll* sampled 1125 voters in representative precincts, asking voters: "To what extent did Obama's race alone make you more or less likely to vote for him as President?" Over half of the white respondents (54.6%) said that they were less likely to vote for Obama because of his "race alone." Specifically, 21.1% of the white voters answered "A little less likely," another 12.7% said "Somewhat less likely," while 21.8% said that they were "A lot less likely" (Warren 2008). Once again, the actual role played by racism in any election is difficult to measure. Nonetheless, white votes for Obama in 2008 and 2012 were very low and certainly deviated a lot from when Missouri, as a bellwether state, voted for white winning Democratic presidential candidates such as John Kennedy, Lyndon Johnson, Jimmy Carter, and Bill Clinton, reflecting quite closely the nation's winning vote percentage for these victorious candidates.

As we look toward future presidential elections, the question must be asked: Did Missouri drift from its swing-state status because Missourians are evidently reluctant to vote for a black presidential candidate or will it return to its previous swing-state role, possibly even its bellwether status, when both the Republican and Democratic presidential candidates are white?

The Awakened Evangelical Vote: Perhaps the Most Obvious Reason for Why Missouri Has Lost Its Swing-State Status

As senior political advisor for George W. Bush's presidential campaigns in 2000 and 2004, Karl Rove realized that there was a potentially large voting bloc in America that needed to be awakened, organized, and lured to the voting booths. This bloc was the evangelical bloc and he knew that these socially conservative evangelicals, if they turned out to vote, would vote overwhelmingly Republican. Rove believed that the key to future Republican presidential wins was to get these evangelicals to vote. However, in 2000 Rove calculated that about four million evangelicals did not vote for George W. Bush in part because they were not targeted very well, but also because of Bush's well-publicized DUI charge discouraged evangelicals from turning out and voting for Bush. Rove did not want this large evangelical vote to be wasted again, so in the 2002 congressional elections and in the 2004 presidential elections, he developed a micro-targeting strategy to identify evangelicals and bring them to the polls (Rove 2010; Moore and Slater 2011; Miller 2012). His efforts paid off. In the 2004 presidential race 23% of the voters identified themselves as evangelicals and 78% of them voted for Bush, while only 21% of them voted for Democratic presidential candidate, John Kerry (CNN Exit Poll 2004). The evangelical vote for Bush constituted a 10% gain from 2000 where he received 68% of the evangelical vote (Pew Research Center for People & the Press 2004), but enough more to help Bush easily win the 2004 presidential election, 53.2% to 46.7% over Kerry.

Learning from Rove, Republicans continued to target evangelicals in the 2008 and 2012 presidential campaigns, using vast amounts of money from American Crossroads, as well as its sister conservative PAC, Crossroads GPS, controlled by Rove (Moore and Slater 2011; Miller 2012). The key was not to target so much the evangelicals in general, but to target evangelicals in swing states where a heavy vote by evangelicals could turn the battleground state from the Democratic column to the Republican column. Republican strategists found many evangelicals to tap in many of the battleground states, but found an "evangelical goldmine" in Missouri.

Table 2.8 displays the percentage of evangelicals in each swing state in 2008 and 2012, as well as the percentage of votes cast for Obama by evangelicals in 2008 and 2012. Since there were only token third-party candidates in these two presidential elections, it can be assumed that virtually all votes not cast by evangelicals for Obama were cast for McCain in 2008 and Romney in 2012. Table 2.8 makes one thing perfectly clear; that is, relatively few evangelicals in these swing-states voted for Obama, as few did for Kerry and Gore four years and eight years before. Although racist voting likely had some impact on evangelicals' vote choice, it appears that race may have played a minor role since other values play a more influential role in motivating evangelicals. And it must be acknowledged that Gore and Kerry also did poorly among evangelicals. Consequently, it appears that the evangelical vote has a weighty, independent status as a determinant of vote choice.

What is also clear is that the evangelical vote made more of a difference in the presidential elections in Missouri and North Carolina in 2008 and 2012 than in any other swing state, but especially in Missouri because Missouri was the only battleground state in 2008 to give McCain a victory. The large impact of the evangelical vote on Missouri may have contributed to Missouri moving from its swing-state status more than any other single factor.[4] Table 2.8 reveals that in 2008 39% of the total votes cast in Missouri were cast by those who identified themselves as evangelicals to exit pollsters, and only 29% of them voted for Obama. Parenthetically, 26% of the national exit poll respondents in 2008 and 2012 identified themselves as evangelicals, so the fact that Missouri was found to have 39% evangelicals places the state well above the national average. Only North Carolina in 2008 had more voters identifying themselves as evangelicals (44%) in combination with a smaller percentage of them voting for Obama (25%). These large blocs of evangelicals voting overwhelming against Obama likely made the vote for president very close in both North Carolina and Missouri, off-setting a wave of other factors in 2008 favoring Obama. Although Obama pulled out a squeaker in North Carolina in the 2008 presidential race, despite the few votes he received from evangelicals, he lost an even closer squeaker in Missouri largely because of a massive turnout by evangelicals voting for McCain, mostly from Missouri's rural counties.

In 2012 Missouri and North Carolina were the only swing states that voted for Romney, yet only Missouri stood out because Missouri voted so overwhelmingly for Romney by almost 10%, while in North Carolina Obama lost by just 2%. Table 2.8 shows that in 2012 no swing state came close to matching Missouri's ratio of the "percent of evangelicals voting" versus the "percent of evangelicals voting for Obama." In 2012, 37% of Missouri's voters identified themselves as evangelicals, more than any other state except Iowa's 38%. However, while 35% of Iowa's evangelicals voted for Obama, only 22% of Missouri voters did. This may have very well made the difference between Iowa voting for Obama and Missouri voting for Romney.

Table 2.8. Percent of Evangelicals in Swing States Voting for Obama in 2008 and 2012

Swing States	% Evangelicals Voting 2008	% Evangelicals For Obama 2008	% Obama Win/Loss 2008	% Evangelical Voting 2012	% Evangelical For Obama 2012	% Obama Win/Loss 2012
Colorado	21%	23%	54-45% W	25%	22%	51-46% W
Florida	24%	21%	51-48% W	24%	21%	50-49% W
Iowa	31%	33%	54-44% W	38%	35%	52-46% W
Michigan	27%	33%	57-41% W	28%	24%	54-45% W
Missouri	**39%**	**29%**	**49-49% L**	**37%**	**22%**	**54-44% L**
Nevada	16%	27%	55-43% W	18%	28%	52-46% W
New Hampshire	NA	NA	54-45% W	12%	25%	52-46% W
New Mexico	16%	18%	57-42% W	NA	NA	53-43% W
North Carolina	44%	25%	50-49% W	35%	20%	50-48% L
Ohio	30%	27%	51-47% W	31%	30%	51-48% W
Pennsylvania	NA	NA	54-44% W	NA	NA	52-47% W
Virginia	28%	20%	53-46% W	23%	17%	51-47% W
Wisconsin	26%	35%	56-42% W	24%	27%	53-46% W

Sources: CNN Exit Poll 2008, http://www.cnn.com/ELECTION/2008/results/polls.main/
CNN Exit Poll 2012, http://www.cnn.com/election/2012/results/race/president
David Leip's Atlas of U.S. Presidential Elections, http://uselectionatlas.org/

The fact that Missouri's rural, Republican voters have turned out in much greater numbers since 1996, as shown in this chapter's section on the "swelling Republican turnout numbers," cannot be ignored, especially since so many of these rural Republicans are evangelicals, voting overwhelmingly for Republican presidential candidates. The percentages presented in Table 2.8 also cannot be ignored because they show so starkly what an enormous role the evangelical vote played in Missouri in the 2008 and 2012 presidential elections compared to all other swing states. In sum, although we have provided other plausible explanations, the rise of the evangelical vote in Missouri since 2000 may in fact be the most obvious reason for why Missouri has lost its swing-state status.

CONCLUSION

For a century, Missouri stood uncontested as the nation's ultimate swing state. As a political microcosm and a harbinger of how things would play out nationally, the Show-Me-State came second to none until the dawn of the twenty-first century. However, due to an ensemble of factors (most significantly, the ideological, geographical, cultural, and racial backgrounds of the most recent presidential nominees; certain major policy issues; the swelling of GOP voters; and the awakening of the evangelical vote), Missouri has been moving briskly toward the Republican column, at least at the presidential level.

The intriguing question is whether Missouri will continue to stay in the Republican column or once again shift back to its previous swing state status. At this time, either path is entirely possible. Since many of the electoral factors that have removed Missouri from the list of hotly contested swing states could be temporary (for example, the personal traits of presidential candidates; major policy issues on the national agenda), it is conceivable that Democrats could avoid these pitfalls in future presidential elections, allowing Democratic presidential candidates to win in Missouri.

We can also not ignore the changing demographics that have allowed Democrats to win more easily in key swing states in recent presidential elections, but not in Missouri. That is, while the minority population, especially the Hispanic and Latino population, has been steadily increasing nationally, as well as in many battleground states, Missouri's demographics have remained rather stable and, therefore, quite white. This trend has allowed the Democratic Party to do better in swing states with larger and expanding "pro-Democrat minorities," but less well in those states that have not experienced significant increases in their minority populations such as Missouri.

It is also true that Democratic presidential candidates in the future may simply "write off" Missouri, perceiving it as a non-competitive red state, as Obama did when he withdrew from active campaigning in Missouri in early October of 2008, while totally ignoring Missouri in 2012. Missouri's large bloc of conservative white, evangelical voters, its relatively small percentage of minority voters, and its declining weight in the Electoral College (once with 18 electoral votes, but dwindling to only 10 today), make it a state that Democrats may just want to ignore. This is especially possible when considering that other formerly red states such as Virginia, North Carolina, New Mexico, Colorado, and Nevada have emerged as swing states Democrats can and have won in recent years. Clearly, such a decision by the Democratic Party would cause Missouri to leave the swing state ranks for the foreseeable future.

However, the future of Missouri as a red state or swing state is not certain. Not so long ago Missouri elected a Democrat, Bill Clinton, to two presidential terms. His wife, Hillary Clinton, the odds-on favorite to capture the Democratic presidential nomination in 2016, may become as popular as her husband was in 1992 and 1996, and go on to win the 2016 presidential election nationally, as well as capturing Missouri's ten electoral votes on her way. Having roots in neighboring Illinois and Arkansas, being a white woman (women have done quite well in Missouri politics; for example, Democratic U.S. Senator Claire McCaskill), and espousing an agenda more moderate than Gore, Kerry, or Obama, she might be the Democratic candidate to bring Missouri back into the Democratic column. While Missouri's swing state and bellwether status may currently be in hibernation, the Show-Me-State may not yet be through giving us presidential races to get excited about.

NOTES

1. An important distinction should be made between the concepts of a "swing state" and a "bellwether state" because both concepts are employed in this chapter. While the former broadly refers to a competitive state that either party can win and where candidates logically spend much of their time and resources (also known as a battleground state), the latter encompasses something more specific: the best of the swing states in predicting which way the nation will side. It is a reputation earned during a period of many decades—over successive elections where the split between the state-level and the national-level results were close.

2. In 2000, in a postelection interview with the *Washington Post* Kenneth Warren, one of the authors of this chapter, explained that Missouri had not adhered to its bellwether status because technically a bellwether state is a state that mirrors the popular vote of the nation, not the electoral vote. The reporter consulted with her editor and

called Warren back, explaining that this was too confusing to distinguish between the popular vote winner and the electoral vote winner in determining a state's bellwether status, so the *Post* went with a story saying that Missouri still retained its bellwether status because Bush had won the election and Missouri voted for Bush, ignoring the critical fact that the popular vote nationwide had actually gone to Gore. In 2004 reporters, ignoring this reality, flocked Missouri from all over the nation and the world because they believed that Missouri was still the best bellwether state. In 2004 Missouri did return to its bellwether status, but the 2008 and 2012 presidential elections would prove that Missouri was rapidly drifting away from its bellwether role.

3. "Race alone" is put in quotation marks because *The Warren Poll* in 2008 asked Missouri voters in an Exit Poll whether they voted against Obama because of his race alone. The poll's results are discussed later in this section.

4. On October 1, 2004, CNN's Jeff Greenfield interviewed me (Kenneth Warren, one of this chapter's authors) on the presidential race in Missouri, assuming that Missouri was still in play as a battleground state. Two days later I met him and he told me that he had to drop the interview because he had just been informed by the Kerry camp that they had given up on Missouri because the evangelical vote was causing Kerry to trail in Missouri by about 5%. Greenfield was told by Kerry's campaign staffers that they regarded the evangelical vote "as a nut too hard to crack" and it would be unlikely that they could pull out a victory in Missouri because of it. This tale conveys in real terms the impact the evangelical vote has had on Missouri and underlines one of the reasons Missouri has gone from a swing state to a red state.

FURTHER READING

Campbell, Tracy. 2013. *The Gateway Arch*. New Haven, CT: Yale University Press.

Carmines, Edward G., and James A. Stimson. 1989. *Issue Evolution: Race and the Transformation of American Politics*. Princeton, N.J., Princeton University Press.

CNN. 2008. "Study: Obama Most Liberal Senator Last Year." Online. <http://politicalticker.blogs.cnn.com/2008/01/31/study-obama-most-liberal-senator-last-year/>.

Flanigan, William H., and Nancy H. Zingale. 2009. *Political Behavior of the American Electorate*, 12th edition. Washington, DC: CQ Press.

Ganey, Terry. 2008. "What Bellwether: Did Race Make the Difference in Missouri?" *Columbiatribune.com*. Online. <http://archive.columbiatribune.com/2008/Nov/20081109Feat004.asp>.

Miller, Lisa. 2012. "The New Evangelical Vote." *Faithstreet*. Online. <http://www.faithstreet.com/onfaith/2012/01/06/iowa-caucuses-dispel-the-myth-of-monolithic-narrow-evangelical-voters/22367>.

Piston, Spencer. 2010. "How Explicit Racial Prejudice Hurt Obama in the 2008 Election." *Political Behavior*, vol. 32, no. 4, pp. 431–51.

Sniderman, Paul M., and Edward G. Carmines. 1997. "The Two Faces of Issue Voting." *American Political Science Review*, vol. 74, no. 1, pp. 78–91.

Wagner, Michael W., and William H. Flanigan. 2014. *Political Behavior of the American Electorate*, Washington, D.C., CQ Press.

Warren, Kenneth. 2008. "The Warren Poll, Exit Poll." *St. Louis Beacon*. Online. <https://www.stlbeacon.org/#!/content/13546/obama_draws_strong_support_in_st._louis_area_poll_shows>.

BIBLIOGRAPHY

Ansolabehere, Stephen, and Phillip Edward Jones. 2010. "Constituents' Responses to Congressional Roll-Call Voting." *American Journal of Political Science*, vol. 44, no. 3, pp. 583–97.
Campbell, Tracy. 2013. *The Gateway Arch*. New Haven, CT: Yale University Press.
Carmines, Edward G., and James A. Stimson. 1989. *Issue Evolution: Race and the Transformation of American Politics*. Princeton, N.J., Princeton University Press.
CNN. 2008. "Study: Obama Most Liberal Senator Last Year." Online. <http://politicalticker.blogs.cnn.com/2008/01/31/study-obama-most-liberal-senator-last-year/>.
Death Penalty Information Center. 2014. "Number of Executions by State and Region Since 1976." Online. <http://www.deathpenaltyinfo.org/number-executions-state-and-region-1976>.
Engel, Brent. 2010. "Cap-and-Trade Could Be Sore Spot on Obama Visit." *Hannibal Courier-Post*. Online. <http://www.hannibal.net/article/20100427/NEWS/304279883
Enten, Harry. 2014. "Republicans Have Regained the Foreign Policy Edge." *FiveThirtyEight*. Online. <http://fivethirtyeight.com/datalab/republicans-have-regained-the-foreign-policy-edge/>.
Flanigan, William H., and Nancy H. Zingale. 2009. *Political Behavior of the American Electorate*, 12th edition. Washington, DC: CQ Press.
FOX News. 2004. "Raw Data: Bush Speech in Springfield." Online. <http://www.foxnews.com/story/2004/07/30/raw-data-bush-speech-in-springfield/>.
Ganey, Terry. 2008. "What Bellwether: Did Race Make the Difference in Missouri?" *Columbiatribune.com*. Online. <http://archive.columbiatribune.com/2008/Nov/20081109Feat004.asp>.
Harris, John F. 2004. "Truth, Consequences of Kerry's 'Liberal' Label." *Washington Post*, p. A1.
Hartman, Ray. 2012, "White Power and Missouri Politics." *St. Louis Magazine*, Nov. 8, 2012. Online. <http://www.stlmag.com/news/politics/White-Power-and-Missouri-Politics/>.
Holbrook, Allyson L., Melanie C. Green, and Jon A. Krosnick. 2003. "Telephone Versus Face-to-Face Interviewing of National Probability Samples with Long Questionnaires. Comparisons of Respondent Satisficing and Social Desirability Response Bias." *Public Opinion Quarterly*, vol. 67, no. 1, pp. 79–125.
Leip, David. 2012. "David Leip's Atlas of U.S. Presidential Elections." Online. <http://uselectionatlas.org/RESULTS/>.
Miller, Lisa. 2012. "The New Evangelical Vote." *Faithstreet*. Online. <http://www.faithstreet.com/onfaith/2012/01/06/iowa-caucuses-dispel-the-myth-of-monolithic-narrow-evangelical-voters/22367>.

Missouri Secretary of State. 2014. "Election and Voting: Election Results: Previous Elections." Online. <http://www.sos.mo.gov/elections/s_default.asp?id=results>.

Moore, James, and Wayne Slater. 2011. *Bush's Brain: How Karl Rove Made George W. Bush President.* New York: Wiley.

National Institute on Money in State Politics. 2012. "Proposition B: Creation of a Health and Education Trust Fund." Online. <http://www.followthemoney.org/database/StateGlance/ballot.phtml?m=1038>.

Pasek, Josh, Tobias H. Stark, Jon A. Krosnick, Trevor Thompson, and B. Keith Payne. 2014. "Attitudes toward Blacks in the Obama Era: Changing Distributions and Impacts on Job Approval and Electoral Choice 2008–2012." *Public Opinion Quarterly*, vol. 78, no. S1, pp. 276–302.

Pasek, Josh, Alexander Tahk, Yphtach Lelkes, Jon A. Krosnick, B. Keith Payne, Omair Akhtar, and Trevor Tompson. 2009. "Determinants of Turnout and Candidate Choice in the 2008 Presidential Election: Illuminating the Impact of Racial Prejudice and Other Considerations." *Public Opinion Quarterly*, vol. 73, no. 5, pp. 943–94.

Pew Research Center for the People & the Press. 2004. "Religion and the Presidential Vote." Online. <http://www.people-press.org/2004/12/06/religion-and-the-presidential-vote/>.

Pilkington, Ed. 2008. "Obama Angers Midwest Voters with Guns and Religion Remark." *The Guardian.* Online. <http://www.theguardian.com/world/2008/apr/14/barackobama.uselections2008>.

Piston, Spencer. 2010. "How Explicit Racial Prejudice Hurt Obama in the 2008 Election." *Political Behavior*, vol. 32, no. 4, pp. 431–51.

Public Policy Polling. 2009. "Healthcare in the States." Online. <http://publicpolicypolling.blogspot.ca/2009/12/health-care-in-states.html>.

Rabinowitz, Joshua, David O. Sears, Jim Sidanius, and Jon A. Krosnick. 2009. "Why Do White Americans Oppose Race-Targeted Policies? Clarifying the Impact of Symbolic Racism." *Political Psychology*, vol. 30, no. 5, pp. 805–28.

Rove, Karl. 2010. *Courage and Consequence: My Life as a Conservative in the Fight.* New York: Threshold Editions.

Shesgreen, Deirdre, and Maureen Groppe. 2014. "New EPA Rules Could Force Big Changes in Missouri." *Springfield News-Leader.* Online. <http://www.news-leader.com/story/news/local/missouri/2014/06/02/new-epa-rules-force-big-changes-missouri/9886701/>.

Sides, John H., and Lynn Vavreck. 2013. *The Gamble: Choice and Chance in the 2012 Presidential Election.* Princeton: Princeton University Press.

Silver, Nate, and Allison McCann. 2014. "Are White Republicans More Racist Than White Democrats?" *FiveThirtyEightPolitics.* Online. <http://fivethirtyeight.com/features/are-white-republicans-more-racist-than-white-democrats/>.

Sniderman, Paul M., and Edward G. Carmines. 1997. "The Two Faces of Issue Voting." *American Political Science Review*, vol. 74, no. 1, pp. 78–91.

Tesler, Michael. 2013. "The Return of Old-Fashioned Racism to White Americans' Partisan Preferences in the Early Obama Era." *Journal of Politics*, vol. 75, no. 1, pp, 110–123.

Tesler, Michael. 2012. "The Spillover of Racialization into Health Care: How President Obama Polarized Public Opinion by Racial Attitudes and Race." *American Journal of Political Science*, vol. 56, no. 3, pp. 690–704.

Tourangeau, Roger, and Yan Ting. 2007. "Sensitive Questions in Surveys." *Psychological Bulletin*, vol. 133, no. 5, pp 859–883.

U.S. Census Bureau. 2014. "U.S. Census." Online. <http://www.google.com/search?q=population+of+St.+Charles+County%2C+MO&ie=utf-8&oe=utf-8&aq=t&rls=org.mozilla:en-US:official&client=firefox-a&channel=np&source=hp>.

U.S. Census Bureau. 2014. "State and County QuickFacts." <http://quickfacts.census.gov/qfd/states/29/29189.html>.

VandeHei, Jim. 2004. "Kerry Drops the Ball with Packers Fans." *Washington Post*, p. A9.

Wagner, Michael W., and William H. Flanigan. 2014. *Political Behavior of the American Electorate*, Washington, D.C., CQ Press.

Warren, Kenneth. 2008. "The Warren Poll, Exit Poll." *St. Louis Beacon*. Online. <https://www.stlbeacon.org/#!/content/13546/obama_draws_strong_support_in_st._louis_area_poll_shows>.

Chapter Three

Ohio

The "Battleground of Battlegrounds"?

Henriët Hendriks and Bas van Doorn

At a November 2 campaign event in West Chester, Ohio, 2012 vice-presidential candidate Paul Ryan characterized Ohio, home to his *alma mater* Miami University, as "the battleground of battlegrounds" (Foley 2012). Media accounts at the time agreed. A *Time* magazine article published two weeks prior to the 2012 election was titled "Why Ohio Will Decide the Presidential Election" (Altman & Sherer 2012). The article argued that although Ohio has "a history as a bellwether for the nation" it was "behaving differently from the rest of the country this year." Unlike other competitive states, according to the piece, Ohio was resisting a late Romney surge and, as such, was positioning itself as "the President's firewall." A week later, the *New York Times* similarly characterized Ohio as "seen by both sides as critical to victory" and it concluded that Ohio, in particular, was "the biggest focal point of the race" (Zeleny 2012). It should be no surprise then, that on election night, the Ohio results were eagerly anticipated and widely discussed. Between 8 pm and midnight, for example, CNN's live TV coverage of election night mentioned Ohio 123 times,[1] and even once it was apparent Obama had clinched the state and thus in all likelihood the election, Karl Rove was seen arguing on Fox News that outstanding votes in the southwest of the state would deliver a narrow Romney victory.

On this evidence, Ohio is perhaps the most prominent of all modern swing states. Candidate strategy bolsters this point: as we will discuss in more detail below, during the most recent election Ohio received the most candidate visits and the second-to-most advertisement spending of all states. Ohio's status as a swing state is beyond dispute: in the last fourteen elections, it swung back and forth between Republican and Democratic presidential candidates seven times. But despite the fact that Ohio is a *swing* state, a careful look at historical election data shows Ohio has not always been closely contested.

During the 1980s, for instance, Ohio's election outcomes closely mirrored national outcomes with landslides for the winning candidate. More recently, and perhaps surprisingly, both Al Gore and George W. Bush viewed Ohio as leaning Republican in 2000 and spent less time and money there than in what they saw as that election's true battlegrounds (Shaw 2006).

In this chapter, we argue that from a long-term temporal perspective Ohio is more accurately described as a bellwether, whose results tend to mirror the national popular vote, than as a consistent battleground. The Buckeye State has voted with the winning candidate in every election since 1964 and, what is more, Ohio's margins of victory between the two major-party candidates approximate national margins of victory. In other words, when the national election outcome is close, Ohio's election outcome is close, and when presidential candidates comfortably win the national election, they tend to do so in Ohio as well. Moreover, even in landslide elections, when both national and state expectations and the eventual results clearly favor one of the candidates, Ohio is still one of the few states that receive a lot of attention from the campaigns. However, we also show that during the last two decades it *has* consistently been a closely contested state.

To illustrate this argument, we first document national and state-level historical voter trends and then present data from recent elections in which Ohio was, in fact, a battleground state, including patterns of campaign activity, voter turnout, and vote choice. Next, we discuss possible reasons for Ohio's bellwether status as well as its current importance as a swing state. We argue that a combination of national political dynamics and the experiences of the 2000 and 2004 elections set the stage for its rise to prominence. Finally, we address whether we can expect Ohio to remain a closely and vehemently contested state. We speculate that, assuming that the political climate remains polarized and that presidential contests remain close on a national level, Ohio will continue to be a battleground in future presidential elections.

Presidential Elections Results in Ohio Since 1960

With respect to presidential elections it is a political truism to state that "as Ohio goes, so goes the nation." In fact, since the 1904 election, Ohio has voted for the winning candidate with only two exceptions. Perhaps most surprisingly, in 1944 the Buckeye State voted for Thomas Dewey instead of incumbent president Franklin D. Roosevelt, though by less than 1% of the vote. The fact that Dewey's running mate was Ohio Governor John Bricker may have made the difference. In the 1960 race, an extremely close election nationwide, Richard Nixon beat John F. Kennedy quite comfortably in Ohio, much to JFK's chagrin because he had spent much time and effort campaigning in the state and he believed he had it sown up (White 1961: 22).

Generally speaking, then, Ohio's results have been quite predictive of overall presidential election outcomes as measured simply by who eventually won the presidency. In and of itself, however, this in no way means that Ohio is consistently a battleground state in the sense that presidential contests are always closely contested there, but it suggests that Ohio cannot simply be counted on by either party. Table 3.1 serves as a good illustration of this point.

A quick glance at these numbers makes clear that presidential elections are not always close affairs in Ohio. In fact, they are often not. Five out of the last fourteen contests were decided by margins exceeding 10% and three of those approached or exceeded 20% (1964, 1972, and 1984). All in all, the mean margin of victory during this period is 8.44%.

A closer look suggests that one is on more solid ground saying that Ohio has recently become a regularly closely contested state. The period stretching from the 1960s through the 1980s was particularly uncompetitive, including all double digit margins and with only two out of eight races featuring margins of less than 5%. The mean margin of victory in these elections was 12.1%. Of the last six presidential elections, in contrast, only one was decided by more than 5% in Ohio and the mean margin of victory was 3.58%.

For more context, it is useful to compare the Ohio vote margins to the national vote margins. This allows us to conclude whether Ohio's vote trends are similar or different from developments at the national level. Table 3.2

Table 3.1. **Presidential Election Results in Ohio Since 1960**

Year	Democrat %	Republican %	Margin
1960	46.7	53.3	6.6
1964	62.9	37.1	25.9
1968	42.9	45.2	2.3
1972	38.1	59.6	21.5
1976	48.9	48.7	.2
1980	40.9	51.5	10.6
1984	40.1	58.9	18.8
1988	44.1	55.0	10.9
1992	40.2	38.3	1.9
1996	47.4	41.0	6.4
2000	46.5	50.0	3.5
2004	48.7	50.8	2.1
2008	51.5	46.9	4.6
2012	50.7	47.7	3.0

Source: http://www.sos.state.oh.us/elections/Research/electResultsMain.aspx

Table 3.2. Nationwide versus Ohio Vote Margins (in percentages)

Year	Nationwide	Ohio	Difference
1960	.2	−6.6	−6.8
1964	22.6	25.8	3.3
1968	.7	2.3	1.6
1972	23.2	21.5	−1.7
1976	2.1	.2	−1.9
1980	9.7	10.6	.9
1984	18.2	18.8	.6
1988	7.8	10.9	2.1
1992	5.6	1.9	−3.7
1996	8.5	6.4	−2.1
2000	.5	−3.5	−4.0
2004	2.4	2.1	−.3
2008	7.2	4.6	−2.6
2012	3.9	3.0	−.9

Sources: http://www.presidency.ucsb.edu/elections.php and http://www.sos.state.oh.us/elections/Research/electResultsMain.aspx

compares the national vote margins to the Ohio vote margins. The first column indicates the margin by which the victorious presidential candidate won the national popular vote. Percentages in the second column are the margins by which a presidential candidate won Ohio. Negative numbers indicate that the candidate who won Ohio lost the nationwide popular vote whereas positive numbers indicate the candidate won both Ohio and the nationwide vote. Finally, positive numbers in the Difference column indicate stronger than nationwide support for the winner in Ohio, whereas negative numbers indicate that the nationwide winner of the popular vote had less than average support in the state. In other words, a zero in this column indicates that the national margin of victory equals Ohio's margin of victory.

The first conclusion we can draw from these numbers is that Ohio is not a consistently accurate barometer for the nationwide popular support for presidential candidates. While the difference in margins occasionally approaches zero, it is sometimes also considerably higher than that and in two instances (1960 and 2000) the state supported a candidate other than the one who won the nationwide popular vote. The numbers show that in the competitive era (1992–2012), Ohio consistently shows less than average support for the winner of the nationwide popular vote. This is further evidence that Ohio's status in presidential election is different than before: the state is now more competitive than it used to be and it is now consistently more competitive than the nation as a whole.

One final way to consider the competiveness of the state is to compare its margins of victory to that of other states that are routinely considered swing

Table 3.3.   Ohio, Florida, and Pennsylvania Vote Margins*

Year	Nationwide	Ohio	Florida	Pennsylvania
1960	.2 (D)	−6.6 (R)	-3.0 (R)	2.4 (D)
1964	22.6 (D)	25.9 (D)	2.3 (D)	30.2 (D)
1968	.7 (R)	2.3 (R)	9.6 (R)	−3.6 (D)
1972	23.2 (R)	21.5 (R)	44.4 (R)	20.0 (R)
1976	2.1 (D)	.2 (D)	5.3 (D)	2.7 (D)
1980	9.7 (R)	10.6 (R)	17.0 (R)	7.1 (R)
1984	18.2 (R)	18.8 (R)	30.7 (R)	7.4 (R)
1988	7.8 (R)	10.9 (R)	22.4 (R)	2.3 (R)
1992	5.6 (D)	1.9 (D)	-1.9 (R)	9.0 (D)
1996	8.5 (D)	6.4 (D)	5.7 (D)	9.2 (D)
2000	.5 (D)	−3.5 (R)	.0 (TIE)	4.2 (D)
2004	2.4 (R)	2.1 (R)	5.0 (R)	−2.5 (D)
2008	7.2 (D)	4.6 (D)	2.8 (D)	10.3 (D)
2012	3.9 (D)	3.0 (D)	.9 (D)	5.5 (D)
Mean	8.0	8.44	10.8	8.3

Source: http://www.presidency.ucsb.edu/elections.php

*A negative number indicates the state was won by the nationwide popular vote loser. For example, in 1960 Richard Nixon won Ohio, even though he lost the nationwide popular vote.

states (see Table 3.3). In this case, we selected Ohio's neighboring state Pennsylvania and, because of its importance in the 2000 election and after, Florida.

Several things are of note here. First, consistent with their bellwether reputations, Ohio and Pennsylvania both only voted with the nationwide loser twice in this period. Counting Bush's 2000 win in the state, Florida voted with the nationwide loser three times. When we look at partisan patterns, we see that Ohio voted Republican eight times and Democratic six times, Florida Republican eight times, Democratic five times, and tied once (2000), while Pennsylvania shows a more unbalanced pattern voting Democratic 10 times and Republican only 4 times. Notably, Pennsylvania has now voted for the Democratic presidential candidate 5 times in a row.

Using the more precise measure of mean margin of victory, it becomes clear that, looking at the entire period, Florida's margins are furthest removed from the national margins, whereas Ohio and Pennsylvania's are quite close to the national mean. Once again, though, it is useful to break the numbers down by period. The mean nationwide vote margin is 4.68% for the 1992–2012 period. Ohio, as discussed above, has a mean average margin of victory of 3.58% over the last 6 presidential elections compared to a mean of 12.1% for the elections from 1960–1988. At 2.72%, Florida, which has a higher mean for the full period, has a smaller mean margin for the 1992–2012 period than Ohio does. Pennsylvania's mean margin of victory, meanwhile, is quite a bit higher at 6.78%. In sum then, Ohio is more competitive than neighboring Pennsylvania and slightly less competitive than Florida over the last six elections.

Candidate and Media Perceptions of Ohio

The numbers indicate that Ohio has become a consistently competitive state over the last two decades. But how do presidential candidates think about the state? Do they view it as crucial to their (re)election strategy? Do they also perceive it as consistently competitive?

In 1960, Nixon campaigned hard in Ohio and JFK definitely believed the state was competitive, but for the taking. In fact, the state "caused him bitterness" (White 1961: 22) when it became clear on election night that Nixon was going to win there. According to White's classic account (ibid. 23), Kennedy lifted his hand, grotesquely swollen and calloused from shaking so many hands during the campaign, and said "Ohio did that to me—they did it there." Pollsters and journalists, meanwhile, had been convinced that Kennedy would carry the state, with White calling the result "the greatest upset of the election" (363).

In 1964, Goldwater, who was counting on the deep South, Oklahoma, Kentucky, and his home state of Arizona, identified Ohio as one of the four swing states that would help him win the race, with Illinois, California, and Indiana being the other three (White 1964: 332–334). Lyndon Johnson, meanwhile, "felt good about Ohio" (395) and, as the polls and the eventual result showed, for good reason. Still, the fact that one of the two major party candidates once again regarded Ohio as crucial to his strategy, attests to its special status in presidential electoral politics.

During the 1968 race, conventional wisdom from the start of the general election campaign right up until election day held that Nixon would comfortably win Ohio. On September 1 of that year, for example, the *Cleveland Plain Dealer* reported that according to "private polls and politicians' judgment," Nixon had a "definite lead" in Ohio (Broder 1968). Nonetheless, the article suggests Ohio was one of the "Big Seven" states where "Nixon and Humphrey will concentrate their campaigns." Subsequent reporting, for example *New York Times* articles from October 23 (Apple 1968) and October 29 (Frankel 1968), indeed suggests that both major party candidates spent significant time campaigning in the Buckeye state and the final result, a Nixon win by 2.3%, was closer than initially anticipated.

The 1972 election was a huge landslide, with Nixon beating McGovern by a nationwide 23.2% margin. Ohio, like most other states, was never realistically in play for McGovern. However, Ohio still received special attention during the campaign. In his nomination acceptance speech at the tumultuous Democratic National Convention in Miami Beach, Florida, McGovern said:

> This is going to be a national campaign, carried to every part of the nation— North, South, East and West. We're not conceding a single state to Richard Nixon. I should like to say to my friend, Frank King, that Ohio may have passed a few times in this convention, but Tom Eagleton and I are not going to pass Ohio. I shall say to Governor Gilligan, Ohio is sometimes a little slow in counting the votes, but when those votes are counted next November, Ohio will be in the Democratic victory column.

The next presidential election, the 1976 race between Ford and Carter, was much closer. In fact, it featured the narrowest margin of victory in Ohio in the 1960–2012 period. Contemporary media reports indicate Ohio was in play for both candidates. A September 22 piece from the *New York Times*, for example, cites several polls that indicate that Carter was leading Ford in Ohio (Apple 1976). Two days earlier, however, the *Los Angeles Times* reported that Ford was ahead though only by "a few points" and the outcome of the race is characterized as "uncertain" (Reich 1976).

Judging from the eventual results, the presidential elections of the 1980s were quite uncompetitive in Ohio, with Ohioans supporting Reagan (twice) and Bush Sr. by margins exceeding 10%. Nonetheless, the state received plenty of press and candidate attention in 1980 and accounts published in mid-October suggest that the state "has become a serious battleground" and the race was "Expected to be Close" (Clymer 1980). The 1984 election was another blowout, with Reagan winning all states but Mondale's home state of Minnesota. Yet, once again Ohio was among a select group of states that "strategists count as vital" to Mondale's hopes (Gailey 1984). In 1988, the *New York Times* wrote that analysts considered Ohio as "all but essential" to Bush's chances (Apple 1988). A later article describes the Ohio contest as "a fierce battle" and the state, according to the Bush campaign, was "one of its best three targets, along with New Jersey and Michigan, among the states the Democrats have said they need to win" (Dowd 1988).

CANDIDATE STRATEGY:
CAMPAIGN APPEARANCES AND SPENDING IN OHIO

The anecdotal evidence from the 1980s suggests that a shift in candidate perceptions was starting to take place, with Ohio increasingly being seen as a pivotal state on the road to the White House. In this section, we present data on candidate appearances and advertisement spending in Ohio over the 1988–2012 period, election years for which reliable data is available.

As we illustrate above, margins of victory as well as media and candidate statements are one way to gauge a state's competitiveness and thus far, the evidence suggests Ohio has been a true bellwether state and only more recently, a truly closely contested state. Candidate strategy in the form of campaign visits and advertisement spending are other indicators that can help us understand Ohio's crucial role in recent presidential elections. Different than election outcomes, these strategies reveal how candidates perceive states *leading up to election day.* In that sense, they are often more dependent on previous election years than margins of victories are. Candidates often look back to previous election outcomes to determine which states to focus on in the current campaign (Shaw 2006). In particular, the extreme closeness of the 2000 general election and the controversies in Ohio during the 2004 election seem to have served as catalysts for the amount of subsequent campaign visits and spending in Ohio.

Despite the ever-growing amount of money spent in American elections, candidates' resources (including time) are limited and thus allocated strategically. In presidential elections, campaign strategy is by and large the result of a curious institution called the Electoral College. Under this system, each state is awarded a number of electoral votes equal to its total number of U.S. Senators and members of the House of Representatives.[2] For presidential candidates to win office, they need to win 270 of 538 electoral votes. While not required by the Constitution, all states except Maine and Nebraska award all their electoral votes to the winner of the statewide popular vote.[3] Even a single vote margin in Ohio, then, provides the winner with all of Ohio's current eighteen Electoral College votes, the seventh largest share of electoral votes among the fifty states.[4] This potential big win in combination with its competitiveness means presidential candidates shower Ohio with attention while they all but ignore other often smaller and decidedly more Republican or Democratic states. In fact, during the 2012 election cycle, 34 states (including the District of Columbia) received no campaign spending at all from either Republican candidate Mitt Romney or incumbent President Obama.[5]

So how does Ohio fare in comparison with other states in terms of candidate attention? Tables 3.4 and 3.5 show candidate appearances and advertisement spending in Ohio going back to 1988. Candidate appearances include all unique appearances by presidential candidates in Ohio during the two months leading up to election day, with the exception of 2008, for which appearances as far back as June 11, 2008, are counted (see Huang and Shaw 2009). In other words, candidates might make three appearances on the same day at three different events. Advertisement spending can be measured in two dif-

Table 3.4.   Presidential Candidate Appearances in Ohio, 1988-2012

Year	Democratic Candidate	Republican Candidate	Total
1988	7	11	18
1992	7	6	13
1996	10	9	19
2000	5	7	12
2004	17	17	34
2008*	13	16	29
2012	20	32	52
Mean	**11.3**	**14**	**25.3**

Sources: 1988, 1992, and 1996 data from Shaw (1999); 2000 and 2004 data from Shaw (2006); 2008 data from Huang and Shaw (2009) and 2012 data compiled by the authors themselves.

*Unlike the other years which only include visits during the ten or so weeks leading up to election day, 2008 includes visits from June 11 through November 4.

ferent ways: Gross Rating Points (GRPs)—an industry measure of the potential reach of a campaign—or total dollar amount. For years 1988–2008, GRPs are available whereas for years 2000–2012 total dollar amounts are available.

First, looking at the number of candidate appearances, we see that Ohio has been on candidates' minds going back as far as 1988, which is consistent with statements found in media reports of the time. Moreover, the general trend seems to be one of increase, going from a combined 18 visits in 1988 to 52 in 2012. In 1988, Ohio received the third largest number of visits among all states. Only California (34) and Illinois (23) received more. In 1992, only Michigan received more visits than Ohio and in 1996, California and the District of Columbia took the number one and two spots before Ohio. With

Table 3.5.   Ad Spending by Democratic and Republican Candidates, 1988-2012

Year	Dem. GRPs	Rep. GRPs	Total GRPs	Dem. $	Rep. $	Total $
1988	2,078	5,259	7,337	n/a	n/a	n/a
1992	8,760	9,100	17,860	n/a	n/a	n/a
1996	5,626	4,980	10,606	n/a	n/a	n/a
2000	11,132	12,624	23,756	7,828,493	9,045,793	16,874,286
2004	8,354	12,493	20,847	7,652,379	11,057,010	18,709,389
2008*	64,822	51,993	116,815	48,292,479	38,734,581	87,027,060
2012	n/a	n/a	n/a	28,610,000	15,590,000	44,200,000

Sources: 1988, 1992, and 1996 data from Shaw (1999); 2000 and 2004 data from Shaw (2006); 2008 data from Huang and Shaw (2009) and 2012 data compiled by the authors themselves.

*Unlike the other years which only include spending during the ten or so weeks leading up to the election and only spending by the major party candidates, 2008 spending includes spending from June 11 through November 4 and also includes spending by the parties and interests groups with clear ideological leaning.

the average number of appearances per state equaling between four and five for most election years, Ohio consistently receives at least twice as many. For instance, in 1996, the average number of candidate appearances for all states was five. With 19 visits between September 1 and election day, Ohio received almost four times as many.

Ironically, during the closest presidential election in recent memory, that of 2000, Ohio received the fewest combined campaign visits (12) of all elections during the period 1988–2012. This might have been due to a miscalculation on the candidates' parts, especially Al Gore, who saw Ohio as leaning Republican rather than a battleground (Shaw 2006). In the two months leading up to the election, Al Gore only appeared in Ohio five times and Bush followed suit with only seven appearances as his campaign also deemed it a leaning Republican state.

Spending data reveal similar trends in the sense that the amount of spending in Ohio has overall increased over the last two decades. However, whereas Ohio saw a dip in candidate appearances in the 2000 election, ad spending did not follow this trend, with the exception of Kerry's 2004 campaign. Shaw (2006) reveals that Kerry and his team had difficulty spending all their money in the final weeks of the campaign since little television time was left available. This is especially ironic given that, according to Shaw's estimates, "an extra ten million dollars in Ohio would have produced a virtual tie in the Buckeye State" (149).

Table 3.6. Comparison of Candidate Appearances in Ohio, Florida, and Pennsylvania

Year	Total # of appearances			Ad Spending (in GRPs)		
	OH	FL	PA	OH	FL	PA
1988	18	0	9	7,337	1,540	6,353
1992	13	8	7	17,860	6,470	16,650
1996	19	16	7	10,606	10,011	13,592
2000	12	23	20	23,756	24,345	32,828
2004	34	43	19	20,847	21,172	20,394
2008*	29	15	27	116,815	47,644	54,219
2012	52	39	4	n/a	n/a	n/a
Mean**	25.3	20.6	13.3	16,081	12,708	17,963

Sources: 1988, 1992, and 1996 data from Shaw (1999); 2000 and 2004 data from Shaw (2006); 2008 data from Huang and Shaw (2009) and 2012 data compiled by the authors themselves.

* 2008 data includes appearances as far back as June 11 and spending by outside groups in addition to the candidates alone.

**The average GRPs do not include 2008 as this would artificially bring up the mean as it includes spending by outside groups as well.

Once again, it is helpful to compare Ohio data to two other modern swing states: Florida and Pennsylvania (see Table 3.6). This comparison reveals that Ohio has more reliably received candidate visits than the other two states, even though one or both states eclipsed Ohio in appearances in 2000 and 2004. In fact, on average, candidates have appeared a whopping 25 times in Ohio during the months leading up to the election compared to almost 21 and 13 times in Florida and Pennsylvania, respectively. Spending data reveal fewer differences between the states, perhaps an indication that appearances are truly a finite campaign resource (a candidate can only be in one place at one time), whereas campaign dollars don't face that same limitation.

Ohio's perceived importance is also highlighted when we take into account that Florida has many more Electoral College votes than Ohio (currently 29 to 18). One would expect candidates to focus on the states that would offer them the biggest bang for their buck, yet Ohio receives more visits than Florida in all elections except two. In fact, in the final week of the 2012 election, it seemed that nothing *but* Ohio was on candidates' minds. Both the Obama and Romney campaigns appeared at multiple rallies in Ohio during those final days. Mitt Romney and vice-presidential candidate Paul Ryan made ten appearances (some at the same event) whereas Obama and Biden made a total of eleven appearances. In contrast, Romney and Obama only made one appearance each in Florida during that same week.

While drawing conclusions based on just seven consecutive elections is always somewhat speculative, we believe that the last three elections (2004, 2008, and 2012) stand out as elections during which Ohio truly became "the battleground of battlegrounds." For instance, in 2004 Kerry and Bush combined spent close to $20 million in Ohio and this amount was more than doubled eight years later, with Obama and Romney spending over $44 million in the Buckeye State. Tellingly, the average number of visits for the period 1988–2000 is about seven whereas the average for the last three election is almost 17. And after the notorious 2000 election, both campaigns about tripled their visits to the Buckeye state.

An area of the state that has received outsized attention in the past two presidential elections is Hamilton County, which encompasses Cincinnati and some of its surrounding suburbs. In 2008, Barack Obama became the first Democratic candidate to win the county since LBJ's 1964 landslide. He did so with a voter margin that mirrored the national voter margin, 52% to 47%. In 2012, both Obama and his opponent Mitt Romney allocated large amounts of campaign resources to the county and with good reason: of the three most populated counties in the state, it is decidedly the most competitive and has swung both ways in local elections. Romney's campaign director in Ohio, Scott Jennings, called the county "one of the most important places in

America."[6] Moreover, it became a big battleground over collective bargaining rights in 2011, when Republican Governor John Kasich signed a law that curbed unions' negotiating powers. The backlash was especially fierce in Hamilton County, which might have led to a more favorable climate for President Obama in 2012: he was able to win the county again by exactly the same voter margin as in 2008. Hamilton County illustrates firstly, how candidates think in terms of swing *counties*, not just swing states, and secondly, how local issues can drive national campaigns.

It stands to reason that the 2000 and 2004 elections served as catalysts for the 2008 election and beyond. Clearly, the 2000 election was an extremely close affair nationally and highlighted the decisive role one state can play in the overall election outcome. Al Gore's underestimation of Ohio's importance was not lost on both campaigns in 2004 and as a result, it became the center of attention. But not only was the 2004 election extremely close, with President Bush winning with 2.5 percent of the vote, or just 136,483 votes, immediately following the election, many stories appeared in the media of election irregularities and possible fraud. Democrats on the House Judiciary Committee even conducted an official investigation and, on January 5, 2005, published a report called "Preserving Democracy: What Went Wrong in Ohio." While the ranking Democratic member, Rep. Conyers, made sure not to claim that anything criminal had happened in Ohio, the report contained allegations of "serious election irregularities in the Ohio presidential election, which resulted in a significant disenfranchisement of voters." This only seems to have heightened the stakes in Ohio as evidenced by Karl Rove's assessment of Ohio in August 2008: "Then there is Ohio. Ground zero in '04, its 20 electoral votes will be hotly contested again this year. No Republican has won the White House without winning the Buckeye State." Ohio voters seem to agree with Rove's assessment: In mid-August 2008, a Rasmussen Reports poll asked Ohioans whether it was likely that Ohio would determine the election outcome. 38% of the sample believed it very likely that Ohio could determine the general election outcome and another 47% believed this somewhat likely. Only 7% believed it not very likely or not likely at all.[7] It was no surprise then that both John McCain and Barack Obama spent so much time and money there.

The disproportional attention Ohio now receives appears to translate into higher turnout rates. Looking at turnout data since 1988 (see Table 3.7), we see that Ohio tends to have higher turnout than the national rate, but the extent of the margin is considerably more pronounced in more recent elections, exceeding 5% in 2004, 2008, and 2012.

Table 3.7. Ohio Turnout versus National Turnout (in %)

Year	Ohio	National	Margin
1988	55.8	52.8	3
1992	61.3	58.1	3.2
1996	55.4	51.7	3.7
2000	56.7	54.2	2.5
2004	66.8	60.1	6.7
2008*	66.9	61.6	5.3
2012	64.5	58	6.5
Mean	**61.1**	**56.6**	**4.4**

Source: http://www.electproject.org/home/voter-turnout/voter-turnout-data.
Turnout rates based on Voting Eligible Population.

Why Ohio?

So far, we have argued that Ohio can be best characterized as a swing *and* bellwether state as evidenced by historic voting patterns and candidates' strategic behavior. We noted Ohio is attractive to candidates because of its relatively large share of Electoral College votes. But states like California and New York have even more electoral votes (55 and 29, respectively); yet neither is a swing or battleground state. This raises the question "Why Ohio?" A closer look at the demographics of Ohio makes clear why the state is unusually competitive and how this competitiveness combined with the state's relatively high number of electoral votes leads candidates to spend so much time and resources there.

Ohio is, and has been for a long time, an incredibly diverse state and, in many ways, it is a microcosm of the country as a whole. The state features major urban centers in Cleveland, Columbus, and Cincinnati, and several other midsized cities such as Toledo, Dayton, Akron/Canton, and Youngtown, but also many rural, suburban, and exurban communities. Economically, the state has prominent manufacturing industries, high tech, large scale commercial farming, and many white collar industries.

Another common and helpful way to grasp Ohio's diversity is to acknowledge that rather than being one state, it is composed of, as a *Cleveland Plain Dealer* special report called it, "Five Ohio's" (Smith and Davis 2004). Rather than one Ohio, we have a state composed of a handful of regions that are culturally, economically, and politically distinct (see also Coffey et al. 2011; Green 2004).

Northeast Ohio, which includes Cleveland, Youngstown, Akron/Canton, and the surrounding suburban, exurban, and rural areas, is still a major manufacturing center and it is Ohio's most liberal region and most reliable Democratic stronghold. Southeast Ohio is the Appalachian part of the state and it is in many ways more similar to West Virginia than to other parts of Ohio. Containing no major city, it is rural, and thinly populated. It is the state's most economically downtrodden area, especially since the downturn in mining. Politically, there is strong support for certain positions that favor Republicans (for example, Second Amendment rights, social conservatism), but given the region's economic woes there is also support for economic and welfare state policies traditionally favored by Democrats. Because of this, the region is more open than others to swinging from one party to the other. Southwest Ohio, meanwhile, is Ohio's most culturally southern region and it is also its most socially and economically conservative. Northwest Ohio is Ohio's most archetypically Midwestern region. Its economy is dominated by commercial farming and manufacturing and politically it is socially conservative, but occasionally prone to voting Democratic. Central Ohio, finally, is dominated by Columbus, Ohio's capital and now by far Ohio's largest city. As a whole, this region's population has grown dramatically over the last few decades, even as other Ohio regions have lost residents. Central Ohio's economy is sound, with particular strengths in the public sector (state government, The Ohio State University, and the U.S. Government), white collar industries, and some manufacturing. Politically this area is divided between Columbus' inner core, which is predominantly Democratic, and its suburbs and exurbs which, by and large, are more Republican.

To further explore Ohio's diversity and to determine how it compares to the country as a whole, Table 3.8 presents some of Ohio's demographic statistics juxtaposed to the national numbers. On most of these indicators, Ohio's numbers are quite close to the country as a whole's. The lone exception is that the proportion of Hispanics is significantly lower in Ohio than in the nation as a whole.

Table 3.8. Ohio versus National Demographics

	Ohio	USA
% Persons 18-65 years old	62	62.6
% Persons 65+ years old	15.1	14.1
% White	83.2	77.7
% Black	12.5	13.2
% Hispanic	3.4	17.1
% high school graduate or higher	88.2	85.7
% Bachelor's degree or higher	24.7	28.5
% Persons below poverty level (2008-12)	15.4	14.9

Source: U.S. Census Bureau

Another way to approach the question of "Why Ohio?" is from the perspective of partisanship and ideology. Using Gallup Data[8] we can compare Ohio's partisan profile to that of other states and to that of the country as a whole. Nationwide, data from 2013 suggest Democrats have a 5.1% edge in party identifiers, but there is plenty of variance across states. In Wyoming for example, Republicans have a 40.1% edge on Democrats and in New York Democrats have a 24.8% margin over Republicans. Ohio, meanwhile, is closest to 0 of all 50 states, with Democrats holding a slim .4% margin over Republicans. Gallup also provides state-level data on ideology. The numbers here suggest Ohio is close to the national mean, with the percentage of respondents identifying as conservative being 36.8 nationwide and 37.9% in Ohio. The proportion of Ohioan respondents who identify as moderate is also similar to the national number, with the former amounting to 38.9% and the latter to 36.6%, whereas 19.9% of Ohioans and 22.2% of Americans identify as liberal.

Overall, then, Ohio is a diverse state, with five distinct regions and a variety of cultural, economic, and political profiles. What is more, the state as a whole resembles the nation as a whole on a variety of demographic and political variables, thus explaining why the state's presidential election results are often remarkably similar to those of the national popular vote.

Concluding Remarks and Looking Ahead

When vice-presidential candidate Paul Ryan named Ohio "the battleground of battlegrounds," this rang true in most political experts' ears. In fact, it is difficult to remember a time when Ohio was not at or near the top of candidates' priority lists. Yet, as we have shown in this chapter, election outcomes in Ohio have not always been so incredibly close, nor have candidates always vied over the Buckeye State with quite the kind of ferocity they do today.

The evidence also shows Ohio to be one of the few states that has consistently voted with the winning candidate and it has therefore rightfully earned the labels "bellwether" and, thereby, "swing state." But with increasingly close elections on the national level and given the dramatic events during both the 2000 and 2004 elections, Ohio has now solidified its status as a regular battleground. Presidential candidates simply cannot afford to ignore Ohio. This is illustrated by the fact that Quinnipiac University already ran a poll in Ohio in early 2015, pitting Hillary Clinton against several potential Republican candidates, including Ohio's current Governor John Kasich.[9]

In sum, all empirical evidence points to one conclusion: Going forward, Ohio will remain at the top of candidates' priority lists of states they must win to secure the seat in the White House. To be sure, demographic and political shifts may diminish Ohio's importance over time, but the state is likely to be pivotal to presidential election strategies in the foreseeable future.

NOTES

1. Transcripts accessed here: http://transcripts.cnn.com/TRANSCRIPTS/se.html

2. For instance, Minnesota currently has eight representatives and two senators for a total of ten electoral votes.

3. Maine and Nebraska award two votes to the winner of the statewide popular vote and the remaining by congressional district.

4. As the state's population size relative to the national population has been shrinking, Ohio's number of electoral votes has also shrunk. It currently stands at 18, down from 20 in the previous decade and down from its peak number of 26 out of 538 in the 1964 and 1968 elections.

5. This does not include spending by interest groups, PACs, Super PACs, or other politically motivated groups in elections.

6. http://www.wcpo.com/news/local-news/hamilton-county-is-a-key-national-battleground

7. This was before Ohio received 34 candidate visits and millions of dollars in television advertisements (numbers based on the *New York Times'* 2008 election coverage and press releases from the Wisconsin Ad Project).

8. http://www.gallup.com/poll/125066/State-States.aspx

9. http://www.quinnipiac.edu/news-and-events/quinnipiac-university-poll/ohio/release-detail?ReleaseID=2066

FURTHER READING

Altman, A., and M. Scherer (2012, October 25). Why Ohio will decide the presidential election. *Time Magazine.* Retrieved from time.com.

Coffey, D.J., Green, J.C., Cohen, D.B., and Brooks, S.C. (2011). Buckeye battleground: Ohio, campaigns, and elections in the twenty-first century. Akron, OH: The University of Akron Press.

Green, J.C. (2004). Ohio: The heart of it all. *The Forum* 2(3): Article 3.

Huang, T., and Shaw, D.R. (2009). Beyond the battlegrounds? Electoral College strategies in the 2008 presidential election. *Journal of Political Marketing,* 8(4), 272–291.

Shaw, D.R. (1999). The methods behind the madness: Presidential Electoral College strategies, 1988–1996. *The Journal of Politics,* 61: 893–913.

Shaw, D.R. (2006). *The race to 270: The Electoral College and the campaign strategies of 2000 and 2004.* Chicago: The University of Chicago Press.

Smith, R.L., and Davis, D. (2004, July 4). Differences create invisible borders. *Cleveland Plain Dealer.*

White, T.H. (1961). *The making of the President 1960*. New York: Atheneum Publishers.
White, T.H. (1965). *The making of the President 1964*. New York: Atheneum Publishers.

BIBLIOGRAPHY

Altman, A., and M. Scherer (2012, October 25). Why Ohio will decide the presidential election. *Time Magazine*. Retrieved from time.com.
Apple, Jr., R.W. (1968, October 23). Nixon intensifies blows at Humphrey on Ohio train tour. *New York Times*.
Apple, Jr., R.W. (1976, September 22). Carter surprises Ohio politicians by his show of strength in state. *New York Times*.
Apple, Jr., R.W. (1988, October 16). Strategist for G.O.P. plays key role in Ohio race. *New York Times*.
Broder, D.S. (1968, September 1). Two also-rans of other years: Can one win? *Cleveland Plain Dealer*.
Clymer, A. (1980, October 16). Ohio race expected to be close as labor mobilizes for President. *New York Times*.
Coffey, D.J., Green, J.C., Cohen, D.B., and Brooks, S.C. (2011). Buckeye battleground: Ohio, campaigns, and elections in the twenty-first century. Akron, OH: The University of Akron Press.
Dowd, M. (1988, October 22). Bush assails use of chemical weapons. *New York Times*.
Foley, E. (2012, November 2). Mitt Romney, Paul Ryan in Ohio, "Battlegrounds of battlegrounds." The *Huffington Post*. Retrieved from huffingtonpost.com.
Frankel, M. (1968, October 29). Humphrey pleads for key Ohio vote in push for upset. *New York Times*.
Gailey, P. (1984, October 27). Mondale fights President's lead in industrial rim of Great Lakes. *New York Times*.
Green, J.C. (2004). Ohio: The heart of it all. *The Forum* 2(3): Article 3.
Huang, T., and Shaw, D.R. (2009). Beyond the battlegrounds? Electoral College strategies in the 2008 presidential election. *Journal of Political Marketing*, 8(4), 272–291.
Reich, K. (1976, September 20). President reportedly now is leading Carter in 3 big Middle West states. *Los Angeles Times*.
Sewell, Dan. (2012, November 1). Hamilton County is a key national battleground. *WCPO Cincinnati*.
Shaw, D.R. (1999). The methods behind the madness: Presidential Electoral College strategies, 1988-1996. *The Journal of Politics*, 61: 893–913.
Shaw, D.R. (2006). *The race to 270: The Electoral College and the campaign strategies of 2000 and 2004*. Chicago: The University of Chicago Press.
Smith, R.L., and Davis, D. (2004, July 4). Differences create invisible borders. *Cleveland Plain Dealer*.

White, T.H. (1961). *The making of the President 1960*. New York: Atheneum Publishers.

White, T.H. (1965). *The making of the President 1964*. New York: Atheneum Publishers.

Zeleny, J. (2012, October 31). Ohio working class may offer key to Obama's reelection. *New York Times*.

Chapter Four

Florida

The Purple Sunshine State

Sean D. Foreman

Florida, the third most populated state in the nation, is the biggest presidential swing state in American politics. California is reliably Democrat and Texas has been solidly Republican. Florida's voting behavior is more complex. Florida has sided with the winner of each presidential election since 1928 except for 1960 and 1992 (see Table 4.1). It has swung for the winner of the White House in each of the last five presidential elections. Bill Clinton won Florida in 1996 after losing the "sunshine state" in 1992 to George H.W. Bush on the way to defeating the incumbent nationally. In 2000, Florida's result infamously handed the presidency to George W. Bush by 527 votes of those properly cast and counted in the election. Bush won Florida more easily in 2004 on the road to reelection. Alternatively, Barack Obama's campaign energized Florida Democrats to carry him to victory in 2008 and again in 2012.

Florida voters have swung between Democrats and Republicans in recent presidential elections and in their selection for U.S. Senate seats. However, it has been dominated by Republicans in statewide races since 1998. Republicans continue to have a strong hold on the state legislature despite an advantage for Democrats in voter registration. There are also more Republican than Democrat members of the Florida delegation to Congress due to gerrymandered districts that have become more entrenched in favor of the GOP since 2000. This trend continued even after a citizens' initiative for state constitutional amendments requiring fair districts for both legislative and congressional districts won approval in 2010.

While Florida has been Republican "red" in state-level elections starting in 1994 the state also has some larger, solid "blue" counties that helped fuel Obama's two victories. This provides a purple strain of a swing state, one that has rapidly gained electoral votes in recent decades (see Table 4.2).

Table 4.1. Presidential Vote Results in Florida, 1980–2012. (Statewide winner in bold)

Year	Democratic Candidate	Democratic Percentage	Republican Candidate	Republican Percentage	Third Party Candidate (Party)	Third Party Percentage
1980	Jimmy Carter	38.5	**Ronald Reagan**	**55.5**	John Anderson (Independent)	5.1
1984	Walter Mondale	34.7	**Ronald Reagan**	**65.3**	n/a	n/a
1988	Michael Dukakis	38.5	**George H.W. Bush**	**60.9**	Ron Paul (Libertarian)	.5
1992	Bill Clinton	39	**George H.W. Bush**	**40.9**	Ross Perot (Reform)	19.8
1996	**Bill Clinton**	**48**	Bob Dole	42.3	Ross Perot (Reform)	9.1
2000	Al Gore	48.8	**George W. Bush**	**48.8**	Ralph Nader (Green)	1.6
2004	John Kerry	47.1	**George W. Bush**	**52.1**	Ralph Nader (Green)	.4
2008	**Barack Obama**	**51**	John McCain	48.2	Ralph Nader (Ecology)	.3
2012	**Barack Obama**	**50**	Mitt Romney	49.1	Gary Johnson (Libertarian)	.5

Source: Florida Division of Elections

Table 4.2. Florida Electoral Votes, 1960–2012

Year	Electoral Votes
1960	10
1964	14
1972	17
1984	21
1992	25
2004	27
2012	29

Florida moved from being a solidly southern conservative Democrat state in the 1950s and 1960s to a more moderate Democrat one in the 1970s and 1980s. It shifted to moderate Republicans in the late 1990s and 2000s followed by more conservative Republicans from 2010 forward. The reasons for this swing in political identity in the state leaders is based on three factors. The first is cultural. The second is geographical. And the third is political.

The political culture of the state has switched from being traditional southern to being more minority and internationally influenced. This cultural change accompanies demographic changes in the ethnic and racial identity of its citizens.

The geography of the state encompasses territory from the northern panhandle to the Florida Keys with several sub-cultural groups. There are large swaths of agricultural and rural areas represented by conservative members and urban areas represented by liberal candidates.

Political factors have also made Florida a state swing. Democrats have long held and continue to hold a voter registration advantage. But as that advantage has shrunk over time so has the number of Democrats to win in Florida elections. And once Republicans captured the legislature, through gerrymandering and superior fundraising, they consolidated their hold on the state legislature and in statewide elections.

An overview of the state's political history will be followed by a review of presidential election outcomes in Florida since 2000. A closer examination of 2012 election polls will show where Florida stood in comparison with opinions in other state swings. This will set the stage for seeing factors that may influence how Florida voters may cast their votes in 2016 and beyond.

FROM CONSERVATIVE
DEMOCRATS TO CONSERVATIVE REPUBLICANS

Florida was a typical southern Democrat state from the Civil War through the 1960s. Democrats dominated the state legislature and governor's mansion for most of the twentieth century.[1] It was a traditional "Dixiecrat" state in its politics and the profile of most of its state and federal public officials.

While state government was purely dominated by Democrats, Florida voters did back Dwight D. Eisenhower in 1952 and 1956 and his vice president Richard M. Nixon in 1960. The shift to more statewide party balance started in 1966 when Claude R. Kirk, Jr. became the first Republican to win the governorship since Reconstruction and continued in 1968 and 1972 when Nixon won Florida and easily won the presidency.

The one-party control consisted of a coalition of conservative Democrats and progressive Democrats in an alliance of convenience through the 1970s. Talented Democratic politicians like governors LeRoy Collins, Reuben Askew, Lawton Chiles, and Bob Graham appealed to independents and moderate Republicans due to their reputations for strong leadership and integrity.[2] These popular leaders also enjoyed having quality party members occupy state cabinet and legislative leadership positions. Despite being an uneasy coalition between the two wings of the Florida Democratic Party, the numbers were in their favor into the 1990s. But a failure of the party to rapidly modernize and reorganize—and the lack of a leader with the stature of the aforementioned governors—led to the structural decline of the Democratic Party in Florida.

Meanwhile the Republican Party of Florida began to have superior organizational and fundraising skills in the 1980s. Three developments that aided the Republican Party's growth were "the gradual shift of natives/ Crackers to the Republican Party; the rapid population growth of the central and southwestern regions of Florida; and the shift of Cuban voters to the Republican Party."[3] These major developments along with several more subtle demographic and social changes shifted the sand to favor more conservative, anti-tax, tough on crime candidates that emerged in the Republican Party. Demographic changes included more military retirees remaining in the state, especially in the northern panhandle, other retirees settling throughout the state, and particularly migrants from the Midwest moving to the Florida west coast and maintaining their more conservative political identification.

As a result, the State Senate, dominated by Democrats through the 1980s, shifted to a 20 seat to 20 seat tie in 1991 and moved to a 22 to 18 Republican advantage in 1995. The State House followed suit in a shift from a 63–57 Democrat advantage in 1995 to a 61–59 Republican advantage in 1997. John Ellis "Jeb" Bush lost the 1994 gubernatorial race to incumbent Lawton Chiles by 1.8 percent or 63,940 votes out of more than 4.2 million cast (see Table 4.3). Bush won the governor's mansion in 1998 by 55.3 percent to 44.7 percent over Lt. Gov Buddy MacKay, a 418,051 vote margin.[4] In 1998, Democrats and Republicans split the then six statewide cabinet seats. Bush easily

Table 4.3. Selected close election outcomes in Florida, 1994-2014

Year–Race Winning Candidate	Losing Candidate	Total Votes	Vote Margin
1994–Governor Lawton Chiles (D)	Jeb Bush (R)	4,206,076	63,940
2000–President George W. Bush (R)	Al Gore (D)	5,963,031	537
2010–Governor Rick Scott (R)	Alex Sink (D)	5,359,735	61,550
2012–President Barack Obama (D)	Mitt Romney (R)	8,474,179	74,309
2014–Governor Rick Scott (R)	Charlie Crist (D)	5,951,561	64,144

Source: Florida Division of Elections

won reelection in 2002 and Republicans consolidated power in the elected cabinet and governor's seat in 2010 that continued through 2014.[5]

In 2010 Republicans increased their advantage to a super majority in both chambers and elected their third governor in a row, Rick Scott. Aided by increased turnout for the reelection of President Barack Obama Democrats cut the legislative voting advantage slightly in 2012 and defeated two incumbent Republican members of Congress. In 2014, the Republican governor and four cabinet members were all reelected and Republicans regained their state House super majority.

This Republican electoral advantage in the state occurred despite the voter registration advantage Democrats have historically held over Republicans (see Table 4.4). In 2012, there were 4,821,859 registered Democrats compared to 4,263,587 Republicans. While Democrats hold numerical advantage their challenge is in motivating their voters to go out to the polls.

The fastest growing segment of the Florida electorate includes registered independents called "no party affiliation" (NPA) which locks them out of voting in closed party primaries. In 2012, there were more than 2.5 million NPAs out of the 2.9 million voters registered with no party or a party other than Democrat or Republican. The NPAs play an important swing vote role in elections for president but are less active in races for governor and other statewide offices where turnout in off-year, midterm elections is usually dominated by party base voters.

Table 4.4. Florida Registered Voters, 1972-2012

Year	Republican	Democrat	Other	Total
1972	974,999	2,394,604	117,855	3,487,458
1982	1,500,031	3,066,351	299,254	4,865,636
1992	2,672,968	3,318,565	550,292	6,541,825
2002	3,610,992	3,956,694	1,756,873	9,324,559
2012	4,263,587	4,821,859	2,953,125	12,038,571

Source: Florida Division of Elections

Since 2000, it is commonly thought that for a Republican to win the White House they must win Florida's electoral votes. The recent national electoral map heavily favors Democrats. A Democrat can afford to lose Florida and still win (that is, Bill Clinton in 1992) while a Republican must win Florida and some other swing states (that is, George W. Bush in 2000 and 2004) to secure 270 electoral votes. Barack Obama won Florida in both 2008 and 2012 with superior ground organization and strong airwaves advertising support. Obama gained Florida's 27 votes in 2008 and 29 in 2012 but would have won the presidency both times without Florida. It was a show of strength of his overall campaign organization nationally which was particularly strong in Florida.

In 2014, Florida's two senators were Bill Nelson, a Democrat, and Marco Rubio, a Republican. Nelson, known as a moderate, easily won reelection to a third term in 2012. Rubio, who leans more conservative, was backed by both the tea party and the establishment in 2010.

The state's two seats have essentially been occupied by politicians from opposing parties since 1980. This is with the exception of 1987 to 1989 after Bob Graham (D) defeated Paula Hawkins in the 1986 election until Connie Mack III (R) succeeded Chiles in 1989 after winning the 1988 election. Mack defeated Buddy McKay by 35,000 votes out of more than 4 million cast.

Rubio emerged as an underdog to take on the frontrunner, then-Governor Charlie Crist, for the Republican nomination.[6] Rubio, who served for eight years in the State House (the final two as Speaker) started with little name recognition outside of his home county, Miami-Dade. Due to his charisma on the campaign trail and public speaking abilities he gained national attention. With support both from the tea party movement and from Florida establishment Republicans like former governor Jeb Bush, whom Rubio considered as a political mentor, Rubio overtook Crist in polls for the Republican primary. Crist ended up withdrawing from the Republican primary and running as an independent with no party affiliation.

Late in the 2010 campaign reports surfaced that former president Bill Clinton met with the Democratic candidate, Kendrick Meek, a four-term U.S. Representative from Miami, to try to convince him to withdraw from the race and endorse Crist as the choice for Democratic voters.[7] Meek declined. Rubio won the race with 48.9 percent to 29.7 percent for Crist and 20.2 percent for Meek. If, hypothetically, all voters who supported Meek (1,092,936) instead voted for Crist (1,607,549) that would have been 2,700,485 votes for Crist to 2,646,743 for Rubio.

Nelson, a career politician from Central Florida who keeps a low profile and focuses on Florida issues, was elected to the Senate in 2000 over then-Attorney General Bill McCollum by 51 percent to 46.2 percent. Nelson easily won reelection over former Florida Secretary of State Katherine Harris in 2006 by 60 percent to 38 percent. In 2012, Nelson was reelected to a third term with 55.2 percent to 42.2 percent for Connie Mack IV. Mack, a four-term Congressman and son of former Senator Connie Mack III (and great-grandson of the legendary baseball manager), did not gain traction. Nelson actually got 4.5 million votes, nearly 300,000 more than President Obama did in winning reelection. The vote totals drop off from more than 8.4 million votes cast for president but less than 8 million cast in the U.S. Senate race in Florida in 2012.

THE FLORIDA MOSAIC

Florida is a swing state because it has several important voting constituencies. Florida was the fourth most populous state in the 2010 Census with 18,801,310 residents. In December 2014 it officially passed New York to become the third most populated state with 19.9 million to 19.7 million for New York.[8] Many move south on Interstate 95 from New York and New England bringing liberals to the state's east coast. Others take I-75 from the greater Chicago area increasing conservatives on Florida's west coast. People migrate from across the globe especially from Latin American and Caribbean countries adding diversity to the mixture.

Florida has a reputation as a retirement refuge due to the weather and the low tax environment. According to the 2013 Census estimate, 18.7 percent of the population was 65 years and over compared to 14.1 percent nationally. This makes the senior vote an important one and Medicare and Social Security core issues. Senior voters in Florida favored Democrats for several decades but that trend is reversing. The Republican candidates won the 65 and older vote in both the 2010 and 2014 gubernatorial elections (Scott) and in the 2012 presidential election (Romney).[9]

There are 21 military bases in Florida (five Air Force bases, one Army base, three Coast Guard bases, one Marine Corps base, and 11 Navy bases) and U.S. Central Command is located in Tampa and U.S. Southern Command in Miami.[10] This provides generally conservative voters who place issues of national security and military readiness at the top of their agenda.

The white population is 78.1 percent of the state. The Hispanic population is growing and at 23.6 percent is higher than the 17.1 percent national average. The white, non-Hispanic portion is 56.4 percent, lower than the 62.6 percent nationally. The black population is 16.7 percent of Florida, higher than the 13.2 percent across the nation.[11] Florida's rich racial and ethnic diversity impacts its politics and foreshadows where the rest of the nation is heading.

Hispanics are the fastest growing segment of the population. Immigrants from Cuba have steadily increased in size and influence in south Florida since the 1950s. There are Hispanics from all over Latin America throughout the state. People from Puerto Rico and the Dominican Republic predominantly settle in the central part of the state. Puerto Ricans make up a large portion of the Hispanic population in Florida and helped to tip the Latino vote from 57 percent for Obama in 2008 to 60 percent support in 2012.[12] Democratic gubernatorial candidate Charlie Crist had a 49–47 percent advantage among all Hispanics in 2014 in part by winning Puerto Rican and all other Hispanic support by 57–40 percent while losing the Cuban vote by 65–30 percent.[13]

Cuban-Americans have been heavily conservative and traditionally have voted for Republicans. The Cuban connection to the Republican Party has two main origins. First, under Democrat John F. Kennedy, the Cuban community felt they were betrayed during the Bay of Pigs invasion in 1961, an armed revolt against Cuban president Fidel Castro.[14] Secondly, the Ronald Reagan administration with its staunch anti-communist stance appealed directly to the Cuban exile community. A visit by Reagan to Miami in 1983 helped to crystallize that support. Jorge Mas Canosa, a Bay of Pigs veteran, and some colleagues established the Cuban American National Foundation (CANF) in 1981 at the urging of Reagan's National Security Advisor, Richard Allen.[15] The CANF, also called The Foundation, headed the "Cuba Lobby" that held significant sway with both the Reagan and George H.W. Bush administrations and helped to get the first Cuban-American elected to Congress, Representative Ileana Ros-Lehtinen in 1989.

African Americans, despite being higher than the national percentage of the population have had limited political success in Florida. There was one major party black candidate for Senate, Democrat Kendrick Meek in 2010. Meek was not widely known or wildly popular statewide. Still, the move to try to get him to drop out of the 2010 race did not sit well with African American leaders who felt that Obama and Clinton were snubbing their candidate.

After the contested 2000 presidential election results there were efforts to increase black voter turnout. This occurred in conjunction with the reelection campaign for Governor Jeb Bush in 2002. In 1999 Bush launched his One Florida education initiative which replaced affirmative action admissions in higher education with guarantees that the top 20 percent of graduates in a high school class would gain college admissions in state schools. Meek, then a state senator, helped organize a 10,000 person sit-in at the state capitol to show displeasure with the policy change.

There was an African American candidate for lieutenant governor in 2006 (former state lawmaker Daryl Jones) on a losing ticket. Overall black voters in Florida have lacked candidates or causes for which to get excited. Barack Obama was an exception in 2008 and 2012.

Florida is culturally like three states in one with ten major media markets (Pensacola, Panama City, Tallahassee, Gainesville, Jacksonville, Orlando, Tampa-St. Petersburg, Ft. Myers-Naples, West Palm Beach, Miami).[16] This makes running statewide campaigns expensive and nuanced. The party advantage in each market and past voting patterns differ across the state. North Florida is mainly rural and conservative; much like the traditional U.S. south. South Florida is largely liberal with urban areas, diverse populations, and international cultural influences. In Central Florida, the Interstate 4 (I-4) corridor—one of the most watched battleground territories in the country—is home to generational Floridians, Midwestern transplants, and growing numbers of people from Puerto Rico and the Dominican Republic.

The I-4 corridor that runs through the middle of the state and connects Orlando to Tampa has gained a reputation as being one of the most influential areas for politicians to mine for votes. "There's no bigger swing state on the electoral map than Florida, and there's no bigger swing area in Florida than the Interstate 4 corridor. While the northern, panhandle part of the state is solidly conservative and the south goes more Democratic, the I-4 corridor decides the state. In fact, this area includes three of the four counties in the state that flipped from Republican to Democrat in 2008 and could very well determine the winner of the state."[17] This was a key strategic reason for the Republicans to select Tampa to host their 2012 national convention. Pinellas and Hillsborough counties surrounding Tampa were two of only four Florida counties that flipped from Republican to Democrat voting for Bush in 2004 and Obama in 2008. Osceola, south of Orange County (Orlando), was a third one.[18] (Flagler County was the fourth one.)

However, a closer examination of the vote totals along the I-4 corridor can show a different story. As the demographics of the central region of the state have changed so has the tendency of the vote to swing. In 1992 Republicans had a 26,000 vote advantage in six counties along the corridor (Hillsborough, Polk, Osceola, Orange, Seminole, and Volusia) which dwindled to 1,000 in 1996. Democrats enjoyed an advantage overall in those counties in each presidential election from 2000 to 2012. President Obama had an 85,000 advantage along the I-4 corridor in 2008 and won by 84,000 votes there in 2012. Four of the six counties have trended Democratic while one, Polk, has been solidly Republican, and one, Volusia, has trended Republican.[19] Hillsborough, Orange, and Osceola have had their non-white populations more than double with significantly higher percentages of Hispanics, blacks, and Asian voters. Meanwhile Volusia and Polk have retained larger percentages of white populations which tend to be more conservative and support Republican candidates.

A quarter of Florida's Republican voters live in the Tampa/St. Petersburg/ Sarasota market.[20] Another 21 percent live around Orlando/Daytona Beach/ Melbourne. That means 41 percent of the state's Republicans live in the I-4 corridor. The Miami/Ft. Lauderdale area is home to 16 percent of Republicans. Of the state's registered Republicans 11 percent are Hispanic with more than two-thirds of them living in south Florida.

Jewish voters are also significant in the Miami/Ft. Lauderdale market. There are around 640,000 Jewish residents in Florida, third most in the nation behind New York and California.[21] Jewish voters lean toward liberal policies and the Democratic Party but could vote for Republican candidates with strong support for Israel and a hard line against Iran.

FLORIDA POLITICAL ISSUES

At the state level, education, guns, gay marriage, taxes, health care, water conservation and environmental policies, and voting access are significant policy issues. Since the 2000 election several electoral reforms were put in place. Florida has had early voting as an option since 2004. The requirements for obtaining an absentee ballot were eased and absentees were encouraged. With absentee and early in-person voting the voter turnout rate has not increased but it has remained consistent. The conventional thinking is that Democrats take more advantage of early voting and Republicans benefit from absentee voting.

The Republicans in the legislature and especially the leadership tend to be more conservative. Gun laws have been strongly influenced by the statewide chapter of the National Rifle Association (NRA). A controversial "stand your ground" law that exasperated Democrats passed in 2005 eliminating a citizen's duty to retreat if they face a mortal threat.

Social conservatives push for more protection of unborn life with bills aiming to limit choice and impose requirements such as the mother viewing an ultrasound picture of the fetus and a twenty-four-hour waiting period before having the procedure. A state constitutional amendment requires minors to get parental consent before obtaining an abortion.

Same-sex marriage was prohibited through a statewide constitutional citizen initiative in 2008. Incidentally this initiative passed at the same time Obama won the state in 2008. African American and non-Cuban Hispanic voters heavily supported Obama but many of them also voted for traditional marriage. Court challenges ultimately led to the judicial overturn on the state ban and homosexual couples began getting married in January 2015.

Environmental issues are a big concern especially dealing with protection of the Everglades.[22] Water conservation policies enjoy bipartisan support in theory but there is a large divide in terms of funding priorities and the proper role of government in these efforts.

International policy, especially related to the western hemisphere, finds its way into Florida's political debates. In 2012 the legislature passed a law that tried to ban municipalities from awarding contracts to firms that have business ties to Cuba. Governor Scott signed the law even though there was concern that it would be found unconstitutional, which it eventually was.

Health care and Medicaid expansion have been major issues. The state of Florida was a lead plaintiff in the case of 26 states challenging the constitutionality of the Patient Protection and Affordable Care Act that the Supreme Court upheld in 2012. The state legislature has refused to expand Medicaid coverage directly under the ACA and rejected about $5 billion in federal money.[23] Meanwhile, Florida had the highest numbers of registrations nationally in the first two years of the Affordable Care Act.[24]

Health care, employment, and taxes will be important issues in 2016. The economy was the primary issue in 2008 and 2012 and likely will again top voters' minds. With the significant military presence in the state, foreign policy could also be an important issue.

2000 PRESIDENTIAL ELECTION: GROUND ZERO

Florida appeared into the national spotlight in presidential politics with the 2000 election. On election night the news networks initially projected that Democrat Al Gore would win the state's 25 electoral votes. Before the end of the evening, the networks retracted this decision and declared that the race was too close to call. As the election outcome between Gore and Republican George W. Bush, whose brother Jeb Bush was Florida's governor, was so close, there was no winner declared until Florida certified its vote count 36 days later.

Recounts ensued in several of Florida's 67 counties most notably in south Florida's Miami-Dade and Palm Beach Counties. Miami-Dade had more registered Democrats and the Bush team worried that a recount could increase Gore's totals. Palm Beach County had suffered from an additional problem in that the design of its ballot had caused confusion with some voters. The so-called "butterfly ballot" had candidate names listed on each side of the page with the small place to cast the vote down the middle. Some elderly voters allegedly voted for Reform Party nominee Pat Buchanan, a more conservative candidate, but intended to vote for Gore.[25]

The Bush campaign hired a legal team headed by former U.S. Secretary of State and Bush family advisor James A. Baker. Gore had a team headed by noted attorney David Boise. The Gore team brought a law suit saying that votes should be counted by hand in order to determine the full intent of the voters. In the case of *Gore v. Harris* (Katherine Harris, a Republican, was the elected Florida Secretary of State) the Florida Supreme Court ruled 4–3 on December 8 to order a statewide recount.

Bush appealed that decision to the U.S. Supreme Court arguing that the justices should stop the recount process and have the election certified using the counts determined from election night. The Supreme Court ruled on December 12 in a 7–2 opinion that the Florida Supreme Court scheme for recounting the ballots was unconstitutional and violated the equal protection clause of the Constitution. In a concurrent 5–4 decision they held that no recount could bring remedy in the time remaining before the Florida legislature was required to certify the vote. That part of the decision was controversial and split along ideological lines. It was the first (and to date only) time the Supreme Court weighed in on the election of a U.S. president and, in effect, decided the outcome of the presidency.[26]

Florida's 25 electoral votes ultimately went to Bush. That gave him 271 to Gore's 266 votes. While Bush's victory in Florida was controversial due to systemic efforts to purge the voter rolls of ineligible voters, the flawed ballots, the recounts, court decisions, and public perceptions with his brother as the state's governor, later studies of the ballots actually cast found that Bush did receive more votes than Gore.

For 36 days after the 2000 election all eyes were on Florida to determine the outcome. After the Supreme Court decision Gore immediately and graciously conceded the race. The move was applauded by the public in general but angered more partisan Democrats that wanted him to continue to fight politically even though there were no more legal options. Bush was sworn in as president on January 20, 2001, and the transition from the Democratic administration of Clinton-Gore to the Republican Bush-Cheney team was peaceful, even if bitter.

2004 PRESIDENTIAL CAMPAIGN

In 2004 Florida was again one of the handful of battleground states as Democratic U.S. Senator John Kerry challenged George W. Bush. The Bush campaign put additional emphasis on Hispanic voter outreach in 2004 and those efforts paid off in Florida. Kerry was hurt late in the campaign by the Swift Boat Veterans for Truth ads which questioned Kerry's leadership and the reasons for his earning three Purple Hearts in Vietnam. The Kerry campaign did not effectively respond to these allegations and that may have hurt him in states like Florida with a large portion of active duty and military veteran voters. Bush beat Kerry in Florida and won reelection. But if Kerry would have been able to beat Bush in Florida—or in Ohio which had the more controversial outcome in 2004—then Kerry could have won the presidency.

2008 PRIMARY CAMPAIGNS

Until 2008 Florida generally held late presidential primaries and by the time they occurred the party nominees were essentially decided. State leaders wanted Florida to play a more important role in selecting both party nominees in 2008 and moved the primary to the front of the campaign calendar.

The Republican-led legislature voted to move the primary to January against the will of both national party committees. After Florida front-loaded their primary to follow Iowa, New Hampshire, and South Carolina, both national parties penalized the state parties by stripping them of delegates to their national conventions. They also urged candidates not to campaign in the renegade state but Republican candidates competing in a wide open race sought an advantage.

2008 Republican Primary

Rudy Giuliani, the former mayor of New York City, engaged in a risky primary strategy. Knowing that his moderate Republican views would not play well in Iowa and that Mitt Romney was somewhat of a hometown favorite in New Hampshire, Giuliani skipped the first caucus and primary states and put all of his electoral eggs in Florida's basket. Giuliani was an early favorite in the polls but did not raise and spend the money needed to solidify his position. Then-Republican Governor Crist promised to endorse Giuliani prior to the primary but later reneged and threw his support to McCain (presumably because McCain put Crist on his short list for vice presidential nominee). With strong support among military personnel and Hispanic voters, and with endorsements from Crist and Republican lawmakers, McCain won the Florida primary. This was a springboard for the Arizona Senator, who had little money financing his campaign and was viewed as not conservative enough for the base, to ultimately win the Republican nomination.

2008 Democratic Primary

The Florida Democratic Party was placed in a tough situation due to the legislation passed by the majority Republican legislature in 2007. Because of the January 29 primary breaking the calendar rules, the DNC announced that it would punish Florida by not seating its delegates or super delegates. They also convinced candidates to sign a pledge to not campaign in Florida.

Despite national party leaders calling for a boycott of Florida's primary Hillary Clinton still visited Florida while Barack Obama toed the party line. Hillary Clinton (50 percent) beat Obama (33 percent) and John Edwards (14 percent) in the primary but with an asterisk noting that the candidates did not fully engage in the campaign there.

Ultimately the Democrats made a deal to seat Florida's delegates at the convention and count them with half of the votes. The DNC scaling back the punishment on Florida and Michigan, which engaged in a similar situation, was an acknowledgement of how important Florida would be to the eventual winner of the White House. It was also an indication of some of the flaws of the nomination process including the awkwardness of the schedule and the difficulty of penalizing states that do not fully comply with party rules.

2008 GENERAL ELECTION

On the way to winning the presidency Obama beat McCain by 51–48 percent in Florida in 2008.

Voter turnout measured 75.2 percent statewide including a high of 85.5 percent in Leon County, home to state capitol Tallahassee and a majority African American county where Democratic voters outnumber Republicans by nearly two to one.

On the same ballot, a statewide constitutional amendment banning same-sex marriage passed with 63 percent support. The majority win by the liberal Obama at the same time that the conservative traditional marriage amendment received strong support showed that many black voters supported the president but sided with the conservative view on marriage. This apparent ticket splitting by many Democrats went against the grain of the Republican-led strategy to put marriage initiatives on ballots in several states in order to drive out the conservative base.

The 2008 exit polls showed Obama got 96 percent of the black vote. Obama won 57 percent of Hispanics in Florida to 42 percent for McCain. McCain had an advantage of 56–42 percent with white voters.[27] By comparison, in 2004 Kerry got 86 percent of black voters to 13 percent for George W. Bush. Bush won white voters 57–42 percent and a majority of Hispanics by 56–44 percent went for Bush over Kerry.

With higher than usual turnout among black voters and young voters, a strong showing with Hispanics, women, and senior citizens, Obama easily won Florida as well as the presidency.

2012 REPUBLICAN PRIMARY

In 2012, the frontrunners for the Republican nomination were Mitt Romney and Newt Gingrich. Rick Santorum gained momentum but did not have enough money to run in large states like Florida. Florida again front-loaded its primary but this time got the approval of the Republican Party which also selected Tampa as the site of its national convention. Florida Democrats did not have a competitive primary as incumbent Barack Obama was not significantly challenged.

Herman Cain, the former CEO of Godfather Pizza, actually won the Republican Party convention straw poll in September 2011. Cain was the "flavor of the month" on the campaign trail at that time. His campaign appealed to younger voters and his message on a simplified tax code ("9–9–9") gained popular traction. Texas Governor Rick Perry had recently entered the race and hoped for a strong showing in the straw poll. Cain's 37 percent was more than Perry (15 percent) and Romney (14 percent) combined.[28]

Florida's Republican electorate did not generally favor any one candidate. With fewer white evangelicals than South Carolina, the Gingrich primary win in the Palmetto state did not translate into widespread support in the Sunshine state. More than two-thirds of South Carolina's Republican primary voters were white evangelicals while in Florida they were less than 30 percent. A Quinnipiac poll heading into the Florida primary showed that Gingrich was getting around 40 percent support from these voters while Romney was picking up almost 30 percent.[29]

Florida is also more densely populated and has more urban voters than the rural Republicans of South Carolina. 2008 exit polls found more moderate Republican voters in Florida than in South Carolina. Furthermore, with around 12 percent of Republican primary voters being of Hispanic origin, that made the Florida Republican electorate different than other primary states, being less evangelical, more moderate, more urban, and more Hispanic. Romney ultimately won the 2012 Florida primary, tacitly backed by the Bush political machine, and this gave him a significant boost along the way to winning a spirited and contested nomination.[30]

OBAMA AND ROMNEY IN THE 2012 QUINNIPIAC UNIVERSITY SWING STATE POLLS

President Obama held a polling advantage in Florida over his challenger, former Massachusetts Governor Mitt Romney, throughout the 2012 campaign (see Table 4.5). Once the Democratic Party realized that Romney had

Table 4.5.   Barack Obama vs. Mitt Romney polls, 2012.

Date of Quinnipiac poll release	Barack Obama	Mitt Romney
March 28, 2012	49	42
May 3, 2012	43	44
June 27, 2012	45	41
August 1, 2012	51	45
August 23, 2012	49	46
September 26, 2012	53	44
October 31, 2012	48	47
November–Actual election result	**50**	**49**

Source: Quinnipiac Polls.

the inside track on the Republican nomination they started running negative ads against Romney as early as January.

In a March 28 poll Obama had a 49–42 percent lead over Romney and was ahead of Santorum by 50–37 percent. Obama's noticeable advantage was greater than in a poll two months prior that had Obama and Romney in a statistical dead heat. Still, the news was not all rosy for Obama as 48 percent said Romney would do a better job on the economy while 45 percent said that Obama would be better on the issue that was on top of voter's minds. The economy rated "extremely important" or "very important" to 90 percent of the respondents. It was followed by 81 percent identifying unemployment, 78 percent citing the healthcare law, and 76 percent saying the federal budget deficit was important to them. Next in line was the war in Afghanistan with 67 percent closely followed by gas prices at 66 percent. Immigration ranked as important with 55 percent while social issues were important to less than 50 percent of the respondents.

These seemingly schizophrenic selections showed the seriousness of Florida as a swing state. Obama registered "a split 47–49 percent job approval rating" while 50–47 Florida voters said he deserved to be reelected.[31] Oddly, 69 percent responded that they were either somewhat (26) or very dissatisfied (43) with the way things were going in the nation today while 31 percent were either somewhat (27) or very (4) satisfied. Romney had a favorable rating of 41 percent with 36 percent unfavorable and 19 percent saying they had not heard enough about him. Obama had a 51 percent favorable with 44 percent unfavorable and two percent said they had not heard enough about the president.[32] Meanwhile the Democratic Party was split with 45 percent each favorable and unfavorable and the Republican Party was 39 percent favorable compared to 50 percent unfavorable. Republican Governor Rick Scott also had disapproval of his job by 36 to 52 percent. Still, Florida voters indicated that they were more enthusiastic about the presidential election than their counterparts in swing states Ohio and Pennsylvania with 35 percent more enthusiastic, 27 percent less enthusiastic and 37 saying their level of enthusiasm was about the same as for other presidential elections. In the key demographic of female voters, the Democrats were viewed by 58 to 28 percent advantage for which party voters trusted to do a better job with women's issues in that March poll.

By May, the perceived advantage that Romney held with voters about his ability to handle the economy helped him to catch Obama overall. This poll showed Romney with 44 percent support compared to 43 percent for Obama. It was also within a similar 44–42 percent advantage for Romney in Ohio at that time. The May poll came as Romney became the *de facto* Republican nominee and the negative attacks from Santorum and Gingrich and ultra conservative groups subsided.

In May, Romney had a small lead among men (46–42) while women were slightly supporting Obama (44–42). Obama's job approval was underwater at 50–46 disapproval while by 50–45 percent respondents said he did not deserve to be reelected. Interestingly, it found 51–38 percent in favor of the U.S. Supreme Court overturning the Affordable Care Act. The poll reflected a decline for Obama more than an increase in support for Romney. The president's favorability rating dropped to 46–47 percent while Romney's remained largely the same as in March at 40–34 percent favorable.[33]

June's poll showed Obama ahead by 45 to 41 percent. The four point advantage in Florida was less than the nine point lead the president had in Ohio and six point benefit in Pennsylvania. This poll showed a greater advantage for Obama with Hispanic voters by 56 to 32 percent compared to a 49–39 percent lead with Hispanics prior to both candidates making major speeches about immigration. Obama announced an executive order that would prevent the deportation of some younger illegal immigrants, a move that was popular with many Hispanic residents. The poll still showed that voters favored Romney on the economy but gave Obama higher marks than in prior polls and a 46–45 percent advantage in who would be better for voter's personal economic future.[34]

This June poll also included data on Florida's race for the U.S. Senate seat. Incumbent Bill Nelson had 41 percent to 40 percent for U.S. Rep. Connie Mack. In a sign of how little attention the Senate race was getting up to that point, 17 percent of voters were still undecided.

Early August marked the first time Obama broke 50 percent in Florida. The poll released on August 1 showed Obama with 51 percent to 45 percent for Romney. Part of the reason for Obama's rise, according to Peter A. Brown, assistant director of the polling institute, was the drop in the unemployment rate in Florida. Governor Scott, a Republican, and Obama's Democratic supporters were both trying to take credit for the decrease. Obama was strong with female voters prompting Brown to suggest "it is this dynamic that argues for Romney to pick a female running mate" while Senator Marco Rubio could have also helped Romney in Florida.[35] Obama had 51–44 percent support with female likely voters but was at 45–46 with men. Obama was slightly ahead by 47 to 46 percent with independents.

Obama's lead started to show as the intensity of his support was stronger than Romney's. The likely Obama voters were 65 percent strongly behind him while Romney's were 49 percent with strong support. Alternatively, 10 percent said they would vote for Obama because they disliked Romney and 19 percent said their support for Romney was motivated by a vote against Obama. The economy was the top issue identified by 52 percent of voters but by 47 to 45 percent voters said they thought Romney would be better on the economy. Strangely, "One of the few positives for Romney in Florida is that voters are split on whether his election would help or hurt their pocketbook, but by 38–23 percent they say the president's re-election would leave their wallets thinner," said the pollster Brown.

Another poll was released in late August after the Republicans met in Tampa and the Democrats in Charlotte, North Carolina, for their national conventions.[36] It marked the debut of Paul Ryan as Romney's running mate. Obama's lead tightened to 49–46 percent. As far as post-convention bumps go it was small and insignificant. Obama's favorability result rating was at 50–45 percent while Romney was at 45–42 percent. Ryan got a 35–29 percent favorability in Florida compared to 37–44 for Vice President Joe Biden.

The economy was identified as "extremely important" to 60 percent of respondents. Medicare was viewed as "extremely important" to 50 percent including 60 percent of likely voters over age 65. Respondents said Romney would do better by 48–45 on the economy while Obama was seen as better on Medicare.

On a contentious issue of cleaning (or purging) the voter rolls, 65 percent of respondents said it would prevent ineligible people from voting while 28 percent thought it would suppress voting. The national narrative was that efforts like this one were done to suppress minority voting. But the respondents in this poll did not see it that way.

By September, Obama's lead started to widen with a 53–44 percent gap. The president also topped the challenger in the question over who was better able to handle the economy by 51–46 percent. This came in the wake of Romney's comment that 47 percent of citizens did not pay taxes and would never vote for him, comments that were secretly recorded at a Florida fundraiser. Coincidentally, the economy was the most important issue for 47 percent of survey respondents. At the same time, Obama's lead widened in

Ohio and Pennsylvania and indicated that the president was on the road to being reelected. More potential voters felt that Obama cared about their needs and problems (57–40 percent) while more said they thought that Romney did not care by 55–41 percent.

Obama's lead extended to 58–39 percent with women while men went for Romney by 50–47 percent.[37] Obama had a comfortable 55–41 lead with Hispanics. Independent voters favored Romney by 49–46 percent. Obama also had an advantage on the question of which candidate would make the right decisions on Middle East policy, 53 percent for Obama compared to 46 percent for Romney.

In the final Quinnipiac poll before Election Day, released on October 31, the race again tightened. Obama held a 48–47 edge, a statistical tie and a five point decline for the president from the September poll.[38] Obama still held a more comfortable 50–45 percent lead in Ohio, but was also at a close 49–47 percent advantage in Virginia. Brown, the pollster, cited an increase in support from women for Romney as a reason that made these swing states too close to call. Obama had a 53–43 advantage with likely female voters which was down from 58–39 percent in September. Romney had an advantage with independent voters by 49–44 percent.

"Much of the difference between Obama's solid lead at this point four years ago and today in the swing states and nationally is the drop in the president's support among white voters, especially in Florida, where he trails 59–37 percent among whites, a group he lost 56–42 percent in 2008, when he got 43 percent of the white vote nationally," according to Quinnipiac.[39]

Obama had an advantage in empathy among voters (60–38 percent) compared to 47–49 for Romney. But Romney got higher marks for strong leadership (65–31 percent) than Obama at 55–43 percent. Obama had an advantage with Hispanic voters at 57–39 percent.

In the Senate race, Nelson led Mack by 50–41 percent in late August. That compared to a 47–40 lead for Nelson earlier in the month. In both polls Nelson held a slight lead with independents. By September Nelson's lead jumped to 53–39 percent. The October poll showed Nelson ahead by 52–39 percent and a solid 52–36 percent lead with independents. Ultimately, Obama won by 50–49 percent while Nelson had a 55–42 percent victory.

PURPLE SUNSHINE STATE

A view of the map of election results by county in 2012 and 2014 is revealing. The colors of the 67 counties are exactly the same in both elections. Obama won a majority of votes in 13 out of 67 counties making the map look predominately red despite Obama's victory. In 2012 Democrat Obama was reelected as president and in 2014 Republican Scott was reelected as governor. The difference, of course, is in voter turnout. Obama was still popular with Democratic voters and benefited from strong organizational support and Democrat turnout in relatively high numbers in the key southeastern counties of Palm Beach, Broward (Ft. Lauderdale), and Miami-Dade and in the Tampa Bay area in Hillsborough (Tampa) and Pinellas (St. Petersburg) counties. The Romney campaign actually flipped two northeastern counties that McCain lost in 2008 by winning a majority of voters in Flagler (St. Augustine) and Volusia (Daytona Beach) counties.

Going into the 2014 gubernatorial campaign the Charlie Crist campaign knew what they needed to do. They needed to maintain those high levels of Democratic voter enthusiasm in the urban counties and particularly focused their efforts on Broward and Miami-Dade. Despite placing his campaign headquarters in Broward County (rather than his home county of Pinellas) and selecting Annette Taddeo, a Colombian-American and the chair of the Miami-Dade Democrats, as his running mate, the campaign was not able to muster better Democratic turnout than the 2010 candidate, Alex Sink.

It may be that Florida is a red state in gubernatorial elections and blue in presidential elections. As one columnist put it, "Florida isn't purple. It's schizophrenic."[40] President Obama and Governor Scott are notably politically and personally different yet both of them won two elections. Candidates matter as do campaigns and issues. Obama had an historic campaign with effective, albeit simplistic, messages ("Hope," "Change," and "Yes, We Can"), and an outstanding political organization. Florida Democrats have been notoriously disorganized for the past two decades yet Obama was able to unify and motivate them. Scott was an awkward political neophyte in 2010 who spent $72 million of his own money to run an effective outsider strategy with tea party grassroots support and a catchy campaign theme ("Let's Get to Work").

An example of the importance of Florida as a swing state can be seen in the number of ads and visits by the candidates. Romney visited Florida 33 times and Obama made 24 trips to the sunshine state during the 2012 campaign. Obama outspent Romney on ads in Florida but both spent significant resources, $69.5 million to $42 million.[41] Obama's campaign operation blanketed the state with 104 field offices, second only to 131 in Ohio of their 690 overall. Team Romney had their most field offices, 48, in Florida followed by 40 in Ohio out of 262 in total. There were 23 events held by Romney or Ryan in Florida (behind 45 in Ohio and 26 in Virginia) while Obama or Vice President Biden appeared 17 times in Florida (compared to 28 in Ohio) during the campaign's peak.[42]

On election eve in 2000 Al Gore held a midnight rally on Miami Beach prefaced by musical performances by Bon Jovi and Stevie Wonder. The Republicans held their national convention in Tampa in 2012 and Florida hosted one of the three presidential debates at Lynn University in Boca Raton in 2012. Bill Clinton stumped for gubernatorial candidate Crist in Orlando the day before the 2014 election.

Democrats both in Florida and nationally may need a candidate to thrill them. An old saying goes that Democrats fall in love while Republicans fall in line.[43] Democrats did not fully love Clinton in 1992 but most of them did by 1996. In 2000, they were not in love with Al Gore, in part because he separated himself from Clinton in his campaign. Kerry was a steady and well credentialed candidate but he did not excite the party. Obama was a different kind of candidate with a special appeal to both traditional Democratic voters and potential new voters. At the gubernatorial level Democratic candidates since 2002 have been lackluster campaigners and lacked mass popular appeal. In 2014 the Republican-turned-Democrat Crist had a reputation for being personable and likable, but he was not beloved largely because he switched parties and flipped policy positions on a host of issues.

2016 AND BEYOND

2016 provides an optimal view of Florida's political future. Both Jeb Bush and Marco Rubio are quite popular with Florida Republicans and with many independents in the state. If a Floridian is the Republican nominee they will be hard to defeat in their home state. The real test will be whether a Republican other than Bush or Rubio will be able to enthuse Republican voters more than McCain and Romney did and model the party's off-year election success in Florida. It will also be a challenge for any candidate other than Hillary Clinton to motivate and mobilize Democratic voters in the way that Bill Clinton or Barack Obama were able to do.

Florida is a true swing state because any number of groups could prompt a shift in the alliance or their turnout and alter the results of the election. A significant swing or fluctuation among Jewish voters, African-Americans, Cuban-Americans, Puerto Ricans, Catholics, conservative Republicans, military personnel and veterans, LGBT voters, senior citizens, or younger voters can shift the election results. When you have more than 11 million registered voters and the 2012 and 2014 statewide elections being determined by between 64,000 and 74,000 votes, a controversial campaign ad, a major candidate gaffe, a significant endorsement, or even a momentous weather event can impact the results.

Florida should continue to be a swing state into the foreseeable future. Democrats have had a voter registration advantage but a challenge turning out voters in non-presidential elections. People registering with no party affiliation are the fastest growing group of voters and those voters in the middle of the ideological spectrum are up for grabs in each election.

Demographic trends could work against Republicans if current political trends continue. Immigration from South and Central America brings people who may be liberal and more connected to Democrats on social issues like education and health. But they could also become Republicans if that party works to find solutions on immigration policy. Marco Rubio could be a catalyst for bringing more Hispanic voters to the conservative side, not simply because he is descended from Cuban parents but because he speaks about the American Dream and American exceptionalism in his appearances. But if Republicans mishandle immigration reform they could lose a generation of Hispanic voters.

African Americans continue to strongly support Democratic candidates. The big question will be whether they turn out in high percentages for future Democratic Party candidates in the way that they did for Obama. They did not turn out for recent gubernatorial candidates.

Older Floridians are favoring Republicans in recent elections. How Republicans in the state legislature handle health care policy may influence them. Property taxes and homeowners' insurance are major concerns in the state for all but disproportionately for older residents.

Younger voters were expected to be motivated to vote in 2014 for a statewide constitutional amendment on legalizing medical marijuana. The proposal got 57.5 percent of the vote but 60 percent is needed for approval. The presence of the amendment did not have a significant impact on Democratic turnout. Proponents plan to gather signature petitions in order to put the item on the ballot again in 2016 unless the legislature passes a more permissive bill.

For the 2016 presidential election Florida is sure to be in the spotlight. Hillary Clinton, the Democratic frontrunner, is popular in the state and would be expected to continue heavy fundraising and grassroots organizing efforts there. Congresswoman Debbie Wasserman-Schultz has served as chair of the Democratic National Committee since May 2011 and would be an important resource for Democratic candidates as long as she holds that position. Any other Democratic candidates would be able to draw on the funding from wealthy liberals and organization from the Obama campaign—but to what extent is yet to be determined. With an open Senate seat vacated by Rubio it may help to further energize and mobilize Democrats.

Florida has never had a homegrown presidential or vice presidential nominee.[44] Two-term governor Reubin Askew (D) ran "an ill-timed and underfunded campaign for president in 1984" though he may have had a better chance had he run in 1976.[45] Bob Graham, a two-term governor and then three-term U.S. Senator, ran an unsuccessful campaign in 2004. Neither came close to winning the nomination.

If Bush or Rubio, both declared candidates, secure the nomination then Florida Republicans will be highly motivated for one of the home state candidates. They are likely to be the strongest competitors in Florida against a Democrat in 2016 especially if it is Hillary Clinton. While polls show Hillary Clinton easily defeating most Republican candidates, Jeb Bush and Marco Rubio hold the best chance of beating Clinton in Florida according to several polls released in early 2015. Other Republican candidates for president could have a harder time motivating Florida voters especially if they go negative on Bush and/or Rubio in the primaries.

In December 2014 Bush announced that he was exploring forming a campaign for president. Bush created a leadership PAC called Right to Rise in January 2015, announcing it on social media in both English and Spanish. Bush also released thousands of emails from when he was governor and resigned from some boards on which he served. Bush has a challenge in appealing to more conservative Republican primary voters nationally but he would likely have to do little to win their loyalty in Florida where his conservative *bona fides* are well established.

Rubio followed suit by pushing his own presidential aspirations in early 2015, hiring the finance director of the conservative super PAC American Crossroads to work with his Reclaim American PAC simultaneous with the release of his second book, *American Dreams: Restoring Economic Opportunity for Everyone*, which discusses his policy proposals. Rubio's Senate seat is up in 2016 but he has declared that he would not run for president and Senate reelection simultaneously. Rubio believes that he can appeal to middle- and working-class voters based on his own upbringing and the experience of his immigrant parents. He also hopes to represent generational change in the Republican Party that is attempting to reach younger voters.

One thing is clear; Florida's sunshine will continue to bring purple electoral results in the near future. The voter demographics, the relative strength of the state political parties, and the amount of money needed to run a competitive campaign in the state will result in a back and forth struggle for red or blue political dominance. It may well be that the characteristics of the candidates and their particular appeal to Florida voters rather than their party affiliation will be what make the difference in earning Florida's electoral votes.

NOTES

1. David R. Colburn. *From Yellow Dog Democrats to Red State Republicans: Florida and Its Politics since 1940.* (Gainesville, FL: University Press of Florida, 2007).
2. Colburn, 2007, 103.
3. Colburn, 2007, 104.
4. Florida Department of State. Division of Elections.
5. Florida voters approved a Constitutional Amendment proposed by the legislature and supported by Governor Bush to consolidate the state cabinet and reduce the number of elected officials from six to three positions.
6. Sean D. Foreman. "Florida Senate Race (Crist v. Meek v. Rubio): The Rise of Rubio and the Fall of Crist," In *The Roads to Congress 2010*, edited by Sean D. Foreman and Robert Dewhirst. Lexington Press, Lanham, MD. 2011.
7. Ben Smith. "Bill Clinton pushed Kendrick Meek to quit Florida race," *Politico.* October 28, 2010. http://www.politico.com/news/stories/1010/44337.html.
8. "Florida Passes New York to Become the Nation's Third Most Populous State, Census Bureau Reports," 2014. United States Census Bureau. December 23. http://www.census.gov/newsroom/press-releases/2014/cb14-232.html.
9. Susan A. MacManus and David Bonanza. "Changing Vote Patterns in 2010, 2012, 2014 and Their Potential Impact on 2016," SayfieReview.com. January 20, 2015. http://www.sayfiereview.com/featured_column?column_id=54.
10. Military Bases in Florida. http://militarybases.com/florida/.
11. State & County QuickFacts, Florida. United States Census Bureau. http://quickfacts.census.gov/qfd/states/12000.html.
12. Alessandra Hickson. "Analysis: Puerto Ricans turned Florida blue," NBCLatino. November 7, 2012. http://nbclatino.com/2012/11/07/analysis-puerto-ricans-turned-florida-blue/.
13. MacManus and Bonanza. 2015.
14. Kennedy inherited a CIA-backed plan to train, equip, and support a 1,400 man force of Cuban exiles to attack the Castro regime. The botched operation that was essentially abandoned by Kennedy at the eleventh hour led to the killing of more than 100 and capture of nearly 1,200 members. "The Bay of Pigs," John F. Kennedy Presidential Library and Museum. http://www.jfklibrary.org/JFK/JFK-in-History/The-Bay-of-Pigs.aspx.
15. William M. Leogrande. "The Cuba Lobby," *Foreign Policy.* April 11, 2013; Daniel C. Walsh. "An Air War with Cuba: The United States Radio Campaign Against Castro." (Jefferson, North Carolina: McFarland & Company, Inc., 2012).
16. Kevin Hill, Susan A. MacManus, and Dario Moreno, eds. Florida Politics: Ten Media Markets, One Powerful State. (Tallahassee, FL: Florida Institute of Government, 2004).
17. "Swing counties along Florida's I-4 corridor," *The Washington Post.* August 25, 2012. http://www.washingtonpost.com/politics/swing-counties-along-floridas-i-4-corridor/2012/08/25/8c01136a-ef27-11e1-afd8-097e90f99d05_graphic.html.

18. Aaron Blake. "Why the GOP gambled on Tampa," *The Washington Post.* August 25, 2012. http://www.washingtonpost.com/blogs/the-fix/wp/2012/08/25/why-the-gop-gambled-on-tampa/.

19. Dominico Montanaro. "Demographics show why 1-4 Corridor is no longer a swing area," NBCNews First Read. November 8, 2012. http://firstread.nbcnews.com/_news/2012/11/08/15023352-demographics-show-why-i-4-corridor-is-no-longer-a-swing-area?lite.

20. Micah Cohen. "The Political Geography of Florida," FiveThirtyEight. January 31, 2012. http://fivethirtyeight.blogs.nytimes.com/2012/01/31/the-political-geography-of-florida/?_php=true&_type=blogs&_r=0.

21. Cohen, 2012.

22. Michael Grunwald. "The Swamp: The Everglades, Florida, and the Politics of Paradise" (New York: Simon & Schuster, 2006).

23. An estimated 760,000 Floridians would benefit from Medicaid expansion. Daniel Chang. "Florida hospitals could lose billions without Medicaid expansion, group warns," *Miami Herald.* November 10, 2014. http://www.miamiherald.com/news/local/community/miami-dade/article3727590.html.

24. Chabeli Herrera, "1.6 million Floridians sign up for Obamacare coverage," *Miami Herald.* February 18. http://www.miamiherald.com/news/health-care/article10610435.html.

25. Jonathan N. Wand, Kenneth W. Shotts, Jasjeet S. Sekhon, Walter R. Mebane, Jr., Michael C. Herron, and Henry E. Brady, "The Butterfly Did it: The Aberrant Vote for Buchanan in Palm Beach County, Florida," American Political Science Review 95 (2001): 793-810.

26. Cass R. Sustein and Richard A. Epstein (eds). "The Vote: Bush, Gore & the Supreme Court," (Chicago: The University of Chicago Press, 2001); Steve Bickerstaff. 2001. "Counts, Recounts, and Election Contests: Lessons from the Florida Presidential Election," Florida State University Law Review. Col. 29: 425.

27. Mark Hugo Lopez. "The Hispanic Vote in the 2008 Election: Results for Florida," PewResearch Hispanic Trends Project. November 5, 2008. http://www.pewhispanic.org/2008/11/05/vi-results-for-florida/.

28. Marc Caputo, Alex Leary, and Michael C. Bender. "Herman Cain wins Presidency 5 straw poll," *Tampa Bay Times.* September 24, 2011. http://www.tampabay.com/news/politics/national/herman-cain-wins-presidency-5-straw-poll/1193524.

29. Allison Kopicki. "Polls Highlight Florida's Diverse Electorate," *New York Times*, The Caucus blog. January 27, 2012. http://thecaucus.blogs.nytimes.com/2012/01/27/polls-highlight-floridas-diverse-electorate/.

30. Sean D. Foreman. "Mitt Romney—The Republican Choice: Inevitability, Electability, and Lack of Enthusiasm" (pp. 219-244) in *The 2012 Nomination and the Future of the Republican Party: The Internal Battle.* Edited by William J. Miller. (Lanham, MD: Lexington Books, 2013).

31. "Women Favor Obama in Florida, Ohio, Pennsylvania, Quinnipiac University Swing State Poll Finds: Economy, Health Care Top Voter Concerns," March 28, 2012. http://www.quinnipiac.edu/news-and-events/quinnipiac-university-poll/presidential-swing-states-(fl-oh-and-pa)/release-detail?ReleaseID=1727.

32. Four percent refused to answer the favorability of Romney question and three percent on Obama.

33. "Romney bounces back in two of three key states, Quinnipiac University Swing state poll finds; Obama widens lead in Pennsylvania; Ohio, Florida tied," May 3, 2012. http://www.quinnipiac.edu/news-and-events/quinnipiac-university-poll/presidential-swing-states-(fl-oh-and-pa)/release-detail?ReleaseID=1743.

34. "Florida, Ohio, Pennsylvania swinging to Obama, Quinnipiac University swing state poll finds; voters back president on immigration, split on economy," June 27, 2012. http://www.quinnipiac.edu/news-and-events/quinnipiac-university-poll/presidential-swing-states-(fl-oh-and-pa)/release-detail?ReleaseID=1767.

35. "Obama hits 50% in Florida, Ohio, Pennsylvania, Quinnipiac University/CBS News/New York Times Swing State Poll Finds," August 1, 2012. http://www.quinnipiac.edu/news-and-events/quinnipiac-university-poll/presidential-swing-states-(fl-oh-and-pa)/release-detail?ReleaseID=1781.

36. "Ryan Micro-Bump in Florida, Wisconsin, But Not Ohio, Quinnipiac University/CBS News/New York Times Swing State Poll Finds," August 23, 2012. http://www.quinnipiac.edu/news-and-events/quinnipiac-university-poll/presidential-swing-states-(fl-oh-and-pa)/release-detail?ReleaseID=1789.

37. "Obama has big leads in Florida, Ohio, Pennsylvania, Quinnipiac University/CBS News/New York Times Swing State Poll Finds," September 26, 2012. http://www.quinnipiac.edu/news-and-events/quinnipiac-university-poll/presidential-swing-states-(fl-oh-and-pa)/release-detail?ReleaseID=1800.

38. "Obama up in Ohio; Florida, Virginia too close to call, Quinnipiac University/New York Times/CBS News Swing State Poll Finds," October 31, 2012. http://www.quinnipiac.edu/news-and-events/quinnipiac-university-poll/presidential-swing-states-(fl-oh-and-pa)/release-detail?ReleaseID=1812.

39. Ibid, October 31.

40. Marc Caputo. "10 takeaways from Florida's 2014 elections," *Miami Herald.* November 9, 2014. 1B.

41. "Obama to win Florida, CNN projects, sweeping all battlegrounds," 2012. CNN.com. November 10. http://politicalticker.blogs.cnn.com/2012/11/10/obama-wins-florida-cnn-projects/.

42. Andrea Levien. "Tracking Presidential Campaign Field Operations," The Center for Voting and Democracy, FairVote.com. November 14, 2012. http://www.fairvote.org/research-and-analysis/blog/tracking-presidential-campaign-field-operations/.

43. James Walcott. "Looking for Love in All the Right Places," *Vanity Fair.* June 2011. http://www.vanityfair.com/politics/features/2011/06/james-wolcott-republicans2012-201106.

44. Andrew Jackson, seventh President of the United States, was the military governor of Florida in 1821.

45. Steve Bousquet. "Former Florida Gov. Reubin Askew dies art 85," *Miami Herald.* March 3, 2014. http://www.miamiherald.com/news/politics-government/article1961313.html.

BIBLIOGRAPHY

David R. Colburn. 2007. *From Yellow Dog Democrats to Red State Republicans: Florida and Its Politics since 1940.* Gainesville, FL: University Press of Florida.

36 Days: The Complete Chronicle of the 2000 Presidential Election Crisis. 2001. Correspondents of *The New York Times.* New York. Times Books. Henry Holt and Company.

J. Edwin Benton. 2008. *Government and Politics in Florida.* Third Edition. Gainesville, FL: University Press of Florida.

Robert P. Watson (ed). 2004. *Counting Votes: Lessons from the 2000 Presidential Election in Florida.* Gainesville, FL: University Press of Florida.

Chapter Five

The Bluest Red State in America

Exploring North Carolina's Political Past, Present, and Future

Christopher A. Cooper and H. Gibbs Knotts

North Carolina is a puzzling state. V.O. Key Jr. (1949) called North Carolina a "Progressive Plutocracy" and for years it was the home of a southern-bred style of progressive politics (Fleer 1994). But, while moderate Democrats lived in the Governor's Mansion and dominated the General Assembly, the state's voters also elected ultra-conservative U.S. Senator Jesse Helms to five consecutive terms and supported Republican presidential candidates in nine out of the ten elections from 1968 through 2004 (Eamon 2014). Veteran North Carolina political journalist Rob Christensen calls this *The Paradox of Tar Heel Politics* and political scientist Charles Prysby (2014, 175) describes this as a "stable competitive pattern," noting that "Democrats tended to win elections for state government, whereas Republicans did better in congressional elections, and elections generally featured competitive races, at least below the presidential level."

Today, North Carolina stands as a true swing state, a state that could be picked up by Republicans or Democrats in 2016. The Tar Heel state is perceived by some as one of the Democrats' best hopes in the South and by others as the last piece of the puzzle for Republican domination in the region. Highlighting this political tension, the state legislature passed some of the most conservative legislation in the country in 2013 and 2014, while hundreds of liberal protestors gathered for "moral Mondays" where they made national headlines for their organization and activism (Fuller 2014). Despite, or perhaps because of, this ideological push-and-pull, the *Wall Street Journal* maintains that "North Carolina is still the prototype swing state" (Moore 2013).[1] Prysby (2014, 176) echoes this sentiment noting that "the state will be on the list of contested states in future presidential elections."

Using a combination of U.S. Census reports, election return data, a profile
of the state's voters, and available survey data, we argue that North Carolina
is not as red as the Republican legislature would lead you to believe, and not
as blue as the protestors outside of the General Assembly would like it to be.
It is, as we will argue in more detail below, the bluest red state in America.
And, as one of the few swing states in the politically important South, North
Carolina's 15 Electoral College votes will continue to play a key role determining who sits in the White House.

North Carolina is a swing state precisely because it has never been a purely
red or blue state. Democrats certainly dominated Tar Heel politics in the
early part of the twentieth century, but there were always a sizable minority
of Mountain Republicans in the General Assembly. In more recent elections,
when one party wins, they tend to win by a small amount, thus giving both
parties a chance in the succeeding election. The parties and candidates, of
course, see this potential and invest significant sums of money into North
Carolina's elections—reinforcing its reputation as a political battleground.[2]
Like other swing states, North Carolina is a place where campaign strategy
and electioneering can yield a significant shift in electoral votes. In fact,
North Carolina allocated the third-most electors of any swing state in 2012
(Politico 2012).

In this chapter, we begin with a political overview of North Carolina,
focusing on the three regions of the state. We then examine the partisanship
and ideology of North Carolina voters, showing that they are similar to the
average voter in the rest of the country. Because presidential politics do not
exist in a vacuum, but are rather affected by politics at multiple levels, we
also examine officeholding at the state and local levels. We conclude with a
look to the future and return to some of the recent debates over the state that
have taken place in the headlines of major newspapers like the *New York
Times* and *Wall Street Journal*.

We'll spoil the ending now: we don't know who's going to win future
presidential elections in North Carolina, but, were we the gambling type, we
would bet on close contests. In fact, short-term factors like the quality and
characteristics of Democratic and Republican presidential nominees, the dynamics of gubernatorial elections (unlike many southern states, these contests
are held during presidential elections years in North Carolina), and even the
ripple effects from changes in voting procedures will likely be important. In
fact, the odds of a landslide victory for the Republican or Democratic presidential nominee are about as likely as Duke University basketball fans paint-
ing their faces light blue and cheering for the University of North Carolina
Tar Heels.

WHERE AND WHAT IS NORTH CAROLINA?

An increasing number of people call North Carolina home. The state ranks ninth in total population and continues to grow at a higher rate than most other states (U.S. Census Bureau 2014). Although the state includes a relatively small proportion of some ethnic groups, over a fifth (22%) of North Carolina's population is African American (U.S. Census Bureau 2015) and the Tar Heel state has the seventh fastest growing Latino population in the country (Pew 2013). On other economic indicators, North Carolina typically ranks in the middle of all states and in the top one-third of southern states (Cooper and Knotts 2008). In terms of economic health, North Carolina ranked 23 out of 50 in a 2010 comparison of the best- and worst-performing state economies (24/7 Wall St. 2010).

Like many southern states (Key 1949), demographic and political patterns in North Carolina vary by intrastate regions (see Table 5.1 for some descriptive statistics on the three regions). The central region, known as the Piedmont, has the largest number of people. Based on 2010 Census figures, 53% of the state's 9.5 million residents reside in the Piedmont. This region also includes the state's five largest cities in North Carolina: Charlotte, Durham, Greensboro, Raleigh, and Winston Salem. Given the Piedmont's population, it is no surprise that it is has considerable influence over state politics. Some political observers differentiate between the Urban Piedmont and Western Piedmont when writing about Tar Heel politics (Kazee 1998; Knotts 2005). The more Democratic-leaning urban Piedmont includes the counties that are home to the five cities above, plus Orange County, where the state's flagship university, the University of North Carolina at Chapel Hill, is located. Conversely, the Western Piedmont has provided much stronger support for Republican candidates (Kazee 1998; Knotts 2005) than the urban Piedmont. As a whole, the Piedmont is racially diverse. According to the 2010 U.S. Census, 21% of the Piedmont's population is African American and 10% is Hispanic.

Table 5.1.   North Carolina's Three Regions

	Western	Piedmont	Eastern
Number of Counties	23	24	53
Total Population	1,078,667	4,961,202	3,310,614
Percent of N.C. Pop.	11%	53%	35%
Percent Black	4%	21%	28%
Percent Hispanic	5%	10%	8%

Source: U.S. Census of Population and Housing

Far fewer people reside in Western North Carolina (also called the Mountain region), generally defined as the 23 westernmost counties in the state. According to the 2010 Census, just 11% of the state's residents live in Western North Carolina and the region is less racially diverse than the other regions. Western North Carolina has also been politically distinct from the rest of the state. Because of the mountainous topography, making it difficult to grow cotton and rice, Western North Carolina had fewer slaves than other regions, and today is much more racially homogeneous. There were political differences as well. Much like East Tennessee, and the Ozark region of Arkansas, Western North Carolina supported Republican politics when the rest of the South was solidly Democratic (McKinney 1998), a trend that holds today.[3]

Eastern North Carolina (also known as the Coastal Plain) covers 53 counties (Kazee 1998) and is home to about a third of the state's population. The region includes the cities of Greenville, Fayetteville, and Wilmington, and is also a region with the most racial diversity. Given its history of plantation agriculture, the region has the highest percentage of African Americans in the state, at 28%. The region also has a growing Hispanic population, which make up 8% of the region's residents.

Eastern North Carolina represents the part of the state where Democrats have their deepest political roots. Before the enfranchisement of African-American voters, conservative white Democrats utilized Jim Crow laws and a variety of discriminatory practices to uphold the racial order. In the decades following the Civil Rights Act of 1964 and the Voting Rights Act of 1965, whites and newly registered blacks formed bi-racial coalitions to help Democrats maintain their political dominance (Black and Black 2002). At the same time, however, the adoption of blacks into the Democratic Party led many white conservatives to fear that they were losing control. As a result, they fled the Democratic Party and took over the (then fledgling) Republican Party. This theory of partisan transformation, known as "Relative Advantage Theory" (Hood, Morris, and Kidd 2012) helps explains the partisan shift, not just in Eastern North Carolina, but throughout the Tar Heel State and the South.

WHO ARE NORTH CAROLINA VOTERS?

As most students of political science know, partisanship is the strongest predictor of a person's vote choice. Key (1959) referred to partisanship as a voter's "standing decision" and there is considerable evidence that partisanship is relatively stable over the course of a person's life. Fortunately, North Carolina is a state where voters register by party and these party registration data are contained in publically available state voter files so we do not have to rely solely on self-reports in surveys to study party identification in the state. When examined over a period of time, voter files provide a host of voter registration statistics, help identify political trends, and provide a window into the state's electoral dynamics (Cooper, Knotts, and Haspel 2009).

Overall, there has been a decline in Democratic voter registration (from a high of near 80% of the state's registered voters in 1966 to a low-point of 45% in 2014). The steepest and most sustained decline occurred in the mid-1980s and early 1990s, an important time in North Carolina's changing partisan landscape. An exceedingly popular president, Ronald Reagan, was elected to a second term by landslide margins in 1984. In North Carolina, Reagan won with 62% of the popular vote, up from 49% in 1980. In addition, Tar Heel voters elected Governor Jim Martin in 1984, only the second Republican governor since Reconstruction. By the early 1990s, North Carolinians were much less likely to identify as Democratic than they had been in previous decades.

There was also an unmistakable rise of Republican voter registration during the mid-1980s and early 1990s. While Republican voter registration increased from less than 20% in 1966 to over 30% in the early 1990s, GOP registration has not risen dramatically in the two decades since. In fact, unaffiliated registrants have increased at a higher rate than Republicans during this time period. While this is important, we should note that unaffiliated voters in North Carolina are to decide whether they would like to vote in the Democratic or Republican primary. Graph 5.1 summarizes these trends and shows the percent Democratic, Republican, and unaffiliated between 1984 and 2014.[4]

The ideological makeup of registered voters also provides important clues about the state's political leanings. Of course, partisanship did not always line up with political ideology—especially in the American South (Abramowitz and Saunders 1998), but the ideological breakdown is particularly relevant today since the two major parties are much more ideologically distinct than they were in the past (Noel 2013). More so than at any other time in U.S. history, Democrats tend to be liberals and Republicans tend to be conservatives.

Graph 5.2 presents the results of a February 2014 survey asking registered voters to classify themselves as very liberal, somewhat liberal, moderate, somewhat conservative, or very conservative. This figure illustrates the current balance among Tar Heel registered voters with the ideological makeup somewhat normally distributed, albeit one that leans slightly to the right. Looking across the five categories, one-third of North Carolina registered voters identify as moderates. Conservative candidates do have a slight edge in North Carolina, however. For example, 39% of registered voters are either

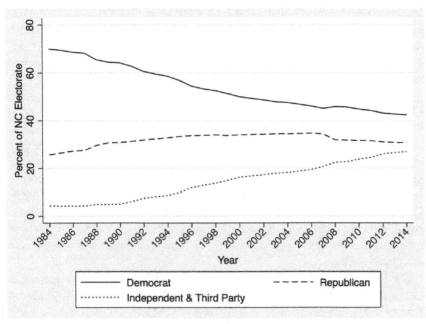

Graph 5.1. Partisan Composition of NC's Registered Voters, 1984–2014

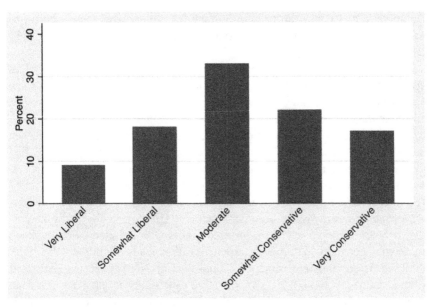

Graph 5.2. Political Ideology in the North Carolina Electorate

"somewhat conservative" or "very conservative" compared to 27% identifying as "somewhat liberal" or "very liberal."

How does the ideological makeup of North Carolina voters compare to the nation as a whole? Based on the 2012 Exit Polls, 22% or North Carolina voters identified as liberals, 38% identified as moderates, and 40% identified as conservatives (CNN 2012). As you might expect, North Carolina voters were slightly more conservative than the nation in 2012. According to the national Exit Poll, 25% of voters said they were liberal, 41% moderate, and 35% conservative (CNN 2012).[5]

Public Opinion, writ large, influences both electoral outcomes and public policy (Erikson, Wright, and McIver 1993). Although there are exceptions, states that have a large proportion of conservatives are likely to elect Republican candidates and pass conservative policies. Liberal states tend to exhibit the opposite trend. Here too, evidence derived by aggregating a variety of public opinion sources suggests that the public in North Carolina is largely centrist, although it leans slightly to the conservative side (Lax and Phillips, 2012).[6]

The message from this review of partisanship and ideology in North Carolina is clear: we find little evidence, at least thus far, that the Tar Heel state leans heavily toward one party or the other. While the relative size of Democratic registration in North Carolina has declined considerably, the plurality of voters in the state are still registered as Democrats. At the same time, the ideology of North Carolina voters leans slightly towards the conservative side. Thus far, the evidence supports the notion that both parties have a shot at winning the state's 15 Electoral College votes in 2016.

LOCAL POLITICAL OFFICEHOLDING

An important but understudied measure of a state's partisan competition is local officeholding (Bullock 1993; Knotts 2005). Local officeholding can provide a glimpse into voter decision-making, the future of partisanship in the state, as well as substantive information about policy-making in the state. Examining the political make-up of county commissioners in North Carolina's 100 counties, therefore, can provide a detailed picture of ground-level partisanship in the state.

Fortunately, the N.C. Association of County Commissioners compiles data on local office holding back to 1974. This organization collects descriptive information about the state's county commissions including the number of seats, the number of new commissioners, the number of female, African-American, and Native American commissioners, and most importantly for our purposes, the partisan makeup of each county commission.

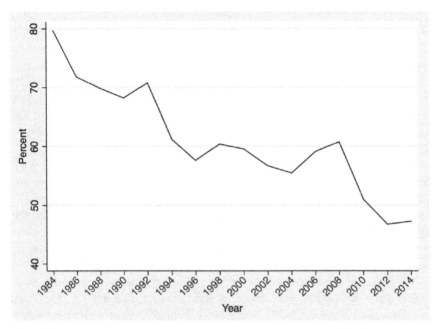

Graph 5.3.   Partisan Composition of North Carolina County Commission Seats 1984–2014

Graph 5.3 displays the percent of the state's county commission seats held by Democrats from 1984–2014. To provide some historical context, the percent of Democrats hovered between 80% and 90% during the 1970s and early 1980s, but a steep decline in Democratic officeholding occurred between 1982 and 1984. As mentioned above, the election of Reagan to a second term in office and the selection of Governor Martin likely helped shape politics at the county level.

As the graph indicates, another sharp decline occurred in the early 1990s. After a small bump coinciding with the 1992 election of Bill Clinton, Democratic officeholding took another steep drop in 1994 and 1996. Of course, these elections occurred alongside the Republican Party's successful 1994 efforts to nationalize congressional races. Declining support for Clinton, particularly in the South, likely also contributed to the decline in Democratic officeholding.

After hovering just below 60% for most of the late 1990s and 2000s, the Democratic share of local office holding dropped even further in 2010. In fact, Democrats held only 51% of seats, down from a high of just over 90%

in 1976. Of course, the 2010 elections were important in North Carolina for another reason. As previewed above, Republicans took control of both chambers of the General Assembly for the first time in over a century. By 2012, Democrats held just 47% of county commission seats, ceding majority status to the Republican Party for the first time. Although Republicans are still in the majority, the Democrats picked up 4 seats, and the Republicans lost 1 in 2014 (the other 3 seats were held by Independents).

This brief look at local officeholding leads us to two key conclusions. First, the Democratic Party has lost a considerable amount of its strength in the state. In fact, Democrats lost about 1% of county commission seats per year since 1974. This story is not all negative for the Democrats, however. Today there is virtual partisan parity at the local level in North Carolina. Republicans have only a small majority and based on this measure, the GOP is a long way from one-party domination. From the bottom-up, at least, North Carolina once again looks like a swing state—one where neither party has a competitive advantage.

STATE GOVERNMENT OFFICEHOLDING

The partisan composition of the state government officeholding is another important barometer of the state's political condition. In this section, we focus on the governor's office and the state legislature to gain a better since of North Carolina's recent political history.

Like most southern states, Democrats dominated gubernatorial politics in North Carolina during the twentieth century—electing Democratic governors from 1900 to 1972. Mountain Republican James Holshouser was elected governor in 1972, breaking the Democratic stranglehold, followed by Martin's election in 1984 and successful reelection in 1988. Former Charlotte Mayor Pat McCrory became the third Republican elected governor since 1900 when he was elected in 2012.

It is also important to consider the partisan makeup of the North Carolina General Assembly. Graph 5.4 presents the percentage of Democrats in the state legislature from 1984 2014. Prior to the time-series represented in the graph, Democrats dominated the legislature during the 1950s, but it is important to note the presence of a small group of Republicans. Most southern state legislatures during this time period were entirely composed of Democrats, but in large part because of the strength of Mountain Republicanism mentioned above, North Carolina had some Republican legislators (Cooper and Knotts 2014). There was also a steady decline in Democratic officeholding through the 1960s and early 1970s. The Watergate scandal and the election

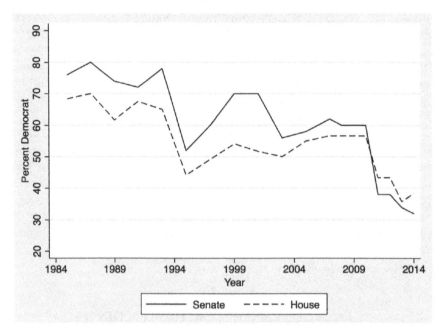

Graph 5.4.   Partisan Composition of the North Carolina General Assembly 1984–2014

of Democratic Governor Jim Hunt in 1976 likely contributed to a Democratic resurgence in the mid- to late 1970s. As the graph indicates, by the 1980s, the percentage of Democrats in the legislature declined again, falling below the 60% threshold in 1992.

From the early 1990s to the early 2000s, the General Assembly was much more balanced between Democrats and Republicans, highlighting the competitive nature of Tar Heel politics. As a result of the 2002 elections, the House was split evenly between Democratic and Republican members. In fact, Democrat Jim Black and Republican Richard Morgan served as co-speakers during the 2003-2004 legislative session. As noted above, it was not until 2010 that Republicans gained majorities in both chambers. The same basic story continues today, although the Democrats did rebound slightly in 2014—gaining 3 House seats and 1 in the Senate.

Previously, we reviewed data at the voter and county commission levels—both of which demonstrated that neither party has a clear advantage in North Carolina. The state legislative data, however, show a more dominant Republican Party and provide more reason for concern for Tar Heel Democrats. Nonetheless, the North Carolina General Assembly still has more two-party competition than many of its southern neighbors (Cooper and Knotts 2014), and more recent survey data suggest that the current state legislature in North Carolina is fairly unpopular—making it possible for the Democrats to gain seats in upcoming contests (Public Policy Polling 2015b).

NORTH CAROLINA'S CONGRESSIONAL DELEGATION

Much like the other political measures we have highlighted, North Carolina's congressional delegation has also shifted considerably over the past 40 years. Graph 5.5 presents a graphical representation of this shift from 1984 to 2014. Since the percentages in Graph 5.5 are based on a small number of seats, they fluctuate more radically than other political indicators. Congressional Democratic officeholding dropped considerably in 1996 and hit a low point in 2014.

There are, of course, many reasons for the recent Republican rise/Democratic decline, but redistricting has likely had a larger influence in North Carolina than in other states. While political scientists are divided on the effects of redistricting, even studies arguing that redistricting has little effect on officeholding tend to find that North Carolina's redistricting was politically consequential. For example, McGhee's (2012) analysis of expected partisan

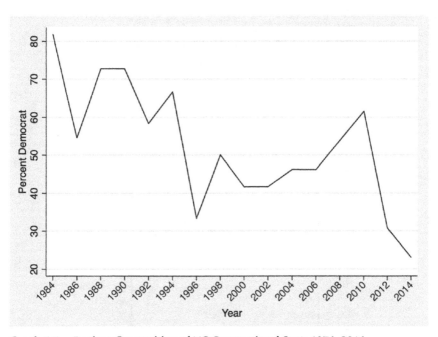

Graph 5.5.   Partisan Composition of NC Congressional Seats 1974–2014

Table 5.2. The Partisan Effects of Redistricting in the North Carolina Congressional Delegation

District #	113th Congress Occupant	112th Congress Occupant	2012 % McCain	2010 % McCain
1	Butterfield (D)	Butterfield (D)	31%	37%
2	Ellmers (R)	Ellmers (R)	56%	47%
3	Jones (R)	Jones (R)	56%	61%
4	Price (D)	Price (D)	28%	36%
5	Foxx (R)	Foxx (R)	57%	61%
6	Coble (R)	Coble (R)	55%	63%
7	McIntyre (D)[t]	McIntyre (D)	55%	52%
8	Hudson (R)	Kissell (D)	55%	47%
9	Pittinger (R)	Myrick (R)	55%	55%
10	McHenry (R)	McHenry (R)	57%	63%
11	Meadows (R)	Shuler (D)	58%	52%
12	Watt (D)	Watt (D)	22%	29%
13	Holding (R)	Miller (D)	56%	40%

Source: North Carolina Free Enterprise Foundation

Note: Seats in grey changed from Democrat to Republican in 2012. [t] indicates that the district flipped from Democrat to Republican in 2014.

shifts as a result of redistricting predicted that two seats would shift from Democrat to Republican in North Carolina as a result of redistricting. This is the only state where he found such an effect, even after controlling for reapportionment. Table 5.2 makes this conclusion even clearer. After the 2010 election, 7 of North Carolina's 13 congressional districts were represented by Democrats; after 2012, that number shrank to 4 of 13. After the 2014 election, 1 of the 4 Democrats lost, leaving Democrats with their lowest level of congressional representation since Reconstruction.

Table 5.2 also shows the support for 2008 Republican presidential candidate, John McCain, in each of North Carolina's congressional districts before and after the redistricting process. In the three congressional districts that changed hands from Democratic to Republican (NC-8, NC-11, and NC-13), McCain's support increased rather dramatically. For example, in NC-8 support for McCain increased from 47% in the old district to 55% in the new district, making it much more hospitable ground for Republicans. An even more dramatic change occurred in NC-13, where support for McCain went from 40% before redistricting to 56% after redistricting. But, while Republicans now hold a large majority of North Carolina's congressional seats, our analysis of voter returns demonstrates that about 80,000 more people voted for Democratic than Republican candidates in the 2012 U.S. House of Representatives contests in North Carolina. In 2014, this advantage reversed and the Democrats garnered about 80% as many votes for Congress as did the Republicans. While this would, of course, portend a Republican advantage, keep in mind that the Democrats only hold 23% of the congressional seats in North Carolina. Simply put, while the share of officeholding might suggest that the Republicans have a large advantage, the voters in these congressional contests are more split.

PRESIDENTIAL ELECTIONS IN NORTH CAROLINA

Only a decade ago, North Carolina was considered one of the most reliably Republican states in presidential contests. The Tar Heel state supported Republican presidential candidates in every election from 1980–2004. Many argue that Obama's 2008 victory in North Carolina was an anomaly, and that the state remains reliably red—at least at the presidential level. We disagree with this view. While North Carolina's electoral votes have consistently gone to the Republican nominee because of the winner-take-all system, this fact masks the true level of competitiveness in the state. The reality, of course, is that some Republican victories are greater than others—and the margin of victory can give us important clues about the degree to which a state is or is not a swing state.

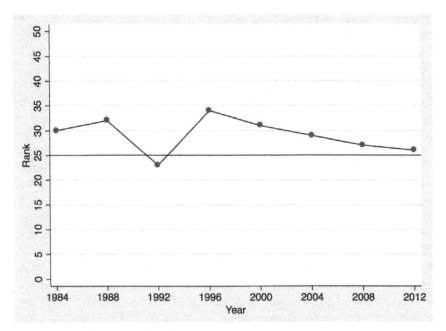

Graph 5.6.　Ranking of North Carolina Vote for Democratic Presidential Candidates 1980–2012

To place North Carolina in a broader context, Graph 5.6 presents North Carolina's Democratic vote share rank, compared to the other 49 states from 1984–2012. For example, if North Carolina has a 10 in a given year, that would indicate that North Carolina had the 10th largest vote share for the Democratic candidate (out of 50). A 40, on the other hand, would indicate that the Democratic candidate did not do well in North Carolina—at least when comparing to other states. We have highlighted the 25th rank, as it represents the median state.

As you can see, North Carolina has become more, not less of a swing state. In 2012, North Carolina was only one position away from the median state in terms of Obama vote share. Despite the fact that North Carolina supported Obama in 2008 and did not in 2012, the Tar Heel State was actually closer to the median vote share in 2012 than it was in 2008. North Carolina may be colored red on maps of the 2012 election, but it is best characterized not as bright red, but rather as the bluest red state in America.

This brief exercise also reinforces the importance of the Electoral College for electing presidents. While North Carolina's presidential elections have been among the closest in the country, the national media tends to focus on where all 15 of North Carolina's electors are allocated, thus ignoring the closeness of the race, and over-interpreting small movements in one direction or another as a mandate, a radical shift in state public opinion, or evidence of an unusually effective mobilization campaign. Given that advocates for Electoral College reform in North Carolina have not gotten very far,[7] this is likely to remain the case going forward.

CONCLUSION

A *New York Times* editorial summed up a common perspective about North Carolina stating, "North Carolina was once considered a beacon of farsightedness in the South, an exception in a region of poor education, intolerance and tightfistedness. In a few short months, Republicans have begun to dismantle a reputation that took years to build" ("The Decline of North Carolina" 2013). Comedian Stephen Colbert agreed, noting that the General Assembly was turning North Carolina into "a conservative Shangri-La" and poked fun at recently passed legislation allowing concealed handgun permit holders to carry a weapon on a playground (Seaton 2013).

These quips came less than a year after the Democratic Party held their biggest and most important event, the Democratic National Convention, in Charlotte—the state's most populous city. Had North Carolina changed that much in less than a year? Were the Democrats delusional in thinking they had a chance in the Tar Heel State? Eminent political observer Stu Rothenberg (2012) would have us believe so, as he argued in his pointedly titled piece, "On Second Thought, Maybe North Carolina Was a Mistake." While the North Carolina General Assembly has certainly passed conservative legislation, the state as a whole, has not undergone a radical political transformation. It was likely never as progressive as some would have had us believe, but is not as conservative as the *Times*, Rothenberg, and others have argued. As another example of the state's political competitiveness, early public opinion polls place Hillary Clinton in a dead heat with potential Republican candidates (Public Policy Polling 2015a).

Given the parity in North Carolina politics, short-term factors will likely play an important role in the state's presidential contests. For instance, we expect that the outcome of the 2016 election could hinge on who the Democrats and Republicans nominate. Given the slight conservative tilt among North Carolina voters, a Democratic nominee too far to the left will certainly push independents toward the GOP. Likewise, a far right Republican would be unlikely to gain the support of enough moderate voters to win the state. We will also be watching to see if there is a backlash against Republican control in Raleigh. Incumbent Republican Governor McCrory will likely be on the ballot in 2016 and the 2014 state legislative elections demonstrated small gains for the Democrats in Raleigh—perhaps suggesting that North Carolina voters may want to return to a closer balance of power in state government.

Voter turnout will, of course, be important in 2016. The Democrats were quite successful with voter mobilization efforts in 2008 and 2012, but Barack Obama will not be the party's nominee in 2016. Will the 2016 Democratic nominee be able to replicate Obama's substantial mobilization effort? In addition, will Democrats match the high levels of turnout among black voters if an African American is not atop the ticket? Moreover, a host of changes to the election process including new voter identification rules, fewer days for early voting, elimination of pre-registration for 17-year-olds, and elimination of same day registration could also change the composition of the electorate. After all, there is some evidence that voter ID laws reduce turnout among minorities (Dropp 2014; Smith and Heron 2012), and thus, may hurt Democrats in subsequent presidential contests. Likewise, eliminating pre-registration has the potential to reduce youth voter registration (McDonald and Thornburg 2010) and youth voter turnout (Holbein and Hillygus 2014). Although some have begun to speculate on the effects of some of these electoral changes in 2014 (Barrett 2014), most of the most politically controversial changes, like the 2013 Voter ID, do not go into effect until 2016, thus the 2014 election results may only provide a weak indication of their eventual effects.

In sum, we expect North Carolina to remain a swing state. North Carolina has more registered Democrats than Republicans and a demographic profile that doesn't appear to lean heavily towards one party or the other. At the same time, Republicans enjoy unified control of government in Raleigh—as well as leads at the county commission and congressional levels. Perhaps most importantly, North Carolina has moved closer to the median state in terms of presidential vote share in each of the last four election cycles. Some may call it red, some may call it blue. But, North Carolina is, and has been for quite a while, a purple state—situated in the political center. It is likely to swing from election to election, depending on the candidates and their campaigns.

NOTES

1. Political scientist Tom Eamon (2014, 287) agrees, stating "North Carolina emerged as a major swing state in presidential politics."

2. For example, the 2014 US Senate race in North Carolina between Kay Hagan (D) and Thom Tillis (R) was both the most advertised and the most expensive senate campaign in the country. This race featured over 60,000 television advertisements that aired between September 1st and Election Day at a cost of over $52 million (Fowler and Ridout 2015). In total, spending in this race came it at $111 million—$14 million more expensive than the next most expensive race (Wallack and Hudak 2014).

3. For example, Buncombe County (home to the liberal city of Asheville) was the only county in Western North Carolina to support either Democrat Walter Dalton in the 2012 gubernatorial election, or Democrat Barack Obama in the 2012 presidential election.

4. At various times, people have also been able to register as members of the Labor, Reform, and Libertarian Parties, but the numbers are relatively small and we do not display those data in this figure.

5. We considered using 2014 exit poll data, but the lack of a presidential election means that the data are less comparable across states. Nonetheless, North Carolina's exit poll data in 2014 look fairly similar to 2012—differing only by a few percentage points. In 2014, 20 percent of North Carolina voters in exit polls were self-professed liberals, followed by 38 percent who were moderates and 42 percent who were conservative. Nationally, 23 percent claimed to be liberals, 40 percent moderates, and 37 percent conservatives (CNN 2014).

6. Interestingly, the policies that emerge from North Carolina tend to lean farther right than the public will (Lax and Phillips 2012).

7. For example, the National Popular Vote Plan (http://www.nationalpopularvote.com/) passed the NC Senate in 2007, but has never passed the House and has not been introduced again since 2011.

FOR FURTHER READING

Christensen, Rob. 2008. *The Paradox of Tar Heel Politics: The Personalities, Elections, and Events that Shaped Modern North Carolina.* Chapel Hill, NC: University of North Carolina Press.

Cooper, Christopher A., and H. Gibbs Knotts. 2008. eds. *The New Politics of North Carolina.* Chapel Hill, NC: University of North Carolina Press.

Eamon, Tom. 2014. *The Making of a Southern Democracy.* Chapel Hill, NC: University of North Carolina Press.

Fleer, Jack D. 1994. *North Carolina Government and Politics.* Lincoln, NE: University of Nebraska Press.

Hood, M.V., and Seth C. McKee. 2010. "What Made Carolina Blue? In-Migration and the 2008 North Carolina Presidential Vote," *American Politics Research* 38(2010): 266–302.

Key, V.O. 1949 [1984]. *Southern Politics in State and Nation.* Knoxville, TN: University of Tennessee Press.

Luebke, Paul. 1998. *Tar Heel Politics 2000.* Chapel Hill, NC: University of North Carolina Press.

Prysby, Charles. 2014. "The Shifting Sands of Tar Heel Politics." In *The New Politics of the Old South*, 5th edition, edited by Charles S. Bullock and Mark J. Rozell, 157–180. New York: Rowman & Littlefield, 157–80.

Walden, Michael L. 2014. *North Carolina in the Connected Age: Challenges and Opportunities in a Globalizing Economy.* Chapel Hill, NC: University of North Carolina Press.

BIBLIOGRAPHY

Abramowitz, Alan I., and Kyle L. Saunders. 1998. "Ideological Realignment in the US Electorate." *Journal of Politics* 60: 634–52.

Barrett, Mark. 2014. "Turnout Sheds New Light on Election Law Changes." *Asheville Citizen Times,* December 21. Accessed January 4, 2015. http://www.citizen-times.com/story/news/local/ 2014/12/20/turnout-stats-new-light-election-law-changes/20711193/

Black, Earl, and Merle Black. 2002. *The Rise of Southern Republicans.* Cambridge, MA: Harvard University Press.

Bullock, Charles S. III. 1993. "Republican Officeholding at the Local Level in Georgia." *Southeastern Political Review* 21: 113–131.

Christensen, Rob. 2008. *The Paradox of Tar Heel Politics: The Personalities, Elections, and Events that Shaped Modern North Carolina.* Chapel Hill, NC: University of North Carolina Press.

Cooper, Christopher A., and H. Gibbs Knotts. 2008. "Introduction: Traditionalism and Progressivism in North Carolina." In *The New Politics of North Carolina,* edited by H. Gibbs Knotts and Christopher A. Cooper, 1–14. Chapel Hill, NC: University of North Carolina Press.

Cooper, Christopher A., and H. Gibbs Knotts. 2014. "Partisan Change in Southern State Legislatures: 1953–2013." *Southern Cultures* 20: 75-89.

Cooper, Christopher A., H. Gibbs Knotts, and Moshe Haspel. 2009. "The Value of Voterfiles for U.S. State Politics Research." *State Politics and Policy Quarterly* 9: 102–121.

CNN 2012. "Presidential Exit Polls." Accessed January 4, 2015. http://www.cnn.com/election/2012/results/race/president.

CNN 2014. "2014 Exit Polls." Accessed January 4, 2015. http://www.cnn.com/election/2014/results/exit-polls.

"The Decline of North Carolina." 2013. *New York Times.* July 9. Accessed January 4, 2015. http://www.nytimes.com/2013/07/10/opinion/the-decline-of-north-carolina.html.

Dropp, Kyle. 2013. "Voter ID Laws and Voter Turnout." Working Paper: Dartmouth University. Accessed January 4, 2015. http://kyledropp.weebly.com/uploads/1/2/0/9/12094568/dropp_voter_id.pdf.

Eamon, Tom. 2014. *The Making of a Southern Democracy: North Carolina Politics from Kerr Scott to Pat McCrory.* Chapel Hill, NC: University of North Carolina Press.

Erickson, Robert, Gerald C. Wright, and John P. McIver. 1993. *Statehouse Democracy: Public Opinion and Policy in the United States.* New York: Cambridge University Press.

Fleer, Jack D. 1994. *North Carolina Government and Politics.* Lincoln, NE: University of Nebraska Press.

Fuller, Jamie. 2014. "80,000 people protested in NC this weekend. Here's Why." *The Washington Post.* February 10. Accessed January 4, 2015. http://www.washingtonpost.com/blogs/the-fix/wp/2014/02/10/why-tens-of-thousands-of-people-were-rallying-in-raleigh/.

Holbein, John, and D. Sunshine Hillygus. 2014. "Making Young Voters: The Impact of Preregistration on Youth Turnout. Working Paper. Available at http://papers. ssrn.com/sol3/papers.cfm?abstract_id=2483860 or http://dx.doi.org/10.2139

Hood, M.V., Quintin Kidd, and Irwin Morris. 2012. *The Rational Southerner: Black Mobilization, Republican Growth, and the Political Transformation of the American South.* New York: Oxford University Press.

Kazee, Thomas A. 1998. "North Carolina: Conservatism, Traditionalism, and the GOP." In *The New Politics of the Old South*, edited by Charles S. Bullock and Mark J. Rozell. New York: Rowman & Littlefield, 141–166.

Key, V.O. 1949 [1984]. *Southern Politics in State and Nation*. Knoxville, TN: University of Tennessee Press.

Key, V.O. 1959. "Secular Realignment and the Party System." *Journal of Politics* 21: 198–210.

Knotts, H. Gibbs. 2005. "Grassroots Republicanism: Evaluating the Trickle Down Realignment Theory in North Carolina." *Politics & Policy* 33: 330–345.

Lax, Jeffrey R., Justin H. Phillips. 2012. "The Democratic Deficit in the States." *American Journal of Political Science* 56: 148–66.

McDonald, Michael and Matthew Thornburg. 2010. "Registering the Youth: Preregistration Programs." *New York University Journal of Legislation and Public Policy* 12: 551–71.

McGhee, Eric. 2012. "The 2011 House Redistricting, State by State." *The Monkey Cage*, September 28. Accessed January 4, 2015. http://themonkeycage. org/2012/09/28/the-2011-house-redistricting-state-by-state/.

McKinney, Gordon. 1998. *Southern Mountain Republicans, 1865–1900*. Knoxville, TN: University of Tennessee Press.

Moore, Stephen. 2013. "Why are North Carolina Liberals so @&%*! Angry?" *Wall Street Journal* July 19. Accessed January 4, 2015. http://online.wsj.com/news/ articles/ SB10001424127887324448104578615701537475998.

Noel, Hans Noel. 2013. *Political Ideologies and Political Parties in America*. New York: Cambridge University Press.

North Carolina Board of Election. 2014. "Voter ID Requirements in North Carolina." Accessed January 4, 2015. http://www.ncsbe.gov/ncsbe/Voter-Id.

Politico. 2012. "2012 Swing States." http://www.politico.com/2012-election/swing-state/ Accessed on February 18, 2015.

Public Policy Polling. 2015a. "Bush Leads GOP Field in NC, Clinton Up On Most Republicans." Accessed July 2, 2015. http://www.publicpolicypolling.com/ main/2015/06/bush-leads-gop-field-in-nc-clinton-up-on-most-republicans.html.

Public Policy Polling. 2015b. "Gay Marriage Reaches Record Support in North Carolina." Accessed July 2, 2015. http://www.publicpolicypolling.com/main/2015/06/ gay-marriage-reaches-record-support-in-nc.html.

Prysby, Charles. 2014. "The Shifting Sands of Tar Heel Politics." In *The New Politics of the Old South*, 5th edition, edited by Charles S. Bullock and Mark J. Rozell, 157–180. New York: Rowman and Littlefield.

Ridout, Travis N., and Erika Franklin Fowler. 2015. "Political Advertising in 2014: The Year of the Outside Group." *The Forum* 12: 663–684.

Rothenberg, Stu. 2012. "On Second Thought, Maybe N.C. Was a Mistake." *Roll Call*, April 30. Accessed January 4, 2015. http://www.rollcall.com/issues/57_129/On-Second-Thought-Maybe-NC-Was-a-Mistake-214176-1.html?pg=1.

Seaton, Jake. 2013. "Daily Show the Latest in Line of Satirists Taking Aim at North Carolina." *WNCN News*, September 17. Accessed January 4, 2015. http://www.wncn.com/story/23060184/daily-show-the-latest-in-line-of-satirists-taking-aim-at-nc.

Smith, Daniel A., and Michael C. Herron. 2012. "Souls to the Polls: Early Voting in Florida in the Shadow of House Bill 1355." *Election Law Journal* 11: 331–347.

24/7 Wall St. 2010. "The Best- and Worst-Performing State Economies in America." *The Atlantic*, October 11. Accessed January 4, 2015. http://www.theatlantic.com/business/archive/2010/10/the-best-and-worst-performing-state-economies-in-america/64307/

U.S. Census Bureau. 2014. "Florida Passes New York to Become the Nation's Third Most Populous State, Census Bureau Reports." Accessed January 4, 2015. https://www.census.gov/newsroom/ press-releases/2014/cb14-232.html.

U.S. Census Bureau: State and County QuickFacts. 2015. Data derived from Population Estimates, American Community Survey, Census of Population and Housing, State and County Housing Unit Estimates, County Business Patterns, Nonemployer Statistics, Economic Census, Survey of Business Owners, Building Permits. Available at http://quickfacts.census.gov/qfd/states/37000.html. Accessed on February 17, 2015.

Wallack, Grace, and John Hudak. 2014. "How Much Did Your Vote Cost? Spending Per Voter in the 2014 Senate Races." *Brookings Institution*. http://www.brookings.edu/blogs/fixgov/posts/2014/11/07-spending-per-voter-2014-midterm-senate-wallack-hudak. Accessed on February 18, 2015.

Chapter Six

The Badger State as a Battleground

Wisconsin Politics Past, Present, and Future

Neil Kraus and Aaron C. Weinschenk

In recent presidential elections, the national political media has spent a considerable amount of time discussing so-called red and blue states, with red identified as solidly Republican and blue as reliably Democratic. Yet much more important than these predictable states are what have come to be called swing states—those states that are conceivably "up for grabs" for either the Democratic or Republican candidate. As a mix of red and blue, these states have been described by many observers as "purple," and elect statewide candidates of different parties fairly regularly. Because of the functioning of the Electoral College, swing states have become incredibly important as they essentially determine the outcome of presidential elections. Thus swing states are also called battlegrounds, given the intense political competition they typically attract. The list of such states is rather small, and some of the most widely discussed swing states include Ohio, Florida, Nevada, Iowa, and Wisconsin.

The main reason for Wisconsin's status as a swing state is its long-standing clash of political cultures. Several decades ago, Daniel Elazar pioneered the study of regional political cultures in the United States, and Elazar argued that Wisconsin has historically been dominated by a moralistic political culture. This type of culture views the political system as a commonwealth in which "politics is focused on issues and the purpose of political activity is to create and maintain a government that advances the interests of the whole society" (Conant 2006, 17). Yankee migrants from New England and New York as well as Scandinavian and German immigrants in the nineteenth century brought the moralistic political culture to Wisconsin and other parts of the upper Midwest, most notably Minnesota.

Yet in competition with the moralistic approach has been the individualistic political culture in Wisconsin, which sees the political system as more of a marketplace in which "politics is viewed as a bargaining process among self-interested individuals and groups. . . . Those who participate expect to gain rewards for their efforts, and they can be expected to distribute benefits to the people who help them" (Conant 2006, 17). In an analysis of the historic conflict between these two conceptions of the political order in Wisconsin, Conant has argued that "[w]hether visible or not, the results of the electoral competition between those who hold the commonwealth and marketplace views has had profound consequences for the state and its people" (Ibid., 2). Historian John Buenker has made a similar point arguing that the state's internal conflicts have made it a microcosm of the entire nation (Buenker 1988).

The early period of the state's history saw a handful of powerful industries, most notably timber and railroad interests, exercising significant influence over the political and economic systems, which established and strengthened the individualistic culture in terms of elections and public policy. Then in the late nineteenth century, within the context of a changing state population resulting from immigration and internal migration, the emergence of Robert M. LaFollette ushered in the ascendance of the moralistic political culture under the guise of the Progressive Party, which was initially allied with many Republicans.

For the remainder of the twentieth century, while alternating political party control of state government as well as Congressional seats, Wisconsin leaders have generally maintained the policies established beginning early in the twentieth century reflecting the moralistic political culture, including those aimed at increasing political participation, opening up the political process, limiting political corruption, preserving natural resources, and mitigating the effects of the free market economy. Yet in the contemporary period, the state's Republican Party more closely exhibits Elazar's individualistic political culture in which the power of business has increased and elected officials are more intent on rolling back laws passed decades ago in an attempt to undo the legacy of the moralistic political culture. Indeed, Conant's analysis, published in 2006, eerily foreshadowed the intense polarization that has engulfed the state since the election of Governor Scott Walker in 2010. After surviving a recall effort in 2012, Governor Walker has become a favorite among national Republicans and conservative organizations. His reelection in 2014 increased his national political profile and contributed to speculation that he will run for president in 2016. Indeed, the governor has only furthered speculation about his future by writing a book, appearing frequently in the national media, travelling extensively to conservative fundraising events around the country, and sounding increasingly like a presidential candidate.

Despite the Republican dominance of the state legislative and executive branches of late, the results of recent national elections continue to reveal the ongoing conflict between political cultures in Wisconsin. The state's two sitting U.S. Senators, Ron Johnson and Tammy Baldwin, represent the conservative wing of the Republican Party and the liberal wing of the Democratic Party, respectively. Senator Johnson defeated one of the more liberal U.S. Senators in recent decades, Russ Feingold. And while Democratic candidates have won the last several presidential elections, the state remains consistently competitive at the presidential level.

Graph 6.1 illustrates the divided nature of the electorate in terms of the distribution of political ideology in the state in the contemporary period. While self-described conservatives consistently outnumber liberals, moderates outnumber both, illustrating the competitive nature of state politics today. Moreover, the relatively large numbers of residents who consider themselves moderate (40 percent as recently as 2012) lends itself to a type of politics in which conservatives, liberals, and moderates all have a reasonable chance at winning statewide office. To get a quick sense of how Wisconsin compares to the nation as a whole, it is useful to compare the results of recent exit polls. In 2012, exit polls showed that at the national level, 25% of people identified as liberal, 35% identified as conservative, and 41% identified as moderate. In 2012 in Wisconsin, exit polls found that 24% of Wisconsinites identified as liberal, 35% identified as conservative, and 40% identified as moderate. So, the state's ideological composition is nearly identical to that of the U.S., which has become evident in presidential elections as well as elections for statewide office. In recent decades, presidential candidates from both major parties have believed that they could win in Wisconsin, which has made the state the target of a great deal of campaign advertising, candidate visits, and media attention.

This chapter proceeds in a straightforward manner. In the next section, we provide some basic information on the economic and demographic characteristics of Wisconsin. We then move to a discussion of the political

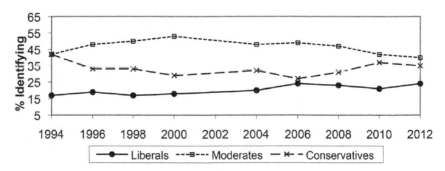

Graph 6.1. Political Ideology in Wisconsin

history of the state, which argues that Wisconsin has evolved into a politically competitive state over time. Next, we provide a discussion of the nature of contemporary politics in Wisconsin, focusing on recent gubernatorial and presidential elections. We conclude by discussing recent data on presidential campaign visits, campaign spending, and field offices and by discussing the future of politics in the Badger state.

CHANGING ECONOMY AND DEMOGRAPHICS

As an agricultural and industrial state, Wisconsin was built on farming—primarily dairy—along with several industries, most notably lumber and heavy manufacturing. And the strength of industry in the state's early history corresponded with the development of the individualistic political culture, as noted above. Yet the growth in agriculture and unionization beginning early in the twentieth century, in conjunction with increasing immigration, helped to strengthen the state's burgeoning moralistic political culture, and provided a counterweight to the power of large industrial firms. However, similar to many other Midwestern and Northeastern states, Wisconsin began to lose industrial jobs after World War II. This weakened organized labor, once the backbone of the Democratic Party. According to a report by the Bureau of Labor Statistics, the union membership rate in Wisconsin hit a low point (11.2 percent) in 2012. It is worth noting that unions have been a salient and controversial topic in Wisconsin over the past several years. In 2011, the state legislature passed and Governor Scott Walker signed into law Act 10, which suspended most collective bargaining powers for public unions. Act 10 led to a series of intense protests and ultimately a recall election for Walker. Although Walker survived the recall attempt, unions and their impact on the state are still a hot topic in Wisconsin, and in 2015 the Republican-led state legislature pushed through "right-to-work" legislation, which Governor Walker also signed into law, the dynamics of which are discussed in more detail below.

The state's racial and ethnic makeup has changed in recent years as well. While still largely white (Wisconsin was 88.1% white as of 2013), the numbers of African Americans, Hispanics, and Asian Americans has increased in recent decades. According to the U.S. Census Bureau, from 2000 to 2010 the size of the Asian population increased by 46 percentage points, the size of the Hispanic population increased by 74 percentage points, and the size of the African American population increased by 18 percentage points. The numbers of Asian Americans, African Americans, and Latinos in Wisconsin remain relatively small in comparison to the U.S. as a whole. Today, the state consists of roughly 2.5% Asian Americans, 6.5% African Americans, and 6.3% Latinos, whereas these numbers for the U.S. are 5%, 12%, and 15% respectively. While the demographic changes in Wisconsin are certainly not as pronounced as the changes that other states have experienced in recent years, if the state's population continues to become more diverse, there may be important implications for Wisconsin politics, especially if minority groups consistently vote for a particular party.

A BRIEF POLITICAL HISTORY OF WISCONSIN

With a bit of information on Wisconsin's economic landscape and demographic features in mind, it is now important to consider how the state's political system has changed over time. Wisconsin's current pattern of party competition is a post-World War II phenomenon. Throughout most of the state's history, the Republican (GOP) Party dominated Wisconsin government and politics. The current nature of Wisconsin political parties, therefore, owes much to the unique circumstances of its evolution from one-party Republicanism to a system of two-party competitiveness.

Republican One-Partyism, 1855-1934

Nineteenth-century Wisconsin politics was characterized by Republican dominance as the party won the governorship in all but three of 19 contests from 1855 to 1894. In the 1920s, Democratic gubernatorial nominees averaged only 28.4% of the vote and in 1922 the party's candidate gained only 10.6% of the popular vote. The most meaningful competition occurred in the Republican primaries between the conservative stalwart faction and the Progressive followers of Robert M. La Follette. Between 1894 and 1934, intra-party struggles between these two factions produced a system of bi-factional one-partyism, as stalwart and Progressive Republicans alternated control of Wisconsin government. This division within the Republican Party highlighted the tension between the individualistic and moralistic political cultures discussed above.

The Democrats won statewide elections only under the most unusual circumstances, such as the Great Depression when they carried the state for Franklin Roosevelt, elected a U.S. senator and governor, and gained a majority in the state Assembly in 1932. This electoral sweep was accomplished with the support of the La Follette Progressives, who had defected from the Republican Party after Governor Philip La Follette had been defeated by the stalwart Walter Kohler, Sr. in the 1932 Republican primary. The La Follettes and their Progressive followers did not intend to form a permanent alliance with the Democrats. To the Progressives, Wisconsin's Democratic Party was electorally weak and no less conservative than the Republicans.

Third-Party Politics, 1934-1946

Senator Robert M. La Follette, Jr., who had been elected as a Republican, faced reelection in 1934. However, the Depression had temporarily discredited the Republican label—whether it was worn by a Progressive or a stalwart. In addition, his brother Philip's defeat in the 1932 GOP primary demonstrated that he was not assured a re-nomination as a Republican. Faced with these circumstances, Robert La Follette, Jr. led his family's followers out of the Republican Party and formed a separate Progressive Party. During the 1934-1946 era, therefore, Wisconsin had three parties contesting elections (Epstein 1986; Sundquist 1983). The departure of the Progressives left the Republican Party dominated by conservatives. The Progressives were a moderate to liberal force and were largely supportive of the domestic policies of Franklin Roosevelt's New Deal. The Democratic Party had a narrow ethnic base—a coalition of Irish, Polish, and some German Catholics—and a distinctly conservative policy orientation. During this period, major electoral competition for state and congressional offices was between the Republicans and the Progressives. Even the national Democratic Party recognized this political reality and supported Robert La Follette, Jr. in his campaigns for the Senate in 1934 and 1940 (Thompson 1988).

In the mid-1940s, an electoral realignment occurred that foreshadowed the development of regular two-party competition between the Republicans and Democrats. Liberal and labor elements in the state started to move into the Democratic Party. This movement toward the Democrats was aided by President Franklin Roosevelt's fourth term. In 1944, Wisconsin Progressives were confronted with Franklin Roosevelt leading the Democratic presidential ticket, no La Follette on the ballot, and a popular Republican governor with some Progressive inclinations, Walter Goodland, seeking reelection. In these difficult circumstances, the Progressive gubernatorial candidate received only 5.8% of the vote. However, the Democratic nominee, Daniel Hoan (Socialist mayor of Milwaukee from 1916 to 1940), captured 41% of the vote, an indication that Wisconsin politics was moving toward two-party competitiveness between the Republicans and the Democrats.

Two-Party Competition, 1946-Present

The Progressive Party voted in 1946 to disband and re-enter the Republican Party. Robert M. La Follette, Jr. sought to retain his Senate seat by seeking the GOP nomination. He was, however, defeated in the Republican primary by Joseph McCarthy, who went on to win the general election. La Follette's decision to re-enter the GOP and his defeat in the Republican primary killed the Progressive Party, which had always been heavily dependent upon the La Follette family's personal following rather than a strong organizational base.

Although many Progressives in metropolitan areas did not follow their leaders back into the Republican Party, the return of many older and rural Progressives to the GOP helped the Republicans to maintain their electoral dominance of the state for another decade (Dykstra and Reynolds 1978). The demise of the Progressive party did, however, result in many rank and file Progressive voters shifting their allegiance to the Democrats. As a result, the Democratic share of the gubernatorial vote rose in the 1940s from 12.3% in 1942 to 44.1% in 1948, as the Democrats became the principal opposition force to the dominant GOP (Thompson 1988, 433–34).

The election of Wisconsin Senator Joseph McCarthy and his emergence as a controversial national figure affected both the Republican and Democratic parties. McCarthy had never been close to the state GOP leadership. Indeed, he had won the party endorsement for the Senate in 1946 largely by default because no well-known party leader emerged to challenge La Follette. McCarthy's greatest asset among Republican activists was that he was not La Follette. McCarthy's controversial "red baiting" in the 1950s, however, created a high level of divisiveness within state Republican ranks, as evidenced by his relatively weak showing (54%) in the 1952 elections when the GOP presidential and gubernatorial nominees, Dwight Eisenhower and Walter Kohler, Jr., were winning landslide victories in the state.

Although they never succeeded in defeating McCarthy at the polls, the senator did have some beneficial consequences for the Democrats. McCarthy was so controversial and divisive that he proved to be a potent basis for recruiting workers and voters for the Democratic Party and thereby contributed in an unintended way to making Wisconsin a two-party state. The first breakthrough for the Democrats came in the 1957 special election for United States senator to fill the vacancy caused by the death of Senator McCarthy. William E. Proxmire, who had been defeated three times as Democratic nominee for governor, was elected. The following year, he was reelected and Gaylord Nelson became the first Democratic governor since 1932. In addition, three Democrats won state constitutional offices, and the party won control of the Assembly. Wisconsin has had competitive two-party politics in contests for major statewide offices ever since.

CONTEMPORARY PATTERNS OF TWO-PARTY COMPETITION

While electoral politics are competitive in Wisconsin, there is substantial variation in relative levels of support for the two major parties across the state. In the period of GOP electoral dominance from 1938 through 1956, the vast majority of Wisconsin counties were either strongly or marginally Republican (Donoghue 1974). The GOP was particularly strong in the more prosperous southern half of the state, especially in rural areas, small towns, medium sized cities, and Milwaukee's northern and western suburbs. Democratic electoral strength was concentrated in the southeastern corner of the state–the highly urbanized, industrialized, and unionized counties of Milwaukee, Racine, and Kenosha; Dane County (which is where the city of Madison, home of the state capitol and the University of Wisconsin, is located); industrial centers of Manitowoc, Sheboygan, and Two Rivers along Lake Michigan and Eau Claire in the northwest; Portage County (Stevens Point); and the economically depressed northern Wisconsin-Lake Superior region. The shift toward the Democrats that began in the late 1950s and ran through the 1970s was particularly pronounced in the northern counties close to the Minnesota border. Counties containing medium sized cities—Green Bay, Janesville, Beloit, La Crosse, and Wausau—also moved toward the Democratic column.

A Closer Look at Gubernatorial Elections

The Republicans and Democrats have been locked in tight competition to control Wisconsin government since the Democrats emerged as a major electoral force in the 1950s. In the 19 gubernatorial elections between 1956 and 2006, only one candidate, Republican Tommy Thompson in 1994 and 1998, has received in excess of 58% of the major party vote (see Graph 6.2). Thompson's 67% in 1994 was the largest majority any candidate had received since 1922 when John J. Blaine (Rep.) garnered 76%. In recent years, the state has shifted between Democratic and Republican control—from 1987 to 2001 Republican Tommy Thompson served as the governor, from 2003–2011 Democrat Jim Doyle served as the governor, and since 2011 Republican Scott Walker has been the governor.

As shown in Graph 6.2, with only a few exceptions, two-party competition in gubernatorial elections has been fairly consistent in the state over the last several decades. The 2010 Wisconsin gubernatorial election featured Milwaukee Mayor Tom Barrett, the Democratic candidate, and Milwaukee County Executive Scott Walker, the Republican candidate. Incumbent Jim Doyle (D) decided not to seek a third term. Although many perennial issues were at the forefront of the campaign, several themes emerged more prominently than others, including taxes, budget reform, and job growth. The Walker campaign tried to use the national political climate—an unpopular Democratic president and voter concern over economic conditions—to their advantage. Both candidates were well financed, though Walker outspent Barrett by a large margin ($11,072,433 to $6,781,584 according to data from the

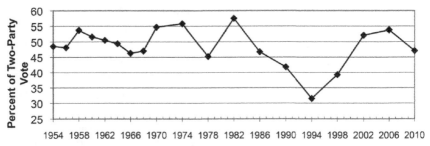

Graph 6.2. Democratic Percent of the Two-Party Vote for Governor

Wisconsin Democracy Campaign). A great deal of money was also spent by independent expenditure groups and by interest groups, some of whom spent millions of dollars on campaign advertising. The 2010 Wisconsin gubernatorial election was the most expensive in the state's history. In the end, Walker won the election with 52.3% of the vote (Barrett won 46.5% of the vote), and Republicans won majorities in both houses of the state legislature.

Despite Walker's victory in November of 2010, his election and policies spurred a significant amount of controversy, much of which centered around disputes about public unions and collective bargaining. Plans to recall Walker began shortly after he introduced his plans on collective bargaining, although Wisconsin law stipulates that an official must serve for at least 1 year before they can be subject to a recall election. Although Governor Walker could not be put through a recall election immediately, his supporters and opponents went into action rather quickly in pursuit of recalls of both Democratic and Republican state senators. In the summer of 2011, six Republican and three Democratic state senators faced recall elections, with all but two Republicans surviving; and in 2012 four additional Republican state senators faced recalls, with one of them losing to his Democratic opponent. In 2014, incumbent Governor Walker defeated former State Secretary of Commerce and Madison School Board member Mary Burke by a 52.3 to 46.6 percent differential, again illustrating the competitive nature of party politics in statewide races. Further, Governor Walker's three elections revealed the extreme partisan divide that has become apparent in the state as the individualistic political culture has, once again, become the dominant framework, at least among a majority of elected officials at the state level.

National Elections

The pattern of two-party competition found in gubernatorial elections is also found in elections for federal office. For instance, in presidential contests since 1948, the Republican candidate has won seven times and the

Democratic nominee has carried the state eight times. However, Democratic candidates have carried the state in the last seven presidential contests (1988 through 2012). In presidential elections, Wisconsin has tended to follow national trends and has voted for the winning candidate in eleven of the last fifteen elections, with 1960, 1988, 2000, and 2004 as the exceptions.

Graph 6.3 tracks the two-party vote for Democratic presidential candidates in Wisconsin in comparison to the nation as a whole. A couple of trends stand out in this figure. First, while Wisconsin typically voted somewhat more Republican than the nation as a whole in the 1952, 1956, and 1960 elections, it has tilted more Democratic than the U.S. in most elections from 1972 to 2012. Second, while the Democratic candidate has every presidential election in Wisconsin since 1988, the deviation from the national outcome in the last four elections has been very slight.

One interesting idea to consider is whether the election of Governor Scott Walker, a conservative politician, will have implications for future presidential elections. Walker has now won two gubernatorial elections (in 2010 and 2014) and survived a recall election (in 2012). In addition, both houses of the Wisconsin state legislature are now controlled by the Republican Party. One interpretation of these trends is that they signal that Wisconsin is tilting in the more conservative direction. It is certainly the case that Walker and his Republican colleagues in the legislature tend to be ideologically conservative. However, we would caution against inferring too much about presidential elections from recent state-level elections. It is important to note that the political context that informs elections often varies considerably from state level to national elections. It is also important to note that over the past several decades the state has tended to tilt more Democratic than the nation as a whole when it comes to the presidential vote.

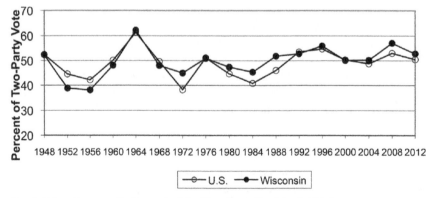

Graph 6.3. Democratic Percent of the Two-Party Presidential Vote

Despite its relatively modest number of electoral votes (10 in 2012), the level of two-party competition in Wisconsin has made it an important battleground state in the last few presidential elections. Given that the state is relatively evenly divided politically, and that no party has a built-in advantage, both parties have gravitated to Wisconsin in pursuit of its electoral votes. A number of indicators illustrate the extent to which Wisconsin is viewed as a competitive state in presidential elections. The number of campaign field offices is one potential signal about the importance of a state. Campaign field offices generally engage in a wide range of campaign activities, from voter mobilization drives to asking for campaign donations. There is quite a bit of variation in the number of campaign offices per state; some states have just one or two offices, while other states have dozens. In 2012, although Wisconsin did not have the highest number of field offices, it certainly stands out in light of the fact that it had 93 field offices in total, behind only Florida and Ohio (Center for Voting and Democracy 2012). Presumably, the presidential campaigns would not locate that many campaign offices in Wisconsin if they did not think that the state was important.

Another way of assessing the perceived value of a state is to look at how many times the presidential candidates visited it during the campaign. Once again, in 2012 there was considerable variation in the number of campaign visits. Some states did not see the candidates at all, while other saw them many times. Wisconsin stands out as a state that received quite a few visits from the Obama and Romney campaigns. In total, the state saw 31 visits from Barack Obama, Joe Biden, Mitt Romney, and Paul Ryan (a Wisconsin native), placing it in the top tier of most frequently visited states during the campaign (*Washington Post* 2012). Once again, it is doubtful that the candidates would spend a great deal of time in a state if they did not view it as a valuable one.

One final way of assessing the value of a state is to examine patterns of campaign spending. Money is a valuable resource during political campaigns, and, like campaign offices and candidate visits, campaigns tend to use it strategically. And in 2012, once again, Wisconsin stands out as a state that garnered a lot of attention from the campaigns, with over 30 million spent by the two campaigns combined through the end of August 2012 (*Slate.com* 2012). In fact, this figure actually placed Wisconsin second nationally, and first among swing states, in this spending category (Illinois led the nation in campaign spending during this period because it was the location of President Obama's headquarters). While this statistic does not include spending by outside groups, when considered alongside the data discussed above, it seems reasonable to conclude that if Wisconsin were not considered "up for grabs," it would not have attracted this much attention from the two major candidates.

THE FUTURE OF PRESIDENTIAL
POLITICS IN THE BADGER STATE

In this chapter, we provided insights into how Wisconsin has changed over time. The state has seen a clash of political cultures since the nineteenth century. Historically, there have been periods during which either the individualistic or moralistic political culture has appeared dominant. Yet neither has ever gone away entirely. Although Wisconsin has experienced periods in which one political party dominated, it is now safe to say that the state has been consistently competitive in the contemporary era. Voters have clearly shown that they are willing to elect candidates who come from very different parties and ideological positions. Although the Democratic presidential candidate has won the state in the last 7 elections, presidential candidates in both parties have certainly viewed Wisconsin as competitive in recent years. Indeed, data from 2012 on campaign offices, candidate visits, and campaign spending illustrate the high level of attention given to the state by both President Obama and Governor Romney.

As this is being written, in April 2015, Governor Scott Walker is gearing up for a likely presidential run. Walker's political style and the nature of his major policy accomplishments illustrates how just how closely divided Wisconsin remains in the contemporary period. When first elected in 2010, Walker did not run on the issue of ending collective bargaining for public workers. Moreover, fact checkers found that few of the specifics of his far-reaching 2011 budget bill (including, of course, the new restrictive rules on collective bargaining for public workers) were even discussed by candidate Walker during the campaign (Umhoefer 2011). Further, the right-to-work legislation that the governor signed in early 2015 reveals a similar, yet even more deceptive political pattern. During his first term, Governor Walker said on several occasions that right-to-work legislation was not a priority for his administration. In 2012, he even went so far as to say that: "It's not going to get to my desk. . . . I'm going to do everything in my power to make sure it isn't there because my focal point (is) private sector unions have overwhelmingly come to the table to be my partner in economic development" (Marley 2012). Yet early in 2015, Walker signed a right-to-work law, and, rather remarkably, claimed his previous comments only applied to his first term (Bice 2015).

In light of the history of labor unions in Wisconsin, it stands to reason that had Governor Walker decided to push either of the two anti-labor laws during his campaigns, he may well not have won. After all, Walker only won his initial election by a 5.5% margin, and his reelection by 5.7%, despite significantly outspending his opponents. As noted above, Wisconsin has been reliably blue in presidential elections in recent years (albeit closely contested), and is a state the Barack Obama won twice. Thus Governor Walker had to essentially use misleading tactics in order to enact significant anti-union legislation in a state that is not rabidly anti-union. Immediately upon passage, Walker trumpeted the right-to-work law in fundraising appeals and speeches gearing up for his inevitable White House run in light of the popularity of this policy with much of the Republican primary electorate, and, even more so, with major Republican donors.

Given the attention that Wisconsin received from the presidential candidates in 2012, we believe that it is unlikely that presidential campaigns will ignore the state in future elections. Wisconsin was considered a swing state in the 2004, 2008, and 2012 elections, and we suspect that it will make the list of swing states in 2016 and beyond. Given the closeness of recent elections (Kerry won Wisconsin by 0.38 percent in 2004 and Gore won Wisconsin by 0.22 percent in 2000), and the fact that slight changes in campaign strategies can potentially alter the outcome of a state (Masket 2009), we are confident that future presidential elections will be contested by the two major parties in Wisconsin.

BIBLIOGRAPHY

Bice, Daniel. (2015). Scott Walker says 2012 pledge to fight right to work applied only to first term. *Milwaukee Journal Sentinel*, 25 February.

Buenker, John D. (1988). Wisconsin as maverick, model, and microcosm. In *Heart Land: Comparative Histories of the Midwestern States*, ed. James H. Madison. Bloomington, IN: Indiana University Press.

Center for Voting and Democracy. (2012). Tracking Presidential Field Operations. http://www.fairvote.org/research-and-analysis/blog/tracking-presidential-campaign-field-operations/.

Conant, J. K. (2006). *Wisconsin Politics and Government: America's Laboratory of Democracy*. Lincoln, NE: University of Nebraska Press.

Donoghue, J. (1974). How Wisconsin voted, 1848–1972. Madison, WI: Institute of Governmental Affairs, University of Wisconsin-Extension.

Dykstra, R., & Reynolds, D. (1978). In search of Wisconsin progressivism. In *The History of American Electoral Behavior*. Eds. Joel H. Sibley, Allan G. Bogue, and William Flanigan. Princeton. Princeton University Press.

Epstein, L. (1986). *Political parties in the American mold*. Madison, WI: University of Wisconsin Press.

Marley, Patrick. (2012). Walker says he will do 'everything in my power' to prevent right-to-work bill. *Milwaukee Journal Sentinel*, 11 May.

Masket, S. (2009). Did Obama's ground game matter? The influence of local field offices during the 2008 presidential election. *Public Opinion Quarterly*, 73, 1023–1039.

Slate.com. (2012). Where is Romney Spending Ten Times More than Obama? A Map of Campaign Expenditures by State. http://www.slate.com/articles/news_and_politics/map_of_the_week/2012/10/campaign_spending_map_shows_where_obama_romney_campaigns_spend_.html.

Sundquist, J. (1983). *Dynamics of the Party System: Alignment and Realignment of Political Parties in the United States.* Washington, DC: Brookings Institution.

Umhoefer, Dave. (2011). Wisconsin Gov. Scott Walker says he campaigned on his budget repair plan, including curtailing collective bargaining. *PolitiFact Wisconsin,* 21 February. http://www.politifact.com/wisconsin/statements/2011/feb/22/scott-walker/wisconsin-gov-scott-walker-says-he-campaigned-his-/.

Washington Post. (2012). Presidential Campaign Stops: Who's Going Where? http://www.washingtonpost.com/wp-srv/special/politics/2012-presidential-campaign-visits/.

FURTHER READING

Alperin, D. and Kraus, N. (2012). Voting Restriction Politics in Minnesota and Wisconsin. *New England Journal of Political Science* 6, 2: 334–357.

Elazar, D. J. (1966). *American Federalism: A View from the States.* New York: Thomas Y. Crowell Co.

Elazar, D. J. (1970). *Cities of the Prairie.* New York: Basic Books.

Holbrook, T. M., Johnson, T., Clouse, C., and Weinschenk, A.C. (2013). Elections and Political Parties in Wisconsin. In *Wisconsin Government and Politics,* 10th edition, Editor Thomas M. Holbrook. McGraw Hill.

Nichols, J. (2012). *Uprising: How Wisconsin Renewed the Politics of Protest, from Madison to Wall Street.* New York: Nation Books.

Phelps, C. (2011). The Wisconsin Idea. *The Chronicle of Higher Education.* April 21. http://chronicle.com/article/The-Wisconsin-Idea/126553/.

Secter, B. (2012). Bruised-purple Wisconsin takes political beating State's near-even red-blue split fuels barrage of attack ads in tight races for Senate, president. *Chicago Tribune.* 2 November.

Stein, Jason, and Marley, P. (2013). *More than They Bargained For: Scott Walker, Unions, and the Fight for Wisconsin.* Madison, WI: University of Wisconsin Press.

Unger, N. C. (2008). *Fighting Bob La Follette: The Righteous Reformer.* Madison, WI: Wisconsin Historical Society Press.

Walker, Scott, with Marc Thiessen. (2014). *Unintimidated: A Governor's Story and a Nation's Challenge.* New York: Sentinel.

Chapter Seven

New Mexico

A Swing State No Longer?

Donald W. Beachler

NEW MEXICO IN AMERICAN PRESIDENTIAL POLITICS: THE LONG VIEW IN SHORT

With just five electoral votes, New Mexico might seem to be an unlikely candidate for battleground or swing state status. The comparative closeness of recent presidential campaigns and the various combinations of electoral votes that campaign strategists perceive as routes to the 270 required for an Electoral College victory have meant that all states might be contested states. States with fewer electoral votes than New Mexico such as New Hampshire (four) or a state with just one more, such as Nevada (with six electoral votes after the 2010 census), have been fiercely contested. (Like 48 states, New Mexico awards its five electoral votes to the statewide winner of the popular vote.) The candidates' assessment of the probability of winning a state, rather than number of electoral votes the state casts, is the determining factor in whether a state will be a swing state in an election, or will be relegated to the status of what George C. Edwards III, a trenchant critic of the Electoral College, calls a "spectator state" that is ignored by both major party presidential candidates (Edwards 2011).

New Mexico, with its large Hispanic and Native American populations, is in some ways one of the most peculiar American states demographically. And yet, despite its demographic distinctiveness, New Mexico has generally been an accurate indicator of the outcome of the presidential election. For the entire century it has been a state, (New Mexico attained statehood in 1912), New Mexico has been carried by the winner of the national popular vote for president except in 1976 when Jimmy Carter lost the state by 2.5 percent while winning the national popular vote by 2.1 percent.[1]

New Mexico has evolved into a swing state in many recent elections. In 2000, Al Gore won the state by just 366 votes, the narrowest popular vote margin in any state that year. (Measured by percentage of the popular vote, Gore's .06 percent victory margin in New Mexico in 2000 was a relative landslide compared to the .01 percent margin by which George W. Bush carried Florida's 25 electoral votes that same year.) In 2004, New Mexico was again the state decided by the narrowest absolute popular vote margin as George W. Bush won the state by 5,988 votes in his successful reelection bid. The state flipped from one party to the other in presidential elections between 1988 and 1992, from 2000 to 2004 and from 2004 to 2008.

In an era in which there has been seemingly endless discussion of the partisan implications of the changing demography of presidential electorates, New Mexico may be the proverbial canary in the coal mine (Beachler 2009).[2] New Mexico has the largest Hispanic population of any U.S. state, with the 2010 Census reporting that Hispanics were 46 percent of the state's population. New Mexico was the only state where Hispanics comprised a greater percentage of the population than the non-Hispanic white population, though trends would indicate California will also reach this status by 2015. New Mexico's Hispanics are unusual in that a majority of them trace their roots in the state back several generations. The Hispanic population in New Mexico has, as in the rest of the country, been increasing at a rapid rate. Between 2000 and 2010 the Hispanic population increased from 42 to 46 percent of the statewide total population. Finally, about ten percent of New Mexico's population is Native American, the second highest percentage in the country after Alaska. New Mexico's non-Hispanic white population of 40.5 percent is the second lowest in the United States after Hawaii (22.5 percent).

It will be argued in this chapter that after several elections as a swing state, New Mexico is likely to become a Democratic base state. As in many other states, non-white voters have been constituting a greater percentage of the electorate in New Mexico in recent elections and casting a greater share of their votes for the Democratic presidential nominee. The large Hispanic and Native American vote in New Mexico will keep it in the Democratic column in 2016 and beyond unless and until the current voting patterns of these two ethnic groups (especially Hispanics) shifts substantially towards the Republicans.

NEW MEXICO AND THE NATIONAL ELECTORATE

Table 7.1 compares the Democratic presidential candidates' margin of victory or defeat in the popular vote nationally and their margin of victory or defeat in the popular vote in New Mexico over the past eleven presidential elections (1972–2012) (Leip 2014). An examination of Table 7.1 indicates that in most

Table 7.1. New Mexico & the National Popular Vote in Presidential Elections, 1972–2012

	Democratic Margin Popular vote Nationally	*Democratic Margin New Mexico*	*Difference in Margin Nationally & New Mexico*
1972	−23.1	−24.5	−1.4
1976	2.0	−1.7	−3.7
1980	−10.7	−18.7	−7.4
1984	−17.1	−20.5	−3.4
1988	−7.6	−5.0	2.6
1992	5.5	8.5	3.0
1996	8.5	7.3	−1.2
2000	0.5	0	−0.5
2004	−2.5	−0.7	1.8
2008	7.3	15.2	7.9
2012	3.9	10.0	6.1

elections from 1972 to the present, Democrats did worse in New Mexico than they did in the nation as a whole. There have been a few exceptions, however. In 1988 Michael Dukakis, who emphasized his Spanish-speaking skills and chose a Texan as his running mate, lost New Mexico by a smaller percentage than his margin of defeat in the national popular vote. In his first presidential campaign in 1992, Bill Clinton carried New Mexico by 8.5 percent points while his national popular vote victory was just 5.5 percent. Clinton's margin of victory in 1992 was in all likelihood affected by the strong showing of independent presidential candidate Ross Perot who ran well in many western states. Perot's 16 percent of the vote in New Mexico was easily his weakest showing in a Mountain West state (Perot did not do well in most states with large black or Latino populations), but as in other states in the region, his candidacy appeared to harm the incumbent president George H. W. Bush more than Bill Clinton. When Perot's vote declined by about half both nationally and in New Mexico in 1996, Clinton won New Mexico by a smaller vote margin than he achieved in his national reelection victory.

It was only in the 2008 presidential election that the Democratic presidential margin in New Mexico greatly exceeded the party's national result. Barack Obama defeated Republican John McCain by 7.3 percent in the national popular vote while carrying New Mexico by 15.2 percent. This electoral disparity between New Mexico and the nation was especially notable because McCain was from the adjacent state of Arizona, had been a co-sponsor of immigration reform legislation, and was regarded as having good relations with Hispanic constituents in his state (Rohter 2008). Furthermore, Republicans had hoped that Barack Obama's weak showing among Hispanic voters in his protracted 2008 nomination battle against Hillary Clinton would continue in his general election matchup against McCain, and that Obama's perceived weakness among Hispanics would make the Republican ticket especially competitive in New Mexico and other western battleground states such as Nevada and Colorado (Todd and Gewisser 2009). McCain made an election eve visit to Roswell, in the eastern part of New Mexico, in an effort to win the state's five electoral votes. In 2012, Obama won reelection with a smaller margin of 3.9 percent of the national popular vote, however, while his margin of victory in New Mexico was also smaller than in 2008, Obama still won the state by ten percentage points.

For two consecutive elections, the popular vote margin of the Democratic candidate in New Mexico was more than double his national vote margin. Writing after the 2008 election, Chuck Todd and Sheldon Gewisser classified New Mexico as a "receding" battleground state. Todd and Gewisser predicted that Republicans would need to repair their strained relations with many Hispanic voters before they have the opportunity to successfully compete with Democrats in New Mexico in close presidential elections. (Of course, swing states are not really relevant in landslide elections) (Todd and Gewisser 2009).

The dramatic shift in New Mexico voting in 2008 and 2012 can also be seen in the swing in the margin of the vote captured by Obama in his two presidential bids compared to the swing in other states. From 2004 to 2008 the change in the margin of victory or defeat for the Democratic candidate in New Mexico was among the highest in the nation. Obama improved on Kerry's −.7 margin by 15.8 percent as he won the state by 15.1 percent of the vote.[3] Indiana, which Kerry ignored as a safe Republican state in 2004, was carried by George W. Bush by a margin of 20 points. In 2008, Obama won Indiana by the very tight margin of .1 percent, but four years later with the state regarded as out of reach for the President by both political parties, Mitt Romney carried Indiana by 11 points in a state that saw no active campaigning by either candidate. If we examine changes in margin of victory or defeat for the Democratic candidate in each state from 2004 to 2012, New Mexico's eleven point swing to the Democrats was the largest in the nation.[4]

THE CHANGING ELECTORATE IN NEW MEXICO

Whites have constituted a declining percentage of the national vote in presidential elections for several decades and this trend has been evident in New Mexico in the past four presidential elections. In 2000, when Al Gore narrowly won New Mexico's five electoral votes, whites were 59 percent of the electorate according to the exit polls conducted for the consortium of news

Table 7.2. Ethnicity & New Mexico in Presidential Voting, 2000–2012

	Latino % of the electorate	Latino Democratic	White % of Electorate	White Democratic	Other	Other Democratic
2000	32	66	59	37	5	N/A
2004	32	56	57	41	9	65
2008	41	67	50	42	8	79
2012	37	66	51	41	10	65

outlets. In 2004 similar polling pegged the white percentage of the electorate in New Mexico at 57 percent and by 2008 whites were just 50 percent of the presidential electorate. In 2012 the exit polls recorded a slight uptick and whites were reported at 51 percent of the state's electorate although polling margins of error would indicate that little importance should be placed on such a small change. Hispanics were reported as constituting 32 percent of the presidential voters in 2000 and 2004. The Hispanic share of the vote surged to 41 percent in 2008 and receded to 37 percent in 2012.

Over a somewhat longer period of time, it is clear that New Mexico's general electoral demographic trends resemble those of the rest of the United States. When George H.W. Bush carried the state by a 52–47 percent margin over Michael Dukakis in 1988, whites constituted 61 percent of the electorate. Since 1988, the decline in white electoral influence has been accompanied by a 13 percent increase in the Hispanic share of the electorate increasing from 28 percent in 1988 to 41 percent in 2008. Although as indicated, there was a decline to 37 percent in 2012, the overall trend is clear. The white portion of the electorate has declined while Hispanics play a significantly larger role in New Mexico elections.

New Mexico's African American (2.1 percent) and Asian-American (1.4 percent) populations are much lower than the national percentage. When exit polls report an "other" category it is reasonable to assume that the bulk of these voters are Native-American. The "other" category has increased from 5 percent in the 2000 presidential election to 10 percent in the 2012 election. The "other" voters have been strongly Democratic as their percentage of the state electorate has risen.

The voting patterns of Hispanic and white voters in New Mexico have closely resembled those of the national electorate in the last three presidential elections. In 2004, white voters in New Mexico were two percent more supportive of John Kerry than were whites nationally, while in 2008 they were one percent less supportive of Barack Obama than whites across the nation. When Obama's support among white voters nationally dipped to 39 percent in his successful reelection bid in 2012, he won 41 percent of the white vote in New Mexico. All of these variations are within the margin of error for the exit polls and one can say that white voting trends in New Mexico have rather closely mirrored those of whites across the country in the last three presidential elections.

There has been slightly more variation between national and state voting trends among Hispanics in recent elections, although the difference, as with whites, is not terribly great. When exit polls reported George W. Bush had performed well among Hispanics across the country, John Kerry received the support of 56 percent of Latinos in the national electorate which matched his 56 percent share in New Mexico. In New Mexico, Obama's popular vote totals among Hispanics were two percent less than his national percentage in 2008 and a full six points less in his 2012 reelection bid. In 2012, Obama's percentage of the national Hispanic vote jumped to 71 percent while exit polling indicated that he won 65 percent of the Hispanic vote in New Mexico (CNN 2012).[5]

In explaining the shifts in electoral voting patterns, Ruy Texeira and John Judis have argued that a number of demographic changes, but most especially the growth of minority voters and college-educated whites, bode well for the future of Democrats in U.S. elections (Judis and Teixeira 2004). Moreover, in a 2012 book on the politics of the Mountain West, Teixeira and William Frey argue that the two biggest demographic trends impacting New Mexico were a decline in the white working-class percentage of the electorate and a growth in the Hispanic percentage of the voting population (Frey and Teixeira 2012).

Frey and Teixeira define working-class whites by educational status rather than income. Whites of working age who have not graduated from college are classified as working-class white voters. Between 2000 and 2010, working-class whites declined from 27.6 percent of the eligible voters in New Mexico to 24 percent. Working-age whites with a college degree also declined slightly as a share of the eligible electorate from 13.8 to 13.0 percent. The minority proportion of the eligible New Mexico electorate grew by 3.9 percent. Most of the gain in voting age minority voters was among Hispanics, who increased their share of the eligible electorate from 36 to 39 percent (Frey and Teixeira 2012).

These basic changes in the composition of the state population have been to the Democrats advantage. In 2008 Obama carried the Hispanic vote in New Mexico by 69 to 30 percent margin. Obama defeated McCain by a 70 to 20 percent margin among voters who were not classified as white, African American, or Hispanic. As noted earlier, the majority of the "all other" vote is almost certainly Native American voters (CNN 2008).

There was a substantial distinction in the voting patterns of whites according to educational attainment, in New Mexico in 2008. Whites who had not graduated from college voted for McCain by a margin of 62 to 36 percent. Whites who had received at least a bachelor's degree split their votes evenly between the two candidates. New Mexico deviated from the nation with a higher percentage of white voters who were college graduates (58 percent of white voters were college graduates as opposed to 47 percent nationally), but the partisan preference pattern was similar. In New Mexico, Obama benefitted more than he did in some other states by the tendency of white voter turnout to skew by levels of education at a greater rate than it did nationally, with citizens with higher levels of education voting at much higher rates than those who had not obtained a bachelor's degree. According to exit polling, college-educated whites constituted 29 percent of the total electorate in the state in 2008 while whites who had not finished college were just 21 percent of the electorate even though they constituted nearly twice as a high a percentage of the eligible electorate. (Nationally, McCain carried white college graduates by a four percent margin, while he won among whites who had not graduated from college by an eighteen percent margin.)

REGIONAL DIVERSITY IN NEW MEXICO'S ELECTIONS

Another factor that would appear to be changing the nature of presidential politics in New Mexico is the growing and changing role of the Albuquerque metropolitan region in the state's elections. Traditionally, geographical analysis of New Mexico divided the state into three distinct regions. The largest city in the state and its environs—Albuquerque—is located in Bernalillo County. Bernalillo is by far the state's most populous county and by sheer dint of its population has always been an important factor in New Mexico politics.

LITTLE TEXAS

Much of Eastern New Mexico and parts of the southern area of the state were dubbed Little Texas, after the state which is adjacent to the region. Ranching and oil production have long been key parts of the economy of Little Texas and these economic mainstays of the region were thought to be a major reason why this part of New Mexico has to this day shared the conservative politics of West Texas. Little Texas counties have been voting for Republican presidential candidates for several decades. Writing in an early edition of the bi-annual *Almanac of American Politics*, Barone, Ujifusa, and Matthews described Little Texas in quite vivid terms, "With small cities, plenty of oil

wells, vast cattle ranches, the region is economically and politically similar
to the adjacent plains of west Texas. The oil is important here, but not as
important as the military installations. They include a couple of Air Force
bases and the Army's White Sands Missile Range, near Alamogordo, where
the first atomic bomb was detonated" (Barone, Ujifusa, and Mathews 1973,
636-37). In 2012, while losing New Mexico by a wide margin, Mitt Romney
won several counties in Little Texas with majorities of landslide proportions.

In recent elections, fast-growing Dona Ana County, part of the El Paso,
Texas Metropolitan Statistical Area, has been an exception to the Republicanism of Little Texas. Home to the city of Las Cruces and New Mexico
State University, the county had a 66.6 percent Latino population in 2010
(U.S. Census 2013). In 1980 when Dona Ana County had 96,340 residents,
the Hispanic percentage of the population was 51.1 compared to 2010 when
the Hispanic population surged to 209,333 or 66.6 percent of the population.
Dona Ana was once a bellwether county within New Mexico, voting for the
statewide winner in every presidential election since statehood except 2004
when it backed John Kerry. In 2012 Barack Obama carried Dona Ana by a
margin of 14 percent, exceeding his statewide win by more than four percent.
In the current political atmosphere in the United States it is most unlikely that
a Republican could win a county with a two-thirds Latino population that also
contains an academic community.

NORTH AND WEST:
THE LATINO AND NATIVE AMERICAN BELT

Finally, the northern and western counties in the state as well as Santa Fe
have consisted of counties with large Hispanic and/or Native American
populations. Historically, these areas have been heavily Democratic in their
politics and these trends have continued in the present era of presidential
politics. In 2012, Barack Obama won more than 70 percent of the vote in
six New Mexico counties all of which were located either north or west of
Albuquerque. In four of these counties (McKinley, Mora, Rio Arriba, and San
Miguel) the combined Hispanic and American Indian share of the population exceeded 80 percent. The two other counties that voted most heavily for
Barack Obama, Taos (62 percent Hispanic and Native American) and Santa
Fe (54.7 percent Hispanic and Native American), are also noted for large arts
and cultural communities that in much of America, tilt communities to the
Democrats. Just as Little Texas forms the core of the Second Congressional
District, which nearly always elects a Republican, the Northern and Western
regions of New Mexico constitute the core of the Third Congressional Dis-

trict which has elected a Republican representative for just a single term (in a special election) in its 32-year history.

BERNALILLO COUNTY (ALBUQUERQUE)

As Table 7.3 illustrates, over the past 30 years Bernalillo County has become more Democratic relative to the rest of the state in nearly every presidential election. The state's most populous county had a decidedly more Democratic tilt than the state as a whole in 2004 when it was 5 percent more Democratic than New Mexico's statewide electorate. In the two elections in which Barack Obama was the presidential nominee, Bernalillo County has been significantly more Democratic. In 2008 and 2012, Bernalillo County became even more Democratic leaning than the state as a whole as Barack Obama won, what was once seen as a politically balanced county, by decisive double digit margins. As the state's most populous county, casting 34.6 percent of the statewide vote in 2012, grows more Democratic only strong countervailing trends elsewhere in the state would prevent the closely divided state from trending heavily to the Democrats. (As noted, Little Texas and the rural, heavily non-Anglo counties of the Western and Northern parts of the state have been persisting in their long-standing partisan preferences for the Republicans and the Democrats, respectively.)

Bernalillo County's tilt to the Democrats has occurred while the county's population has approached majority-Hispanic status. In 1980 Hispanics constituted 36.8 percent of the Bernalillo County population. By the 2010 census, the county was 47.9 percent Hispanic and a 2013 estimate of the population by the Census Bureau put Bernalillo County's Hispanic population at 48.8

Table 7.3. Bernalillo County (Albuquerque) & the Popular Vote in New Mexico, Presidential Elections 1988–2012

	Democratic % of Popular vote in Bernalillo County	Democratic % Margin Bernalillo County	Deviation of Bernalillo democratic vote from state vote
1988	45.3	−8.3	+3.3
1992	45.3	+6.8	−1.8
1996	48.3	+5.1	+0.1
2000	48.7	2.0	2.1
2004	51.5	4.2	5.0
2008	60.0	21.3	6.1
2012	56.6	17.4	7.4

Note: The figure in Column 3 is the percentage by which the Democratic margin in Bernalillo County exceeded the Democratic margin in New Mexico as a whole.

percent (U.S. Census 2013).[6] The University of New Mexico is also in Bernalillo County and as was noted with regard to Dona Aña County, a large Hispanic population and a university in most instances give Democrats a distinct electoral advantage in a county.

Writing on the eve of the 2012 election, longtime New Mexico blogger Joe Monahan proclaimed that Bernalillo was no longer a swing county, but a Democratic county (Monahan 2012). Such a strong partisan move in a county casting a third of the state vote, if it persisted, would make it very difficult for a Republican presidential candidate to be competitive in New Mexico in a close national election.

SANTA FE COUNTY

Political and population change in Santa Fe also has had an important impact on presidential elections in New Mexico. The state capital and its eponymous county have grown at an even faster rate than the state as a whole over the past three decades. Santa Fe's population grew by 95 percent between the 1980 and 2010 census, while New Mexico's statewide population increased by 58 percent over the same period of time. Against the general pattern of New Mexico and indeed of much of the United States, Santa Fe County has seen a decline in the percentage of population that is of Hispanic descent from 55.5 to 50.6 percent from 1980 to 2010. Of course, given the near doubling of the population in just 30 years, in absolute numbers the Hispanic population has risen substantially. White migrants are an important part of the transformation of politics in Santa Fe County.

As Table 7.4 demonstrates, Santa Fe, long a Democratic county in presidential politics, has become even more strongly Democrat in recent elections.[7] In both of his presidential campaigns, Barack Obama carried Santa Fe County by margins of over fifty percent which was a considerably larger margin than his Democratic predecessors had achieved. In the past three elections, Santa Fe County presidential election results indicate that the county has become even more Democratic than New Mexico as a whole.

Santa Fe has grown as a center for the arts and is widely cited as having the second largest art market in the United States and to a lesser extent a "counter culture" community. In many ways Santa Fe is a good illustration of what some have referred to as the political self-sorting or self-segregation that occurs among much of the population (Fiorina and Abramowitz 2013).[8] That is, conservative and liberal voters move to locales where they will be joining a community of many like-minded citizens. Describing the state's politics in 2003, the *Almanac of American Politics* attributed Santa Fe's political lean-

Table 7.4. Santa Fe County & the Popular Vote in New Mexico Presidential Elections, 1988-2012

	Democratic % of vote in Santa Fe	Democratic % Margin in Santa Fe County	Deviation of Santa Fe Margin Santa Fe Margin/ statewide margin
1988	63.9	29.0	+34.0
1992	63.4	40.4	+31.8
1996	62.1	36.5	+31.5
2000	64.7	36.4	+36.5
2004	71.0	43.2	+43.9
2008	76.9	55.0	+39.8
2012	73.4	51.1	+40.0

Note: The figure in Column 3 is the percentage by which the Democratic margin in Santa Fe County exceeded the Democratic margin New Mexico as a whole.

ings in part to "liberal newcomers" (Barone and Cohen 2003, 1065). Later editions of the *Almanac* referred to the city's new residents as "affluent bohemians and hippies who have flocked to Santa Fe by the thousands" (Barone and McCutcheon 2011). Santa Fe city and county would seem to have little attraction for those who desire to reside in a culturally or politically conservative area. The Mountain West has many other locales for those who wished to live among their fellow political and cultural conservatives.

Finally, as the state capital, Santa Fe is naturally the home of many government employees who in much of the country are not inclined to view the very conservative Republican party of the Obama era very favorably. Santa Fe turned in Democratic margins larger than well-known liberal bastions with large universities and/or state capitals such as such as Dane County (Madison), Wisconsin; Washtenaw (Ann Arbor), Michigan; and Lane County (Eugene), Oregon, though it has no large institution of higher education.[9]

Santa Fe's development as a Democratic stronghold that casts a somewhat larger share of the statewide vote in recent years and was carried by the Democratic candidate by margins of more than fifty percent in 2008 and 2012, has important implications for presidential politics in the state. It is difficult to imagine how a Republican candidate would win the state while losing Santa Fe by such large margins.

2012: OBAMA'S SECOND GO ROUND

In the 2012 election Barack Obama faced a far more challenging electoral environment than he had in 2008. The economic recovery was regarded by many as tepid, the president's health plan, the Affordable Care Act, now widely dubbed Obamacare, evoked ferocious opposition in conservative circles, and Republicans had gained control of the House of Representatives in the 2010 midterm elections leading to intense partisanship in Washington. Many Republican strategists were quite confident that their nominee, former Massachusetts governor and long-time private equity executive, Mitt Romney, would defeat Obama.

Romney did, however, face the daunting task of adding at least 97 electoral votes to the 173 captured by John McCain in 2008. Naturally, Romney's strategists were especially optimistic about the nine states that George W. Bush won in 2004 that were then captured by Obama in 2008. Three of these states—Colorado, Nevada, and New Mexico—were in the Mountain West region. Obama had won each of these three states by rather decisive margins in 2008, scoring margins of 15 percent in New Mexico, 12.5 percent in Nevada and 9 percent in Colorado. These margins were larger than Obama scored in five of the other six Bush states he won in 2008 (he did carry Iowa by a margin of 9.5 percent).

Despite the impressive Obama victory margins in 2008, the Romney campaign planned to contest the three battleground states of the Mountain West. The Republican nominee's challenge in states with fast-growing Latino populations was made harder by a Republican nomination process in which Republican candidates engaged in a battle to be the most virulently opposed to immigration policies that would permit undocumented immigrants to remain in the United States. Romney famously declared that he would make life for these immigrants so miserable that they would "self-deport" (Blake 2013).

A June 2012 Gallup Poll of Hispanic voters across the nation indicated health care, and not immigration, was the issue most important to them in the upcoming presidential election. Unemployment was rated as the second most important issue by 20 percent of Hispanic voters just short of the 21 percent who chose health care. Immigration policies were fifth behind not only health care and unemployment, but also economic growth (17 percent) and the gap between rich and poor (16 percent). Despite widespread vituperative criticism of Obamacare by conservatives, and in parts of the media, seventy percent of those who listed health care as the most important issue indicated that they intended to vote for Obama, the same percentage he received from those who rated immigration as the most important issue, as did 66 percent of those who listed unemployment as the most important issue (Saad 2012). Eighty-six percent of those who listed the gap between rich and poor as the most important issue voted to reelect the president. It would appear that Barack Obama was receiving a great deal of support from Hispanic voters based on economic concerns and was even receiving a measure of support for his much maligned "Obamacare."

A September 2012 article in the *New York Times* described New Mexico as the least contested among the swing states that year. Two months before the presidential election many Republicans believed that New Mexico was out of reach for their nominee, Mitt Romney. In addition to alienating Latino voters with his harsh immigration rhetoric, Romney's infamous characterization of 47 percent of the U.S. population as indolent malingerers, craving government handouts was regarded as harmful in New Mexico, one of the nation's poorest states. The state's Republican governor Susana Martinez declined to appear at an event with Romney in August even as she was willing to campaign for him in Nevada and Florida, where Hispanic voters were regarded as important to the outcomes of those states still in play. In mid-September, the Republican National Committee withdrew key personnel from the state, essentially ceding New Mexico's five electoral votes to Obama (Santos 2012). New Mexico had been a battleground state in 2012, but it was in many ways the first to be removed from the target list of Republican strategists.

Writing after the election, *Washington Post* political reporter Dan Balz asserted that when it considered the nine states that had switched from Republican to Democrat in 2008, the Romney campaign had decided that only New Mexico was probably not worth contesting. According to Balz, Romney strategists had concluded that the Latino vote in New Mexico put the state out of reach for their candidate (Balz 2013). Later efforts by the national Republican Party to put the state back in play were limited and short lived.

NEW MEXICO: A SWING STATE NO LONGER?

The noted philosopher and baseball personality Yogi Berra once famously said that predictions are difficult, especially when they are about the future. Most social scientists have disregarded Berra's admonition to caution and intellectual modesty and attempt to prognosticate about the next election before all the votes are counted in the current presidential election. The last section of this chapter will also abandon caution and seek to make some predictions about the future of presidential politics in New Mexico.

Writing about the 2012 election, political scientist Alan Abramowitz argued that the growing ethnic diversity of the electorate and, most especially the surge in the Hispanic population, was changing the political balance in many states. Abramowitz argued that as the state with the largest Hispanic electorate, New Mexico had become a safe Democratic state, while the smaller, but significant Hispanic electorates in Colorado and Nevada had given Democrats an advantage in both states in presidential elections. If Abramowitz is correct, New Mexico would have been transformed from a quintessential swing state to a safe Democratic state in just two elections (Abramowitz 2013).

New Mexico political blogger Joe Monahan offered a similar, if blunter, assessment of the state's partisan leanings in November 2012. Monahan stated that, "New Mexico is now blue when it comes to national politics. That is until the GOP finds a way to appeal more to Hispanic and Native American voters. Yes, it is as simple as that" (Monahan 2012).

In winning reelection with 39 percent of the white vote nationally, Barack Obama became the first candidate to ever win the presidency with less than 40 percent of white voters. Obama did only marginally better with white voters in New Mexico winning 41 percent of the vote (CNN 2012).[10] The nation and New Mexico have been moving in the same direction with Democratic presidential victories provided by a growing non-white electorate that voted heavily Democratic in the last two presidential elections. With a much larger non-white electorate than the nation as a whole, New Mexico produced larger Democratic margins of victory than Barack Obama won nationally in 2008 and 2012.

The single most important factor in declaring New Mexico as a receding swing state or even a safe Democratic state in presidential elections is the assumption that the Hispanic vote will remain as heavily Democratic as it was in 2008 and 2012. From the vantage point of 2014, it is hard to imagine the GOP doing better with Hispanic voters as House Republicans steadfastly refuse to permit a vote on an immigration reform bill and assiduously seek to repeal the Affordable Care Act, which should especially benefit Hispanics, an ethnic group with a high rate of people without health insurance.

Another factor that would damage Democratic prospects in New Mexico and elsewhere in the country would be a further sharp decline in the party's percentage of the white vote. Lyndon Johnson was, of course, the last Democratic presidential candidate to actually win the white vote (exit polls indicate that Bill Clinton lost the white vote nationally by a single point in 1996). As was previously noted, Barack Obama was reelected with a historically low percentage (for the winning candidate) of the nationwide white vote. Should the Democrats' percentage of the white vote decline at a faster rate than the increase in minority voter participation, it would endanger Democratic prospects in New Mexico and many other states.

It is possible that New Mexico could become an idiosyncratic swing state in the absence of broader demographic shifts in partisan voter preference if Republican Governor Susanna Martinez were the GOP candidate for Vice-President. As a woman of Mexican-American descent, Governor Martinez might enhance Republican appeal to two constituencies that have been vital to Democratic success in recent presidential elections. (Unfortunately, New Mexico was not one of the states where an exit poll was conducted in 2014, so it is not possible to gauge Martinez's success among Hispanic voters in her reelection bid.) Elected in 2010 and reelected by an impressive 14 percent margin in 2014, Martinez has compiled a generally conservative record as governor, but she has displayed a pragmatic streak. Martinez was one of the minority of Republican governors who accepted the expansion of Medicaid for poor New Mexicans under the Affordable Care Act (ACA)/Obamacare and the state committed to establishing its own health insurance exchange in the near future (Young 2013). Martinez joined Republican governors in Arizona and Nevada, two other states with large Hispanic populations, in going against her party's adamant resistance to all aspects of Obamacare. In fact, Martinez's ambiguous stance on health care is worth considering in comparison to the vehement denunciation of the program by so many conservative Republicans. Just ten days before her 2014 reelection Martinez told a reporter that "There's [*sic*] so many issues—and that may be one of them—but I have to hope we don't get hung up on one and forget all the important issues that impact families every day" (Burns 2014).

Martinez also refused to renounce the Common Core education standards that were opposed by most conservative Republicans. Martinez criticized President Obama for ineffective leadership on immigration matters, but declined to state specific policies she would support, though the New Mexico governor did call for the GOP to adopt a more "respectful" tone on immigration matters (Burns 2014). The interesting question about a prospective Martinez candidacy would be whether she would have less appeal in her state if she were running on a Republican ticket that took the very conservative policy positions that Martinez had often declined to adopt in her gubernatorial campaigns. Repealing Obamacare is not likely to be a winning strategy in a state that has among the highest poverty rates in the country and enrolled 150,000 new patients in Medicaid during the first year Obamacare was in effect. It is worth recalling that former Massachusetts governor Mitt Romney won just 37 percent of the vote in his home state when the previously moderate governor of the liberal state ran as the conservative Republican presidential nominee in 2012.

With his very controversial 2014 executive order staying the deportation of millions of undocumented immigrants, Barack Obama raised the profile of the already controversial issue of the fate of illegal immigrants already in the United States. In the 2012 Republican presidential nominating process, the candidates competed to appear as the most zealous advocate of harsh policies toward these immigrants, with Mitt Romney famously promising to be so harsh as to induce them to "self-deport." A similar tact by the Republican presidential nominee in 2016 would make it difficult for the GOP to win more Hispanic voters in New Mexico and elsewhere in the country. As the state with the highest percentage of Hispanic voters, the negative impact of a harsh anti-immigrant tone for the GOP, in all likelihood would be most pronounced in New Mexico.

The impact of the immigration issue might be quite different if former Florida governor Jeb Bush won the Republican nomination while sticking to his position in favor of an immigration policy that is generally benign towards those who entered the country illegally. Like all segments of the population, Hispanics are not single issue voters and Bush takes orthodox conservative positions on most issues. Still, Bush, who in 2014 characterized illegal immigration as, in many cases, an act of love for one's family might do better among Hispanic voters in New Mexico and elsewhere than John McCain in 2008 and Mitt Romney in 2012.

Absent the presence of a New Mexican on the national ticket, it seems most unlikely that the Democrats would suffer substantial declines in either white or Latino votes in New Mexico without experiencing a corresponding decline in many other parts of the United States. Therefore, it would seem that if a Democratic presidential candidate were to be in difficult straits in New Mexico, it is highly likely that the Democrats would be in deep trouble across the nation. It is always worth remembering that swing states are only relevant in relatively close elections. For the foreseeable future, it would appear that in elections where the popular vote margin between the major party presidential nominees is as close or closer nationally than it was in 2012, New Mexico will be a solid Democratic state.

NOTES

1. New Mexico voted narrowly for Al Gore in 2000. This claim also assumes that John F. Kennedy is classified as the winner of the popular vote in the 1960 election. For a consideration of the 1960 election, see Edwards, 2011.

2. For an argument that Barack Obama's 2008 victory is more attributable to demographic change than the economic collapse of 2008, see Beachler, 2009.

3. Virginia was just behind New Mexico, as Obama improved on Kerry's margin by 15.5 percent as he became the first Democrat to win the state since 1964.

4. This is a conclusion based on calculations from the Dave Leip website.

5. For exit poll data on the 2012 election in New Mexico, see CNN's website.

6. For the 2013 estimates, please see the U.S. Census website.

7. Richard Nixon, in 1972, was the last Republican presidential candidate to carry Santa Fe County.

8. For a discussion of political sorting, see Fiorina and Abramowitz, 2013.

9. Barack Obama's winning margin in these three counties did not exceed the 44 percent by which he carried Dane County, Wisconsin.

10. For New Mexico data see the David Leip website. For national exit poll results, see CNN Election Center, 2012.

BIBLIOGRAPHY

Abramowitz, Alan. 2013. "Voting in a Time of Polarization: Why Obama Won and What it Means." In *Barack Obama and the New America: The 2012 Election and the Changing Face of American Politics,* edited by Larry Sabato, 45-58. Lanham, MD: Rowman Littlefield.

Balz, Dan. 2013. *Collision 2012: Obama vs. Romney and the Future of Elections in America.* New York: Viking.

Barone, Michael and Richard E. Cohen. 2003. *The Almanac of American Politics, 2004.* Washington, D.C: National Journal.

Barone, Michael and Chuck McCutcheon. 2011. *The Almanac of American Politics, 2012.* Chicago: The University of Chicago Press.

Barone, Michael, Grant Ujifusa, and Douglas Mathews. 1973. *The Almanac of American Politics, 1974.* Boston: Gambit.

Beachler, Donald W. 2009. "The Economy and Domestic Policy." In *Winning the White House 2008: Region by Region, Vote by Vote,* edited by Kevin J. McMahon, David M. Rankin, and John Kenneth White. New York: Palgrave MacMillan.

Blake, Aaron. 2013. "Priebus: Romney's Self-Deportation Comment Was 'Horrific.'" *Washington Post,* August 16. Accessed August 30, 2014. http://www.washingtonpost.com/blogs/post-politics/wp/2013/08/16/priebus-romneys-self-deportation-comment-was-horrific/.

Burns, Alexander. 2014. "Found: The First Post-Obama Republican." *Politico,* October 26. Accessed December 27, 2014. http://www.politico.com/story/2014/10/susana-martinez-new-mexico-112204.html.

CNN Election Center, 2008. Accessed September 14, 2014. http://www.cnn.com/ELECTION/2008/results/polls/#USP00p1.

CNN Election, 2012 New Mexico. Accessed December 23, 2014. http://www.cnn.com/election/2012/results/state/NM/president#exit-polls.

Edwards III, George C. 2011. *Why the Electoral College is Bad for America, Second Edition.* New Haven: Yale University Press.

Fiorina, Morris P. and Alan I. Abramowitz. 2013. "Polarized or Sorted: Just What's Wrong with our Politics Anyway?" *The American Interest,* March 11. Accessed September 20, 2014. http://www.the-american-interest.com/articles/2013/03/11/polarized-or-sorted-just-whats-wrong-with-our-politics-anyway/

Frey, William H. and Ruy Teixeira. 2012. "America's New Swing Region: The Political Demography and Geography of the Mountain West." In *America's New Swing Region: Changing Politics and Demographics in the Mountain West,* edited by Ruy Teixeira. Washington: Brookings Institution Press, 2012.

Judis, John and Ruy Teixeira. 2004. *The Emerging Democratic Majority.* New York: Scribner.

Leip, Dave. *Atlas of U.S. Presidential Elections.* http://uselectionatlas.org/

Monahan, Joe. 2012. *New Mexico Politics with Joe Monahan,* November 4. Accessed July, 30, 2014. http://joemonahansnewmexico.blogspot.com/

Rohter, Larry. 2008. "McCain is Faltering among Hispanic Voters." *New York Times,* October 22. Accessed July 8, 2014. http://www.nytimes.com/2008/10/23/us/

politics/23latino.html?pagewanted=all&module=Search&mabReward=relbias%3 Ar%2C%7B%222%22%3A%22RI%3A14%22%7D&_r=0.

Saad, Lydia. 2012. "Hispanic Voters Put other Issues before Immigration." *The Gallup Poll*, June 25. Accessed July 14, 2014. http://www.gallup.com/poll/155327/ hispanic-voters-put-issues-immigration.aspx.

Santos, Fernando. 2012. "New Mexico Offers Look at U.S. Elections of the Future." *New York Times*, September 29. Accessed July 1, 2014. http://www.nytimes. com/2012/09/30/us/politics/new-mexico-gives-look-into-politics-of-future.html?p agewanted=all&module=Search&mabReward=relbias%3As%2C%5B%22RI%3A 10%22%2C%22RI%3A13%22%5D.

Todd, Chuck and Sheldon Gewisser. 2009. *How Barack Obama Won: A State-By State Guide to the Historic 2008 Presidential Election*. New York: Vintage Books.

U.S. Census, 1980. Accessed August 17, 2014. http://www2.census.gov/prod2/decennial/documents/1980/1980censusofpopu80133unse_bw.pdf.

U.S. Census, 2013. Accessed July 26, 2014. http://www.census.gov/popest/schedule. html.

Young, Jeffrey. 2013. "New Mexico Medicaid Expansion Will Move Forward, Republican Governor Susanna Martinez Announces." *The Huffington Post*, January 10. Accessed September 2, 2014. http://www.huffingtonpost.com/2013/01/09/ new-mexico-medicaid-expansion_n_2442640.html.

Chapter Eight

Contesting Colorado

The Politics of Change in the Centennial State

Robert R. Preuhs, Norman Provizer,
and Andrew Thangasamy

Longtime Colorado political observer and academic, Robert Loevy dryly views the state as "Sometimes Red and Sometimes Blue" (Loevy 2011, 19). This apt description highlights the vacillating nature of Colorado's political orientations and its centering in the swing state phenomenon. In 2008, Colorado favored Democratic presidential candidate Barack Obama by a 53.7% to 44.7% margin over Republican nominee John McCain. It marked the first time Colorado voted for a Democratic candidate in presidential elections since 1992 when Bill Clinton secured Colorado's Electoral College votes with 40.1% of the vote in a three-way race that included Reform Party candidate Ross Perot. In fact, from 1952 to 1992, Colorado favored Republican presidential candidates in all but Lyndon B. Johnson's 1964 victory over Barry Goldwater. Barack Obama's 2012 victory by a margin of just over five percent highlights two aspects of Colorado presidential politics. First, it solidified Colorado's role as a swing state that it will likely retain in the 2016 presidential elections. Second, the transformation of Colorado from a Red, or Republican, state in presidential politics to one with a purple tint is a story of both demographic trends and state-specific politics that reveals a more complex picture of its swing state status, and its potential to maintain that equilibrium over the next several presidential elections.

In what follows, we examine Colorado's evolution to swing state status. In many ways, "sometimes red, sometimes blue" aptly describes Colorado's history in presidential elections. In other ways, structural trends in demographic composition and their impact on overall voter preferences, state-specific policy issues, and long-standing preferences for divided government and increasing proportions of unaffiliated voters, suggest a narrowing of the historic long-cycles of red versus blue presidential preferences and a much more state-specific and nuanced explanation for Colorado's recently established swing state status.

We begin at the birth of the state, where Colorado may be described as born to swing presidential elections as the timing of Colorado's statehood led to a likely reversal of the fortunes of Democratic presidential candidate Samuel J. Tilden in 1876, the last time a state legislature in the U.S. chose electors without a popular vote. Then, we provide an historic overview of Colorado presidential elections and subsequently move on to the major demographic shifts in Colorado's electorate over the last several decades. Following the introduction of the historic and contemporary political and demographic context, the state's voter preferences reveal that the demographic shifts in Colorado foretell a continuing role as a swing state in presidential politics. Finally, we examine a variety of state-level political factors, in particular policy factors, that add to the state's cyclical nature of red versus blue preferences. In short, Colorado has historically witnessed long waves of alternating partisan support in presidential elections, but recent demographic shifts and state-specific policy issues have resulted in much closer elections than previously experienced in Colorado politics. We conclude with a brief discussion of the direction of Colorado's political landscape going forward and its prospects for swing state status in 2016 and beyond.

COLORADO—BORN TO SWING PRESIDENTIAL ELECTIONS

You might say that Colorado was born to swing—presidential elections that is. Of course, in order to swing the outcome of any presidential election, Colorado first had to achieve statehood, a process that itself reflected Electoral College politics. Following several failed attempts at statehood, and fearing a close presidential election in 1876, Republican officials saw Colorado as a solidly Republican state with three electoral votes that could make a world of difference in a close presidential election. Thus, following three unsuccessful attempts, a fourth Constitutional Convention in Colorado was held; and voters approved the move to become a state by an 11,381-vote margin (15,443 to 4,062) on July 1, 1876. One month later, on August 1, 14 weeks before the presidential election, Republican President Ulysses S. Grant proclaimed Colorado the nation's 38th state (Cronin and Loevy 1993, 87).

Interestingly enough, there was Democratic support for statehood in Congress as well, though, as Robert Dudley and Eric Shiraev note, if the Democrats had "simply stalled on Colorado admission, putting it off just one year" their candidate Samuel J. Tilden, not Republican Rutherford B. Hayes, would have emerged from the 1876 election as the 19th president of the United States and the most bizarre presidential election in American history would just have been a normal one (Dudley and Shiraev 2008, p. 49). The irony here is that in the mid-term election of 1874, the Democrats in the House of Representatives gained 90 seats to take control of that body, though the Republicans still had a clear majority in the Senate (Holt 2008, p. xii).

Any thoughts among Democrats that Colorado might actually vote Democratic in 1876 disappeared nine weeks after the August 1 statehood proclamation. Elections for state government occurred and they resulted in a Republican governor and a Republican state legislature. Now, with only five weeks left before the November 7th presidential vote, the decision was made to have the state legislature appoint the state's three electors without any popular vote on the matter. Those three Republican electors from the Centennial State would play a critical role in the constitutional crisis that would soon mark the nation's presidential election in its centennial year.

William Rehnquist observed that the 1876 election provided Democrats with an even chance "for the first time in 20 years" to capture the White House (2005, p. 32). When the results were tallied, it looked like the Democrats had done just that. The party's candidate Samuel J. Tilden received 254,235 more votes nationwide than his Republican opponent Rutherford B. Hayes. Additionally, in terms of the electoral vote, Tilden led Hayes 184 to 165. The only hitch was that there were 20 disputed electoral votes. Nineteen of those were in three southern states (Louisiana, South Carolina, and Florida) and one was from Oregon. Thus Tilden was one vote short of the 185 needed for a majority that would have sealed the results. To allot the 20 disputed votes, Congress formed an Election Commission of fifteen members, five each from the U.S. House, Senate, and Supreme Court. On each and every one of the 20 disputed electoral votes, the Election Commission voted 8 to 7, along party lines, in favor of Hayes. That meant that Hayes was elected with 185 electoral votes to Tilden's static 184 electoral votes.

If Colorado had not become a state three months prior to the election, then there would have been 366 electoral votes up for grabs instead of 369 votes. A majority of 366 votes is 184 which is the number Tilden had without having to decide the fate of any of the disputed votes. The election would have thus ended on time, without the need for an Election Commission and the frequently discussed political maneuvers to gain support that took place and brought Reconstruction to an end in 1877. It's hard to imagine swinging an election more than that.

After its dramatic debut on the presidential election scene in 1876, Colorado settled into a much more conventional Republican role. For example, in the 22 presidential elections that occurred from 1920 until 2004, Colorado went Democratic five times: 1932 and 1936 for Franklin D. Roosevelt; 1948 for Harry Truman; 1964 for Lyndon B. Johnson; and 1992 for Bill Clinton (aided considerably by Ross Perot's third-party candidacy). But starting in 2008, it once again approached its swing state label.

COLORADO'S PRESIDENTIAL
PREFERENCES IN HISTORIC PERSPECTIVE

The 2012 presidential election results in Colorado reflected nationwide preferences. President Barack Obama's 51.5% of Coloradans' votes came within just 0.44 percentage points above his national popular vote. The proximity of Colorado's 2012 vote total to the national average reflects the general pattern of the last three decades in which the winner in Colorado's presidential election also won the overall national election. In the eight presidential elections between 1984 and 2012, only once did a candidate win in Colorado and not win the national election. The one exception came in 1996 when Republican Bob Dole won the vote in Colorado.

This bellwether status of reflecting national outcomes may have gone unnoticed as other more populous states played prominent roles in contentious elections during this timeframe. Presidential elections in Colorado, however, display a bit more of a contrarian tendency than recent history would indicate. In the 34 presidential elections determined by popular voter since 1880, Coloradans preferred a candidate that did not win the national election in twelve contests or approximately 35% of the time. Much of these deviations from national trends occurred in the early decades of statehood and therein lies the historic basis for an independent-minded Colorado electorate. Nevertheless, recent presidential contests provide the best evidence in terms of future preferences, and thus Colorado remains a key state in terms of both national presidential outcomes, and as we shall discuss below, a competitive context for presidential elections.

While Colorado's recent consistency with national presidential outcomes highlights its bellwether status, its battleground status, where either party's candidate perceives a legitimate chance at winning Colorado's now nine, winner-take-all, Electoral College votes, emerged over the last several decades as well. Graph 8.1 presents the percentage of Colorado's popular vote for the Democratic and Republican candidates in each of the presidential elections determined by popular voter since statehood (the 1880 election to the 2012 election). Several points are noteworthy. First, while the 1952 to 2004 period certainly favored Republicans in general (and thus a Red State reputation), the longer history displays a more vacillating political orientation where a party's dominance seems to hold for two or three election periods

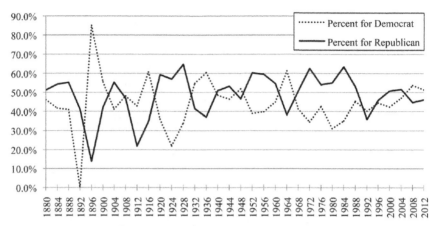

Graph 8.1. Percent of Popular Vote for Democratic and Republican Presidential Candidates in Colorado, 1880–2012.

and then reverses course. These longer wave swings, not to be confused with contemporary swing state status, mark a long history of changes in the political orientations of voters in Colorado.

Second, the contested nature of contemporary Colorado elections seems to elude much of the political history in the state. Over the entire 34 elections depicted in Graph 8.1, the average margin of victory was 16.05%—hardly reflective of close contests. The most recent period of Republican dominance (from 1952 through 1988) provided an even greater edge for the winner, with an average margin of victory of 18.25%. It is only recently, since 1992, as can be seen by the smaller amplitude and degree of separation between party candidates' votes, that presidential elections reflect the more competitive status that is required of a battleground state and thus approaches the 5% margin this volume employs to determine swing state status. The average margin of victory from 1992 through 2012 fell to 5.5%, or roughly 1/3 of the size of the average margin of victory over the previous nine presidential elections in Colorado. Colorado's swing state status can thus be confirmed, but it is not simply a result of contested elections in 2008 and 2012, but a shift from Republican dominance (and large margins) to an ebbing of Republican dominance and recent Democratic victories by fairly narrow margins. Colorado did not simply change overnight in 2008, but the emergence of contested presidential elections seems to have roots over the last two decades. It is no surprise that Colorado garnered much attention since 2008, but it should be noted that close contests began to materialize in the preceding decades.

PARTISAN AFFILIATION AND A CHANGING ELECTORATE

The shift from the four decades long advantage for Republican candidates in Colorado's presidential elections largely follows multiple changes in the composition of the electorate. The most proximate of these, however, is the shifting partisan allegiances of registered voters. As is the norm across the United States, partisan attachment ranks as the most efficient predictor of presidential voter choice. Thus, as shifts in partisan attachments, or the stated partisan affiliation of voters, occurs, so follows the fortunes of presidential nominees within the state (Erikson, Wright, and McIver 1993, chapter 8).

In Colorado, voters proclaim a partisan affiliation, or claim unaffiliated status, when registering to vote. The affiliation does not commit them to vote for a party, but with a closed caucus and primary process, affiliated voters are the only ones able to participate in these pre-general election nominee selection decisions (which are most significant in state offices given the recent front-loading of the presidential nominating process). The Secretary of State's office compiles and releases figures on voter registration by party on a monthly basis.

Graph 8.2 depicts the yearly partisan affiliation of registered voters as of January of each year, from 2004 to 2014. The period offers a glimpse into the changing dynamics of the partisan makeup of Colorado's voters as well as covering the shift from Republican presidential victories (the last in 2004) to Democratic victories (in 2008 and 2012). The electorate has long been fairly divided and highly independent in terms of party affiliation. This ten-year period highlights several important changes occurring in the electorate that help emphasize both the shift away from Colorado's Republican dominance and its centering as a swing state. First, note that as recently as 2004, Republicans held a seven point voter registration advantage over Democrats. The 37% to 30% advantage translated into a general disposition toward Republican presidential candidates, as well as a *prima facia* case for continued GOP victories in both national and state election contests. Moreover, Democratic voters were outnumbered by unaffiliated voters during this year, and thus Democratic candidates needed to not only mobilize co-partisans, but also move non-partisans toward a Democratic vote for a chance to win statewide elections. The Democrats had done so with some success in gubernatorial elections, and given the splits in presidential election votes presented in Graph 8.1, were able to capture some unaffiliated voters in presidential choices as well. However, the seven point advantage for the GOP meant that even if Democratic candidates swayed 55% of the 32% of voters who registered as unaffiliated, they would still only garner about 48% of the vote. In fact, if partisanship perfectly predicted presidential voter preference (all Democrats

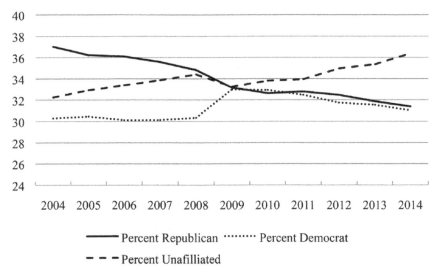

Graph 8.2. Partisan Affiliation of Registered Voters in Colorado, 2004 to 2014.

voted Democratic and Republicans voted for the Republican candidate), the Democrats would have to convince about 64% of unaffiliated voters to vote for the Democratic candidate to win the election (under the assumption that the affiliation of actual voters reflected the affiliation of registered voters—an assumption that gives the Democrats a generous starting point). In short, in 2004, the voter registration rolls favored Republican presidential candidates. The almost six percent reelection victory of George W. Bush in Colorado's election of that year confirmed this advantage, and the margin closely approximated by the seven point GOP advantage in partisan affiliation.

The political landscape changed by 2008. Measured just two months after the election in January 2009 (and thus reflecting the buildup of support and dynamics of voter affiliation shifts through the 2008 election), Republicans made up just 33.15 percent of registered voters—a drop of almost four percentage points from January 2004. Democratic affiliation rose as a percentage of overall registrants by about 2.75 percent, to 33%, and unaffiliated voters increased their share of registered voters by one percent (from 32.24% to 33.24%). This essentially even split between Republicans, Democrats and unaffiliated voters fundamentally altered the election calculus for 2008 and beyond. The buildup of Democratic support was a result of a massive voter registration drive that was supported by national Democratic Party and liberal non-partisan groups—efforts that paid off with the 2008 Obama victory. However, it is important to underscore these changes as the allegiances of potential voters shifted the political landscape in Colorado. Under the assumptions discussed above, rather than convincing 64% of the unaffiliated voters to support Democrats (or equivalently the GOP needing to convince 37% to support Republican candidates), this new baseline meant that the Democrats only needed to sway about 54% of unaffiliated voters. Republican candidates still held a real advantage, but the numbers were no longer so widely in their favor that a national Democratic tide (as witnessed in 2008) would be stalled in the face of an overwhelming disadvantage in partisan affiliation.

By the election of 2012, the registration landscape continued to shift. Republicans lost just over a half of a percentage of the registered voters from January 2009 to January 2013. Democrats, however, lost even more as they come off their peak of 33% in 2009 to just over 31.5%. The loss of registered voters relative to the overall electorate for both parties meant that unaffiliated voters increased their influence. In January of 2013, just over 35% of registered voters were unaffiliated, a high point for the decade. The winnowing of Republican registered voters meant that Democrats could win elections by relying on only 53% of unaffiliated voters. The unaffiliated, always a key voting block, were now solidly contestable.

The trends in voter affiliation seem to favor continued swing state status for Colorado. While each party will undoubtedly attempt to persuade and register voters to up their baseline level of support among registered voters, the continued reduction of affiliated voters and increase in unaffiliated voters suggests even closer and more hotly contested presidential races in 2016. The past is no guarantee of the future, but with unaffiliated voters accounting for just over 36% of the registered voters in Colorado in January 2014, and the major parties representing about 31% each, Democratic and Republican candidates both need to reach just over half of the unaffiliated to secure a victory.

The preferences of unaffiliated voters in Colorado matched presidential outcomes fairly closely in Colorado in 2008. Exit polls in 2008 indicated a 54/45 split favoring Obama and almost exactly the state's overall split (CNN 2008). In 2012, independent voters shifted toward the Republicans, with Mitt Romney's 49/44 split not enough to overcome a high level of Democratic mobilization (*Washington Post* 2012). This shift suggests both the need for mobilization, and the significance of Get out the Vote (GOTV) drives, but also the potential for unaffiliated voters, in aggregate, to shift party and presidential allegiances in Colorado in a relatively short time frame—a shift that seemingly followed national trends. Given the presumption that non-partisan registrants, in aggregate, are the true swing voters, Colorado will continue to experience the attention it has received as a swing state in the future as the voting pool continues to trend toward including more and more individual swing voters.

In addition, the rise in unaffiliated voters, and the equalizing of partisan attachments, suggests an explanation for why Colorado's recent presidential preferences closely match those of the nation. The large number of independents is not completely new. In fact, in their study of state-level self-identified party identification in the mid-1970s to late 1980s, Erikson, Wright and McIver found that Colorado ranked 12th in percentage of independents and 11th in terms of the margin between the percent of Republicans versus Democrats. The large proportion of unaffiliated voters, then and now, and a balance between identifiers with the major parties, would lead one to anticipate that national trends affecting the voting decisions of independent, or swing, voters is perhaps more likely to alter Colorado's overall vote totals than in other states lacking either the large contingent of independents, partisan balance in affiliated voters, or both. In short, the characteristics of Colorado's partisan composition not only lead to competitive presidential elections, but are also likely to reflect national trends as independents ebb and flow with national political tides.

DEMOGRAPHIC SHIFTS

The emergence of Colorado as a swing state over the last several decades accompanied changing demographics in the state as well. Since relative group size remains the granite foundation of how we predict and understand election outcomes, the shifting soils of Colorado's population provide some hints as to why the shift in political orientation from Red State to swing state occurred over the last several decades. Demographic shifts by no means explain all the change, but they are an important component of understanding both the dynamics of swing state politics and the future of swing state status in Colorado (Erikson, Wright and McIver 1993).

Table 8.1 presents several key aspects of Colorado's population from 1980 to 2010 and how they compare to averages based on the fifty states' demographic components. First, note that in terms of urbanization, education, income, and size of its Latino population, Colorado's population falls above the fifty-state average in each category. It remains significantly lower than average in terms of its African American population, and thus might be best termed ethnically/racially bifurcated as opposed to diverse. The 2010 demographic picture is somewhat fuzzy in terms of general patterns of voter behavior in national level contests. Its high level of urbanization and sizeable Latino population suggest a Democratic advantage. Higher incomes and a relatively small black population provide a counterbalance. Education, while related to income, is less an indicator of partisan orientation or voter prefer-

Table 8.1.   Colorado and Fifty-State Average Population Characteristics, 1980 to 2012.

	1980	1990	2000	2010
Percent Urban				
US	59	61	65.5	68.2
CO	78.3	80.4	82.8	84.7
CO as % Fifty-State Avg	132.7119	131.8033	126.4122	124.1935
Percent College				
US	16	19.7	23.8	27.5
CO	22.9	26.9	32.7	36.3
CO as % Fifty-State Avg	143.125	136.5482	137.395	132
Median Income				
US	16639	29102	41371	49880
CO	18056	30140	47203	60233
CO as % Fifty-State Avg	108.5161	103.5668	114.0968	120.7558
Percent Latino				
US	4.5	5.3	7.8	10.6
CO	12.4	12.9	17.1	20.7
CO as % Fifty-State Avg	275.5556	243.3962	219.2308	195.283
Percent Black				
US	9.2	9.5	9.9	10.3
CO	3.7	4	3.8	4
CO as % Fifty-State Avg	40.21739	42.10526	38.38384	38.83495

Source: Minnesota Population Center. National Historical Geographic Information System: Version 2.0. Minneapolis, MN: University of Minnesota 2011. Fifty-State Average calculated by the authors.

ence but suggests a level of voter sophistication that seemingly rests above the national average.

The shifts in Colorado's demographics over the four decades presented in Table 8.1, however, provide some clues to Colorado's dynamic political landscape. Colorado's urban population has increased steadily during this time period. Moreover, this increase masks the high concentration of growth in the major metropolitan region surrounding Denver and the 120-mile corridor from Fort Collins to Colorado Springs which is centered in Denver. It should be noted that great variation in political leanings emerges along this corridor (including consistently conservative Colorado Springs and the southern suburbs of Denver, and communities surrounding Fort Collins; consistently liberal Denver and Boulder; and moderate/swing counties of suburban Denver to the east, west, and north). Nevertheless, the population growth is clearly centered outside of traditionally conservative rural communities.

Latino population growth is perhaps most pronounced, increasing from about 12% of Colorado's population in 1980 to just over 20% in 2010. As others have noted, this growth comes from a variety of sources, from high native birth-rates to immigration (both documented and a significant portion of undocumented immigration from Mexico and Central/South America) (Preuhs 2015). Thus, while Latino population growth has increased, its influence is complex as the increase in eligible voters certainly does not match its overall population size. At the same time, Latinos have recently exerted significant influence in political and policy debates. These complexities are an important part of the swing state story in Colorado that is discussed in more detail below.

The last major dynamic is income growth. Along with urbanization, Colorado rests above the fifty-state average in median household income in each of the last four decades but also displayed an income growth rate that outpaced the average as well. With median incomes reported in non-adjusted dollars, the income as a percentage of the fifty-state average is the most valid measure of relative income. While 1980 witnessed a Colorado median income that fell at 108% of the fifty-state average, by 2010, typical Colorado households earned just over 120% of the fifty-state average. In other words, while always producing more income, Colorado currently provides salaries higher than the national average than in the preceding decades. Descriptions of demographic components are useful, and again, paint a picture of a state in the midst of cross-currents in terms of potential presidential preferences. Next, we turn to specific preference splits between demographic groups to better assess the underlying effect of these demographic shifts.

PRESIDENTIAL CHOICE WITHIN COLORADO'S ELECTORATE

While Colorado's changes in preferences for presidential candidates, partisan affiliation and demographic components provide a definitional basis for its swing state status in the case of the first aspect, and some hint as to why it has emerged as a swing state, in the case of the latter two, for whom different segments of Coloradans vote is an important element of understanding its emerging swing state status. It becomes a key element for drawing some predictions based on basic demographic shifts, but also highlights the potential for longer term swing state status in the absence of consistent or growing orientations towards one party's candidate or the other's.

With this end goal in mind, Table 8.2 presents the results of an average of key polls taken during and after the presidential elections of 2008 and 2012. Polling sources are discussed in the note below the graph, but it is useful to underscore that the values presented are averages across two or more state-wide polls which should provide some additional level of validity and accuracy over a single poll. Nevertheless, given the inherent random sampling

Table 8.2. Exit Polling of Colorado Presidential Preferences and Margins by Group, 2008, 2012 and Change from 2008 to 2012.

	2008			2012			Change in Democratic Margin, 2008 to 2012
	Obama	McCain	2008 Democratic Margin	Obama	Romney	2012 Democratic Margin	
Actual Overall Vote	53.7	44.7	9	51.5	46.1	5.4	–3.6
Race/Ethnicity							
White	48.75	48.25	–.5	42.75	52.5	–9.75	–9.25
Hispanic	61.25	30.75	30.5	67	30.75	36.25	5.75
Age							
18-34	53	42	11	50	39.5	10.5	–.5
30-44	53	46	7	50	48	2	–5
46-64	56	42	14	51	47.5	2.5	–11.5
65+	44	53	–9	42	57	–15	–6
Education							
College Graduate	54	44	10	47.2	49.8	–2.7	–12.7
No College Degree	45	54.3	–9.3	49.8	45.5	4.3	13.6
Household Income							
<$50,000	56.3	42.3	14	56.5	40.6	16.1	2.1
$50,000+	51.9	47.5	4.4	47.9	49.3	–1.4	–5
Location							
Cities	53.5	43.5	10	56	43	13	3
Suburbs	50	48	2	50	46	4	2
Rural	51	48	3	41	55.5	–14.5	–17.5

Polling entries represent average responses across polls. Democratic Margins are the Democratic Percentage minus the Republican Percentage. Change in Democratic Margin is the Democratic Margin in 2008 minus the Democratic Margin in 2012.

Polls utilized for the 2008 averages are: Race/Ethnicity (Quinnipiac June 2008; NYT 2008; CNN 2008; Washington Post 2008); Age (Quinnipiac June 2008; NYT 2008; CNN 2008; Washington Post 2008); Education (NYT 2008; CNN 2008; Washington Post 2008); Household Income (NYT 2008; CNN 2008; Washington Post 2008); Location (NYT 2008; CNN 2008). Polls utilized for the 2012 averages are: Race (Quinnipiac October 2012; Survey USA 2012; CNN 2012; Washington Post 2012); Age (Quinnipiac October 2012; CNN 2012; Washington Post 2012); Education (Quinnipiac October 2012; Survey USA 2012; CNN 2012; Washington Post 2012); Household Income (Quinnipiac October 2012; CNN 2012; Washington Post 2012); Location (Survey USA 2012; CNN 2012).

error in any poll, as well as some variation in polling methodology, one should also take these values to be estimates, and thus group differences and trends are most valued as a way to highlight relative magnitude more than specific values. The data, caveats aside, provide meaningful insights into the nature of political conflict in Colorado and why it may continue to be a pivotal swing state in 2016.

The entries in Table 8.2 present percentage support for each of the major candidates in the 2008 and 2012 elections for Latinos and non-Latino whites, by age category, education level, household income, and rural/suburban/urban contexts. Included in the table are Democratic margins for each group in both elections (percent for the Democrat minus the percent for the Republican), as well as the change in margin, which is the 2012 Democratic margin minus the 2008 Democratic margin. These data thus provide election specific breakdowns and the direction of changing allegiances (if any) for each group between 2008 and 2012.

The 2008 election's nine point actual vote margin for Barack Obama can be attributed to fairly widespread support for his candidacy across the various demographic groups. With the exception of those over 65, and those without a college degree, support for Obama was equal to, or greater than, support for his Republican opponent, John McCain. Variation in levels of support is telling, however. Whites were evenly divided (recall the caveats above regarding the estimation procedure). Latinos, however, were much more supportive, giving Obama a 30% margin over McCain. Voters under 65 years of age tended to support Obama and McCain at about the same rate, although support was lowest among those in the 30–44-year-old age category. Higher income earners supported Obama, but the 4% split was more than three times smaller than the 14 point split among those earning less than $50,000. Those residing in cities generally supported Obama at a much greater rate than those living in suburbs or rural areas. The difference between the college educated and those without a college degree was the most striking difference, with the college educated supporting Obama by ten points, but those without supporting McCain by 10 points. Overall, however, 2008 in Colorado reflected national trends. Support for Obama came from minorities and younger (compared to 65+), more educated, poorer, and urban voters.

The presidential election of 2012 revealed some important shifts in support that foretell a continuance of contested elections in the near future. Overall, the margin of victory in Obama's reelection campaign fell by 3.6%. While Latinos, younger voters, urban/suburban voters, and poorer voters still favored Obama to a greater degree than counterparts in the remaining categories, a comparison between 2008 and 2012 uncovers important shifts in support that underscore the potential for swings in aggregate support for either parties' candidates.

The last column in Table 8.2 presents the change in Democratic margin between 2008 and 2012. It is best interpreted as the degree to which a group's preferences increased for the Democratic candidate (a positive value) or increased for the Republican (a negative value). One can see the fluid nature of Coloradans' support for a party's presidential candidate by noting both a tendency of some major sectors to track toward the Republican nominee, yet other groups seem to strengthen their existing Democratic preferences.

While Colorado's overall support for Obama fell, that shift generally reflected a narrower margin in the national election. A variety of groups among Colorado's voters seem to follow this trend. Among those whose drop in support was greater than the 3.6% overall drop, the most striking was the 17.5% shift among rural voters who favored Romney in 2012 while marginally supporting Obama in 2008. College graduates and middle-aged (46–64) voters also reduced their support by roughly 12% each. Finally, white non-Latinos shifted even further toward the Republican candidate by about 9% between the two elections.

Large shifts favoring Obama over the two elections were rare. Voters without a college education shifted support away from the Republican in 2008 (McCain polled at 54% in 2008) to favor Obama by 4 points in 2012. Obama also widened his margin among Latinos, presumably because of pushback against Republican policy positions on immigration and a mid-summer 2012 immigration policy shift in the Obama campaign, among others (Preuhs 2015). More minor and likely statistically irrelevant increases in Obama support came from the cities and suburbs, as well as the poor. However, the key take-away remains that overall support for the Democratic candidate that was the first to secure victory in Colorado since 1992 fell over four years and this drop was witnessed among large voting blocks, such as whites, the middle-aged, and higher-income earners—groups that will likely vote at higher rates than others.

Voting rates are, of course, an important factor in determining statewide election outcomes that have not been discussed thus far. After all, a rough measure of the statewide turnout would reflect the summation of the products of general group preferences, group turnout, and group size for each group. Such an exact calculation is fraught with estimation problems given the non-mutually exclusive nature of the groups, the fact that estimates with sampling errors would be multiplied by equally variable estimates, and the impossibility of capturing all the potential groups that may diverge in preferences. Nevertheless, the differences across groups with available turnout estimates in 2012 raise important considerations for subsequent elections. The U.S. Census' Current Population Survey (2012) reports that 67.5% of Colorado's voting age population (VAP) participated in the 2012 presidential election.

That number increases to 72.1% of the citizens given the large non-citizen, predominately Latino, population. Turnout rates vary substantially, however, and the trends in support reported above tend to correlate with rates. White non-Latino voters, who shifted support toward the Republican Party, turned out at rates around 75%. This compares to the overall Latino turnout of 38% (or 52% of Latino citizens). Thus, while Democrats widened their margin among Latinos, the concurrent gains by Republicans among non-Latino whites and their significantly higher turnout rates likely will forestall a shift in statewide outcomes proportionate to Latino population gains. Variation in turnout by age groups, the other major grouping reported by the Census Bureau, presents a similar conclusion. Shifting support toward Republicans among 46 to 64 year olds occurred while this group maintained voting rates about 20 points above those aged 18 to 24 and 10 points more than 25- to 44-year-olds (voting rates were 56.1% VEP for 18–24-year-olds; 66.9% for 25–44-year-olds; and 77% for 45–64-year-olds). In short, the major shifts in support toward Republicans occurred in relatively high turnout groups, and thus even with growing Latino populations, their Democratic preferences, and those of young voters, may not lead to the linear increase in Democratic support those preferences and demographic trends might portend. White non-Latinos and older voters, while only a small slice of the demographic cleavages in the state, still maintain disproportionate influence in election outcomes as they are much more likely to show up at the polls or mail in their ballots in future elections.

The victories secured in the 2008 and 2012 elections do not so clearly indicate a continuation of Democratic dominance if one considers both the starting point, direction of shifting support and group participation. The caveat, of course, is that Colorado's demographic dynamics may result in an electorate with a rather different composition in years to come and any long term prediction produces a wide margin of error. Nevertheless, three major shifts seem important.

First, while whites tended to support the Republican candidate in 2008 and to a substantially greater degree in 2012, they are likely to hold a smaller proportion of the electorate in Colorado in the years to come, even with a relatively high baseline turnout rate. Conversely, Latinos, with widening margins of support, are estimated to increase their proportion of the electorate. With just over 20% of the population in 2010 and with estimates of Latinos comprising 12–13% of the electorate in 2012 (Preuhs 2015), it is likely that the Latino population's share of the electorate will rise as it has over the last several presidential elections (from about 10% in 2004). Recognizing that predicting future outcomes from a two-election trend is a risky endeavor, it is still possible to apply some of the data to more clearly conclude if presidential elections will remain contentious in Colorado in the near term. Note that a drop in white non-Latino support for the Democratic candidate of about 10% equates to a shift of about 7% of the vote (based on a rather low estimate of white non-Latinos making up 70% of the electorate). A simultaneous increase of 6% of support for Democratic candidates by Latinos who may likely hold 14% of the electorate would only produce a 0.84% margin for the Democratic candidate. While the exact numbers will certainly vary, the idea is that even with growing support for Democratic presidential candidates, Latinos' already high levels of support and still small, but growing, proportion of the electorate may not offset increasing support for Republican candidates among non-Latino whites. In short, while Latinos can swing elections in Colorado (see Preuhs 2015), large swings from white voters in the opposite direction indicate less predictability in Colorado's electoral trajectory than might otherwise be assumed if either group's preferences were static.

The shift in support among both college educated and higher income individuals provides evidence of a second trend that solidifies Colorado's swing state status in 2016. The polling data in Table 8.2 indicate that both groups increased support for the Republican candidate between 2008 and 2012—to such a degree that both groups favored Obama in 2008 but cast their collective votes for Republican Mitt Romney in 2012. Colorado's growth in both college educated and those in higher income categories, coupled with these groups' generally higher voting participation rates (at least as indicated at the national level), suggests an increasing level of influence at the ballot box. Their willingness to shift party allegiances at the margins, however, underscores a continued level of marginal volatility in aggregate returns—these groups produce swings and likely will continue to do so.

Finally, differences in presidential preferences across geographic contexts matters as Colorado's growth is most concentrated in urban and suburban areas. Like much of the U.S., Colorado continues to experience rural population decline. Thus, while rural populations tended to support the Republican in 2012 (by a wide margin), it is the somewhat static nature of urban support (producing 10 to 13% margins) coupled with suburban support (almost even with a slight Democratic edge (a 2% and 4% margin in 2008 and 2012, respectively) that is likely to influence election outcomes. Urban areas, particularly Denver, experienced positive growth over the last decade, and urban infill continues this trend (Denver's 8.2% increase from 2010 to 2013 outpaced all larger counties in Colorado). The Denver Metropolitan Region, including several larger suburban counties, grew by 16.2% from 2000 to 2012, and the much more conservative Colorado Springs area grew by 20% during the same period (U.S. Census 2014). It is likely that the rise in urban populations will continue to favor Democratic candidates, but perhaps not to as striking a margin as suggested by the polling data. For instance, the counties with the two most populous cities in Colorado split their votes in 2012, with Denver (a combined city and county) giving 74% of their vote to Obama while Colorado Springs-based El Paso county favored Romney with 68% of their vote. Thus, as with many urban areas, the marginal direction of support in the suburbs, and not the general support of core cities, is likely to move election outcomes. With relatively small margins of victories in the surrounding suburbs in both 2008 and 2012, the tendency of suburban voters to swing elections, and continued growth in the Denver suburbs, the geographic nature of growth seems to point to continued swing state status as well.

In short, based on demographic and polling data trends, a decidedly unclear picture emerges as to where Colorado voters will place their votes in 2016 and beyond. Some trends suggest increasing Democratic support (that is, Latino and urban population growth). Other trends, such as reduced support among white non-Latinos, higher income earners, and those with a college education, point to the possibility of Republican gains. Still other more static trends, primarily the consistent swing county status of Denver suburbs, remain consistent with Colorado's swing state status. In short, the demographic arrows, pointing in different directions, tend to cross and lead to the prediction of a very close and highly contested presidential election in 2016. This thus leaves open local politics and policy, as well as national candidates and campaigns, as important marginal factors in the upcoming elections. In the next section, we examine some of the policy issues that lay a backdrop to how and why Colorado might have emerged as swing state after decades of a clear GOP tilt.

POLICY DEBATES AND
ISSUES IN SWING-STATE COLORADO

The even partisan and unaffiliated demographics in Colorado may not be enough to explain the competitive political environment in the state. After all, a solid body of research suggests that the state's citizen preferences remain static relative to other states over time regardless of demographic changes (Erikson, Wright, and McIver 1993), and thus Colorado's road to competitive state status can be explained in part by state-specific politics. Moreover, other states such as Georgia have undergone significant demographic change without changing substantially in their politics (Stolberg 2014). For demographic change to make an effect, such changes have to ripen in the sense that new residents become eligible to vote and participate politically before political changes materialize—a process of longer term change.

THE ROLE OF THE BALLOT INITIATIVE PROCESS,
CONFLICT EXPANSION, AND POLITICAL PARTICIPATION

The vibrant policy milieu that exists in Colorado is due in part to the effects of the availability of the ballot initiative process to influence policy and the surrounding noise can lead to an expansion of conflict to activate both partisans on either side and unaffiliated voters to turn out and vote. The availability of ballot initiative processes and campaigning for initiatives along with the ubiquitous presence of ballot signature gatherers presents a policy environment in Colorado that is lively and vocal. Colorado ranks third in the nation among states with ballot initiative processes in the number of ballot initiatives its citizens have placed on state-wide referendums (Smith 2011). Professionalization of the ballot initiative process in Colorado over the years means that many of these initiatives are supported by well-heeled groups and paid signature gatherers are common in populated areas of the state.

Interestingly, voter turnout rates in Colorado have climbed as the state has grown more competitive. In the 2000 presidential elections, 57.5% of eligible voters turned out to vote in Colorado. The 2002 midterms saw a dip to 46.3% of the electorate turn out to vote. By the 2004 presidential election, the voter turnout had climbed to 66.7%. The most recent election cycles in Colorado (2008, 2010, 2012) have witnessed voter turnout rates exceeding 70% of eligible voters (McDonald 2014). The increased competitiveness of Colorado elections is in part correlated with more Coloradans turning out to vote than before, while varying by group as discussed above. While several factors including better registration of voters and voter drives may help explain increased voter turnout—a key factor is the growth in vibrancy of policy debates in the state.

One function of the ballot initiative process has been to bring into the fold new Coloradans and giving them a route to greater political involvement and investment in state policy issues. The presence of the ballot initiative process may speed up the political integration of newcomers. In addition, the initiative process has been a vehicle for the transmission of populism in the state. As an outlet for bringing populist policy ideas—both on the conservative and liberal ideological spectrums to the forefront, the ballot process has heated up the competitive policy context. The issues on the ballot can have an effect of expanding the scope of conflict among Coloradans—thus activating voters who under other conditions may not be paying attention to politics. In short, the initiative process has provided a mechanism to expand conflict, expand the electorate, and thus bring the contentious nature of Colorado politics to bear on national elections. For instance, 2012's initiative to legalize marijuana brought out young voters who were more likely to support the Democratic candidate, while a 2014 ballot initiative to define life at conception mobilized some pro-life voters. The context and issues will likely affect the nature of the constituency that is affected, but multiple ballot questions certainly lead to an increase in turnout and the expansion of conflict. Given the unpredictability of the exact issues facing voters in the long term, what can be said is that the initiative process in Colorado likely bolsters the continuing competitive environment for national campaigns.

POLITICS AND POLICY IN COLORADO

Cronin and Loevy (2012) identify the following key populist issues among liberals and conservatives in the state. Among conservatives, the issues have been TABOR, term limits for state officials, no special rights for gays and lesbians, and limits on annual increases in state spending. Among progressives, populist issues have included guaranteed funds for K–12 education, legalization of medical marijuana, high stakes gambling in limited areas with tax income set aside for historic preservation and community colleges, lottery funds for open space and recreation, strict limits on lobbyists' gifts to state legislators, and strict limits on campaign contributions to state officials. Some of the more recent key policy debates in Colorado are listed below with a discussion of how they split Colorado voters along various demographic lines and potentially spilled over to increase the contested nature of Colorado presidential politics.

Gun Control

As a western state, some policy issues are more salient in Colorado than in other regions. The right to gun ownership is enshrined in the Colorado constitution and the right to bear arms was well protected in Colorado before the U.S. Supreme Court's nationalization of the 2nd amendment. Colorado has also been the site of two horrific gun-related incidents of mass violence—the 1999 Columbine shootings and the 2012 Aurora theater shooting—which elevated the gun control and gun rights issue in the state. In 2013, Colorado passed a set of stricter gun control measures which led to a successful recall vote against the Democratic State Senate President John Morse and State Senator Angela Giron. A potential recall also forced the resignation of another Democratic legislator. This was the first time state legislators were recalled by voters since the adoption of the recall in 1912.

A Quinnipiac University poll from 2013 showed that a majority of Coloradans (54%) opposed the new gun control laws and only 40% supported them

(Killough 2013). The current Democratic governor, John Hickenlooper, has had to walk a careful middle path on the gun ownership and gun rights issue in the state. Gun ownership and gun control also splits Colorado voters across regions and areas. After the passage of the 2013 gun control bills, 54 of the state's 64 elected sheriffs, mostly from rural counties, filed suit in federal court challenging the new restrictions (Moreno 2013). Gun rights advocates also successfully filled a number of seats in the state legislature in 2014, and in the same year mobilized voters to help Republican Gory Gardner defeat Democratic incumbent Mark Udall for a U.S. Senate seat. Overall, a fairly strong majority of 55% of Coloradans oppose stricter gun control, and that figure includes 61% of independents (Quinnipiac 2013). While gun rights plays a marginal role in presidential politics, the relatively strong pro-gun rights sentiment in Colorado likely plays to the Republican party's advantage in 2016.

Fracking and the Environment

As an energy-producing state, Colorado has a long history of extraction of precious minerals including silver, gold, and other minerals. The oil and gas industry contributes a sizeable chunk to Colorado's gross product, and Denver's recent economic growth spurt can in part be attributed to the industry. Fracking or the process of deep drilling to extract energy has come under criticism by environmentalists for harming air and water quality. This issue is also one fought in public in debates among public officials and advertising for and against fracking by various lobbying groups. Support for and opposition to fracking also breaks across regions and areas. Voters in smaller urban communities proximate to industry activity, such as Longmont, Fort Collins, Lafayette, and Broomfield at one point or another imposed fracking bans in place (Bartels 2014). This is an issue that splits Coloradans across urban/rural lines, but also presents a dilemma for politicians as the economic benefits are weighed against environmental concerns. While a recent poll suggests that Coloradans are equally split in terms of whether fracking policy would affect their likelihood of favoring a gubernatorial candidate, just over half support the use of fracking, and thus oil related policy issues, such as the XL pipeline, may once again favor, albeit marginally, the GOP in a national context .

Immigration

The politics of undocumented immigration is another important policy for many Coloradans. Colorado, among other states in the southwest, has seen a growth in the undocumented immigrant population and has attempted to address issues relating to this population. In summer 2006, the Republican-controlled state legislature and the Republican governor passed a series of laws that restricted access to many public services for undocumented immigrants among other things (NCSL 2006). In 2013, the Democratic-controlled state legislature and the Democratic governor passed a law to include undocumented immigrants in the in-state tuition program at state-supported institutions of higher education and also passed legislation to create a driver's license for this population group. The bill to pass in-state tuition had been introduced in the legislature on an almost yearly basis since 2001 without being passed. The contentious politics of immigration are played out in Colorado with groups on both sides of the issue fairly strong in the state.

Hispanic voters overwhelmingly favored the Democratic candidate for President in the most recent two elections (2008 and 2012) with President Obama increasing his support among this group from 61.25% in 2008 to 67% in 2012. A majority of the undocumented population is Hispanic according to a 2012 study by the U.S. Department of Homeland Security (Hoefer et al. 2011) and the rhetoric against undocumented immigrants may be leading some Latino Americans to vote for the party most sympathetic to the concerns of undocumented immigrants. This may be an issue that splits Coloradans across racial and ethnic lines with Latinos more likely to be sympathetic toward liberal policies for undocumented immigrants. The overall effect of immigration policy debates in Colorado suggests a slant toward the Democratic party as Latinos are mobilized and non-Latinos are more apathetic. President Obama's executive order in 2012 likely helped him in 2012 (Preuhs 2015), and the 2015 vote by the Republican-controlled U.S. House of Representatives to undermine Obama's 2014 orders to extend legal status should help the 2016 Democratic nominee by providing a basis for mobilization among Latino voters in Colorado.

Reproductive Rights

The politics of reproductive rights and abortion are also keenly felt in Colorado. The ballot initiative process has allowed pro-life activists to place so-called "personhood" amendments that would recognize fetuses as persons on the ballot in the past. In 2014, Colorado voters rejected an amendment to the state constitution that would have extended personhood and personhood rights to fetuses. Other such similar attempts in the past have also gone down in defeat. These efforts further charged the polarization between liberal and conservative voters. Nevertheless, strong pro-choice attack ads sponsored by the Democratic candidate and independent groups and aimed at Republican Cory Gardner's support for a national version of the amendment failed to secure a victory by incumbent Democrat Mark Udall in the 2014 U.S. Senate race. While polarizing, without visible policy movement by one party or another, it is unclear the extent to which the issue will affect presidential elections.

Taxation and Spending

Taxation and tax policy is another major area of contention in the state. Colorado voters in 1992 approved strict spending and revenue-raising limits on Colorado government through a ballot amendment called TABOR or the Taxpayers' Bill of Rights (Cronin and Loevy 2011). Anti-tax citizen initiatives have been common in Colorado reflecting the state's fiscally conservative orientation. As a consequence of spending limits due to TABOR, more progressive minded Coloradans have placed ballot initiatives in front of Coloradans to increase funding for K–12 public education. In 2013, Colorado voters soundly rejected a ballot initiative, Amendment 66, that would have more progressively restructured the state income tax and raised taxes in the process to increase funding to K–12 public education (Simpson 2013). Among the supporters of this amendment were the liberal mayor of Denver, Mayor Hancock, and the state's Democratic governor, Governor Hickenlooper. While Colorado may currently have a Democratic governor, progressive issues are not an easy sell—particularly with regard to fiscal issues. Nevertheless, Coloradans were willing to vote twice for Barack Obama who promised to raise taxes on the wealthy.

POLICY ISSUES, PROXY BATTLES, AND NATIONAL POLITICS

Each of the above issues is highly contentious among the various cross-cutting divisions of Colorado voters—rural/urban, Hispanic/non-Hispanic, income, age, and others. However, each of the above issues also reflects a nationally contentious issue—pitting Democrats against Republicans. In particular, these policy debates attract national and out-of-state partisans and entities to Colorado to fight these battles. It is likely that if national campaign themes overlap these particular policy issues that intensity of preferences among voters will increase, and thus mobilize the roughly equal in number bases of the Democratic and Republican Parties.

The mostly even demographic support for opponents and supporters of the various contentious policy matters makes outcomes on these policy debates uncertain and unpredictable—in the same way Colorado as a whole has become unpredictable in terms of its support for the Republican or Democratic candidate for President. The mix of demographics and intensity of partisan conflicts makes Colorado a proxy battleground for many national domestic policy debates. This in turn potentially plays out in presidential politics as wide-ranging groups are mobilized based on not only presidential preferences, but also as state-specific policy issues come to the fore during presidential elections. Colorado's issues thus attract national attention, mobilize voters and percolate up the ballot to affect the fortunes of presidential candidates. And, again, as a divided state on these issues, contested elections are the result.

Moreover, it may be said that specific issues tend toward opposite ends of the ideological spectrum. Fiscal issues or issues successfully framed as fiscal in nature have been more likely to cause a swing in the conservative direction while increasingly non-fiscal issues including some social issues—such as marijuana legalization and the defeat of the various personhood ballot amendments—have tended to swing in the liberal or progressive direction. This has not always been true, with Colorado voters passing a ballot initiative in 1992 titled "the Colorado No Protected Status for Sexual Orientation," also known as Amendment 2, which prohibited the extension of certain protections to GLBT individuals in the workplace and elsewhere against discrimination. This initiative was subsequently overturned by the U.S. Supreme Court in *Romer v. Evans* (1996). But in 2012, Colorado voters by a margin of 54.8% to 45.2% voted to legalize marijuana in the state (Politico 2012) and in the following year voted down Amendment 66 which would have raised taxes to improve funding for K–12 education. The trend appears to favor conservative positions on fiscal issues and liberal positions on non-fiscal issues.

THE 2014 ELECTION AND CONTINUATION OF THE STATUS QUO SWING STATE STATUS

Colorado's 2014 mid-term elections led to two conflicting narratives. On one hand, the Republican Cory Gardner unseated Democrat Mark Udall in the U.S. Senate race, Republicans won three statewide offices, and took control of the State Senate for the first time in ten years from the Democrats. The national Republican wave swept through Colorado. On the other hand, Democratic Governor John Hickenlooper defeated well-known Republican and former U.S. Representative Bob Beauprez. Democrats also held on to the State House of Representatives. Democrats staved off the national wave and retained the governor's office and thus are still able to thwart GOP efforts at any major policy shifts within the state. While these two narratives dominate a media-driven analysis, the reality is that 2014 provided an election where marginal shifts did alter outcomes, but close elections dominated and coalitions remained largely unchanged from 2012. In short, the 2014 elections underscored the status quo of highly contested elections with a nominal trend favoring the GOP.

In terms of margins, midterm elections for statewide and U.S. House elections highlight the continuing course in Colorado politics. Republican Cory Gardner defeated Democrat Mark Udall by 48.2% to 46.3%, a margin of 1.9%. Democratic Governor John Hickenlooper defeated challenger Republican Bob Beauprez 49.3% to 46%, or a margin of 3.3%. All incumbent members of the U.S. House of Representatives handily won seats with the smallest margin of victory at 9%. Issues diverged between the 2014 races and the 2012 presidential election, as well as across Senatorial and Gubernatorial races. Thus, comparisons are limited. But the margins suggest a wash in terms clear movement away from swing state status.

Levels of support for the U.S. Senate candidates across groups cannot be directly compared to previous presidential elections. Nevertheless, exit polls can illuminate the continuing nature of each of the two major parties' electoral coalitions (CBS 2014). As in the presidential elections, divides occurred across racial/ethnic categories, with white non-Latinos supporting the Republican candidate while Latinos supported the Democrat. Older voters were more likely to support the GOP than younger voters, and wealthier voters supported Republican Gardner more than those with lower incomes. Colorado may be moving nominally toward the GOP, but given Democratic wins in 2008 and 2012, and the continuing nature of demographic cleavages, it is tenuous to conclude that a massive shift occurred in 2014. The status quo dominated in many ways. The paradox is that this status quo provides a context for a high visibility contested presidential election in 2016 where tight margins may determine the next President of the United States.

CONCLUSION

Reflecting its role of swinging the 1876 election, Colorado has once again become a swing state after decades as a reliably conservative state—due in part to increasing liberalism in its politics, changing demographics, and unique policy contestation. If there is a trend in Colorado, it is liberals and Democrats have been gaining in power in recent elections for both state and national office, but there is some evidence of the limits of a liberal orientation as declining Democratic margins in 2012 and the 2014 election highlighted. Yet, Colorado continues to experience highly contentious policy debates that mobilize different sectors of the electorate. Large demographic groups seem to point to cross-currents in voting trends, and the expansion of the electorate portends even wider levels of participation among a contentious voter pool.

All of the above suggest that Colorado is likely to remain competitive, and likely more so than in the past two presidential elections, in the near to mid-term future. This is a conclusion that is difficult to counter. Colorado, like Oregon and Washington state, has moved to all-mail ballots which may increase voter turnout among partisans and the unaffiliated. Now ballots in Colorado are sent to registered voters 22 days before Election Day. Registration is available on Election Day itself for those who fail to register in advance (Wilson 2014). As voting becomes easier in Colorado, voter turnout rates are likely to see modest initial growth. It is now a three-week-long election, resulting in both earlier campaigning and heightened competition over individual votes. If the polarization among Colorado voters continues and the roughly equal partisan demographic split remains along with a substantially large unaffiliated population, then Colorado can expect to be consequential as a swing state for some time to come.

Swing state status, by definition, means elections will be close. And close elections, by definition, are hard to predict. Close elections also magnify the impact of candidate and campaign effects, as well as the national political context. Any prediction of competitive swing state elections thus comes with caveats. A reasonable conclusion seems that, all else equal, the slight shifts toward the GOP across several key voting blocs will lead to a closer margin for Democratic candidates and the opening up of the possibility for a GOP win in 2016. If the GOP oversteps their mandate in Congress, that could spur mobilization of low turnout, Democratic constituencies such as Latinos, urban voters, and the poor. Turnout among these groups would likely counter the other groups' movement toward the GOP. On the other hand, an open seat, an unpopular Democratic incumbent, or economic downturns and military missteps should hurt the incumbent party's nominee. Given its tendency to reflect national trends, such a context may push Colorado further toward a GOP victory. In the end, the voters decide. Colorado's voters just happen to be almost equally divided in terms of partisanship, with a plurality of unaffiliated voters who, at the margins, will likely once again reflect the national popular vote.

SUGGESTIONS FOR FURTHER READING

Cronin, Thomas E., and Robert D. Loevy. 2012. *Colorado Politics and Policy: Governing a Purple State*. Lincoln, NE: University of Nebraska Press.

Daum, Courtenay, Robert J. Duffy, and John A. Straayer. eds. 2011. *State of Change: Colorado Politics in the Twenty-First Century*. Boulder, CO: University Press of Colorado.

Donovan, Todd, Daniel A. Smith, and Christopher Z. Mooney. 2012. *State and Local Politics: Institutions and Reform*. New York: Cengage Press.

Erikson, Robert S., Gerald C. Wright, and John P. McIver. 1993. *Statehouse Democracy: Public Opinion and Policy in the American States*. New York: Cambridge University Press.

Issenberg, Sasha. 2013. *The Victory Lab: The Secret Science of Winning Campaigns*. New York: Broadway Books.

Lorch, Robert, and James Null. 2003. *Colorado's Government*, Eighth Edition. Colorado Springs, CO: Center for the Study of Government and the Individual.

Polsby, Nelson W., Aaron Wildavsky, Steven E. Shier, and David A. Hopkins. 2011. *Presidential Elections: Strategies and Structures of American Politics*, 13th Edition. New York: Rowman & Littlefield Publishers.

Rehnquist, William. 2005. *Centennial Crisis: The Disputed Election of 1876*. New York: Vintage Books.

Sanchez, Gabriel, ed. 2015. *The 2012 Latino Vote in Colorado*. East Lansing, MI: Michigan State University Press.

Sides, John, and Lynn Vevreck. 2014. *The Gamble: Choice and Chance in the 2012 Presidential Election*. Princeton, NJ: Princeton University Press.

BIBLIOGRAPHY

Bartels, Lynn. 2014. "Let's Make a Deal: How Colorado Came to a Fracking Compromise." *The Denver Post*, September 23. Accessed October 15, 2014. http://www.denverpost.com/election2014/ci_26394883/lets-make-deal-how-colorado-came-fracking-compromise.

CBS. 2014. *Colorado: Exit Poll for Senate Race*. Accessed January 15, 2015. http://www.cbsnews.com/elections/2014/senate/colorado/exit/.

Cillizza, Chris. 2012. "The Five Closest Swing States." *The Washington Post*, October 31. Accessed October 15, 2014. http://www.washingtonpost.com/blogs/the-fix/wp/2012/10/31/the-5-closest-swing-states/ .

CNN. 2008. *Election Center 2008: Exit Polls*. Accessed August 30, 2014. http://www.cnn.com/ELECTION/2008/results/polls/#val=COP00p3.

CNN. 2012. *2012 Election Center Exit Polls Colorado*. Accessed August 30, 2014. http://www.cnn.com/election/2012/results/state/CO/president.

Colorado Secretary of State. 2014. *Voter Registration Statistics*, various years. Accessed August, 2014. http://www.sos.state.co.us/pubs/elections/VoterRegNumbers/VoterRegNumbers.html.

Cronin, Thomas E., and Robert D. Loevy. 1993. *Colorado Politics and Government: Governing the Centennial State*. Lincoln, NE: University of Nebraska Press.

Cronin, Thomas E., and Robert D. Loevy. 2012. *Colorado Politics and Policy: Governing a Purple State*. Lincoln, NE: University of Nebraska Press.

Daum, Courtenay, Robert J. Duffy, and John A. Straayer, eds. 2011. *State of Change: Colorado Politics in the Twenty-First Century.* Boulder, CO: University Press of Colorado.

Dudley, Robert, and Eric Shiraev. 2008. *Counting Every Vote: The Most Contentious Elections in American History.* Washington, DC: Potomac Books.

Duffy, Robert J., and Kyle Saunders. 2011. "What's Going On? The Shifting Terrain of Federal Elections in Colorado." In *State of Change: Colorado Politics in the Twenty-First Century*, edited by Courtenay W. Daum, Robert J. Duffy, and John A. Straayer, 39–66. Bouder, CO: University Press of Colorado.

Erikson, Robert S., Gerald C. Wright, and John P. McIver. 1993. *Statehouse Democracy: Public Opinion and Policy in the American States.* New York: Cambridge University Press.

Hoefer, Michael, Nancy Rytina, and Bryan Baker. 2012. "Estimates of the Unauthorized Immigrant Population Residing in the United States: January 2011." *United States Department of Homeland Security.* Accessed October 1, 2014. http://www.dhs.gov/xlibrary/assets/statistics/publications/ois_ill_pe_2011.pdf.

Holt, Michael F. 2008. *By One Vote: The Disputed Presidential Election of 1876–American Presidential Elections.* Lawrence, KS: University of Kansas Press.

Killough, Ashley. 2013. "Colorado recall a proxy in national gun control debate." *CNN*, September 10. Accessed September 12, 2015. http://www.cnn.com/2013/09/10/politics/colorado-recall/.

Leip, Dave. 2014. *Dave Leip's Atlas of U.S. Presidential Elections.* Accessed Sept. 1, 2014. http://uselectionatlas.org/.

Loevy, Robert D. 2011. "Colorado: Sometimes Red and Sometimes Blue," In *State of Change: Colorado Politics in the Twenty-First Century*, edited by Courtenay W. Daum, Robert J. Duffy, and John A. Straayer, 19–38. Bouder, CO: University Press of Colorado.

Lorch, Robert, and James Null. 2003. *Colorado's Government*, Eighth Edition. Colorado Springs, CO: Center for the Study of Government and the Individual.

McDonald, Michael P. 2014. "Voter Turnout." *United States Elections Project.* Accesed September 28, 2014. http://elections.gmu.edu/voter_turnout.htm.

Minnesota Population Center. 2011. *National Historical Geographic Information System: Version 2.0.* Minneapolis, MN: University of Minnesota.

Moreno, Ivan. 2013. "Colorado Sheriffs sue over new gun restrictions," *The Denver Post*, May 16. Accessed September 14, 2014. http://www.denverpost.com/breakingnews/ci_23260210/colorado-sheriffs-suing-over-gun-control-measures.

National Conference of State Legislatures (NCSL). 2006. *2006 State Legislation Related to Immigration: Enacted and Vetoed.* Accessed September 17, 2014. http://www.ncsl.org/research/immigration/immigrant-policy-2006-state-legislation-related-t.aspx.

New York Times. 2008. *Colorado Exit Polls.* Accessed August 30, 2014. http://elections.nytimes.com/2008/results/states/exitpolls/colorado.html.

Oleaga, Michael. 2012. "2012 Election Results vs. 2008: Measuring Obama's Margin of Victory in the Swing States, from Colorado, Ohio, Pennsylvania, to Virginia." *Latinos Post*, November 8. Accessed September 12, 2014. http://www.latinospost.

com/articles/6638/20121108/2012-election-results-vs-2008-measuring-obamas. htm.

Politico. 2012. "2012 Colorado Ballot Measures Results." Accessed September 9, 2014. http://www.politico.com/2012-election/results/ballot-measures/colorado/#countySelect.

Preuhs, Robert R. 2015. "The 2012 Latino Vote in Colorado." In *Latinos and the 2012 Election*, edited by Gabriel Sanchez, 61–75. East Lansing, MI: Michigan State University Press.

Quinnipiac University. June 2008. *Battleground Soundings Poll*. Accessed August 30, 2014. http://www.washingtonpost.com/wp-srv/politics/interactives/campaign08/battleground-polls/battlegrounds_co_062508.html.

Quinnipiac University, Oct. 2012. *Presidential Swing States (CO, VA & WI)*. Accessed August 30, 2014. http://www.quinnipiac.edu/news-and-events/quinnipiac-university-poll/presidential-swing-states-(co-va-and-wi)/release-detail?ReleaseID=1804#States.

Rehnquist, William. 2005. *Centennial Crisis: The Disputed Election of 1876*. New York: Vintage Books.

Simpson, Kevin. 2013. "Amendment 66 School Tax Measure Goes Down to Defeat." *The Denver Post*, November 5. Accessed September 2, 2014. http://www.denverpost.com/breakingnews/ci_24461186/colorado-tax-school-finance-amendment-66-rejected.

Smith, Daniel. 2011. "Impact of Direct Democracy on Colorado State Politics." In *State of Change: Colorado Politics in the Twenty-First Century*, edited by Courtenay W. Daum, Robert J. Duffy, and John A. Straayer, 89–114. Bouder, CO: University Press of Colorado.

Stolberg, Sheryl Gay. 2014. "In Georgia, Politics moves past just Black and White," *New York Times*, September 19, A1.

Survey USA. 2012. *Election Poll #19856*. Accessed August 30, 2014 at: http://www.surveyusa.com/client/PollReport.aspx?g=c33f6e0a-00b5-4764-8ee2-525a01ca58b0.

U.S. Census Bureau. 2014. "State and County Quick Facts." Accessed on September 29, 2014. http://quickfacts.census.gov/qfd/states/08000.html.

U.S. Census Bureau. 2012. "Table 4b. Reported Voting and Registration, by Sex, Race and Hispanic Origin, for States: November 2012." Accessed Jan. 12, 2015. http://www.census.gov/hhes/www/socdemo/voting/.

U.S. Census Bureau. 2012. "Table 4c. Reported Voting and Registration of the Total Voting-Age Population, by Age, for States: November 2012." Accessed Jan. 12, 2015. http://www.census.gov/hhes/www/socdemo/voting/.

Washington Post. 2008. *Colorado Survey—October 2008*. Accessed August 30, 2014. http://www.washingtonpost.com/wp-srv/politics/interactives/campaign08/battleground-polls/battlegrounds_co_101408.html.

Washington Post. 2012. *Exit Polls 2012: How the vote has shifted*. Accessed August 30, 2014 at: http://www.washingtonpost.com/wp-srv/special/politics/2012-exit-polls/table.html.

Whaley, Monte. 2013. "51st State Question answered 'no' in 6 of 11 counties contemplating secession." *The Denver Post*, November 5th. Accessed September 4, 2014. http://www.denverpost.com/breakingnews/ci_24461077/11-counties-weigh-secession-from-colorado-formation-51st.

Wilson, Reid. 2014. "With a win on the line in Colorado, Democrats hope to mail it in," *The Washington Post*, September 12. Accessed September 3, 2014. http://www.washingtonpost.com/blogs/govbeat/wp/2014/09/12/with-a-win-on-the-line-in-colorado-democrats-hope-to-mail-it-in.

Chapter Nine

Swing State Politics in the Silver State

David F. Damore and Rebecca D. Gill

Perhaps no state has commanded more attention in recent election cycles than Nevada. Starting with the Democratic National Committee's (DNC) decision to place the Nevada caucuses as the third delegate-allocating event in the 2008 Democratic presidential nomination campaign, Nevada's political clout has increased exponentially. The state figured prominently in both parties' Electoral College strategies in 2008 and 2012; in between, Nevada was the site of one of the most compelling and expensive U.S. Senate races of the 2010 cycle. U.S. Senate Majority Leader Harry Reid's victory over Tea Party challenger Sharron Angle, in the face of considerable headwinds (see Damore 2011a, 2011b), demonstrated the might of the "Reid Machine." This personal political organization is most responsible for shifting Nevada from a Republican state to a Democratic-leaning state during the past decade.

Nevada is, of course, the home of casino mogul Sheldon Adelson. Adelson is one of the biggest financial contributors to Republican candidates and conservative causes in the country. His largesse makes Las Vegas a frequent destination for prominent Republican politicians and potential presidential candidates (e.g., Rucker 2014). This, in turn, has allowed Adelson to shape Republican orthodoxy on a host of issues ranging from support for Israel to opposition to legalized Internet gambling to the GOP's ongoing efforts to limit unionization and the political activities of unions. All of this adds further grist to the notion that the Silver State is the preeminent swing state in the Mountain West.

Underlying much of the recent Nevada "swing state" narrative is the sense that the state provides a compelling case study in how population growth, increased urbanization, and ethnic and racial diversification are reshaping the geography of partisan composition (Teixeira 2012). As a consequence of these dynamics, Nevada has doubled its number of Electoral College votes

193

Table 9.1.   Changes in Party of Presidential Nominee Winning Nevada's Electoral College Votes

Election Year	Party of Winner	Two-Party Margin	Switch?
1984	Republican	33.88	no
1988	Republican	20.94	no
1992	Democrat	2.63	YES*
1996	Democrat	1.02	no*
2000	Republican	3.55	YES*
2004	Republican	2.59	no
2008	Democrat	12.49	YES
2012	Democrat	6.68	no
Election Cycles:	8	Republican Wins:	4
Switched Parties:	3	Democratic Wins:	4

* Plurality Winner

since 1980. Now, instead of being viewed as a political afterthought, electoral outcomes in the state exert outsized influence on the national partisan balance, both in presidential elections and in determining majority control of the U.S. Congress.

As we detail below, Nevada's explosive growth in the past three decades transformed the state from a rural and homogenous outpost to one of the most urbanized and diverse states in the country. This is a key factor in explaining the state's present swing state reputation. Indeed, as Table 9.1 details, in many respects Nevada is the quintessential swing state. In the last eight presidential elections, the eventual Republican winner secured Nevada's Electoral College votes four times (1984, 1988, 2000, and 2004), while in four elections (1992, 1996, 2008, and 2012) the state was carried by the eventual Democratic winner. Moreover, in four of these elections (1992–2004) the margin of victory was less than five percentage points.

Yet, as the data presented in Graph 9.1 make clear, these patterns are nothing new; Nevada has *always* been a bellwether of presidential elections with a strong propensity to swing between parties. In the thirty-eight presidential elections in which the state's voters have cast ballots, Nevada's Electoral College votes have gone to the winner 82 percent of the time; in ten of those elections, the margin of victory was less than 5 percent. Nevadans have also been willing, on occasion, to buck the major parties. In 1892, the state delivered its three Electoral College votes and two-thirds of its popular vote for the Populist Party. A hundred years later, another third party candidate, Ross Perot, secured over 26 percent of the vote in the 1992 presidential election. All totaled, there are 14 instances of Nevadans switching their Electoral College votes from one party to another in successive presidential elections.

What has changed, though, is the competitiveness of the state's presidential elections. Graph 9.1 shows the margin of victory for presidential elections in Nevada dropping precipitously after 1984. Since then, the mean vote margin in presidential elections has been just over seven percentage points. Prior to that, this difference was over 19 percentage points.

In this chapter, we bring together these threads to place Nevada's present swing state status into a broader analysis of the state's political history. First, we present data on electoral outcomes from 1864 to 2014 to assess the ebbs and flows of partisan electoral strength in Nevada since the state's founding. To contextualize these data, we argue that three key periods of economic and demographic change have shaped the state's political development. In the second section, we discuss Nevada's weak party organizations. We consider how the lack of strong parties and a transient population results in political outcomes that are shaped by the broader political environment and the "personal" political organizations of a handful of powerful politicians. This is followed by a discussion of contemporary Nevada politics. Here, we highlight how population growth and demographic change have once again shifted the lines of political competition in the Silver State. The chapter concludes by speculating about Nevada's political future. Given the 2014 Republican sweep in the state and the increased proclivity of Nevadans to split their tickets, it is likely that Nevada will continue to be a partisan battleground for years to come.

EBBS AND FLOWS OF PARTISAN STRENGTH

Despite the recent attention that the state's politics have received, Nevada has not "become" a swing state. Over the course of its history, Nevada's Electoral College votes have gone to the winner of the presidential election in thirty-one of thirty-eight elections. Except for 1976, Nevadans have supported every winning presidential candidate since 1912 (see Graph 9.1). In thirteen of these elections, Nevadans voted for the Democratic candidate who would become president; in seventeen elections, the state supported the eventual Republican president. On three occasions (1884, 1892, and 1972), Nevadans failed to deliver for Democratic presidents and in four cases (1880, 1896, 1900, and 1908), Republicans won the White House without Nevada's Electoral College votes.

The data in Graph 9.1 also suggest significant variation in the margin of victory for presidential elections in the state. While the average vote margin between Republican and Democratic presidential candidates is 17 percent, these values vary from a high of 62 percent in 1896 (when Nevadans

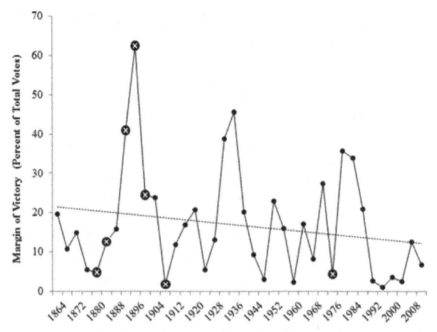

Graph 9.1. Margin of Victory for Presidential Candidate as Percentage of Total Votes in Nevada

overwhelmingly supported William Jennings Bryant) to a low of one percent in 1996 (when Bill Clinton eked out a win against Bob Dole, aided in part by nine percent of the vote going to third-party candidate Ross Perot). Moreover, and as we note at the outset, the margin between the Democratic and Republican vote shares is trending downward, suggesting that Nevada's presidential elections have become more competitive in the last three decades.

Partisan competition in Nevada has not been limited to the presidency. Rather, as the data in Graph 9.2 suggest, the electoral strength of the Democratic and Republican parties has ebbed and flowed throughout the state's history. Specifically, Graph 9.2 presents the Ceaser and Saldin (2005) Major Party Index (MPI), the Federal MPI, and the State MPI for every presidential and midterm election in Nevada's history. The MPI measures Republican strength in federal and state elections, such that larger MPI values indicate greater Republican electoral support and values of 50 indicate equal support between the parties.[1]

To place these data in context, we delineate three periods in the state's political development. Period One runs from the founding of the state until 1950. This captures an era when the state was sparsely populated and its

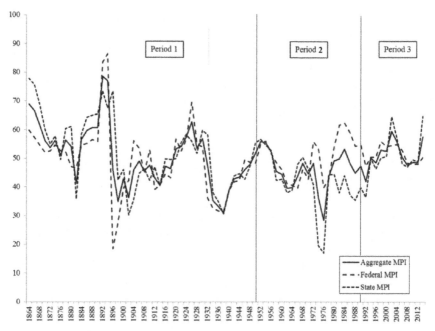

Graph 9.2. Major Party Index Values for Nevada

vitality moved in concert with the cyclical booms and busts of the mining industry. Period Two spans 1950 through 1990, when the emergence of the interstate highway system and advancements in jet air travel laid the foundation for modern Nevada as a tourist and convention destination. Period Three begins in 1990 and continues to the present. It is characterized by unprecedented growth that has created one of the most ethnically and racially diverse and urbanized states in the country.

Consistent with the political machinations that led to Nevada's statehood during the waning days of the Civil War, Nevada was initially a Republican state.[2] Soon thereafter, the Democrats began to gain strength. However, the "Free Silver" movement—the defining issue of Nevada politics throughout the end of the nineteenth century—complicated the party's ascendency. Owing to the state's rich silver and gold deposits, Nevadans adamantly supported allowing both gold and silver to be used as currency. In the 1892 presidential election, Nevada's Electoral College votes went to Populist presidential candidate and "Free Silver" champion James Weaver. Two years later, Silver Party candidates won every statewide office (see note one). By 1896, the various "Free Silver" groups united behind Democratic presidential candidates

William Jennings Bryant, and Democrats enjoyed strong support throughout the Progressive Era.

During the remainder of Period One, party support vacillated back and forth in tandem with the national political environment. There was little variation between state and federal elections in terms of party strength. The Republicans gained support during the 1920s, only to see their electoral support sink dramatically with the onset of the Great Depression. Between the wars, Republicans pointed to "the bipartisanship of the dominant mining and financial interests" as an explanation for Democratic victories (Pomeroy 2003, 241). The Republicans recovered some support during World War II.

The shifts in partisan support in Nevada during the 1890s and the 1930s are consistent with Sundquist's (1983) theory of partisan realignment. In both instances, Nevada changed from Republican to Democratic stronghold. Before each realigning event, the GOP enjoyed its two greatest moments of electoral support. The absence of individual level polling data precludes us from assessing whether these shifts were due to party conversion of existing voters or the mobilization of new voters (Andersen 1979; Campbell 1985; Erikson and Tedin 1981). However, the aggregate patterns are certainly consistent with Sundquist's (1983) thesis.

Period Two, which spans 1950 through 1990, was the era of the most sustained Democratic support in Nevada's history; this is particularly true in state elections. This point is borne out by the data presented in Table 9.2. Specifically, Table 9.2 reports the averages, standard deviations, and ranges for the MPI, Federal MPI, and State MPI values for each period. Although there is substantial variation for each measure during the three periods, only in Period Two do the average values for all of the MPI measures favor the Democrats. However, as we demonstrate in the next section, Democratic voting did not necessarily result in liberal orientations.

The Republicans in Nevada were severely punished electorally by the Watergate scandal, but the effect was largely limited to state elections. In 1974, Mike O'Callaghan received the second highest vote share of any Democratic gubernatorial candidate in the state's history. The Democrats gained an eighteen-to-two seat advantage in the Nevada Senate and a thirty-one-to-nine majority in the Assembly. However, at the federal level, Republican Paul Laxalt defeated Harry Reid by 611 votes to win reelection to the U.S. Senate. Two years later, Nevada's three Electoral College votes went to Republican Gerald Ford. This ushered in a period of increased support for Republicans in federal elections that lasted for the remainder of Period Two and into Period Three. Inspection of the average MPI values (see Table 9.2) indicates relatively small standard deviations for the elections that have occurred thus far in Period Three—another indicator of a highly competitive political environment.

Table 9.2. Summary Statistics for Major Party Indices by Time Period

	Period 1: 1864–1951	Period 2: 1950–1989	Period 3: 1990–2014
Aggregate MPI			
Mean	50.87	46.10	50.91
Std. Dev.	10.87	6.69	4.77
Minimum	31.02	28.38	41.90
Maximum	78.49	55.81	59.53
Federal MPI			
Mean	49.32	49.89	51.54
Std. Dev.	12.71	7.40	3.10
Minimum	18.35	39.38	47.25
Maximum	86.37	62.35	55.92
State MPI			
Mean	52.42	42.32	50.28
Std. Dev.	12.41	10.38	8.12
Minimum	30.27	16.98	36.55
Maximum	77.92	56.60	64.72

At the federal level, the degree to which the Republicans have an electoral advantage stems from the party's dominance in elections for the U.S. House of Representatives.[3] In presidential elections (see Table 9.1), two of the Democratic and Republicans last four wins in the state have come in closely contested races (1992–2004) including three plurality winners (1992–2000). The parties' other wins were less competitive. Ronald Reagan won handily in 1980 (+34) and 1984 (+21), while Barack Obama carried Nevada with margins of +12.5 and +6.7 in 2008 and 2012, respectively. As we discuss below, from an economic and elections perspective, Obama's 2012 victory is particularly notable given the state of Nevada's economy throughout his first term.

At the state level, Republicans have been able to offset Democratic strength in the Nevada Legislature by holding the governorship since 1998. Still, partisan electoral success in Nevada is not guaranteed for either party. This is especially true going forward, given that the fastest growing segment of the Nevada electorate is registered nonpartisans. The recent trend of Democrats winning during presidential elections, with the Republicans rebounding in midterm elections, also hints at this phenomenon.

WEAK PARTIES AND
PERSONAL POLITICAL ORGANIZATIONS

Neither of the two major parties has been able to sustain their electoral strength with any consistency. Most obviously, the data indicate clear instances when the parties have either lost or gained ground in response to the national political environment (e.g., the "Free Silver" movement, the Great Depression, Watergate). The end result is that the state's Electoral College votes tend to end up in the winning presidential candidate's column.

Yet, there are numerous examples of Nevada politicians winning elections even as their party struggled both nationally and in the state. For instance, Republican Paul Laxalt narrowly won reelection to the U.S. Senate in the wake of the Watergate scandal that nearly obliterated his party in the state, if not nationally. In 2010, Democratic Senator Harry Reid survived the Tea Party-infused Republican wave that cost his party six seats in the U.S. Senate. This win was similar to that of Richard Bryan, another Democratic U.S. Senator and former governor, who won in the strong Republican year of 1994.

This illustrates a contradiction between two features of Nevada politics: Nevada's status as a national bellwether and the ability of particular politicians to buck the strong ebbing of their party's national fortunes and avoid being swung out of office. To understand this aspect of the state's politics we examine how the interaction between weak political parties and peculiar patterns of population growth create a context that shapes the very nature of the state's political organizations. Instead of being constituted by grass roots activism or ideological cohesion, political organizations in Nevada are driven by the political acumen of a handful of the state's most successful and determined politicians. Political parties are merely the vehicles through which these ambitions have been realized.[4]

Early political science research suggested that Nevada's status as a swing state might be related to its relative youth. Midcentury observers noted that there was a complete absence of strongly organized political parties in the state. Nevada's voters have traditionally been less attached to parties and are "less stable in their voting patterns" (Wallis 1998, 164). This led some to characterize Nevada's politics as "personal" rather than partisan (Schlesinger 1955, 1128). Nevada has consistently had high levels of interparty competitiveness across a wide range of partisan elections (Bibby et al. 1990; Dawson and Robinson 1963; Holbrook and Van Dunk 1993; Schlesinger 1955).

In all, local party organizations have had a difficult time coordinating efforts. Because of the general political disinterest of Nevadans, these organizations were subject to takeover by the political machines of individual politicians (Driggs 1996). For instance, during the era of Democratic preeminence,

Senator McCarran's machine largely controlled the local party organizations. After his death, the factionalism that emerged damaged the ability of the local organizations to maintain control (Elliot 1987).

By 1980, the local Democratic Party organizations in Nevada were much weaker than their Republican counterparts (Gibson et al. 1985). Even during the periods of Democrat dominance, "the Republican Party was able to maintain a solid state organization" (Elliot 1987, 349). The Republican resurgence in the 1980s is partly a result of the efforts of the Republican National Committee (RNC) and the Republican Governors Association (RGA), which both became heavily involved in state and local politics at a time when the Democrats seemed single-mindedly focused on presidential politics (Bibby 1979). Even still, the local Republican organizations remained vulnerable to takeover by candidate machines or special interests (Driggs 1996). On the Democratic side, it was not until 2002 when Harry Reid asserted control over the party apparatus that the Nevada Democratic Party was transformed from a bastion of political infighting into an electoral force.

A common story underlies much of this analysis. Political disinterest and limited civic engagement in Nevada have allowed political elites and organized interests to exert considerable influence over the state's politics. Why Nevadans have not embraced civic culture can be found in the contours of its demography. Graph 9.3 reports data from the U.S. Census detailing population growth in the state from 1860 to 2010 and growth in the state's two most populous counties (Clark County, home to Las Vegas, and Washoe County, where Reno is located) since the counties were founded. These data are presented again in Graph 9.4, this time with each county's percentage of the population represented in an area graph.

Inspection of Graph 9.3 indicates a dearth of residents throughout much of the state's history. In contrast to Nevada's contemporary growth, in 1890, 1900, and 1920 the state recorded net population losses relative to the prior decade. As we noted earlier, these periods of population gains and losses were driven by fluctuations in the fortunes of the mining industry. Once the price of gold or silver fell and mining operations were shuttered, many simply left the state. Even during the second period of political development (Period Two: 1950–1990), Nevada remained sparsely populated. It was not until 1960 that 100,000 Nevadans cast a vote in a presidential election. The state's population did not exceed a million people until the start of Period Three (post-1990). However, since then, Nevada has been the fastest growing state in the country (see Table 9.4).

Graph 9.4 reveals the shift in the state's population from north (Washoe County) to south (Clark County). At the start of Period Two, Clark and Washoe Counties were similarly populated and each county was home to

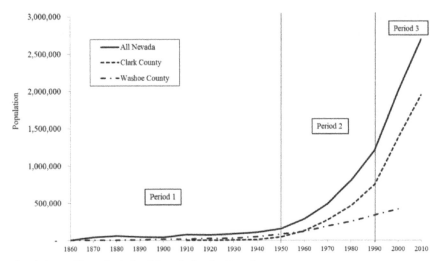

Graph 9.3. Three Periods of Population in Nevada

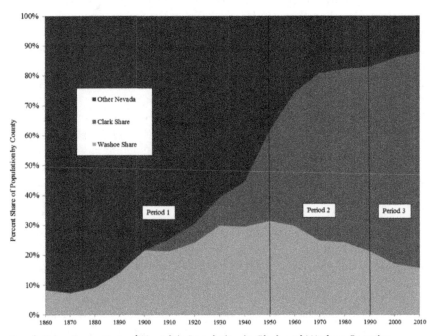

Graph 9.4. Percentage of Nevada's Population in Clark and Washoe Counties

roughly 30 percent of Nevadans. However, between 1950 and 1970 Clark County's population increased more than fivefold. By 1970, more than twice as many people lived in Clark County as compared to Washoe County. To-day, Clark County is home to nearly three out of four Nevadans. Although Washoe County's population has doubled since 1980, just 16 percent of the state's population resides in the county. More generally, the growth of the state's two urban counties has diminished the influence of Nevada's rural counties to the point that now fewer than one in eight Nevadans lives in a county other than Clark or Washoe. Nevada has just six incorporated places with populations exceeding 50,000 residents.[5] In the chapter's third section, we consider the effects that the concentration of Nevada's population in Clark County exerts on the state's politics.

As the data in Graph 9.5 make clear, the growth in Nevada's population throughout its history has largely been driven by migration into the state. Specifically, Graph 9.5 summarizes the place of origin for Nevada residents from 1900 to 2010 as reported by the U.S. Census and compiled by the *New York Times* (Aisch et al. 2014).

Residents not born in the state have always been the largest component of Nevada's population. Even in 1900, when the Census recorded the largest

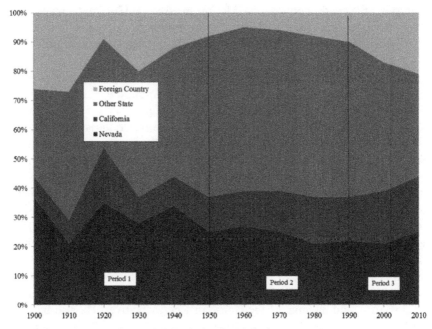

Graph 9.5. Percent of Nevada Population by Birthplace

proportion of native-born Nevadans, this group was only 37 percent of the state's population (less than 16,000 people). Today, the state is home to the smallest share of native-born residents of any state in the country (25 percent). Because Nevada's core economic sectors (i.e., construction, hospitality, and mining) rely on a workforce that requires little formal education, the state is a magnet for migrants from elsewhere seeking employment. Nevada also has a large share of foreign-born residents. They, too, are attracted to the state for its employment opportunities, particularly in the construction and hospitality sectors. In 2010, the share of the state's foreign-born population was 21 percent, slightly less than what it was in 1900 (26 percent).

These characteristics of Nevada's population mean that the composition of the electorate is unlike that of any other state. Drawing on data from the 2010 American Community Survey, Frey and Teixeira succinctly summarize this dynamic, noting that "only about 14 percent of Nevada's eligible voters were born in the state; more than one-fifth were born in California, 12 percent were foreign born, and 40 percent were born in a non-Western state. Nevada has the most non-native electorate of all the states" (2011, 45).

More broadly, the confluence of weak political institutions and a perpetually churning population anchored by a small native-born share has facilitated the development of personal political organization. This point can be nicely illustrated by the careers of the "Big Four" of the twentieth and twenty-first centuries of Nevada politics: Pat McCarran, Alan Bible, Paul Laxalt, and Harry Reid. Except for a brief interruption following McCarran's death in 1954, these four have held Nevada's Class 3 U.S. Senate seat continuously since 1933.[6]

Prior to securing their Senate seats, all four left their marks on state government. Alan Bible is largely credited with transforming the Nevada Attorney General's office from a depository for the state's legal work to an autonomous policy making institution. Under his direction, the office initiated the use of "AGOs" (Attorney General Opinions) to unilaterally interpret the meaning of Nevada's constitution and statutes. He used this to exert significant control over water policy and oversight of the gaming industry (Andrew 1998), among other policy areas. Prior to his service in the U.S. Senate, Laxalt was a lieutenant governor and then a governor, positions that led to a close friendship with former California Governor and future President Ronald Reagan. This relationship paved the way for Nevadan Frank Fahrenkopf to serve as the chair of the RNC during much of Reagan's presidency. For his part, Harry Reid has been a constant presence in Nevada politics since the late 1960s. Before his tenure in the U.S. Senate, he was elected to office as a state legislator, lieutenant governor, and member of the House of Representatives. He also held an appointed post as the Chair of the powerful Nevada Gaming Commission.

All of these politicians suffered one or more electoral defeats in their pursuits of political power. But each of these men went on to build power-ful machines that landed them at the common pinnacle of their respective careers: the U.S. Senate. That the U.S. Senate is the apex of these Nevadans' political careers is no accident. Nevadans have never had influence in the House of Representatives. Rather, for the most part, the House has been a stepping-stone to other ambitions, as evidenced by the fact that the average House tenure for a Nevada Representative is the 46th shortest at 2.71 terms; it is also by far the shortest of any Western state (Ostermeier 2012). Long careers at the state level have been unappealing, given the small size, scope, and capacity of Nevada's state government.

In the U.S. Senate, where seats are apportioned equally regardless of state population, influence accrues through longevity. Those Senators not shy about tapping the federal treasury for parochial interests can amass the power to transcend the ebbs and flows of their own party's national or local fortunes. After all, in what other body could someone literally hitchhike his way from an upbringing near a brothel in a desolate mining hamlet to become arguably the most powerful member of Congress for the better part of a decade, as Harry Reid has done?

The Nevada personal political organization is well exemplified by Senator McCarran's machine. A former member of the Nevada Legislature, district attorney, and chief justice of the Nevada Supreme Court, McCarran won his Senate seat in 1932. This was his third official attempt to become the first native-born Nevadan to serve in the chamber. Although he was elected as part of the 1932 Democratic sweep, McCarran opposed some provisions of the New Deal. Later, he would gain notoriety alongside Wisconsin's Joseph McCarthy as an ardent anti-communist and for using his perch as Chair of the Senate Judiciary Committee to investigate the administrations of his co-partisans, Franklin D. Roosevelt and Harry Truman.

An open admirer of Spanish dictator Francisco Franco, McCarran was one of the authors of the Immigration and Nationality Act of 1952 that imposed national and regional immigration quotas as a means to limit immigration from parts deemed "undesirable." The legislation passed after Truman's veto was overridden. Despite this legacy, McCarran's statue sits in the National Statuary Hall Collection inside the Capitol. He is also the namesake of one of the busiest airports in the world, Clark County's McCarran International Airport.

McCarran's political influence in Nevada stemmed from his network of "McCarran Boys." This was a bipartisan group of nascent Nevada political up-and-comers for whom McCarran secured employment in Washington, D.C., and extended entrée into the corridors of power (Edwards 1982).

Among those benefiting from McCarran's patronage were future governors, attorney generals, and those who would become the state's prominent lobbyists and attorneys.

Foremost among the "McCarran Boys," though, was Alan Bible. He got his start in McCarran's law firm and would eventually succeed McCarran in the Senate. Bible, along with Senator Howard Cannon, sought to extend the McCarran model by, for instance, continuing to find work in and around Washington for Nevada's new law school graduates. They also provided assistance to promising young politicians like Mike O'Callaghan, who would, in turn, help to secure Harry Reid a job as a Capital Police Officer while Reid completed his law degree at George Washington University. O'Callaghan would go on to be a highly popular two-term governor in the 1970s, and it was O'Callaghan who gave Harry Reid his first big political break by including him on the Democratic ticket as the candidate for lieutenant governor in 1970.

The consequences of this personal style of politics can be gleaned from the relatively weak relationship between election outcomes and the two most basic organizing principles of American politics: partisanship and ideology. Specifically, Graph 9.6 presents data summarizing the difference between Democratic and Republican voter registration and the two party margin of victory for presidential elections between 1952, when the state began reporting partisan registration figures, and 2012. Graph 9.7 presents the Berry et al. (1998) revised 1960–2010 citizen ideology series, ADA/COPE measure of state ideology, and NOMINATE measure of state government ideology (Poole 1998; Berry et al. 2010).[7] Table 9.3 summarizes the occurrences of split ticket results in statewide elections in each period of the state's political development.

Examination of Graph 9.6 reveals that, except for the 1990s when the Democrats and Republicans had a similar number of registered voters, the Democrats have held the registration advantage—in some instances by wide margins. However, in a number of presidential elections (that is, 1952, 1956, and 1968–1988), Republican presidential candidates easily carried the state, despite their party's registration disadvantage. It is only in Period Three of the state's political development that the relationship between voter registration and presidential voting tightens.

Perhaps more telling, though, is Graph 9.7, which presents the Berry et al. (1998, 2010) measures of state political ideology from 1960 to 2010, where larger values indicate increased liberalism. While the three series tend to move in tandem, there are at least two important deviations. First, Nevadans have been less liberal as compared to their elected officials, particularly in the 1960s and the mid-1970s when civil rights and social issues were salient.[8]

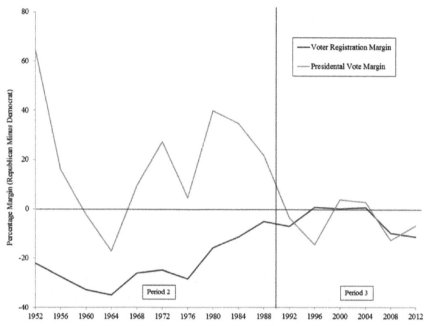

Graph 9.6.   Voter Registration & Presidential Vote Margins (Republican - Democrat)

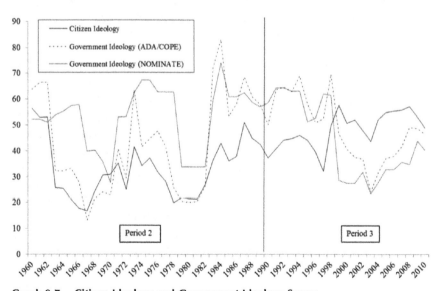

Graph 9.7.   Citizen Ideology and Government Ideology Scores

Table 9.3. Summary Information about Ticket Splitting by Period

	Period 1: 1864–1951	Period 2: 1950–1989	Period 3: 1990–2014
Races Won			
Democrats	55 (54%)	32 (63%)	12 (57%)
Republicans	42 (41%)	19 (37%)	9 (43%)
Other	5 (5%)	0 (0%)	0 (0%)
Total Races	102	51	21
Multi-Office Elections	43	19	8
Split Tickets	9 (21%)	11 (58%)	5 (63%)

This discrepancy also varies across the two measures of government ideology (see note seven) such that the NOMINATE measure of state government ideology values tend to produce more liberal estimates as compared to the ADA/COPE measure of state ideology.

Second, the data suggest that, beginning in the late 1990s, the citizenry in Nevada has become more liberal, while representation in government has become more conservative. Certainly, some of the increased liberalism among Nevadans is a function of the demographic change that we explore below. The conservative turn among the state's elected officials, who have remained much more homogenous than the state's population, suggests a counterresponse that has led to policy misalignment of a different sort than what is observed earlier in the state's history.

Some of the explanation for the dissensus undercutting the sway of party and ideology may be the mixed signals being sent by election outcomes. Table 9.3 presents, for each period, the number of election cycles where Nevadans elected candidates form different parties in statewide races (that is, president, U.S. Senate beginning in 1914, the House of Representatives through 1980, and governor). In total, there are seventy election cycles where a split ticket was a possibility. In twenty-five of these election cycles (36 percent), we observe split ticket outcomes. The percentage of multi-office elections that result in split tickets has increased in each of the three time periods. Indeed, in five of the eight multi-office elections in Period Three, Nevadans returned split tickets. To understand why, we need to examine the effects of demographic diversity and population density on electoral outcomes.

THE POLITICAL CONSEQUENCES
OF DIVERSITY AND DENSITY

The material presented thus far allows us to assess the historical context from which Nevada's present swing state moment has emerged. There is, however, one key variable that we have not addressed in detail: the impact of the state's growth on its political demography. The shifting fabric of Nevada's population is the biggest and most obvious contributor to the state's current social, economic, and political landscape. To be sure, and as Table 9.4 makes clear, many of these same changes are occurring across the United States. Specifically, Table 9.4 summarizes the differences between Nevada's growth rates and the racial and ethnic components of the state's population and those of the nation as a whole using data from the 1990, 2000, and 2010 U.S. Censuses. In 1990, except for a below average share of African Americans (a characteristic that persists through today), the demography of Nevada's population was similar to the U.S. population and in fact, Nevada had a larger proportion of whites as compared to the country as a whole. In the ensuing two decades, growth in Nevada's non-white population, particularly among its Latino and Asian components, and the resulting decrease in the state's white population, has outpaced these shifts nationally.

What distinguishes Nevada, though, is the pace at which these changes are occurring. The state grew five times faster than the country as a whole in the 1980s and 1990s and over three times as fast during the 2000s. As a consequence, Nevada has recently and quickly become incredibly diverse and urbanized, with most of these changes occurring in Southern Nevada. These factors, in turn, have reshaped the state's politics with the end result being an acceleration of many of the themes and trends detailed above.

The data presented in Graph 9.8 and 9.9 tell much of this story. These data draw on the Current Population Survey's P20 reports for the 1994–2012 elections to model the changing racial and ethnic composition of the Nevada electorate.[9] Graph 9.8 uses these data to present changes to the sizes of the white, black, Latino, and Asian shares of the Nevada electorate. Graph 9.9 presents the difference between voting share and population share, such that larger values indicate over voting by a racial or ethnic group and negative values suggest under voting relative to population share. These data, combined with those presented in Graphs 9.3 and 9.4, capture the increasing urbanization and diversification of Nevada's population.

Inspection of Graphs 9.8 and 9.9 suggests three important considerations. First, and most obviously, the white share of the Nevada electorate is decreasing. At the start of the series, whites accounted for 90 percent of the votes cast in Nevada. By 2010, this proportion shrunk to two-thirds. In contrast, the

**Table 9.4.   Comparison of Nevada and Nationwide Population Growth by Race &
Ethnicity**

	National	Nevada	Difference
1990			
Population Growth in Previous Decade	9.8%	50.1%	40.3%
White Share	71.3%	73.9%	2.6%
Latino Share	9.0%	10.4%	1.4%
Black Share	12.1%	6.6%	-5.5%
Asian Share*	2.9%	3.2%	0.3%
Other	4.7%	6.0%	1.3%
2000			
Population Growth in Previous Decade	13.2%	66.3%	53.1%
White Share	62.8%	58.7%	-4.1%
Latino Share	12.5%	19.7%	7.2%
Black Share	12.3%	6.8%	-5.5%
Asian Share*	3.7%	4.9%	1.2%
Other	8.6%	10.5%	1.9%
2010			
Population Growth in Previous Decade	9.7%	35.1%	25.4%
White Share	56.1%	54.1%	-2.0%
Latino Share	16.3%	26.5%	10.2%
Black Share	12.6%	8.1%	-4.5%
Asian Share*	5.0%	7.8%	2.8%
Other	10.0%	3.1%	-6.9%

* Includes Native Hawaiian and Pacific Islander

Latino share of the electorate has increased nearly threefold. Since 1998, the
share of Asian voters has increased by more than 400 percent. Black voters,
too, have become a larger segment of the electorate; their participation was
quite significant in 2008 and 2012 (see Figure 9.9).

Second, the trends depicted in Graph 9.8 capture the beginning of a much
larger transformation of Nevada's electorate. Given the relative youth of the
state's minority communities, in each future election, the replacement of
older white voters by younger minority voters will accelerate. This is most
obvious among the state's Latinos, which as a share of Nevada's population
increased from 10 percent in 1990 to 27 percent in 2010. Drawing on data
from the Latino Decisions 2012 Election Eve Poll, Damore (2015) reports
that a quarter of Latino voters were twenty-nine years old or younger and
that 40 percent of Latinos were first-time voters. As we discuss below, these

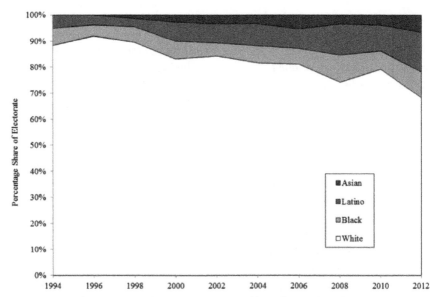

Graph 9.8.   Changing Racial and Ethnic Composition of Nevada's Electorate

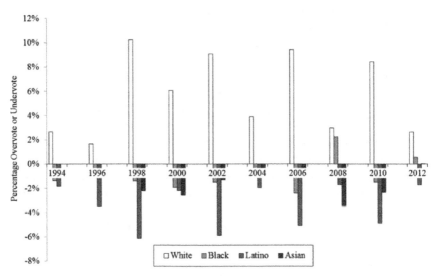

Graph 9.9.   Overvoting and Undervoting by Group Relative to Over-18 Citizen Population

trends provide a structural advantage for the Democrats and a significant challenge for Republicans.

Third, even as white voters are a decreasing segment of the Nevada electorate, these voters continue to turn out at a higher rate relative to their share of the over 18-citizen population.[10] In contrast, minority voters, except for black voters in the last two presidential elections, turn out at rates below their population share. This discrepancy is even more pronounced in midterm elections. For instance, during the 2006 midterm election, white turnout out was nine percentage points higher than its population share, while the Latino under vote was five percentage points. Even in 2010, when high Latino turnout in support of Harry Reid was consequential to Reid's victory (see Damore 2011a, 2011b), white turnout exceeded population share by nearly eight and a half points. In 2012, however, white voter turnout above population share was less than three points, while the Latino under vote relative to population share was less than two points. As in 2008, black voters turned out in excess of their population share in the 2012 election.

Yet, despite the changing contours of the state's electorate, we still observe many of the traditional elements of the state's politics at work. National electoral forces still reverberate as loud as ever as. For instance, Nevada Democrats performed quite well in 2006 and 2008, while Nevada Republicans enjoyed successes in 1994, 2002, and 2014. However, we also see longtime Nevada politicians winning even in unfavorable election environments. Examples include Richard Bryan's victory in 1994 and, more recently, Harry Reid's wins in the weak Democratic years of 2004 and in 2010. Indeed, key to Reid's 2010 campaign was its emphasis on the importance of having the "Senate majority leader" representing the state. This was a point often delivered in campaign spots by some of the dozens of high-profile "Republicans for Reid" who had been enlisted to assist with Reid's reelection effort.

Nevada's mix of personal politics and hyper-responsiveness to the national political environment has resulted in an increase in split ticket voting (see Table 9.3). In addition to the examples noted above, we can add Republican Dean Heller's U.S. Senate victory and Barack Obama's nearly seven-point victory over Mitt Romney in 2012. In 2006, in what was the best midterm election for the Democrats in decades, Republicans won U.S. Senate and gubernatorial elections in Nevada even as Democrats expanded their numbers in the Nevada Legislature.

Another constant is the limited engagement that many Nevadans have in politics. For reasons discussed above, much of this stems from the unique attributes of the state's population. Although those who are registered vote at fairly high rates, particularly in presidential elections, registration rates lag.

There also is a notable decrease in participation when the top-of-the-ticket candidates, particularly Democrats, do not invest in the state. Indeed, it was spending on voter registration and GOTV efforts, particularly in the state's Latino community, that paved the way for victories by Harry Reid in 2010 and Barack Obama in 2012.

From the perspective of traditional political science research emphasizing the reward/punishment nature of the economy, Reid and Obama's wins are rather unexpected. As Damore (2011a and 2015) details, no state was hit as hard by the Great Recession as Nevada. The state had the highest unemployment rate throughout much of this period and it was not far behind in foreclosures and bankruptcies. The ability of Democrats to win in such unfavorable contexts attests to how Nevada's changing demography—when sufficiently mobilized and engaged—can allow Democratic candidates to overcome even the most adverse political environments.

However, absent these resource infusions, the Democrats struggle. This was most obvious in 2014. After three straight election cycles that garnered significant attention and spending, turnout among registered voters decreased from 81 percent in 2012 to 46 percent in 2014. Nearly a half a million fewer votes were cast in 2014 as compared to just two years prior. Given the variation in registration and turnout among different racial and ethnic voting blocs, the composition of the Nevada midterm electorate differs significantly from what is observed in presidential elections (see note 10). In 2014, this resulted in the defeat of a "safe" Democratic incumbent in the newly created 4th House district, a Republican sweep of every statewide office on the ballot, and Republican majority control of both chambers of the Nevada Legislature.

These patterns also reinforce the state's geographic divisions, known colloquially as the "Three Nevadas" (see Damore 2012). When overall turnout dips, rural voters exert outsized influence on outcomes, owing to their higher participation rates and strong Republican inclinations. This was clearly evident in 2014, when rural voters constituted 17 percent of the electorate despite being 11 percent of the population, and the GOP romped. However, in high turnout elections when the Democrats are able to post huge margins in Southern Nevada, rural voters have little sway. Then, the only path for Republicans to win statewide elections is to carry Washoe County and hope that nonpartisan voters break their way. George W. Bush was able to do this in 2000 and 2004, while John McCain in 2008 and Romney in 2012 did not. Washoe County voters were also responsible for split ticket outcomes in 2010 (U.S. Senate and governorship) and 2012 (presidency and U.S. Senate).

IF THE PAST IS PROLOGUE . . .
NEVADA'S FUTURE IS SWINGING

In this chapter, we have examined Nevada's status as a swing state by placing the state's current politics into the context of its political development
since statehood. Besides the decades after the New Deal realignment, neither
party has been able to sustain its electoral support. Moreover, even during
much of the era of Democratic dominance (Period Two), we observe weaker
Democratic electoral support than might be expected given the party's registration advantage. It is not until the state's population begins to diversify
and further urbanize in Period Three that more liberal political orientations
emerge among its citizens. Still, even in the face of the seismic changes that
have reshaped the composition of Nevada's population in recent decades, the
state's Electoral College votes continue to flow to the eventual winner of the
presidential election even as split ticket outcomes in statewide elections have
become more common.

Moving forward, at least on paper, Nevada's changing demographics favor
the Democrats. To realize these structural advantages, however, Democrats
must continue to win the support of minority voters by large margins. Democrats will also have to do more to minimize the drop-off of in participation
among these constituencies in midterm elections when statewide constitutional offices are on the ballot. With this said, it appears that Nevada Democrats will once again benefit from additional resources and attention in 2016
as Nevada has an open U.S. Senate seat and another presidential election
looms. However, the inability of the party to recruit a quality gubernatorial
challenger and the dismal Democratic turnout in 2014 should be a cause for
concern among Democrats.

For Nevada Republicans, 2014 offered a pause in a string of elections when
the party either failed to fully capitalize on a favorable environment (that
is, 2004 and 2010) or was completely overwhelmed by the "Reid Machine"
(that is, 2008 and 2012). There also is evidence suggesting that, unlike the
party nationally, Nevada Republicans are adapting to the country's changing
political demography (Damore 2013b). During the 2013 session of the Nevada Legislature, Republicans played a constructive role in making several
policy innovations a reality: providing drivers' privilege cards for unauthorized immigrants; appropriating—for the first time in Nevada's history—state
funding for English Language Learners; and supporting increased regulation
of the *notario* industry. Most Nevada Republicans serving in Congress have
supported comprehensive immigration reform that includes a pathway to citi-
zenship. This puts Nevada's Republican politicians to the left of their national
party on immigration.

At the same time, the state's demography will continue to be a major obstacle for the Republicans. The GOP cannot sustain itself by hoping that Democratic voters stay home, as they did in 2014. Indeed, the Latino Decisions 2014 Election Eve Poll found that Governor Brian Sandoval won the largest share of the Latino vote among all Republicans in the country. He was able to increase his support among Latinos by more than 30 percentage points as compared to 2010. Yet, even in a low-turnout election and running in such a favorable political environment against only token Democratic opposition, Sandoval received less than 50 percent of the Latino vote in 2014—a telling sign of just how much work the Republicans have in front of them if they hope to remain competitive in states like Nevada.

In sum, there is little reason to suspect that Nevada's politics will look much different in the future. After a lull during the Great Recession, Nevada's population is growing again. While this growth is stimulating Nevada's dormant economy, it is further straining the state's limited infrastructure just as many Nevadans are looking for more activist and effective government. Adding further combustion to this blend is the increasing number of Nevadans who are choosing not to affiliate with either the Democratic or Republican Parties. Nearly a quarter of Nevada's registered voters are either nonpartisan or are aligned with a minor party. This suggests yet another wrinkle to the state's political landscape that is likely to complicate both parties' designs on the Silver State. Taken together, all of this will keep Nevada politics in the headlines for many election cycles to come.

ACKNOWLEDGMENTS

We are thankful to Michael Green for comments and suggestions and to Moritz Rissmann, Michael Trevathan, and Erika Masaki for assistance with data collection.

NOTES

1. As Ceaser and Saldin (2005, 248) explain, the federal component of the MPI is comprised of the Republican share of the two-party vote for the most recent election for president (25 percent) and the House of Representatives (12.5 percent) and the average Republican two-party vote share for the two most recent U.S. Senate elections (12.5 percent). The state component of the MPI is comprised of the Republican share of the two-party vote in the most recent gubernatorial election and the two-party share of seats held by the Republican Party in the upper (12.5 percent) and lower (12.5 percent) chambers of the state legislature as determined by the most recent election.

For the Federal and State MPI measures, the calculation is limited to the federal and state components, respectively, and the weight for each component is doubled. This means that, for the Federal MPI, the presidential component is 50 percent and the two houses of Congress are 25 percent each; for the State MPI, the gubernatorial component is 50 percent and the two houses of the state legislature are 25 percent each. Data for 1970–2010 were retrieved from Saldin's website (http://scholar.harvard.edu/saldin/data). Data for all other years come from *Political History of Nevada* (Parker and George 2006) and the Nevada Secretary of State's website (http://www.nvsos.gov).

There are two caveats associated with the MPI for the early years in the series presented in Graph 9.2. First, like all states, Nevada did not begin electing U.S. Senators until 1914, after the adoption of the 17th Amendment. Thus, for all years prior to 1914, the Republican share of the two-party vote for the U.S. House is weighted at 25 percent in the MPI and at 50 percent in the Federal MPI. Second, throughout the 1890s and into the first decade of the twentieth century, numerous minor party candidates held office in Nevada. This was particularly acute in the 1890s, when the Silver and Silver Democratic Parties were arguably the strongest parties in the state. For 1892 and 1894 (an election in which the Silver Party swept every statewide office), the Silver and Silver Democratic Parties are treated as distinct entities. However, in 1896, these parties coalesced behind the Democratic presidential candidate William Jennings Bryant; thus, they are treated as Democrats in that election and all subsequent elections (members of the Nevada Legislature representing other minor parties are treated as such throughout the entire series). Because the MPI measures are based upon a two party assumption, these coding decisions impact the MPI values such that the Republicans record their highest MPI values for all measures in 1892 and 1894 and their lowest Federal MPI values in 1896.

2. Abraham Lincoln admitted Nevada into the Union on October 31, 1864, a mere eight days before his reelection. However, because one of the state's electors was caught in a blizzard, Nevada registered just two Electoral College votes in 1864. In the end, Nevada's Electoral College votes had little bearing on the outcome, as Lincoln was easily reelected. The state's first member of the House of Representatives, Henry Gaither Worthington cast a key vote in favor of the 13th Amendment banning slavery. Nevada's first U.S. Senators, James Nye and William Stewart, took office on December 15, 1864, but neither voted on the passage of the 13th Amendment; it had been approved by the U.S. Senate the prior spring. Nevada was the 15th State to ratify the 13th Amendment. As one early historian argued, Nevada was "forced, almost, to don the robes of statehood to aid in the reconstruction legislation when she neither had the population nor the wealth to justify such a step" (Wren 1904, 11).

3. Republican candidate have won 22 of the 35 House elections in Nevada since 1990, while Democrats have won five of the eight U.S. Senate elections during this period.

4. Elazar (1966) classified Nevada's political culture as individualistic owning to the state's small government, patronage based political organizations, limited citizen participation, and use of governmental power for private as opposed to public ends; a framing that is certainly consistent with our presentation. In contrast, Erikson,

Wright, and McIver (1993) struggled to make sense of the state's politics and as a consequence, they excluded Nevada from much of their analysis.

5. Damore (2006, 2013a) provides helpful overviews of the effect that urbanization has had on the last two redistricting processes in Nevada.

6. During this same time period, ten different politicians have held Nevada's Class 1 U.S. Senate seat, including Democrat Howard Cannon, who served for twenty-four years.

7. There is a good deal of debate in the state politics literature about the reliability and validity of various ideological measures commonly used in state politics research (see Brace et al. (2007) and Berry et al. (2010) for competing perspectives on this issue). We use the Berry et al. (1998, 2010) measures here because they cover the longest time frame and they vary over time, a characteristic that is consistent with the framing of our broader analysis. With that said, the correlations between the three measures presented in Graph 9.8 suggests some variation and potential inconsistences: $r = .57$ (p<.001) for the citizen ideology series and the ADA/COPE measure of state ideology; $r = -.17$ (p=.22) for the citizen ideology series and the NOMINATE measure of state government ideology; and $r = .62$ (p<.001) for the ADA/COPE measure of state ideology and the NOMINATE measure of state ideology.

8. Nevada is often characterized as libertarian owing to its low taxes, weak government institutions, and embrace of economic activity often outlawed elsewhere (e.g., prize fighting, prostitution, and gambling). Nevada also has a two-thirds requirement for any tax increases in its legislature. However, these same tendencies have not necessarily extended to civil rights and social issues (Pomeroy 2003). The state was long known as "The Mississippi of the West." De jure segregation (marriage) lasted until the 1950s and de facto segregation (employment, schools, and housing) continued into the early 1970s. Nevada's longest serving member of the House of Representatives, Walter Baring Jr., represented the state throughout the civil rights movement (1949–1953, 1957–1973). Baring was an ardent segregationist who aligned himself with the Southern wing of the Democratic Party. On the social front, Nevada has few abortion or gun restrictions, but passed a constitutional provision banning same-sex marriages in the early twenty-first century (see Damore et al. 2007).

9. Specifically, we use the Population Characteristics (P20) Reports and Detailed Tables complied by the U.S. Census Bureau derived from the Current Population Survey (http://www.census.gov/hhes/www/socdemo/voting/publications/p20/index.html, accessed December 27, 2014) for the 1994–2012 elections. Although the series began in the 1960s, prior to 1994 the reports do not differentiate between citizen and non-citizen population shares at the state level. This is a necessity given the large share of foreign-born Nevadans. Also, prior to 1994, the reports do not provide estimates for the Asian component of the state's electorate. Thus, we use the over 18-citizen share of the total population and the ethnic and racial ("Hispanic (of any race)," "White non-Hispanic," "Black Alone," and Asian Alone") subgroups to generate estimates of voter turnout (Graph 9.8) and turnout relative to population share (Graph 9.9). Because these data are from samples, the point estimates used here have error margins, which can be quite large for some of the racial and ethnic subgroups.

10. Although turnout among registered white voters is typically higher than for other groups, there also is significant variation in the rates of registration across racial and ethnic groups. The effects for both are more pronounced in midterm elections. For instance, in 2012 white and Latino registered voters turned out at 90 percent and 87 percent respectively, while the rate of registration for over 18 citizen whites was 67 percent as compared to 60 percent for Latino. In 2010, however, white registration was 64 percent as compared to 42 percent for Latinos and white turnout was 75 percent, while Latino turnout was 66 percent.

REFERENCES

Aisch, Gregor, Robert Gebeloff, and Kevin Quealy. 2014. "Where We Came From and Where We Went, State by State." In *The Upshot*, ed. D. Leonhardt. New York, NY: The New York Times.

Andersen, Kristi. 1979. *The Creation of the Democratic Majority, 1928–1936.* Chicago: University of Chicago Press.

Andrew, Patricia. 1998. "Alan Bible: The Politics of Stewardship." In *The Maverick Spirit: Building the New Nevada*, ed. R. O. Davies. Reno, NV: University of Nevada Press.

Berry, William D., Richard C. Fording, Evan J. Ringquist, Russell L. Hanson, and Carl E. Klarner. 2010. "Measuring Citizen and Government Ideology in the US States: A Re-Appraisal." *State Politics & Policy Quarterly* 10 (2):117–35.

Berry, William D., Evan J. Ringquist, Richard C. Fording, and Russell L. Hanson. 1998. "Measuring Citizen and Government Ideology in the American States, 1960–93." *American Journal of Political Science*: 327–48.

Bibby, John F. 1979. "Political Parties and Federalism: The Republican National Committee Involvement in Gubernatorial and Legislative Elections." *Publius* 9 (1):229–36.

Bibby, John F., Cornelius P. Cotter, James L. Gibson, and Robert J. Huckshorn. 1990. "Parties in State Politics." *Politics in the American States* 5.

Brace, Paul, Kevin T. Arceneaux, Martin Johnson, and Stacy G. Ulbig. 2007. "Reply to 'The Measurement and Stability of State Citizen Ideology.'" *State Politics & Policy Quarterly* 7 (2):133–40.

Campbell, James E. 1985. "Sources of the New Deal Realignment: The Contributions of Conversion and Mobilization to Partisan Change." *Western Political Quarterly* 38 (3):357–76.

Ceaser, James W., and Robert P. Saldin. 2005. "A New Measure of Party Strength." *Political Research Quarterly* 58 (2):245–56.

Damore, David F. 2006. "The 2001 Nevada Redistricting and Perpetuation of the Status Quo." *American Review of Politics* 27 (Summer):149–68.

2011a. "Reid vs. Angle in Nevada's Senate Race: Harry Houdini Escapes the Wave." In *Cases in Congressional Campaigns: Storming the Hill*, ed. D. Dulio and R. Adkins. New York: Routledge.

2011b. "The Tea Party Angle in the Nevada Senate Race." In *Tea Party Effects on 2010 Senate Elections*, ed. W. Miller and J. Walling. Lanham, MD: Lexington Books.

2013a. "Swimming Against the Tide: Partisan Gridlock and the 2011 Nevada Redistricting." In *The Political Battle over Congressional Redistricting*, ed. W. J. Miller and J. D. Walling. Lanham, MD: Lexington.

2012. "The State of Play in the Silver State: Undestadning the Three Nevadas." In *Latino Decisions*. Seattle, WA.

2013b. "What the GOP Can Learn from Nevada Republicans." In *Latino Decisions*. Seattle, WA.

2015. "It's the Economy Stupid? Not So Fast: The Impact of the Latino Vote on the 2012 Presidential Election in Nevada." In *Latinos and the 2012 Election*, ed. G. Sanchez. East Lansing, MI: Michigan State University Press.

Damore, David F., Ted G. Jelen, and Michael W. Bowers. 2007. "Sweet Land of Liberty: Gay Marriage and Mormonism in Nevada." In *Religious Interests in Community Conflict*, ed. L. Olson and P. A. Djupe. Waco, TX: Baylor University Press.

Dawson, Richard E., and James A. Robinson. 1963. "Inter-Party Competition, Economic Variables, and Welfare Policies in the American States." *Journal of Politics* 25 (2):265–89.

Driggs, Don W. 1996. *Nevada Politics and Government: Conservatism in an Open Society*. Lincoln, NE: University of Nebraska Press.

Edwards, Jerome E. 1982. *Pat McCarran, Political Boss of Nevada*. Reno, NV: University of Nevada Press.

Elazar, Daniel J. 1966. *American Federalism: A View From the States*. New York: Thomas Y. Crowell Company.

Elliot, Russell R. 1987. *History of Nevada*. Revised ed: University of Nebraska Press.

Erikson, Robert S., and Kent L. Tedin. 1981. "The 1928-1936 Partisan Realignment: The Case for the Conversion Hypothesis." *American Political Science Review* 75 (4):951–62.

Erikson, Robert S., Gerald C. Wright, and John P. McIver. 1993. *Statehouse Democracy: Public Opinion in the American States*. New York: Cambridge University Press.

Frey, William H., and Ruy Teixeira. 2011. "America's New Swing Region: The Political Demography and Geography of the Mountain West." In *America's New Swing Region*, ed. R. Teixeira. Washington, D.C.: Brookings Institution Press.

Gibson, James L., Cornelius P. Cotter, John F. Bibby, and Robert J. Huckshorn. 1985. "Whither the Local Parties?: A Cross-Sectional and Longitudinal Analysis of the Strength of Party Organizations." *American Journal of Political Science* 29 (1):139–60.

Holbrook, Thomas M., and Emily Van Dunk. 1993. "Electoral Competition in the American States." *American Political Science Review* 87 (4):955–62.

Ostermeier, Eric. 2012. "US House Tenure Varies Wildly Across the 50 States Throughout History." In *Smart Politics*. Minneapolis, MN.

Parker, Renee, and Steve George. 2006. "Political History of Nevada." ed. Secretary of State. Carson City, NV: State Printing Office.

Pomeroy, Earl S. 2003. *The Pacific Slope: A History of California, Oregon, Washington, Idaho, Utah, and Nevada*. Revised ed. Reno, NV: University of Nevada Press.

Poole, Keith T. 1998. "Recovering a Basic Space from a Set of Issue Scales." *American Journal of Political Science* (1998):954–93.

Rucker, Philip. 2014. "Governors Christie, Walker and Kasich Woo Billionaire Sheldon Adelson at Vegas Event." *Washington Post*, March 29.

Saldin, Robert P. 2014. *Major Party Index Data* [Faculty Website]. Robert Wood Johnson Scholars Program, Harvard University [cited December 28 2014]. Available from http://scholar.harvard.edu/saldin/data.

Schlesinger, Joseph A. 1955. "A Two-Dimensional Scheme for Classifying the States According to Degree of Inter-Party Competition." *American Political Science Review* 49 (4):1120–8.

Sundquist, James L. 1983. *Dynamics of the Party System: Alignment and Realignment of Political Parties in the United States*. 2 ed. Washington, D.C.: The Brookings Institution.

Teixeira, Ruy, ed. 2012. *America's New Swing Region*. Washington, D.C.: Brookings Institution Press.

Wallis, John Joseph. 1998. "The Political Economy of the New Deal Spending Revisited, Again: With and without Nevada." *Explorations in Economic History* 35:140–70.

Wren, Thomas. 1904. *A History of the State of Nevada: Its Resources and People*. New York: Lewis Publishing Company.

Chapter Ten

Blue Dawn? New Hampshire and the Limits of the New England Democratic Revival

Niall Palmer

INTRODUCTION

Since the 1950s, New Hampshire has gained a level of political notoriety and media attention greatly disproportionate to the size of its population and to the modest four votes it holds in the Electoral College. On paper, at least, these facts, filtered through a first-past-the-post electoral system, should ensure the "Granite State" receives little serious attention from the major parties in presidential elections, except in extremely close races where voter intentions are fluid and nominees must scramble for every vote. The state is also comparatively low yield in terms of convention delegates and, until recently, had a longstanding reputation for rock-ribbed Republicanism, with the GOP dominating executive offices, the state legislature, and national congressional delegations. Combined, these factors make it all the more surprising that the voting intentions and political culture of a small, conservative New England state have been national talking points for years. In the early twenty-first century, New Hampshire continues to fascinate reporters and political scientists, not only for its controversial "first-in-the-nation" primary but also for an apparent marked change in its partisan make-up, which has converted it into a key 'swing state' in presidential elections.

New Hampshire has occupied a unique position in electoral politics since 1952. Changes to the rules governing presidential nomination con tests, combined with the rapid growth of media coverage of those contests, propelled it into the political limelight. In the pre-reform nomination system, where closed caucuses and behind-the-scenes bargaining determined convention outcomes, New Hampshire's early position in the primary calendar meant little, other than allowing presidential hopefuls such as Franklin Roosevelt to test public opinion and recruit state party activists without serious long-term risk. First place in the nomination calendar only became a positive advantage in the early 1970s, after the Democratic Party's McGovern-Fraser and Mikulski rules commissions produced a new, primary-dominated system reliant on volunteer armies, incessant polling, and saturation media coverage. New Hampshire's verdict became crucial as candidates sought to convert early wins or unexpectedly strong showings into "momentum." New Hampshire, already renowned as a graveyard for the election hopes of established figures such as Robert Taft, Harry Truman, Nelson Rockefeller, and Lyndon Johnson, now also became a beacon of hope for under-funded longshots such as Eugene McCarthy, George McGovern, Jimmy Carter, Gary Hart, and John McCain. The news media responded predictably. New Hampshire's political culture was analyzed in much greater detail than those of larger states whose delegate yields were greater but whose later position in the calendar reduced their ability to significantly influence the nomination race. Under this magnification, a stereotypical image of the state and its voters started to emerge as reporters, hoping for "shock" primary results, sought a re-usable narrative framework for them. Although some of the more famous New Hampshire results, particularly those of 1952, 1968, 1976, 1984, and 1996, reflected the national political or economic mood and thus *confirmed*, rather than upset, expectations, journalists often treated the political culture and libertarian outlook of New Hampshire as factors of equal or greater importance than external political or economic trends. The comparative absence of major urban centers, the noticeable lack of ethnic diversity, the lack of a statewide sales or income tax, the unusually large size of the state legislature, and the twin state cults of "citizen-legislators" and "retail politics" were key components in the entertainingly "quaint" Granite State image served up to audiences. New Hampshire voters were depicted as stereotypical conservative Yankees—cynical, monosyllabic Calvin Coolidge clones as immoveable as the White Mountains—delighting state politicians and media, who played the role for all it was worth.

For some years, the image of the state as a bucolic backwater helped disguise the changes which were occurring by the 1970s. By the end of the century, these changes hardly seemed to matter as front-loading and soaring campaign costs seemed about to end New Hampshire's ability to boost primary underdogs or upset frontrunners. Ironically, however, as critics of the "first in the nation" primary eagerly awaited its demise, New Hampshire's transition from "red state" to "swing state" brought it fresh attention from reporters and campaign strategists and looked set to keep it in the political limelight for years to come.

ERA OF REPUBLICAN DOMINANCE

The Republican Party's dominance in New Hampshire state politics began shortly after the party was formed. Despite claims that the Republican Party was founded in Ripon, Wisconsin, some Granite Staters argue that Amos Tuck, a New Hampshire congressman elected as a Free-Soiler, founded the party at a meeting of fourteen politicians of different parties at Major Blake's Hotel in Exeter, New Hampshire, on October 12, 1853[1] (Gregg and Gardner 2003, 22).

60 of the 81 New Hampshire governors since the Declaration of Independence have been Republican. The party held the governorship for almost the entire period 1857 to 1963 with only short Democratic interregnums—in 1871–1872 and 1874–1875, and in 1913–1914 and 1923–1924. During that period, Republicans also dominated the state legislature. The melting of the Republican ice-sheet in New Hampshire appears to start in 1992 but a closer look at state election outcomes shows that Democrats were already growing more electorally competitive in gubernatorial and congressional elections in the 1960s and 1970s. Democratic Governor John King, elected in 1962, held office for three consecutive terms, a feat no Democrat had achieved before. Elected the same year, Senator Thomas McIntyre was the first Democrat sent to the Senate by New Hampshire voters in thirty years, holding the seat until 1979. Democrat John Durkin held the state's other Senate seat from 1975 to 1980 while Norm D'Amours represented the first House district from 1975 to 1985. Though the party finally lost McIntyre's seat in 1979, Hugh Gallen picked up the governorship in the same year. The end of this wave of competitiveness coincided with the weakening of the New Deal coalition and Ronald Reagan's landslide election in 1980, which renewed the GOP's grip on the state. Clearly, however, New Hampshire's Democrats had competitive potential.

New England was considered safe Republican territory in the pre-New Deal era. In 1916, the GOP carried all but one state in the region (New Hampshire), swept the board in 1920 and 1924, took five of the seven states in 1928 and still won four in 1932 in the depths of the Depression. Regional partisan voting patterns were temporarily reordered by depression and world war, enabling Roosevelt's Democrats to eat into Republican support. Famously, only Maine and Vermont withstood the New Deal coalition which had more or less emerged by 1936, repeating the feat in 1940 and 1944. By 1948, however, with Roosevelt dead and immediate emergencies no longer driving the electoral process, the GOP quickly returned to what Kevin Phillips called the party's "Yankee Era" (Phillips 1969, 7). Until the 1960s, Maine elected only eight Democratic governors, as opposed to thirty-five Republicans. Vermont returned only Republican governors from 1854 to 1961 and even Massachusetts only occasionally strayed to the Democrats before the 1930s. The party relied for its success on small town voters. Andrew Taylor points out that less-populated, rural states tended to vote Republican since the conservative social and economic views characteristic of small towns and villages were not counter-balanced by the more cosmopolitan outlook of larger urban populations (Taylor 2005, 20).

For most of the second half of the century New Hampshire was more loyally Republican than any other New England state. As Table 10.1 shows, it tops the table in choosing Republican presidential candidates in eleven of the seventeen elections since 1948, with Democrats taking the state on just six occasions. Vermont is the next most consistently Republican state, with ten GOP victories to seven for the Democrats. During this period, the Democrats performed strongest in the niches they had carved out in Massachusetts and Rhode Island, notching up thirteen wins to the GOP's four in both states. Over four and a half decades, Democrats could only draw level with Republicans in terms of New England states won in any election year. The exceptions were 1964 and 1968. In these two cycles, however, Republicans' ability to reach out to moderate and independent voters, as well as some conservative Democrats was compromised by right-wing radicalism (the nomination of Barry Goldwater and George Wallace's southern insurgency). Both campaigns disrupted normal patterns of conservative voter behavior across the country by distorting "traditional" conservative messages, resulting in a lopsided Democratic victory in 1964 and a near-win in 1968. As with the earlier Roosevelt and later Reagan eras, the presence on the ballot of a phenomenally popular president tended, in New England, to result in a wipe-out for the opposition. The Democrats lost all of New England in 1952, 1956, and 1984 and only narrowly avoided the same fate in 1972 by holding on to Massachusetts. The Republicans, by contrast, drew a regional blank only once—in 1964. A Republican lock on the region was acknowledged by *The American Voter* in 1960, which noted, "The Northeast, including New England and the Middle Atlantic states . . . is now the strongest Republican area of the country" (Campbell et al. 1980, 152). This makes the appearance of a pro-Democrat fault-line in 1992 all the more interesting. By 2012, the GOP had lost every New England state in five out of six presidential elections.

The presence of an incumbent president on the ballot cannot account for this sudden change in voter behavior. Both Clinton in 1996 and Barack Obama in 2012 were recovering from bruising first terms in which economic growth had been relatively weak, deficits had risen and their parties lost control of one or both houses of Congress. While both retained some popularity, neither was as unassailable as FDR in 1936, Eisenhower in 1956, or Reagan in 1984 and neither president had the advantages of Johnson in 1964 or Nixon in 1972 of running against flawed and ideologically polarizing opponents.

Table 10.1. New England Presidential Election Voting, 1948–2012

Year	CT	ME	MA	NH	RI	VT
1948	R	R	D	R	D	R
1952	R	R	R	R	R	R
1956	R	R	R	R	R	R
1960	D	R	D	R	D	R
1964	D	D	D	D	D	D
1968	D	D	D	R	D	R
1972	R	R	D	R	R	R
1976	R	R	D	R	D	R
1980	R	R	R	R	D	R
1984	R	R	R	R	R	R
1988	R	R	D	R	D	R
1992	D	D	D	D	D	D
1996	D	D	D	D	D	D
2000	D	D	D	R	D	D
2004	D	D	D	D	D	D
2008	D	D	D	D	D	D
2012	D	D	D	D	D	D

The extent of the Democratic surge, covering all states in New England, points to a major realignment, with long-term implications for both major parties.

Election results for New Hampshire's counties show the depth of the shift in voter behavior which occurred during the 1990s. As with the broader New England data, Republican hegemony is more or less complete throughout the period 1972–1992. A sharp disconnect then appears in 1992, after which GOP dominance at county level is either fractured or disappears entirely. Importantly, though, the picture which emerges from New Hampshire's counties is *not* one of unchallenged Democratic hegemony, but a more complex picture in which Democratic performance improves dramatically but Republicans remain competitive.

From Table 10.2 we see that a majority of New Hampshire counties have moved from a position of solid support for the GOP to solid, or almost solid, support for the Democrats. The counties of Strafford and Cheshire to the south, Merrimack in the heartland (containing New Hampshire's largest city, Manchester), and Grafton further to the north had voted Republican in every presidential year from 1972 but moved into the Democratic column from 1992. Sullivan, in the southeast of the state, and Coos, the most northerly county, have followed almost the same pattern. Though both broke away in 2000 to support the Bush-Cheney ticket, some analysts believe this to be an aberration caused by Ralph Nader's third-party challenge and the Gore campaign's failure to target New Hampshire as a battleground state. Both

Table 10.2. New Hampshire voting in presidential elections by county, 1976–2012

County	1976	1980	1984	1988	1992	1996	2000	2004	2008	2012
Belknap	R	R	R	R	R	R	R	R	D	R
Carroll	R	R	R	R	R	R	R	R	D	R
Cheshire	R	R	R	R	D	D	D	D	D	D
Coos	D	R	R	R	D	D	R	D	D	D
Grafton	R	R	R	R	D	D	D	D	D	D
Hillsborough	R	R	R	R	R	D	R	R	D	D
Merrimack	R	R	R	R	D	D	D	D	D	D
Rockingham	R	R	R	R	R	D	R	R	D	R
Strafford	R	R	R	R	D	D	D	D	D	D
Sullivan	R	R	R	R	D	D	R	D	D	D

Source: Office of the Secretary of State. New Hampshire. Elections Division.

counties returned to the Democrats from 2004. In Rockingham and Hillsborough, the Democratic surge weakens. Republicans have kept a 4–2 edge over the Democrats in Rockingham since 1992 while the parties are level in Hillsborough. Both sets of results, however, are still modest improvements for the Democrats. Only Belknap and Carroll have remained loyal to the GOP, with the Democrats managing victory only once in either county since 1972—in 2008, the year of Barack Obama's New England sweep.

Of New Hampshire's ten counties, four have been reliably Democratic for 20 years, while another two only strayed once. Republicans can realistically count upon only two. 1992 was thus, in retrospect, a watershed year in which a long cycle of GOP dominance in presidential elections came to an end in New Hampshire, as well as across New England. Before 1992, Democratic victories in the Granite State were comparatively rare. From 1992, they became commonplace. By 2008, the party was even in a position to inflict on Republicans the same humiliating wipe-out which it had itself suffered three times during the Reagan era. The loosening of the Republicans' grip has enabled Democrats to repeatedly deliver a majority of counties for the national ticket and improve their electoral performances at state and local levels, particularly in the central and southern regions, where much of the population is concentrated.

Significantly, however, these changes have been neither uniform nor entirely in accordance with standard theories of geographical distribution of partisan support. For example, in the less densely-populated counties to the north, which include many small towns but few cities and incorporate the White Mountains and the heavily-forested Great North Woods areas, we might expect to see stronger GOP performances. This is not always the case in New Hampshire. Grafton is highly rural and has only one major city—Lebanon—with a population of roughly 13,000 (U.S. Census, 2010). Yet it has been one of the four most reliable Democratic counties since 1992. In 2014, 21 of the 27 members it sent to the New Hampshire House of Representatives were Democrats. Similarly, Coos, on the U.S.-Canada border, has one small city of just over 10,000 people, Berlin, in a region where population density is 20 people per square mile (contrasted to 773.2 people per square mile in the Greater Nashua region in the south). Nevertheless, Coos has voted Democratic in every national election except 2000. By comparison, Rockingham, further to the south, contains Derry, Londonderry, and Salem, all of which have populations in excess of 24,000 and shares a border with Massachusetts. It might be expected that the county's ideological make-up would become increasingly liberal due to its higher level of urbanization and proximity to the Bay State. Yet Republicans currently hold the seats for Derry, Londonderry, and Salem in the state Senate and 64 of the 90 members the county elects to the House of Representatives are also Republican (with two seats currently vacant). This is in contrast to Nashua, in neighboring Hillsborough county. One of the biggest cities in northern New England, also close to the Massachusetts border, it has 27 seats in the state House of Representatives, of which Democrats currently occupy 24.

If the new electoral vitality of the Democrats produces varied results from county to county, or from town to town, it is also the case that these variations derive from a number of different factors, both internal and external, which have influenced the state's political culture. The economic downturn of the early 1990s almost certainly played a catalysing role, helping Bill Clinton to attract moderates and independents in 1992 with "New Democrat" policies which combined fiscal conservatism with more liberal proposals on healthcare and infrastructure investment. Clinton survived allegations of scandal and ran a strong second to Massachusetts Senator Paul Tsongas in the 1992 New Hampshire primary because his focus on job creation, investment and law and order gave voters disillusioned with "Reaganomics" but distrustful of liberal Democrats' economic competence a reason to switch parties. As a short-term formula for winning votes, this proved effective but it is not sufficient explanation for the longer-term decline in the national Republican Party's influence. Nor does it account for the Democrats' continuing strength after the end of the Clinton era. National events, such as the unpopular Iraq war, a series of sex and ethics scandals in the Republican-controlled Congress and the near-collapse of the financial sector—all taking place during the 2001–2009 Bush administration—would also have taken their toll on the competitive strength of New Hampshire's Republicans. The most fundamental and long-term driver, however, is demographic change—a key characteristic of realignment phases throughout electoral history.

In the early 1930s, the last "critical realignment" was sparked by the Great Depression and subsequent collapse of voter confidence in Republican economic and social policies but the seeds of the change were sown much earlier, in the labor migrations from South to North and the waves of immigration in the first years of the century. These created urban power centers for Democrats in many of the largest cities in the North, where Democratic party machines busily converted newcomers to their cause. Population shifts were also at the root of the next identified realignment at the end of the 1960s, when the decline of traditional heavy industires in the Northeast and Midwest caused a labor migration to the West and South. Richard Nixon's 1968 "southern strategy" capitalized on increasing southern resentment of the centralizing and liberalizing policies of the New Deal and Great Society programs and by the mid-1980s, the "Solid South," a bulwark of Democrat power for decades, had disappeared. Problematically, radical changes in voter behaviour do not always manifest themselves over one presidential election cycle, nor are they necessarily national in their impact. Karl Rove claimed that the 2000 and 2004 elections would, like the McKinley realignment election of 1896, confirm Republican dominance for a generation, this time by uniting southern and Midwestern conservatives and mobilizing a permanently angry Christian voter base. At the same moment, however, the desertion of the West coast of the United States and the entire New England region to the Democrats was already underway. While the changes wrought by one realignment are still working themselves out, the roots of its successor are often already spreading, barely noticed, across the country. Rove's anticipated WASP coalition was vulnerable to higher turnout rates among female, black, Hispanic, and young voters and the shrinkage, through desertion and aging, of the GOP's voter base. Beginning around 2006, when Democrats recaptured Congress, a consensus formed among many analysts that the "Republican realignment" had reached its end. John Judis and Ruy Teixeira claimed a new, center-left realignment was emerging, with the east and west coasts placed beyond Republicans' reach and Democratic inroads forecast in Arizona, Texas, Florida, and parts of the Rocky Mountain west. They argued that rapid changes in lifestyle and demography would mobilize a new cohort of well-educated and comfortably-off voters in favor of the Democrats via the growing influence of the "ideopolis"— flourishing metropolitan areas within the western, southwestern, and upper Midwestern states and also parts of the Northeast. Citizens of the ideopolis are mainly professionals employed in "post-industrial" occupations including media, law, education, design, leisure, and, especially, information technology. Proximity to one or more centers of excellence in education, usually a large university, and access to a major transport hub are also key characteristics. Voters in these areas are more likely to be career-oriented, habitual users of sports and health facilities and café-bookstores. Though predominantly white, the ideopolis was receptive to racial and ethnic diversity, particularly in the lower-paid employment strata (Judis and Teixeira 2002, 70). Ideologically, neither party can completely monopolize the loyalty of these voters, who do not march in lockstep with any party machine or doctrine but the popularity of liberal (or modified libertarian) social values combined with fiscal conservatism makes it a "breeding ground for the new Democratic majority" (Judis and Teixeira 2002, 71).

Alongside demographic and societal change, sudden economic and/or political crises that break established voting coalitions and fundamentally alter the core language and assumptions of political debate can be drivers of realignment. Critical realignments result from larger-than-normal changes in the size of a key element of the voting population leading to a permanent rebalancing of normal patterns of partisanship. Darmofal and Nardulli argue that "conversion" is frequently the main driver of the realignment process, where part of the electorate "converts" to a different party, though an unexpected increase in participation rates can also trigger change (the "mobilization" thesis) (Darmofal and Nardulli 2010, 256). Less frequently, "demobilization," involving the disengagement of a key voting group can affect change. Mobilization and demobilization, they argue, contribute less motive energy to electoral change. Conversion contributes the most.

In New Hampshire's case, a long-term change in the party balance is evidenced in the Electoral College but not precisely mirrored by results at state level or in elections for the U.S. Congress, where Republicans remain successful and highly competitive. While different possible causes exist for the increasing strength of the Democratic Party, voter mobilization cannot be discounted as a factor. Table 10.3 charts fluctuations in voter turnout across New England (with comparative figures for the United States as a whole) in the nine presidential elections between 1980 and 2012. Data is calculated using the method employed by the George Mason University Presidential Elections Project of recording estimated turnout among voting-eligible citizens in elections for highest office (the presidency, Congress, or governorships, dependent upon the year being a presidential or midterm cycle). Voting-eligible turnout, as Michael McDonald argues, serves as a more reliable indicator than voting-age turnout, particularly as the size of ineligible voter populations varies widely from state to state (McDonald, 2014). Immediately noticeable is the gradient of the rise in New Hampshire voter turnout. Grouping the data into a series of three-election cycles, Granite State turnout averages only 56.2 percent during the 1980s, but climbs to 62.7 percent in the 1990s (including 2000) and then to 70.9 percent during the first three elections of this century. This sharp upward curve is unmatched by any other New England state. New

**Table 10.3.   Eligible Voter Turnout Across New England:
Presidential Elections, 1980–2012**

Area	1980	1984	1988	1992	1996	2000	2004	2008	2012
U.S.	54.2	55.2	52.8	58.1	51.7	54.2	60.1	61.6	58.2
CT	63.9	63.8	59.0	68.6	59.6	61.9	65.0	66.6	60.9
ME	65.4	65.8	62.5	74.3	65.2	67.2	73.8	70.6	68.1
MS	61.4	59.9	60.0	63.8	58.4	59.9	64.2	66.8	66.3
NH	58.1	54.1	56.4	66.1	58.3	63.9	70.9	71.7	70.1
RI	61.6	58.8	56.1	62.8	54.4	54.2	58.5	61.8	58.0
VT	58.7	61.5	60.1	69.0	59.3	54.0	66.3	67.3	60.4

Source: McDonald, Michael P., *United States Election Project*. George Mason University. 2014.

Hampshire, of course, started from a lower point than its neighbors. In the 1980s cycle, for example, Maine turnout already averaged 64.5 percent, 8.3 percent above New Hampshire. Nevertheless, New Hampshire voting rates jumped 14 percentage points from 1980 while those of Massachusetts rose only 5.3 percent and Maine only 6.3 percent during the same period. Rhode Island rates remained sluggish throughout while Vermont's climbed only 4.5 percent to a peak of 64.6 percent. Further, New Hampshire produced the second-highest turnout in New England in both 2004 and 2008 and topped the table in 2012—a marked change from 1980 and 1984, when it recorded the lowest levels, and 1988 when it was second-lowest. The turnout spike in New Hampshire, therefore, has been more noticeable and (so far) more sustained than in any other state in the region, possibly a sign that voter mobilization has been a driver for realignment in the state. During the period in which the Democrats have held a lock on New Hampshire's four electoral votes, a substantially higher proportion of the state's eligible voters have been turning out in presidential elections. Voter registration drives are a possible contributory factor but New Hampshire's unique profile offers another, more unusual, explanation. The saturation media coverage given to its "first-in-the-nation" primary may well have helped stimulate turnout. News organizations poured a disproportionate amount of time and resources into coverage of New Hampshire and the Iowa caucuses simply because they had been starved of 'hard' election news for four years. The knock-on effect, at least in New Hampshire, was to galvanize not only the activist bases of both parties but also ordinary voters who were often flattered (or bemused) by the excessive media speculation about their views of national issues and their voting intentions. Although reporters and candidates tended to target southern tier cities and towns such as Derry, Goffstown, Exeter, and Portsmouth, together with Concord and Manchester, communities in the less densely-populated north, such as Berlin, Lincoln, or Conway, still received more attention per voter than their equivalents in other states. As far back as 1980, *New York Times* columnist E.J. Dionne speculated that New Hampshire primary voters "had received a political education from the campaign, displaying far greater knowledge of the issue positions of the candidates" (*New York Times* 1980/03/02).

Another likely reason for increased turnout is that New Hampshire's relatively recent move to "competitive" status prompts candidate organizations and national party strategists to focus more intensively upon it. As Gimpel et al. note, small states considered "competitive" in 2004—including New Hampshire (also New Mexico, Iowa, and Nevada) received significantly higher degrees of candidate and advertising attention than "simplistic mathematical models" would have predicted (Gimpel et al. 2007, 795). Both the George W. Bush and John Kerry camps in 2004 identified New Hampshire as a key state—for Kerry strategists, a potential win; for Bush strategists, a state that was picked up in 2000 but was now "vulnerable." Daron Shaw reveals that while both parties increased their focus on New Hampshire in 2004, more personal appearances were built into the campaign schedules of Kerry and vice-presidential nominee John Edwards than in those of Bush or Vice President Dick Cheney. Additionally, Democrat targeting of an influential media market stretching across Boston, across New Hampshire, and into Vermont increased during the campaign, while GOP advertising investment in the same market decreased over the last weeks of the campaign (Shaw 2006, 55). In 2012, both President Obama and Mitt Romney devoted some of their last critical days of campaigning to rallies in Manchester and in the state capital, Concord. Such degrees of late attention to New Hampshire would have been unthinkable (and electorally irrational) before 1992.

Finally, higher turnout rates are linked to demographic change. As is illustrated in the next section, high rates of immigration and a high birth rate affected New Hampshire's political environment. Beginning in the 1960s, the state experienced an immigration tide unmatched by any other New England state. Many of the newcomers were well-educated and earning salaries in the middle-upper income quartile, making it likely they would also be politically educated and active. The cumulative effect was not felt for some years. By the 1990s, however, the influence of these new New Hampshirites and their children at the ballot box was undermining Republican dominance (Smith 2014).

IMPACTS OF DEMOGRAPHIC CHANGE

Population movement in and around New Hampshire has been the main force driving change in the state's partisan loyalties and political culture. Between

1960 and 1975, the population increased by 33%. By 1990, the rate of increase was 50%, making New Hampshire the second fastest-growing state east of the Mississippi (Palmer 1997, 37). Much of the influx consisted of young and, in later years, middle-aged, baby boomers from Massachusetts whose motivations for relocating ranged from escaping the Bay State's tax system to exchanging the bustle of the Boston metropolitan area for a small town or rural environment. These waves affected political and social attitudes across the state's central and southern tiers, which contain more than sixty percent of Granite State residents (Johnson 2012). Massachusetts businesses often relocated or expanded across the border to cut their tax burden while other companies were attracted to the Granite State by the lack of a strongly-unionized workforce and the potential opportunities for entrepreneurship. After the decline of its textile manufacturing industry, New Hampshire had diversified in the 1960s and 1970s, specializing particularly in electrical components, communications technology, plastics, and industrial tools. This contributed to an economic boom during the Reagan era which raised New Hampshire's average per capita personal income to eighth-highest in the United States. State economic growth rate rocketed from an average of 54.4% in the 1970s to 75.2% during the 1980s (Center for Policy Studies 2014, 9). The economic downturn of the early 1990s hit business hard, with state GDP falling by 25% and failure rates second only to those of California (Palmer 1997, 38–9). Continued immigration and a strong birth rate ensured that the state economy recovered quickly and continued to expand, albeit at reduced levels, until a combination of factors—slowing birth and immigration rates and the 2008 financial crisis and subsequent recession, brought the boom years to an end. In the twenty-first century, state growth rates have been among the lowest in the United States. "Creative well-educated people have driven a lot of what happened in New Hampshire, and most of those people have come from outside of the state," Dennis Delay, in charge of New Hampshire economic forecasting for the New England Economic Partnership, told the Manchester *Union Leader* in October 2014. "If that is not going to happen . . . then that's a source of economic growth that's no longer available to us" (*Union Leader* 2014/10/08).

The partisan political implications of the Massachusetts influx are not as obvious as they might first appear. Teixeira and Judis consider the proximity of Boston, MIT, Harvard, and Route 128 (locally dubbed "America's Technology Highway") to New Hampshire's borders as a key liberalizing influence upon the state's cultural and political development. The movement of workers and their families, especially into the "Golden Triangle" area of Manchester, Salem, and Nashua, injected left-of-center views on state spending and intervention into New Hampshire's political discourse, amplified by the

Boston media market into which the state's southern tier feeds. New Hampshire, they note, "was developing a high-tech corridor whose voters, like professionals elsewhere, were beginning to prefer moderate Democrats" (Judis and Teixeira 2002, 95). The potential for Democrats to achieve dominance-by-ideopolis in New Hampshire was offset, however, by Bay State business influence. Business migrants attracted by the weaker regulatory climate and lower taxes contributed to the Republicans' electoral sweep of New Hampshire counties between 1972 and 1988, during which they took every county in every election except Coos, which defected to Jimmy Carter in 1976. In 2014, Republicans still tend to monopolize political power in towns and cities close to the border. If the power of new liberal migrants had been as great as many expected, New Hampshire's unique brand of fiscal conservatism would almost certainly have been undermined. Instead, the obsession with low taxes continues to box liberal officeholders and candidates into a corner. Most Democrats running for state office take "The Pledge" not to enact broad-based taxes before Republicans even have a chance to confront them with it.

Massachusetts migration is only partly responsible for recent Democratic election successes. Independent or liberal migrants from other New England states and from outside the region have also helped close the gap with Republicans. As mentioned earlier, increased participation by younger voters since the 1990s has advantaged the Democrats. In New Hampshire, the sons and daughters of the big immigration waves form large and politically active student populations, particularly in college towns such as Keene, Hanover, and Durham, which often trend liberal (*New York Times* 2012/06/24). Taken together, these factors tended to dilute the impact of the economic exodus from Massachusetts by increasing voter receptivity to "progressive" social policies. The 1992 Clinton victory, therefore, may have come at precisely the right moment for state Democrats who were demoralized by years of Republican dominance. Clinton's acceptance of much of the conservative economic agenda enabled him to reach out to independents and moderates and softened the edges of his more liberal social policies. Once state Democrats began to follow the "New Democrat" example they were able to fully capitalize on demographic change. Like the national party, they found voters more, rather than less, receptive to their messages as the economy slowed and the Bush administration tarnished the GOP brand.

Research suggests that while the heavy migration had ended by 2006, its impact will be felt until at least mid-century. The median age of New Hampshire's population is not as high as in some neighboring states but it will rise fairly steeply. This carries implications for its future. Large numbers of "boomers" already reaching or past retirement age will seek better leisure, health, and care facilities. These "amenity migrants" have settled in central and northern areas such as Carroll County, while younger families with children have clustered around the seacoast area and along the Massachusetts border. Both regions, Kenneth Johnson of the New Hampshire Center for Public Policy Studies suggests, will confront difficult choices over how best to raise and spend enough revenue to meet the demands of the "silver Tsunami" and the needs of parents with school-age children (Center for Policy Studies 2014, 9). Healthcare has already become a major concern for state legislators, with insurance premiums for families 6% above the national average and 12% higher for individuals. Pressures on the state budget may increase exponentially and the impact on state political dialogue and partisanship may be profound. Republicans are already treading carefully on the issue of Obama's 2010 Affordable Care Act, which proved deeply unpopular in many red states. In New Hampshire, over 40,000 people have signed up to the government scheme, the sixth-highest sign-up rate in the nation (Center for Policy Studies 2014, 27–30).

RELIGION

Until the third quarter of the twentieth century, white Protestants made up nearly half of the New England electorate. This helped entrench Republican regional dominance but was contingent upon the party remaining essentially moderate in its conservatism, since it was non-evangelical whites, Earl and Merle Black note, who generally "set the partisan and ideological tone of Northeastern Protestantism" (Black and Black 2007, 104). During the 1970s, the Nixon administration's failure to actively help evangelicals trying to reverse Supreme Court decisions on abortion and school prayer was instrumental in bringing southern conservative anger with the party's "Wall Street" wing to boiling point. New Hampshire nevertheless supported Nixon in 1972 and opted for Gerald Ford over the "born-again" Christian, Jimmy Carter, in 1976, despite the legacy of Watergate and Ford's pardon of Nixon. Reagan's failure to do much more than scratch the surface of the Christian Right's moral agenda had no impact on his popularity in New Hampshire. State citizens have generally been secular in their views on church-state relations and dislike the more aggressive Christian moralism of Southern evangelicals. This is partly explained by the high concentration of Catholics across the northeast, who comprise 28 percent of the population compared to only 10 percent for evangelical Protestants (Pew Forum 2008, 74). While Catholics are most concentrated in New York, New Jersey, Massachusetts and Rhode Island, they also make up 29 percent of New Hampshire's population (Pew Forum 2008, 99). The hardline theology and tactlessness of the GOP's evangelical activists tends to stoke the concerns of Catholic voters, who often help more moderate Protestants to undermine evangelical candidates such as Pat Robertson (1988) and Rick Santorum (2012) in the presidential primary. The comparative weakness of evangelism's political appeal in the Granite State was evident in the 2008 Republican primary. Former Arkansas Governor Mike Huckabee, after gaining 34.4 percent of the vote in the Iowa caucus, made no headway in New Hampshire. Despite the normal media blizzard surrounding the Iowa winner, Huckabee acknowledged the uphill battle he faced against John McCain in New Hampshire, joking to reporters, "We've got to convert a lot more people in New Hampshire in the next five days. We're going to have a big tent revival out on the grounds of the Concord State Capitol, get them all converted to evangelical faith, then we'll win" (*Washington Post* 2008/01/04, 4). He won just 11.2 percent of the vote, 26 points behind McCain (*New York Times* 2008). In Iowa, 60 percent of caucus attenders had identified themselves as "evangelical Christian," of whom 46 percent voted for Huckabee (Smidt et al. 2010, 84). In New Hampshire, over one-third of McCain supporters told pollsters they never went to church. "New Hampshire," Smidt et al. observe, "is no Iowa in religious terms" (Smidt et al. 2010, 85). In 2012, Santorum and Mitt Romney tied for first place in Iowa but Santorum took 32 percent of the evangelical Christian vote to Romney's 14 percent (Pew Forum 2008). In the New Hampshire primary which followed, Romney's broader appeal helped him to victory. He secured 31 percent of the evangelical vote to Santorum's 23 percent with Santorum finishing in fifth place overall (Pew Forum 2012). Both the 2008 and 2012 contests could be seen to support Adkins and Dowdle's contention that New Hampshire primary results (despite occasional aberrations such as the victories of John McCain in 2000 or Hillary Clinton in 2008) are still more likely than those of Iowa to foreshadow the outcome of nomination and election cycles. Where Iowa's voters are more receptive to evangelical messages and its caucus process more vulnerable to manipulation by a disproportionately right-wing Christian activist base, New Hampshire's more open primary process and the pragmatic inclinations of many of its voters usually subordinates religious or ideological purity to the priority of electability cycles (Adkins and Dowdle 2001, 436).[2] This tendency is only likely to increase, both in primary and general election contests, as demographic shifts continue to erode white Protestant Republican dominance across the northeast. As the numbers of non-WASP racial and ethnic groups and secular white voters have increased, the old conservative white Protestant bloc has been slowly shrinking. This presents difficulties for a party that has, since the 1980s, been increasingly motivated by religious or ideological radicalism. As Black and Black indicate, however, while these changes "greatly facilitate Democratic dominance" across the northeast they have not yet delivered a stable Democratic majority. At the state level in New Hampshire, "close partisan divisions" rather than outright Democratic dominance have resulted from this process, partly due to a simultaneous decline in the traditional *Democratic* advantage among white Catholic voters since the 1970s (Black and Black 2007, 99). This decline may have been driven by Democrats' more liberal policies on social issues, particularly abortion, contraception and homosexuality, leading not to Democratic dominance but to a rise in the number of genuinely competitive races for state and national office.

Demographic change aside, the conflating of the national Republican Party message with Bible-fuelled declarations of hostility to abortion, contraception, and gay marriage, combined with confrontational tactics over immigration and the debt ceiling have harmed the party's competitive strength across the northeast. While it is harder to quantify the impact, it is likely that the party's loss of New England, like the Democrats' loss of the white South, is linked to more than population movements. On paper, both John McCain and Mitt Romney should have performed well in New Hampshire. McCain was extremely popular with mainstream GOP and independent voters while Romney's emphasis on fiscal conservatism and his Massachusetts links should have provided a strong support base. Neither could be credibly linked to the GOP's radical wing. As Bonnie Johnson notes, however, mainstream and social media convert arguments and policies presented by candidates in state and even local campaigns into *national* messages, regardless of whether the message was intentionally tailored to appeal to a narrow voting group in one particular state (Johnson 2005, 354). Since, as Miller and Schofield observe, it is grassroots activists "who give the Party its image to the nation" McCain and Romney often struggled to disassociate themselves from controversial congressional candidates without alienating a religious conservative base with which they were obviously uncomfortable (Miller and Schofield 2008, 446; 433–50).

In 2013, the *Republican Growth and Opportunity Report* urged party members to adopt more considerate and welcoming tones, particularly toward voter groups such as gays and racial and ethnic minorities which, Reince Preibus' RNC admitted, had been alienated by aggressive party rhetoric. The report also urged state and local parties to confront the party's longstanding problem in attracting support from single, young, and career-oriented women. (*GOP Report*, 2013). In the 113th Congress, 82 Representatives and 20 Senators were women. 63 of the House's female cohort were Democrats as were 16 of the 20 women in the Senate. It would not have escaped the attention of Republican leaders that women have been at the forefront of the Democratic Party's resurgence in one of the nation's most competitive states. In 2012, New Hampshire became the first state in American history to return an all-female delegation to Congress. At the start of the 113th Congress in January 2013, three of New Hampshire's four congressional seats were occupied by Democrats (former governor Jeane Shaheen, Ann McLane Kuster, and Carol Shea-Porter) and one by a Republican (Kelly Ayotte). In the same election, Democratic candidate Maggie Hassan defeated Republican Ovide Lamontagne for the governorship, winning every county in a twelve-point sweep. Two years earlier, New Hampshire had become the first state to have a legislative chamber with a female majority when 13 women held seats in the state Senate. Demographic changes in New Hampshire have not noticeably altered its racial and ethnic mix, however. The population is 94.2 percent white. Hispanics make up 3.2 percent, Asian-Americans 2.4 percent, and black Americans 1.5 percent (U.S. Census Bureau 2013). This profile is heavily out of step with the rest of the United States where black Americans account for 13.2 percent and Hispanic Americans for 17.1 percent. The lack of racial and ethnic diversity somewhat disadvantages Democrats, who traditionally do well among such groups.

STATE POLITICS: FLEXIBLE RESPONSE

Party control of the New Hampshire legislature has switched three times in the past four election cycles (from Republican to Democrat and back again) providing further evidence that while the Democrats may be back in the game, neither they nor the Republicans have achieved complete electoral dominance. Since the 1990s, voters have mostly preferred pragmatism to radicalism. GOP right-wingers Newt Gingrich, Rick Santorum, and Rick Perry all fared poorly in New Hampshire's 2012 primary while the more libertarian and thoughtful Ron Paul and Jon Huntsman took second and third spots after Romney. The results did not surprise state party veterans. The state motto, "Live Free Or Die" portrays an electorate perennially receptive to political messages centered upon small government and unintrusive social policies though, ironically, Granite State representatives in Washington have worked hard to secure federal "pork." According to "Citizens Against Government Waste," New Hampshire received more government grants than every state except Alaska and Hawaii (Taylor 2005, 19). In GOP presidential primaries since the nomination reforms of the 1960s and 1970s, only Patrick Buchanan's 1996 win could be seen as a victory for the radical right. Other winners (Nixon, Ford, Bush Sr., McCain, and Romney) have come from the party mainstream, despite the tendency for more ideologically driven party activists to influence primary outcomes. George Bush Jr., the party's most committed evangelical nominee of the modern era, lost to John McCain in 2000. Ronald Reagan's status is more complex. By 2014, definitions of 'radical conservative' had shifted from their 1980 equivalent and the "movement" itself was more organized and aggressive. Moreover, Reagan was a familiar figure, a closet pragmatist and not a practitioner of the train wreck politics later espoused by the Tea Party.

The large numbers of voters describing themselves as "moderate" ensures that both major parties must continually tailor their policies and cultural messages for a broader audience. The impression that New Hampshire's new "swing" status derives from an unusually high number of independent voters, is misleading, according to David Moore and Andrew Smith, who point out that changes to state registration laws have allowed large numbers of voters to stay "undeclared" until Election Day, registering as Republicans or Democrats only at polling stations and then immediately reverting to "undeclared" status before they leave. As a result, "undeclared" voters accounted for 42–44 percent of the state electorate between 2006 and 2014, with 33 percent for Republicans and 29 percent for Democrats (Moore and Smith 2015, 7, 18). Problematically for pollsters, many "undeclareds" were simply Republicans or Democrats who chose not to reveal their party loyalties, perhaps from a merely temporary dissatisfaction with their party's performance at state or national level.

On the Democratic side, polls suggest party voters' liberal self-identification has increased slightly in the last decade but their successes at the gubernatorial and congressional levels have come with strings attached. Democrat candidates have mostly appealed across the ideological divide. Long-serving Governor John Lynch (2005–2013) won four terms in office after taking "The Pledge" and took conservative positions on issues such as the death penalty and parental notification in abortion cases involving minors. He signed the gay marriage law of June 2009 but stated his personal opposition to it. Governor Jeane Shaheen, Lynch's Democratic predecessor (1997–2003), also took "The Pledge" but in 2000 she refused to renew it and tried, unsuccessfully, to enact a sales tax. Her reelection margin dropped dramatically at the next election. As early as the 1950s, political scientist Duane Lockard had observed that Granite State politicians tended to "convert *all* policy to questions of economy in government" (Lockard 1959, 47). Governor Hugh Gallen (1979–1982) was unseated by Republican John H. Sununu on the issue and Democratic nominee Mark Fernold lost his 2002 race against Republican Craig Benson after arguing for a broad-based tax to fund infrastructure investment. Winning Democrats, such as Maggie Hassan, have neutralized Republican exploitation of the issue only by defending what journalist Neil Peirce once called a "jerry-built" budget structure based on property taxes, revenue from tourism and from "sin taxes" on alcohol, cigarettes, hotel rooms, and gambling (Palmer 1997, 44). In other policy areas, Democratic officeholders at national and state levels have sometimes avoided endorsing legislation which might appear "too liberal" for voters' taste. Shortly before the 2014 midterms, Hassan vetoed a bill tackling workplace bullying and discrimination, to the anger of union officials (*Concord Monitor* 2014/09–17). The veto did not prevent her reelection in November 2014, defeating Republican candidate Walt Havenstein.

On the Republican side there have been some opportunities for officeholders to combine right-wing fiscal and social policies, despite the risk of alienating voters. Some candidates, however, have found it harder than others to strike a workable balance. Ovide Lamontagne, a Catholic social conservative, lost primary races for the U.S. House and Senate in 1992 and 2010, while losing gubernatorial elections to Shaheen (1996) and Hassan (2012). His 2012 campaign stressed the need to pare down the state budget and relax regulations on business but also opposed gay marriage and abortion. Lamontagne stressed he did not support invalidating gay marriages already registered in the state but the qualifier failed to help him beat Hassan (*Wall Street Journal* 2012). By contrast, John E. Sununu, serving as First District Representative to the U.S. House from 1997–2003 and as Senator from 2003–2009, was able to match conservative fiscal orthodoxy with more controversial stands against the assault weapons ban and abortion rights. Judd Gregg (Governor, 1989–1993; U.S. Senator, 1993–2011) provided a model profile for pragmatic conservatism. The son of a former GOP governor, Gregg was a fiscal conservative but a social moderate who voted against the proposed 2006 Federal Marriage Amendment and supported an assault weapons ban. Gregg's service on the Senate Budget committee earned him the unusual accolade of nomination for Secretary of Commerce by Democratic President-elect Obama in 2008, a post he eventually declined.

In 2006, Thomas F. Schaller observed that northeastern Democrats had performed well in presidential elections but "have made almost no progress expanding their down-ballot control . . . specifically by eliminating as many as possible moderate Republicans in Congress and electing more Democratic governors" (Schaller 2006, 122). Since 2001, an exodus of moderates out of the GOP, partly due to pressure from grassroots radicals, has seen Vermont's Jim Jeffords switch to independent status and yield his Senate seat to independent Bernie Sanders, Maine's Olympia Snowe replaced by independent Angus King, and Rhode Island's Lincoln Chafee, who became an independent and later a Democrat as state governor, replaced in the Senate by Democrat Sheldon Whitehouse. Democrats in New Hampshire are now performing well by Schaller's regional down-ballot measurement but are unlikely to receive the same help from Tea Party radicals. State Republicans are generally playing a cannier game to preserve their competitive status and seem to understand their own electorate rather better than their counterparts in other states. During primary races for the 2014 midterm elections, two candidates, Daniel Innis and Marilinda Garcia, mounted challenges to more established party figures which went considerably beyond the now-familiar face-off between Washington "insider" and Tea Party populist. Innis, the openly gay and married ex-head of the University of New Hampshire's Paul Business School, campaigned for the first House district seat against ex-Congressman Frank Guinta, a former mayor of Manchester who had won the seat from incumbent Democrat Shea-Porter in 2010, only to lose it to her in 2012. Innis received substantial funding from outside activist groups such as American Unity PAC, an organization donating money to pro-gay marriage Republicans. Innis' support for gay marriage, however, was not the focus of Guinta's campaign, possibly for fear of a backlash among moderates and independents—a problem which Republican candidates in the northeast had encountered as far back as 1998. Fighting for the second district nomination against Gary Lambert, Garcia was conservative on economic and environmental policy but more moderate or nuanced in her stances on immigration and healthcare. This, along with her gender and Spanish and Italian parentage, made her a harder candidate to categorize ideologically but "a demographic trifecta for the party" according to Fergus Cullen, a former head of the state GOP (*Washington Post* 2014/09/09). Recognizing the potential advantages for the November campaign against the popular incumbent Democrat Ann McLane Kuster, the conservative Club For Growth PAC paid out $500,000 for pro-Garcia television ads (*Concord Monitor* 2014/09/10). With support from high-profile national party figures such as Texas Senator Ted Cruz and the influential conservative state newspaper, the Manchester *Union Leader*, Garcia won with a 50–27 percent margin over Lambert, a more traditional Republican conservative and former state senator for New Hampshire's 13th district (*Concord Monitor* 2014/09/10). Innis lost a closer race with Guinta in September 2014 by 41 percent to 49 percent (WMUR-TV 2014).

CONCLUSION

Since 1992, the Democratic Party has moved into a position of either supremacy or rough parity with the GOP in New England, a region once regarded as a Republican bastion. This is partly due to demographic shifts, but also to ideological repositioning by the national parties. From the 1990s, Democrats tended to follow the Clinton "New Democrat" trend by carefully tailoring messages at the national level to accommodate Reaganite fiscal conservatism and right-of-center positions on small government and law and order. Between 1992 and 2014 the national Republican party moved farther to the right. These developments prompted shifts in voting patterns across the United States. In New Hampshire, the consequence has been a modest increase in liberal identification among voters but a very marked improvement in the electoral performance of state Democrats. This did not mean, however, that Republicans have been "locked out" of state politics. Rather, they have faced tougher competition at all levels and are now compelled, as Democrats had been during the 1980s, to adjust their policies to suit the new climate. Both parties now contend for support from voters who tend to be, in Bill Clinton's view, more consistently engaged and informed than many state electorates, partly as a consequence of the heavy media attention lavished upon them since the 1950s. This may also partly explain New Hampshire's relatively robust turnout levels in both state and national elections, even in 2014, when turnout levels for the midterm elections plumbed depths not seen since World War II. An unaggressive but pervasive libertarian ethos constitutes a "glass ceiling" for Democrats with ambitious welfare and spending proposals but voters' lack of sympathy for doctrinal conservatism and Christian moralism simultaneously restrains more radical Republicans. Both sides try to attract "independent" voters but neither now enjoys an in-built advantage. Since 1992, Republicans have found it increasingly difficult to deliver the Granite State for their party but they continue to be highly competitive in congressional and state races. New Hampshire's current political environment, while in step with the general movement of New England states to the left, has stopped short of becoming a "safe" Democrat state. The victory of George W. Bush in 2000 and the see-saw results of congressional and state legislature elections since 2006 suggest that the Granite State, unlike some of its neighbours, is still up for grabs. In the 2014 midterms, Democrats Shaheen, Kuster, and Hassan were all re-elected but Shea-Porter lost the 1st District seat to Republican Frank Guinta and the GOP once again retook the state House of Representatives. New Hampshire's state delegation was thus split evenly between the parties

Rather than changing from a red state to a blue state, New Hampshire has moved, in the words of the *Concord Monitor*, "from ruby-red Republican to a deep shade of purple" (*Concord Monitor* 2012/11/06). As long as both parties remain competitive and state voter registration rules remain unchanged, both Democrats and Republicans will continue to identify New Hampshire as a "swing" state—one of the few in the Northeast region still offering the Republican Party a realistic opportunity to win its electoral votes by moderating its intemperate radicalism and staying in tone with the views and needs of Granite State voters.

NOTES

1. Earl Black and Merle Black, *Divided America: The Ferocious Power Struggle in American Politics* (New York: Simon & Schuster, 2007).
2. U.S. Census Bureau 2013 estimates. http://quickfacts.census.gov/qfd/states/33000.html.

BIBLIOGRAPHY

Black, Earl, and Merle Black. *Divided America: The Ferocious Power Struggle in American Politics* (New York: Simon & Schuster, 2007).

Campbell, Angus, Philip E. Converse, Warren E. Miller, and Donald E. Stokes. *The American Voter*. Unabridged edition (Chicago: University of Chicago Press, 1980).

Concord Monitor. "New Hampshire, once a Republican stronghold, has moved slowly to the middle." Ben Leubsdorf. November 6, 2012. http://www.concord-monitor.com/home/2655386-95/state-hampshire-republican-democrat.

Concord Monitor. "Garcia defeats Lambert, Lawrence in 2nd Congressional GOP race." Sarah Palermo and Casey McDermott. September 10, 2014, A1.

Concord Monitor. "New Hampshire House votes to uphold Gov. Maggie Hassan's veto of anti-bullying bill." September 17, 2014. http://www.concordmonitor.com/news/13586209-95/new-hampshire-house-votes-to-uphold-gov-maggie-hassans-veto-of-anti-bullying-bill.

Darmofal, David, and Peter F. Nardulli. "The Dynamics of Critical Realignments: An Analysis Across Time and Space." *Political Behaviour* 32 (June 2010): 2.

Gimpel, James G., Karen M. Kaufman, and Shanna Pearson-Merkowitz. "Battleground States Versus Blackout States: The Behavioural Impressions of Modern Presidential Campaigns." *The Journal of Politics* 69 (August 2007): 3.

Gregg, Hugh, and William M. Gardner. *Why New Hampshire? The First-in-the-Nation Primary State* (Nashua: Resources NH, 2003).

Interview: Andrew E. Smith, Director of University of New Hampshire Survey Center and Associate Professor of Practice in Political Science. University of New Hampshire. October 24, 2014.

Johnson, Bonnie J. "Identities of Competitive States in U.S. Presidential Elections: Electoral College Bias or Candidate-Centered Politics?" *Publius* 35 (Spring 2005): 2.

Johnson, Kenneth M. *New Hampshire Demographic Trends in the Twenty-First Century* (University of New Hampshire, Carsey Institute, 2012). http://www.carseyinstitute.unh.edu/publications/Report-Johnson-Demographic-Trends-NH-21st-Century.pdf.

Judis, John B., and Ruy Teixeira. *The Emerging Democratic Majority* (New York: Scribner, 2002).

Lockard, Duane. *New England State Politics* (New Jersey: Princeton University Press, 1959).

McDonald, Michael. "2012 November General Election Turnout Rates." United States Election Project. http://www.electproject.org/2012g.

Miller, Gary, and Norman Schofield. "The Transformation of the Republican and Democratic Party Coalitions in the U.S." *Perspectives on Politics* 6 (September 2008): 3.

Moore, David W., and Andrew E. Smith. *Out of the Gate: The New Hampshire Primary and its Role in the Presidential Nomination Process* (University Press of New England, 2015) 7, 18.

New Hampshire Center for Policy Studies. "What Is New Hampshire? An Overview of Issues Shaping the Granite State's Future." September 2014.

New York Times. "New Hampshire Poll Backs View of Volatile Mood Among Voters." E. J. Dionne. March 2, 1980.

New York Times. "Iowa Caucus Results" and "New Hampshire Primary Results" in "Election 2008." http://politics.nytimes.com/election-guide/2008/results/states/IA.html and http://politics.nytimes.com/election-guide/2008/results/states/NH.html.

New York Times. "Presidential Geography: New Hampshire." Micah Cohen. June 24, 2012. http://fivethirtyeight.blogs.nytimes.com/2012/06/24/presidential-geography-new-hampshire/?_php=true&_type=blogs&_r=0.

Office of the Secretary of State. New Hampshire. Elections Division. http://sos.nh.gov/Elections.aspx.

Palmer, Niall A. *The New Hampshire Primary and the American Electoral Process* (Boulder: Westview Press, 1997).

Pew Forum on Religion and Public Life. U.S. Religious Landscape Survey. http://www.journalism.org/search/topics+votor+demographics/?site=pewforum.

Phillips, Kevin P. *The Emerging Republican Majority* (New York: Arlington House, 1969).

Republican Growth and Opportunity Report, 2013. Washington, D.C. http://goproject.gop.com/rnc_growth_opportunity_book_2013.pdf.

Schaller, Thomas F. *Whistling Past Dixie: How Democrats Can Win Without the South* (New York: Simon and Schuster, 2006), 122.

Shaw, Daron R. *The Race to 270: The Electoral College and the Campaign Strategies of 2000 and 2004* (Chicago: University of Chicago Press, 2006).

Smidt, Corwin, Kevin den Dulk, Bryan Groehle, James Penning, Stephen Monsma, and Douglas Koopman. *The Disappearing God Gap? Religion in the 2008 Presidential Election* (Oxford: Oxford University Press).

Taylor, Andrew. *Elephant's Edge: The Republicans as a Ruling Party* (New York: Praeger, 2005).

Union Leader. "Economist says NH No Longer the Economic Driver It Was." Michael Cousineau. October 8, 2014. www.unionleader.com/apps/pbcs.dll/article?AID=/20141008/.

U.S. Census Bureau. 2013 Estimates. http://quickfacts.census.gov/qfd/states/33000.html.

Wall Street Journal. "Election 2012. Profile: Ovide Lamontagne." http://projects.wsj.com/campaign2012/candidates/view/ovide-lamontagne--NH-G.

Washington Post. "Huckabee, Savoring Win and Looking Ahead." Perry Bacon Jr. January 4, 2008, 44. http://voices.washingtonpost.com/44/2008/01/04/huckabee_savoring_win_and_look_1.html.

Washington Post. "Outside groups boost gay man, millennial woman in New Hampshire GOP primaries." Sean Sullivan. September 9, 2014. http://www.washingtonpost.com/blogs/post-politics/wp/2014/09/09/outside-groups-boost-gay-man-millenial-woman-in-new-hampshire-gop-primaries/.

Chapter Eleven

Virginia

Not Leaving the Spotlight

John J. McGlennon

In each of the past two presidential elections, the Commonwealth of Virginia has played a critical role. After a century of highly predictable results, the state suddenly has found itself among those most fiercely contested in the battle for the White House. The emergence of the Old Dominion as a "swing state" has resulted from a confluence of factors including demographic change, emergence of previously quiescent voting blocs, and the realignment of groups both for and against each of the two major parties. The unsettled nature of the electorate promises to keep the state among the small subset of "purple" states in 2016, and allow some better sense of whether the changes that began to appear in George W. Bush's narrow reelection victory were durable or whether the past two elections have been deviations from a continuing pattern.

The expected closeness of Virginia reflects a transformation of the electorate which has given each party unprecedented levels of success among various groups or regions, but in which the Democratic support has more fundamentally altered the state's balance of power. Overall, the changes have advantaged the Democrats in presidential contests, but have been more challenging in the state's midterm and non-federal state election years.

After 1988, Virginia's electoral votes grew from 12 to 13 in large measure due to the surge of population in the Northern Virginia suburbs of Washington, D.C. These votes were awarded to the GOP by margins ranging from more than 20 percent in 1988 to a bare 2 percent in 1996.

The election of 2004 did not appear to signal change in partisan competition in Virginia. For the tenth straight time, the Commonwealth would cast its electoral votes for the GOP nominee as Bush repeated his success of the 2000 election with an eight percentage point victory over Democratic nominee John F. Kerry.

Before long, though, observers noted some subtle changes emerging from the returns, and the Old Dominion began to appear on lists of states that seemed to promise opportunities to Democrats in the future (Marshall 2004). Chief among these changes was a shift of voting among affluent, highly educated suburban voters. In particular, the largest locality in the state gave the win to the first Democrat since Lyndon Johnson in 1964. Fairfax County is home to one out of every eight Virginians, and had been a bulwark of GOP support in Presidential years (McGlennon 2005).

Other changes contributed to the notion that Virginia was an increasingly attractive target for Democrats, and that Republicans would have to invest time and money in defending a state that by common agreement had been effectively uncontested for most of four decades. Growing diversity, a continued movement toward a more urban population, and new efforts to stimulate participation among groups (especially single women, racial minorities, and young voters) which had low voter turnout rates all contributed to moving Virginia from the periphery of the national campaign to a place among the handful of states that would be the center of both the 2008 and 2012 elections (Cable and Claibourn 2012).

Not only has Virginia become a "purple" state, reflecting the closeness of the election outcomes, but it has been one of the most obvious of "swing states," places where regardless of the winner or margin, the state has moved in a new direction.

As we will discuss, candidate schedules, campaign spending, and electoral results all confirm Virginia's status as a "purple" state in both of the elections won by Barack Obama. Increased participation by African-, Hispanic-, and Asian-Americans, urban voters, and young people was accompanied by a growing tendency of these groups to vote for Democrats. Smaller, countervailing trends among rural white voters and disenchantment with President Obama among non-affiliated voters offset the Democratic gains to some extent. Finally, the ability of subsequent Democratic nominees to retain the support of these new groups is an unsettled question. There is ample reason to believe that Virginia will continue to attract the attention of the presidential campaigns in 2016 and beyond.

Both public opinion polling and political punditry showed in early 2015 that Virginia was going to be in the middle of the next Presidential race for just the reasons that put it there in the past two elections (Kidd 2015; Brownstein 2015).

VIRGINIA'S PRESIDENTIAL POLITICS

"Mother of Presidents" may be the nickname enjoyed by Virginia due to its production of Washington, Jefferson, Monroe, Madison, Tyler, Harrison,

Taylor, and Wilson, but its fertility has receded. Although the state dominated the Executive Office in the eighteenth and nineteenth centuries, its contemporary role in the choice of our national leaders has been more modest.

With the emergence of the "Solid South" during the Jim Crow era of American politics, the Commonwealth demonstrated striking consistency in presidential elections. From 1900 to 1948, Democratic nominees for president won the state's electoral votes every four years with one notable exception. In 1928, Virginia voters, like those of four other Southern states, could not countenance the election of a New York Catholic Irish-American who favored ending Prohibition. Even though the state's dominant political organization, the "Byrd Machine" headed by senior U.S. Senator Harry Flood Byrd, did nothing to support the Democratic national ticket from 1940 on, Democrats retained majorities in presidential contests (Key 1949, 336–337).

The second half of the twentieth century provided a mirror image of the first. Republicans scored a major breakthrough in winning Virginia's electoral votes for Dwight D. Eisenhower, and except for the 1964 Lyndon Johnson landslide, the GOP enjoyed uninterrupted success through the last election of the twentieth century. Even the regional appeal of Georgian Jimmy Carter, who carried every other state in the South in 1976, was lost on Virginia, and the all-South ticket of Bill Clinton and Al Gore fell short as well in both 1992 and 1996, as did Gore's presidential campaign in 2000.

The Commonwealth became electorally competitive for statewide and other offices in the 1960s, and while one party or the other may have had successful streaks, overall the outcomes were fairly well balanced. The one-term-limited governorship (it is the only state to still have this restriction), for instance, was held by 5 Democrats and 5 Republicans between 1965 and 2000.

The Democrats' competitiveness in state elections was partly the result of nominating moderates. Candidates for governor like Charles Robb, Gerald Baliles, and even L. Douglas Wilder were able to win nominations in party conventions, an option to primaries allowed under Virginia law. There, party activists hungry for success after a string of GOP victories pragmatically picked nominees who could appeal to traditional Democrats, moderate independents, and even less conservative Republicans. Wilder's 1989 election was historic as the first victory by an African American candidate for governor in the United States, and by multiple accounts, his climb to the governorship was accomplished by his ability to appeal to moderates and conservatives (Baker 1989; Yancey 1988). The fact that gubernatorial elections occurred outside of the federal election cycles also helped insulate Virginia's Democrats from national trends which seemed to benefit the GOP before the new millenium.

As the first decade of the 2000s unfolded, the transformation of the Commonwealth was beginning. Democrats won the first governor's race of the decade while the conventional wisdom held that the GOP cemented its control over the General Assembly (the state legislature) for decades by winning majorities which drew Congressional and state legislative district lines. Though the Republicans have retained wide margins in the House of Delegates, Democrats had at least temporarily won back the Senate by 2007.

In both 2005 and 2006, Democrats won upsets in statewide elections, with Lt. Governor Tim Kaine earning a promotion to governor in the first year and former Reagan Administration Secretary of the Navy James Webb scoring the most improbable of victories over U.S. Senator George Allen in the second, destroying Allen's prospects for a presidential run. In both cases, the Democrats received surprising support among suburban voters in counties which the GOP had routinely carried in Northern Virginia (Brodnitz 2005, 2). All of these developments gave ammunition to those who argued that Virginia was up for grabs in the next presidential race.

THE ELECTION OF 2008

After decades of serving as bystanders in presidential politics, Virginians found themselves front and center in the 2008 election. Democrats had their first meaningful presidential primary, part of a newly minted "Potomac" regional contest, with Maryland and the District of Columbia selecting the same day to vote. Nearly a million Democratic ballots were cast, doubling the vote in the GOP primary contest and shattering all previous primary records. Barack Obama swept the state, winning nearly two-thirds of the vote over Hillary Clinton and John Edwards, who had already ended his campaign but remained on the ballot. Arizona Senator John McCain was believed to have an insurmountable delegate lead by the time of the mid-February contest, but faced a stiff challenge from former Arkansas Governor Mike Huckabee. McCain posted a nine percent win, while losing most of the state's more rural areas to Huckabee (NBC 2008).

The general election campaign brought all four of the major party ticket members in regular rotation to Virginia. Both McCain and Obama suggested prominent Virginians as potential vice presidential running mates. McCain suggested Congressman Eric Cantor would be considered (Allen and Martin 2008). Obama's campaign floated the names of Senator Webb and Senate candidate and former Governor Mark Warner as possibilities until they both demurred and asked to be removed from consideration. Governor Tim Kaine, on the other hand, remained as one of the three finalists (along with Delaware Senator Joseph Biden and Kansas Governor Kathleen Sebelius), and ultimately was prevailed upon to serve as Chairman of the Democratic National Committee at Obama's urging. Kaine had been one of Obama's earliest prominent supporters (Gardner 2008). It was no surprise that Obama chose to include Virginia in his final day of general election campaigning. Even though he focused the bulk of his time on vote-rich Northern Virginia and Hampton Roads, Obama made special efforts to rally support at college campuses across the state. McCain put his emphasis on more rural areas and those with high concentrations of veterans and military installations. Both Alaska Governor Sarah Palin, McCain's running mate, and Senator Biden, the Democratic vice-presidential candidate, regularly included Virginia on their schedules.

Public opinion polling early in the general election showed a slight Obama edge, something that long-time Virginia observers were wary to credit. Even Michael Dukakis in 1988 had managed to post a lead in the Commonwealth following his nominating convention. In September of 2008, polling was inconsistent, but on average provided McCain with a paper-thin advantage, suggesting the normal movement to the GOP seen in previous years. That pattern broke with the financial collapse of late September, and in the last six weeks, nearly two dozen polls of Virginia were published, and not one showed McCain ahead. On average, Obama's lead was 6.5 percent. The evidence all pointed to a clear if small Obama lead, and the Illinois senator wound up carrying the state on Election Day by almost exactly the predicted margin (McGlennon 2009, 219–224).

Turnout in the election surged compared to previous Virginia performance. In 2004, the state had barely exceeded the national voting rate, but in 2008, it was approximately 6 percent higher. V.O. Key had once written of Virginia's voter turnout, "By contrast, Mississippi is a hotbed of democracy" (Key 1949, 20) but the Commonwealth rewarded the attention it was now receiving with a record vote.

In the first "battle of former governors," Democrat Mark Warner swamped Republican James Gilmore with nearly two-thirds of the vote for the U.S. Senate seat being vacated by Republican John Warner. He was joined in the Congressional delegation by three new Democratic House members. This presidential election had upended the previous half-century and assured that Virginia would be front and center in the next presidential contest.

The 2008 election was constructed around mobilizing new voters, especially college students and minorities in central cities, focusing on suburban and urban voters disaffected with the George W. Bush presidency, and utilizing new technology to build a broad and deep voter identification file. That file would prove critical to Obama's reelection effort (Issenberg 2012).

Between 2008 and 2012, Republicans had plenty of reason to believe that Obama's victory in Virginia had been a fluke. Electing its governor in odd years following the presidential contests, voters handed the chief executive office by a wide margin to the GOP candidate, Attorney-General Robert McDonnell. This continued an oddity of the state, which had elected the

Table 11.1. Presidential Voting In Virginia, 2004–2012

Year/Candidates	Percent R vs. D	Total Vote	% Voting Eligible Turnout vs. National	Change in VEP Turnout
2004 Bush (R) v. Kerry (D)	53.7–45.5	3,223,156	61.1%/60.7	6.1% increase from 2000 0.4% above US
2008 McCain (R) v. Obama (D)	46.3–52.6	3,752,858	67.6%/62.2	6.5% increase from 2004 5.4% above US
2012 Romney (R) v. Obama (D)	47.3–51.2	3,896,846	66.6%/58.6%	1.0% decrease from 2008 8.0 above US

Sources: Election data from Virginia State Board of Elections: http://www.sbe.virginia.gov/index.php/resultsreports/ ; Turnout data from U.S. Elections Project: http://www.electproject.org/home/voter-turnout/voter-turnout-data

gubernatorial nominee of the party losing the White House the previous year in every election since 1977. The 2010 Republican midterm "tsunami" washed over Virginia, as three Democrats were swept out of the U.S. House, including a 28-year veteran from Southwestern Virginia's "Fighting Ninth" district. Republicans also solidified their control over the state legislature in 2011.

As the 2012 election approached, the fate of President Obama once again seemed to rest in the hands of voters in a small set of states, and Virginia was once again front and center in this group. Controversy over the president's signature health care reform, a slower than expected economic recovery, and Congressional opposition that seemed to stymie Obama's legislative agenda at every turn left the president with a very small margin for error. For much of this time, however, Obama received approval ratings from Virginians that were slightly above his national numbers.

THE ELECTION OF 2012

Primaries were of little consequence in the Commonwealth during the 2012 nomination phase. Without opposition to Obama, the Democrats were not even on the ballot, and due to failure by most GOP candidates to meet the requirements for competing in the primary, only former Massachusetts Governor Mitt Romney and Texas Congressman Ron Paul qualified. Paul had his best primary performance, but Romney won almost the full slate of delegates, on his way to securing the party nomination (Smith 2012).

Once again Virginia played a prominent role in national ticket speculation. Romney, like McCain, raised the possibility of Eric Cantor, the House Majority Leader, as a potential vice presidential pick, but focused prime attention on Governor McDonnell, who was widely seen as one of three finalists. Though McDonnell did not get the nod, he did get to introduce Romney at the announcement of Congressman Paul Ryan's selection. The choice, in an attempt at misdirection, was held in Norfolk, aboard the retired battleship Wisconsin, named in honor of Ryan's home state (Zeleny and Rutenberg 2012). Given McDonnell's subsequent indictment and conviction on corruption charges, this turned out to be a very lucky choice for Romney.

Obama was focused on Virginia as well, and when Senator Jim Webb announced he would not seek a second term in November, the president used his considerable influence to convince former Governor Kaine to step down from the DNC chair to seek the Senate seat. With George Allen attempting to reclaim the seat he lost to Webb, Kaine's candidacy insured that the Senate contest would be a premier race in the election cycle.

If money was an indicator of the degree to which Virginia was in the cross-hairs of both parties, both sides saw this as a winnable state. By Election Day, television advertising cost the two presidential candidates and their allies a total of $151 million, second only to the much larger state of Florida. Few Virginians could turn on their television sets without being subjected to un-interrupted blocks of presidential campaign ads. While Romney and friends outspent Obama by a clear margin ($83 vs. $68 million), Obama was actually able to run more ads in the state. Romney's reliance on outside groups did not allow him the discounts available to presidential campaigns, which Obama's campaign organization did receive, and more effective targeting allowed the president's campaign greater efficiency.

Between June and the election in November, it was nearly impossible for Virginians to avoid the presidential campaigns in person. The 98 visits made by the presidential and vice-presidential nominees and their respective spouses ranked the Old Dominion third in total visits behind only Ohio (148) and Florida (118). Obama made 20 visits, a pace of nearly once a week, but Romney managed to book travel to the Commonwealth 27 times (McGlennon 2014, 220).

Key to Obama's strategy was the exploitation of the rich trove of data which had been gathered in the 2008 campaign and enhanced throughout the subsequent four years. The president's reelection campaign harnessed a large paid field staff to construct a potent volunteer force which eschewed efforts at persuasion in favor of identifying and mobilizing the president's supporters. Romney's campaign focused on advertising to an electorate which contained self-motivated voters who could be relied upon to show up on Election Day. The president's reelection campaign was constructed around the need to moti-vate Obama supporters, who in many elections were not reliable participants.

With dozens of surveys being conducted throughout the election, Virginia proved to be remarkably stable. The monthly polling averages throughout the election year consistently showed a small Obama advantage, varying from a high of 7.8 percent in March to only 1.7 percent in October. The narrowing lead in polls underestimated Obama's performance, as he bested Romney by slightly less than 4 percent. This was down from his 2008 margin, but less than his national decline. Virginia was identified as the state which provided a kind of "firewall" for the president, as winning here opened a number of paths to the 270 electoral votes he needed and blocked Romney's opportunity.

The 2012 election also produced a win for Kaine over Allen in the U.S. Senate battle, as the Democrat outperformed President Obama and won by a margin of 5.9 percent. No change occurred in the 11 House races. Only one contest wound up with a margin of less than ten percent, and that was in the

Second District, where Republican freshman Scott Rigell was reelected as Obama was narrowly carrying the district at the presidential level.

In Virginia, politics rarely takes a break, and presidential election years are followed by contests for the governor's office the next year. There were plenty of reasons for both sides to believe they had the advantage. Republicans had scored a landslide in 2009, after Obama's solid win nationally and in Virginia. Their nominee, Attorney General Ken Cuccinelli, had crowded out opposition within his party early in the process and was uncontested for the nomination, handed to him at a state party convention in June. Cuccinelli had been elected to the State Senate from a Northern Virginia seat that leaned toward the Democrats and had won his current office in the GOP landslide of 2009.

Democrats had their candidate in Terry McAuliffe, settled when no one filed against him in the party's primary. McAuliffe had run unsuccessfully for the 2009 nomination, and though a 20-year resident of the Northern Virginia suburbs, was better known as a former Democratic National Committee Chair and confidant of President Bill Clinton. McAuliffe had several advantages, including a highly successful fundraising operation built over years of national campaigns, the organizational support of the Obama administration and surprising support among Republican business leaders in Hampton Roads and Northern Virginia, who were angry at Cuccinelli for failing to support a transportation funding plan advanced by Republican Governor McDonnell. McAuliffe actively lobbied the legislature's Democrats to support the transportation plan and was rewarded with several high profile GOP endorsements.

Using the data so effectively collected by the Obama campaign in Virginia, McAuliffe focused on motivating infrequent voters, who turned out for presidential elections in 2008 and 2012 but not others. But even with a huge fundraising edge, crossover support and a technically superior campaign operation, McAuliffe edged Cuccinelli by only a small 2 percent margin, with neither candidate commanding a majority of the vote due to a Libertarian candidate who drew 6 percent (Fisher 2013). Still, for Democrats a win was a win and the satisfaction was tripled when they also won the Lieutenant Governor's race by a wide margin and the office of Attorney General by several hundred votes.

In 2014, Mark Warner retained his U.S. Senate seat over national Republican operative Ed Gillespie by a surprisingly narrow margin, as the Republican Party nationally gained nine senate seats. Warner's might well have proven to be the tenth gain to the shock of nearly all observers, as he clung on to the barest of victories, a winning margin of only 17,000 votes, or less than one percent. His electoral performance tracked closely to the results of the presidential and gubernatorial races of the preceding two years, a sharp contrast to his 30 percent win in 2008, when he carried almost every jurisdiction in the Commonwealth. The result was largely seen as a reflection of the partisan polarization that has overtaken nearly every state, including Virginia, and Warner's challenge as a self-described "radical centrist" in mobilizing his party's faithful to his side in an election where public polling had shown him comfortably ahead.

VIRGINIA'S SWING STATE ROLE IN 2016

As the 2016 election begins to come into sight, Virginia appears likely once again to attract significant attention. Neither side can view the Commonwealth with confidence. Republicans wonder how to reconstruct the dependable majorities of past elections. Democrats face the question of whether another Democrat can stimulate the coalition of voters who emerged in unprecedented numbers to propel Obama to two victories, but whose presence in non-presidential years is far from assured.

LASTING REALIGNMENT OR DEVIATION FROM THE NORM?

To better understand the movement of Virginia into the ranks of "purple states" in the last two presidential elections, it is necessary to deconstruct the Obama majorities, and at the same time, seek to understand its emergence as a "swing state." In particular, did President Obama profit from a changing electorate, which constitutes the new landscape of Virginia politics, or did he uniquely stimulate participation among groups of voters whose turnout in future elections is suspect? Evidence from census data, campaign and Election Day exit polling, and the results of voting in the cities and counties of the Commonwealth help to better predict the future performance of Virginia.

One factor is most clear: the state is moving inexorably toward a more urban population. Year after year, the share of Virginia's population residing outside of metropolitan areas continues to decline. Small towns and hamlets in the rural outposts of the state continue to see rates of growth far less than the healthy statewide population increases, while previously rural areas are appended to metro areas. Most recently, decades of decline in center cities and older, more densely settled suburbs have been reversed and the cities have posted among the highest growth rates in the state. Since 1970, the share of Virginia's population living in urban areas has grown from 63.2% to 75.5%, a rate almost double the national change.

Table 11.2. Virginians Living in Metro Areas by Decade

Year	% VA population in Metro Areas	Change from previous decade	% of US population living in Metro Area	Change from previous decade
1950	47.0	11.7	64.0	7.5
1960	55.6	8.6	69.9	5.9
1970	63.2	7.6	73.6	3.7
1980	66.0	2.8	73.7	0.1
1990	69.4	3.4	75.2	1.5
2000	73.0	3.6	79.0	3.8
2010	75.5	2.5	80.7	1.7

Source: U.S. Census Bureau

Suburban Virginia, which had from the 1960s through 1990 taken on the distinct national pattern of urban flight from city cores, began to reflect a much more diverse pattern of migration, as middle-class African Americans joined newer arrivals (Cable and Claibourn 2012). Fast growing Hispanic populations from Central and South America, and Asian immigrants from the Philippines, Vietnam, Korea, India, and China, among others, contributed to the need for school districts to address students whose home life included dozens of languages other than English. Recent arrivals from Africa both added to and were distinct from centuries-long United States genealogies of African American Virginians.

Many of these new groups, as they joined the ranks of American citizens and voters, contributed to a shifting balance of partisan power in metropolitan areas. The growth of the metropolitan areas had been a consistent development throughout the twentieth century and had not been particularly helpful to the Democrats. The Republican dominance of the Old Dominion in presidential contests throughout the second half of the century had depended on strong support for the GOP in suburban precincts. Particularly in presidential contests, the GOP saw localities like Fairfax County in the Washington suburbs, Henrico County outside of Richmond, and Virginia Beach, a suburban city adjacent to Norfolk, grow to the point that they overwhelmed whatever Democratic advantage might exist in the urban core. So strong was this level of support that it could also cancel out rural areas with their ancestral Democratic loyalties.

Electoral patterns in 2008 and 2012 continued a movement that had first been evident in the 2004 elections. Suburban areas that had been staunchly Republican moved against President George W. Bush in his reelection campaign. While other examples abounded, none was more critical than Fairfax County. Home to approximately one in eight Virginians, Fairfax gave a majority of its vote to Democrat John Kerry in that election. It was the first time

Table 11.3. Presidential Results for Select Virginia Localities, 2004–2012

County	Pty	2004	2004 %	2008	2008 %	2012	2012 %	2004-12 shift
Southwest VA								
Tazewell Co.	D	7,184	41.10	5,596	32.79	3,661	20.64	-20.46%
	R	10,039	57.43	11,201	65.65	13,843	78.06	+20.63
	Tot.	17,480		17,360		18,673		+1,193
Buchanan Co.	D	5,275	53.67	4,063	46.51	3,094	32.07	-21.60
	R	4,507	45.85	4,541	51.99	6,436	66.72	+20.87
	Tot.	9,829		8,961		9,830		+1
Dickenson Co.	D	3,761	50.78	3,278	48.54	2,473	35.81	-14.97
	R	3,591	48.49	3,324	49.22	4,274	61.90	+13.51
	Tot.	7,406		6,904		7,067		-339
Center Cities								
Richmond	D	52,167	70.19	73,623	79.09	75,921	77.81	+7.62
	R	21,637	29.11	18,649	20.03	20,050	20.54	-8.57
	Tot.	74,325		94,352		99,379		+25,054
Norfolk	D	43,518	61.67	62,819	71.02	62,687	72.01	+10.44
	R	26,401	37.41	24,814	28.05	23,147	26.59	-10.82
	Tot.	70,570		88,677		87,652		+17,082
Danville	D	9,436	49.37	12,352	59.12	12,218	60.47	+11.10
	R	9,399	49.18	8,361	40.02	7,763	38.42	-10.76
	Tot.	19,112		21,136		21,138		+2,026
Alexandria	D	41,116	66.84	50,473	71.73	52,199	71.10	+4.26
	R	19,844	32.26	19,181	27.25	20,249	27.58	-4.68
	Tot.	61,515		70,923		74,010		+13,495
Older Suburbs								
VA Beach	D	70,666	40.22	98,885	49.13	94,299	47.95	+7.73
	R	103,752	59.06	100,319	49.84	99,291	50.49	-8.57
	Tot.	175,687		202,377		197,961		+22,274
Henrico Co.	D	60,864	45.62	86,323	55.70	89,594	55.22	+9.62

Fairfax Co.	R	71,809	53.82	67,381	43.48	70,449	43.42	−10.40
	Tot.	133,418		156,527		163,998		+30,580
	D	245,671	53.25	310,359	60.11	315,273	59.56	+6.31
	R	211,980	45.94	200,994	38.93	206,773	39.06	−6.88
	Tot.	461,379		518,094		532,187		+71,808
New Suburbs								
Loudoun Co.	D	47,271	43.60	74,845	53.66	82,479	51.53	+7.93
	R	60,382	55.69	63,336	45.41	75,292	47.03	−8.66
	Tot.	108,430		139,734		160,698		+52,268
Prince William Co.	D	61,271	46.40	93,435	57.51	103,331	57.34	+10.94
	R	69,776	52.84	67,621	41.62	74,458	41.32	−11.52
	Tot.	132,063		163,039		181,084		+49,021
Chesapeake City	D	38,744	42.32	53,994	50.21	55,052	49.85	+7.53
	R	52,283	57.11	52,625	48.94	53,900	48.81	−8.30
	Tot.	91,541		108,139		111,054		+19,513
Chesterfield Co.	D	49,346	36.88	74,310	45.84	77,694	45.43	+8.55
	R	83,745	62.58	86,413	53.31	90,934	53.18	−9.40
	Tot.	133,418		162,390		172,227		+29,809
University Towns								
Charlottesville	D	11,088	71.77	15,705	78.35	16,510	75.74	+3.93
	R	4,172	27.00	4,078	20.34	4,844	22.22	−4.78
	Tot.	15,450		20,122		21,902		+6,452
Harrisonburg	D	4,726	42.85	8,444	57.54	8,654	55.49	+14.64
	R	6,165	55.89	6,048	41.21	6,565	42.10	−13.79
	Tot.	11,030		14,847		15,721		+4,691
Williamsburg	D	2,216	51.30	4,328	63.76	4,903	63.28	+11.98
	R	2,064	47.78	2,353	34.66	2,682	34.61	−13.17
	Tot.	4,320		6,838		7,770		3,450

Source: Virginia State Board of Elections

Table constructed by author.

in 40 years that Fairfax had not supported the Republican nominee. By 2008, the county provided Barack Obama with a 60% majority and 110,000 vote margin, close to half his statewide edge.

The changing vote in suburban counties reflected more than the increased diversity of the affluent communities: polling showed a clear shift of highly educated voters toward the Democrats. While other demographic categories tended to move only marginally, those with advanced degrees (more than a quarter of the Virginia electorate) switched from a GOP majority in 2000 toward the other party by a wide edge. The explanations for this shift came from several factors. Republican candidates and activists increasingly came to align with fundamental religious groups whose policies were unpopular with highly educated voters, who were also unsympathetic to an anti-scientific bias in GOP rhetoric. But just as important, the growth in post-graduate education was particularly evident among minority voters, especially African-Americans.

The historic nature of Obama's candidacy in 2008 had resonated especially well with minority voters and young people. This translated into significant increases in voter participation. Turnout in central cities like Richmond, Norfolk, and Danville increased substantially. Richmond turnout surged by one-third, and produced even fewer votes for Mitt Romney than had been received by George W. Bush. College towns also saw dramatic increases in participation, and even the previously Republican city of Harrisonburg (home of James Madison University), voted for Obama in both 2008 and 2012.

Obama scored a "trifecta" in the Old Dominion: fast growing suburbs moved decisively toward him, newly resurgent cities and inner suburbs saw greater levels of voter engagement benefitting the Democrats, and the enthusiastic mobilization of college students produced new centers of Democratic dominance.

For Republicans, the general shift of Virginia did provide some positive news. Rural communities, especially those in the southwestern sections of the state adjoining Tennessee, Kentucky, and West Virginia, abandoned Democratic identification in 2008, and like other Appalachian communities, produced enormous swings to the Republicans. Counties which had been part of the "Fighting Ninth" Congressional District, where two-party competition had flourished from the 1850s until 2004, suddenly experienced a collapse of Democratic support. Kerry, who had no special appeal to the poor, less-educated voters who had been dispossessed from their mining, furniture, and textile jobs, had won counties like Dickenson and Buchanan, but Barack Obama's weak performance against Hillary Clinton in the Virginia primary in these areas presaged defeat in 2008 and the collapse of Democratic support by 2012.

Obama drew barely half the number of votes that Kerry received when he comfortably carried Buchanan in 2004. Obama lost the county narrowly in 2008, and suffered a 2–1 defeat in 2012 in an electorate that was nearly exactly the same size as the turnout eight years earlier. That last fact reflected the basic problem confronting the GOP: their area of greatest positive change was losing population and share of the statewide vote. While Republicans made slight gains in localities across the state, the most significant changes came in these rural communities with their older, declining populations.

Efforts to understand Obama's lack of appeal to long-time Democrats have largely been unsatisfactory. Low minority populations in the area had in the past led to a relatively low indication of race as a prominent factor in voting. Some have suggested that Obama became associated with "wars" against guns and coal, two mainstays of the Appalachian region, but Obama had no record of advocating strong gun control measures, and had taken pro-coal positions as an Illinois senator. Surely Massachusetts Senator John Kerry would have been more suspect on these grounds.

Without firm evidence, it is hard to understand precisely why Obama declined so precipitously in these areas compared to earlier Democratic nominees. Perhaps it was the combination of his biracial upbringing in exotic Hawaii (and Indonesia), his intellectual and urban background, or his seeming lack of the "bubba" factor so closely associated with President Bill Clinton. Whatever the reason, this region of the country, including southwest Virginia but stretching from western Pennsylvania down through northern Alabama, moved against national trends in 2008 and has emerged as a daunting obstacle to Democratic prospects in a number of Southern states.

Whatever the state of Appalachian Virginia, the Commonwealth produced two clear victories for Democrat Obama. As the metropolitan vote consolidated and increased for the Democrats, the GOP found its base of support increasingly in the declining rural vote. This tendency, reflected in greater influence by these voters in GOP nominating politics, and by the outsized influence of rural members in the GOP state legislative caucuses, has served to exacerbate the division between the parties. This divide was put to a stern test in the 2013 election for governor, a race that at the start of the year most observers thought was the GOP's to lose.

Rather than viewing the presidential contest as a signal of the need to recalibrate the party's appeal to suburbanites, young people, or minority voters, social conservatives declared that the loss in 2012 had resulted from the nomination of a candidate who was not conservative enough. They set about to correct that "problem" before the presidential year had concluded. The party voted in December 2012 to nominate for governor in a state convention in the spring. This decision was regarded as a boon to Cuccinelli and fatal to the chances of the more moderate lieutenant governor, Bill Bolling, who promptly announced his withdrawal from the nomination contest. Bolling pointedly refused to endorse Cuccinelli, and flirted with an independent candidacy. Ultimately, he remained neutral in the governor's race, a move widely interpreted as helpful to the Democratic nominee, Terry McAuliffe.

McAuliffe had diligently pursued the nomination, but other politicians tended to defer to him in part because they were not convinced the nomination was worth having. McAuliffe, however, decided to use his considerable campaign treasury to test the theory that Virginia's movement to the Democrats at the presidential level was in fact more durable and comprehensive.

The Democratic campaign was built on the structure of the Obama campaign, with the singular objective of contacting and stimulating presidential year Democratic voters who typically did not vote in other years to participate. While Democrats certainly spent substantially on television advertising, they constructed a field operation designed to "touch" infrequent Democratic voters multiple times, with mail, phone, personal visits at the door, and any other means of communication to replicate the composition of the electorate from 2012.

The result was a close but decisive victory for McAuliffe and a sweep of all three statewide offices on the ballot, including the separately elected lieutenant governor and the attorney general. The latter was decided by a tiny 973-vote margin in a race that was estimated to cost some $13,000,000 between the two major party candidates. In contrast, the Democrat won the lieutenant governor's race by a ten-point margin, with about $3,000,000 being spent in total. The race for attorney general inevitably drew comparisons to the closeness of Bob McDonnell's election to the office in 2005, when he beat Democrat Creigh Deeds (the same candidate he defeated for governor four years later) by a 323-vote margin.

The Democratic win in 2013 was achieved in large part due to McAuliffe's success in generating a turnout comparable to the presidential vote. While only 55 percent as many voters turned out, the composition of this electorate was very similar to the makeup of the voter group who showed up in 2012 (Teixeira 2013). In particular, African-Americans and unmarried women returned to the polls in sufficient numbers to defeat Cuccinelli. Young voters were notably less visible, accounting for the narrow edge for McAuliffe. In understanding the results, however, it is also important to recognize the overlaps among women, single women and racial minorities. Much has been made of the fact that McAuliffe scored particularly well among single women (Cillizza 2013; Edwards-Levy 2012), but others point to the overwhelming role of minority women in shaping the outcome of this particular demographic group vote (Maxwell 2013). While McAuliffe won among women 51–42 (+9), he lost

Table 11.4.   Exit Poll Results for Virginia, 2004–2013

Characteristic	2013 D vs. R (% of vote)	2012 D vs. R (% of vote)	2008	2004
GENDER				
Male	45/48 (49)	47/51(47)	51/47 (46)	40/59 (46)
Female	51/42 (51)	54/45 (53)	53/46 (54)	50/50 (54)
RACE				
White	36/56 (72)	37/61 (70)	39/60 (70)	32/68 (72)
Black	90/8 (20)	93/6 (20)	92/8 (20)	87/12 (21)
Hispanic	—/— (4)	64/33 (5)	65/34 (5)	—
Asian-American	—/— (1)	66/32 (3)	—	—
AGE				
18-29	45/40 (13)	61/36 (19)	60/39 (21)	54/46 (17)
30-44	56/37 (23)	54/45 (27)	51/47 (30)	40/59 (32)
45-64	46/48 (46)	46/53 (41)	51/48 (38)	45/55 (32)
65+	45/51 (18)	46/54 (14)	46/54 (11)	51/49 (19)
EDUCATION				
No College	47/50 (15)	49/50 (46)	54/45 (48)	—
Some College	40/53 (24)	47/51 (25)	53/46 (28)	—
College grad	46/46 (32)	48/50 (30)	50/49 (29)	—
Post-graduate	57/35 (29)	57/42 (24)	52/47 (23)	—
INCOME				
Under $30K	—/—*	61/38 (18)	69/30 (na)	58/42 (16)
$30-49,999	54/37 (27)	60/38 (18)	55/45 (16)	47/52 (21)
$50,000+	43/51 (33)	47/52 (65)	49/50 (70)	43/57 (61)
$100,000+	49/43 (40)	47/51 (34)	—	—
IDEOLOGY				
Conservative	13/83 (36)	11/87 (31)	18/80 (33)	15/85 (38)
Moderate	56/34 (44)	56/42 (45)	58/41 (46)	57/42 (45)
Liberal	89/4 (20)	92/7 (24)	90/9 (21)	83/17 (17)
MARRIED?				
Yes	—/—	44/55 (62)	—	—
No	—/—	61/37 (38)	—	—
PARTY				
Democratic	95/2 (37)	94/6 (39)	92/8 (39)	92/8 (35)
Republican	4/92 (32)	5/94 (32)	8/92 (33)	5/95 (39)
Independent	38/47 (31)	43/54 (29	49/48 (27)	44/54 (26)

Source: President Exit Polls, *New York Times* on-line. http://elections.nytimes.com/2012/results/president/
exit-polls for 2004-2012 and http://www.nytimes.com/projects/elections/2013/general/virginia/exit-polls.
html for 2013.

*in 2013, one category for "less than $50,000" was provided.

among white women 54–38 (–16), but won among African-American women 91–7 (+84); his loss among married women, who made up 35 percent of the electorate, was substantial (–9) but overwhelmed by his advantage among the 18 percent of voters who were single women (+42).

The 2014 elections provided more evidence of the emergence of a new Virginia electorate. Incumbent U.S. Senator Mark Warner, a very popular former governor who continued to cultivate an image of bipartisanship in his first Senate term, barely edged Ed Gillespie, a long-time GOP national opera-tive who public opinion polls consistently underestimated. With support from numerous prominent Republicans, including former Senator John Warner (whom Mark Warner had challenged in 1996), Warner still barely retained his seat and voting patterns displayed striking similarity to the Virginia results of the preceding two elections.

SUMMARY AND CONCLUSION

As we near the 2016 presidential contest, Virginia is poised once again to be a crucial battleground. Despite its two-fold support of Obama, the even-tual Democratic nominee will face questions about whether they will hold together the successful coalition. Can the new Democratic standard bearer maintain the enthusiasm of black and other minority voters, generate activ-ism and excitement among young voters, especially on college campuses, and will he or she be able to exploit the "marital status gap" by drawing over-whelming support from unmarried women (and men) to overwhelm a closer division among the married?

In the early stages of the election, that nominee appears likely to be Hillary Clinton, a candidate who lost to Obama by a landslide margin in the Virginia primary of 2008. Now she appears to have a unified party behind her, even in Virginia, where she has demonstrated more support among the rural whites who were supporters of her husband's two terms in the White House. Al-though Virginia is home to one of the few challengers to Clinton, former U.S. Senator Jim Webb, he has not yet demonstrated broad popular support in his home state. One early 2015 survey found him to be trailing Clinton among Virginia Democrats by a 65–10 margin. Webb's roots in Appalachia might give him more appeal in this area in a general election, but he faces strong headwinds in winning the nomination.

The white share of the electorate continues to decline. As Hispanic- and Asian-Americans reduce the dominance of white voters, will Democratic victory come more easily? With President Obama's exit from the scene, will rural opposition to Democrats fade, especially if the new nominee is regarded more as "one of us" by residents of the Appalachian region? Or will it matter as the share of the state's vote found in the southwestern "coal counties" continues to decline?

Will a Republican nominee find an effective way to draw some portion of the voters who have been mobilized in opposition to the GOP? Can the party's nominee create excitement among young people or find a way to reconnect with suburban and urban women who provided Democrats with enormous advantage in both presidential years and in the most recent state races?

A key to answering these questions is to simply ask where the GOP is most likely to be able to find the additional electoral votes they need to win the Presidency. It is possible that the path may run through northern industrial states which went heavily Republican in 2010 and gave the GOP some hope in 2012: Ohio, Wisconsin, Michigan, or Pennsylvania. But in the end these states disappointed Romney and his party, often by considerable margins. More likely, the GOP will look to those states that are more closely aligned to their Southern base. The GOP cannot win without the deep South, and their narrow losses in Virginia and Florida must make these states more appealing targets. In the case of the Old Dominion, the prospect of being on the sidelines seems remote.

BIBLIOGRAPHY

Allen, Mike, and Jonathan Martin. 2008. "McCain is Vetting Cantor." *Politico.* August 2, 2008. http://www.politico.com/news/stories/0808/12264.html.

Baker, Donald. 1989. *Wilder: Hold Fast to Dreams.* Washington, D.C.: Seven Locks Press.

Brodnitz, Pete. 2005. "Why Tim Kaine Won." Benenson Strategy Group. http://www.bsgco.com/insights/why-tim-kaine-won.

Brownstein, Ronald. "The States That Will Pick The President: The Sunbelt." *National Journal.* February 8, 2015. http://www.nationaljournal.com/next-america/newsdesk/the-states-that-will-pick-the-president-the-sunbelt-20150204.

Cable, Dustin, and Michael Claiborn. 2012. *Red State, Blue State: Demographic Change and Presidential Politics in Virginia.* Weldon Cooper Center for Public Service, University of Virginia.

Cillizza, Chris. 2013. The Fix: Republicans don't have a woman problem. They have a single woman problem. *Washington Post.* Nov. 6, 2013. http://www.washingtonpost.com/blogs/the-fix/wp/2013/11/06/republicans.

Edwards-Levy, Ariel. "Women, Unmarried Voters Key to McAuliffe's Virginia Victory." *Huffington Post.* November 5, 2013. http://www.huffingtonpost.com/2013/11/05/women-mcauliffe-victory_n_4222645.html.

Fisher, Marc. 2013. "McAuliffe Narrowly Wins Va. Governor's Race." *Washington Post.* November 6, 2013. http://www.washingtonpost.com/local/virginia-politics/

polls-open-across-virginia-in-hotly-contested-governors-race/2013/11/04/06c6205
c-45d2-11e3-bf0c-cebf37c6f484_story.html.

Gardner, Amy. 2008. "Webb Withdraws as Possible Vice President Pick for Obama."
Washington Post. July 8, 2008. http://www.washingtonpost.com/wp-dyn/content/
article/2008/07/07/AR2008070702358.html.

Issenberg, Sasha. 2012. "How President Obama's Campaign Used Big Data to Rally
Individual Voters." *MIT Technology Review.* December 16, 2012. http://www.
technologyreview.com/featuredstory/508836/how-obama-used-big-data-to-rally-
voters-part-1/.

Key, V.O. 1949. *Southern Politics in State and Nation.* New York: Alfred A. Knopf.

Kidd, Quentin. 2015. "Bush Tops Clinton in Battleground Virginia." Judy Ford
Wason Center for Public Policy. April 29, 2015. Newport News, VA: Christopher
Newport University.

Marshall, Will. 2004. "Heartland Strategy: Democrats Can't be a national party if they
cede all of Red America to the GOP." *Blueprint Magazine.* December 13, 2004.
http://www.dlc.org/ndol_cia5a4.html?kaid=127&subid=171&contentid=253055.

Maxwell, Zerlina. "Black Voters, Not the Gender Gap Won Virginia for McAuliffe."
The Nation. Novermber 7, 2013.

McGlennon, John. 2005. "Virginia: The Triumph of Experience over Hope." In *The
American Review of Politics,* 26:245-265.

———. 2009. "Virginia: The New Math of Blue Virginia." In *A Paler Shade of
Red: The 2008 Presidential Election in the South.* Edited by Branwell DuBose
Kapeluck, Laurence W. Moreland, and Robert P. Steed. Fayetteville, Arkansas:
University of Arkansas Press.

———. 2014. "Virginia: Obama's Unexpected Firewall." In *Second Verse, Same as
the First: The 2012 Presidential Election in the South.* Edited by Scott Buchanan
and Branwell DuBose Kapeluck. Fayetteville, Arkansas: University of Arkansas
Press.

NBC. 2008. "McCain Holds Off Huckabee." February 13, 2008. http://www.nbc-
news.com/id/23136322/ns/politics-decision_08/t/mccain-holds-strong-huckabee-
challenge/#.VDvh16OwTHg.

Smith, Kenneth. 2012. "Virginia Primary Results: Romney Wins." *Washington Post.*
March 6, 2013. http://www.washingtonpost.com/politics/virginia-primary-results-
mitt-romney-wins/2012/03/05/gIQA4yravR_story.html.

Teixeira, Ruy. 2013. "Virginia is Now One Step Closer to Being an Official Blue
State." *New Republic.* November 6, 2013.

Weldon Cooper Center. 2014. "July 1, 2013 Population Estimates for Virginia and
its Counties and Cities." January27, 2014. www.Coopercenter.org/demographics/

Yancey, Dwight. 1988. *When Hell Froze Over: The Untold Story of Doug Wilder.*
Dallas: Taylor Publishing.

Zeleney, Jeff, and Jim Rutenberg. 2012. "Romney Chooses Ryan, Pushing Fiscal
Issues to the Forefront." *New York Times.* August 11,2012. http://www.nytimes.
com/2012/08/12/us/politics/mitt-romney-names-paul-ryan-as-his-running-mate.
html?pagewanted=all.

Chapter Twelve

Battleground Iowa

Swing State Extraordinaire

Donna R. Hoffman and Christopher W. Larimer

There should be no doubt that Iowa is a legitimate swing state when it comes to presidential politics. In 2004, Iowa was one of just three states to switch its electoral vote from the previous presidential election, going for Republican George W. Bush just four years after voting for Democrat Al Gore. What is most remarkable, however, is not the switching of partisan presidential preferences, per se, but rather the margin of that switch. Gore's 2000 victory in Iowa over Bush was by a mere 4,144 votes, or 0.3 percent of all votes cast for president in the state. In 2004 the margin for Bush over John Kerry increased to a meager 10,059 votes out of over 1.5 million cast. In every presidential election that has occurred in the 21st century, Iowa has made the list of "battleground" states.[1] In those four election cycles, Iowa is one of only five states deemed a battleground in all of them (the others being Florida, Nevada, New Hampshire, and Ohio). Furthermore, the number of battleground states in the last four election cycles has been dwindling, from 19 in 2000, to just 8 in 2012. Why does Iowa continue to make the cut into the declining universe of states over which presidential candidates wage electoral battle? We find that the explanation for such competitiveness lies, not only in some rather unique structural features of Iowa politics, but also in the political geography of Iowa. Thus, by examining both the impact of unique structural factors, as well as data on party registration and vote share, we show not only why Iowa has been competitive in the past, but also why we expect it to remain competitive for the foreseeable future.

STRUCTURAL ASPECTS
AFFECTING IOWA'S COMPETITIVENESS

How competitive is Iowa at the presidential level? For much of the 20th century, Iowa was considered to be a fairly reliable Republican state. In a string of presidential elections from 1940–1984, the state's Electoral College vote went to the Republican, interrupted only by 1948 (Truman) and 1964 (Johnson). Table 12.1 shows both the popular and Electoral College vote history in Iowa since 1972. One sees the tail end of the mid-twentieth century Republican trend ending with a bang in 1988, when Democrat Michael Dukakis beat George H.W. Bush by ten points; the previous election had seen only a slightly smaller margin going to Republican Ronald Reagan. Since that time, Democratic candidates have fared well, but the state has become hotly contested. However, the real turning point seems to be 2000. George W. Bush would prevail in the national Electoral College tally with one more vote than absolutely necessary to win the presidency. He lost Iowa by a very thin margin of the popular vote, which determined all of Iowa's electoral college votes went to Democrat Al Gore. The following cycle, the state would swing to Bush, again by a very small margin. Iowa's status as a swing state emerged. In an environment where presidencies are won and lost on very slim Electoral College margins, even states with small numbers of Electoral College votes matter. Iowa, since 1972 a player in nomination politics, became competitive in Electoral College math, as well.

There are three main structural features one can consider when examining what is at the root of Iowa's competitiveness. First, Iowa's precinct caucuses lead off the presidential nomination events for each political party in the

Table 12.1.   Iowa's Popular and Electoral College Vote for President, 1972–2012

Year	Dem %	Rep %	Difference	EC Vote
1972	40.5	57.6	17.1	Nixon–8
1976	48.5	49.5	1.0	Ford–8
1980	38.6	51.3	12.7	Reagan–8
1984	45.9	53.3	7.4	Reagan–8
1988	54.7	44.5	10.2	Dukakis–8
1992	43.3	37.3	6.0	Clinton–7
1996	50.3	39.9	10.4	Clinton–7
2000	48.5	48.2	.3	Gore–7
2004	49.2	49.9	.7	Bush–7
2008	53.9	44.4	9.5	Obama–7
2012	51.7	46.0	5.7	Obama–6

Source: *Statistical Abstract of the United States,* various years; Iowa Secretary of State (http://sos.iowa.gov/ elections/results/index.html)

United States. While these events are not pitting Democrat against Republican as in the general election, the caucuses have served to foster strong party organizations in the state. The second structural feature unique to Iowa is its nonpartisan redistricting scheme that puts the drawing of legislative districts (at both the state legislative and congressional level) in the hands of a nonpartisan agency. We find that elections for Iowa's representatives in the U.S. House are often some of the more competitive in the nation. The final structural aspect is the ease with which Iowa voters can change their partisanship. One can arrive at a caucus or primary, which are closed events in Iowa, and change partisan affiliations to enable participation. Because there is little cost to being unaffiliated with a party, there are a disproportionate number of "no-party" registrants in the state. Finally, we should mention one characteristic of the state that is not relevant in its swing state status. Unlike many states, demographics in Iowa are not appreciably changing. Therefore, we cannot attribute Iowa's competitiveness to changing demographic features.

IOWA'S FIRST-IN-THE-NATION PRECINCT CAUCUSES

Years before the Iowa caucuses take place, potential presidential candidates visit Iowa to get a feel for the state and its voters. On November 17, 2012, Senator Marco Rubio attended a birthday bash for Governor Terry Branstad, becoming the first Republican hopeful for 2016 to visit the state of Iowa (Jacobs 2012). This visit occurred just eleven days after the 2012 general election . . . and thus began the 2016 cycle in Iowa. Indeed, out-of-state politicians who visit Iowa need to be prepared to explain their presence in the state to the media. In July 2014, Democratic Governor Jay Nixon of neighboring Missouri visited the state to tour a cellulosic ethanol plant in Emmetsburg (an economic venture in which the state of Missouri and its governor might be interested) and then, when media speculation began, had to assert the visit meant nothing other than he was interested in the new facility (Epstein 2014).

Iowa's first-in-the-nation status began in 1972 as a fluke of national Democratic Party rules changes and the timing needed to accommodate the lengthy caucus/convention method the state party used to both govern itself, as well as pick national convention delegates (Redlawsk, Tolbert, and Donovan 2010). Since that time, if a political party has had a presidential nomination contested, the caucuses have been competitive and drawn attention. The one exception is the 1992 Democratic caucuses when favorite son Senator Tom Harkin vied for the Democratic Party's nomination; other Democrats did not contest the state (Winebrenner and Goldford 2010).

It is no exaggeration to say that what occurs on a cold January or February night in Iowa captures the attention of the world every four years.[2] What is less recognized is that the Iowa precinct caucuses actually take place every *two* years. Precinct caucuses are partisan affairs; they are the first stage (indeed, the grassroots stage) of how the parties govern themselves in the state. They work in conjunction with party conventions, which after precinct caucuses move up to the county, then congressional district, and finally to the state level. In presidential years, this series of events will end at the parties' national conventions; in years with no presidential election, these events end with the state convention. Precinct caucuses elect delegates to the next level of convention (county). In presidential years, Democrats report delegate counts and these delegates are pledged to actual candidates; but, the Republican delegates are elected separately from the straw vote (Presidential Preference Poll) that is taken on caucus night. The media then reports delegate strength for Democrats and the results of the preference poll for Republicans.[3] It is these horse race numbers that are the sole focus of the public in presidential years. Other things, even very important things, take place at precinct caucuses, however.

A precinct is the smallest level of political organization. Precincts are composed of neighborhoods and small rural townships; they are the deepest of the grassroots. As these locally based groups of people meet in their precincts they elect leadership, both for the precinct caucus itself and for representation to the county's central committee (in addition to the delegates that are selected to represent the precinct at the convention as mentioned above). Participants are afforded the opportunity to bring forward platform issues. Attendees engage in face-to-face interaction. They engage in self-governance. Furthermore, convention delegates (at various levels) may be required (in both presidential and non-presidential years) to pick the party's nominee for various offices if no candidate garners 35 percent or more in the primary held in June. In short, what is done at a precinct caucus is important for the health of the party organization at its most fundamental level.

So if these are partisan affairs, how have they fostered competitiveness across the two parties in the state? Since the caucuses are held at the precinct level and receive a disproportionate amount of national media attention, it is imperative that the two parties have the mechanisms in place to successfully put on these events that can be quite organizationally complex; these mechanisms cannot just be at the state level, but must extend downward into the state's 99 counties. The counties' parties are responsible for organizing the precincts and they appoint the temporary chairs of each precinct. In 2000, caucuses were held (in each of the two parties) in 2,131 precincts. In 2012, there were 1,774 precincts. To give an indication of the scope of voters in precincts, if one takes the total active party registrants provided by the Iowa Secretary of State's office from the day of the 2012 caucuses (January 3), and divides by the number of precincts, then Republicans had an average of 347 registered active voters per precinct and Democrats had an average of 363 (Iowa Secretary of State 2012).[4] Both parties in Iowa now have institutionalized mechanisms that enable them to successfully put on the caucuses.[5] It is important to note that this organization is decentralized, taking place simultaneously in 99 counties.

One example can serve to illustrate what can be involved in putting on a caucus. For the last several cycles, the Black Hawk County Republicans have chosen to have every precinct meet in the same location, so that they could attract the attention of candidates to actually appear at the event and thus generate additional excitement. Black Hawk County is the fifth largest county in the state by population and in 2012 had 63 precincts. The party rented the UNI Dome, the University of Northern Iowa's indoor football stadium. All 63 precincts had individual caucus locations within the Dome, thus maintaining their neighborhood character; but before actual caucusing commenced all attendees could hear remarks by Newt Gingrich, Michele Bachmann, and other campaigns' surrogates. Black Hawk County precincts counted 3,642 votes that night (*Des Moines Register* 2012). Another illustration of the decentralized party organization is that this particular county determined their precincts would caucus at a central location, but other counties had Republican precinct meetings in a whole host of locations.

Caucuses are organizational challenges for the parties, but their mechanisms to organize them have become institutionalized. It is, however, the individual campaigns of the candidates in the state that are going to be the most directly responsible for stimulating the grassroots and getting them to turn out to caucus. But, they turn to parties and their organizations in the state to help them mobilize caucus goers. Trish (1999) found that caucus campaigns that successfully created relationships with local party structures had better caucus results (887). Candidates compete for endorsements from state legislators and also from key activists within the party who can serve as precinct leaders. Part of the job of a precinct leader will be to educate potential participants on the party governance that takes place at the caucus (i.e. how caucuses work), and get them to turn out. Caucus campaigns both depend on party infrastructure and seek to build their own. In their survey of 2008 caucus attendees, Redlawsk, Tolbert, and Donovan (2010) found that 84 percent had received a live phone call regarding the caucus and 40 percent had received at least one personal home contact (70) showing just how extensive mobilization efforts in Iowa can be. Furthermore, face-to-face mobilization has been found to be a very effective tool (Gerber and Green 2000).

We know from Patterson and Caldeira (1984) that strong parties in states foster competition. The strong party organizations in Iowa have been nurtured both by the caucus structure that demands grassroots organization, as well as the strong competition we have seen in both parties for critical Iowa caucus goers, which requires grassroots mobilization if an individual is going to, rather than just vote, actually attend a caucus meeting lasting from one to three hours.[6] In turn, we can expect that the interest and attention that has flowed to both the Republican and Democratic parties in the lead up to the caucuses carries over to the general election. Green and Shachar (2000) found in an analysis of ANES panel studies that voting in an election had a sizeable effect on voting in a subsequent election. In an experimental investigation of voting as habit forming, Gerber, Green, and Shachar's (2003) findings imply that campaign contacts may have long-term effects for voting behavior. The time between the caucuses and the general election is roughly ten months. Finally, Stone, Atkeson, and Rapoport's (1992) study of caucus attendees (in Iowa and other states in 1984 and 1988) found evidence that fiercely fought nomination battles did not serve to damage the party in the general election. As they wrote, "Like the quarrelsome family threatened by obnoxious neighbors, the party's common interest is activated in the general election no matter how bitter the internecine conflict has been" (687). Furthermore, if an Iowa caucus candidate is successful in securing the party's nomination, he or she can benefit from the organizational structures that were relied on and developed in the state when moving to the general election, where since 2000 Iowa has been shown to matter in nominees' Electoral College strategies.

We have explored how the unique first-in-the-nation caucuses have served to build decentralized party structures in the state. Furthermore, the presence of national campaigns (not to mention the national media), using party networks and competing for caucus attendees also stimulates the grassroots. But, this is only part of the story.

IOWA'S UNIQUE REDISTRICTING MECHANISM

Another unique feature of Iowa politics is to be found every ten years as reapportionment takes place in the United States. Iowa utilizes a legislative redistricting scheme that is unlike any other state's method for drawing district boundaries. Since 1980 in Iowa, the Legislative Services Agency (LSA)[7] has been charged with drawing legislative districts for both the U.S. House, as well as the state legislature (Cook 2007). The LSA is a nonpartisan staff agency of the Iowa General Assembly. There are only two criteria the Agency may take into consideration when drawing boundaries for Iowa's congressional districts: population and county lines (Cook 2007). After reapportionment has taken place the LSA will map out the new congressional districts, keeping counties intact, and make it public. The guidelines set forth by the LSA are quite restrictive. For example, following the 2010 census, the ideal population for each of Iowa's congressional districts was set at 761,589, meaning each district could not deviate from that total by more than 1 percent or 7,615 persons (Cook 2011, 4). In the plan adopted by the Iowa legislature and signed by the governor, each congressional district deviated by no more than 41 persons from the ideal population (Cook 2011, 12), a remarkable feat given the population and geographic size of each district. A temporary commission (Temporary Redistricting Advisory Commission) is appointed, but its purpose is limited to advising and giving guidance to the Legislative Services Agency, and conducting public hearings. The commission submits its report to the General Assembly and the map will be considered in the normal legislative process. If it fails to pass, the Legislative Services Agency must submit a second plan to the legislature.[8] Should the second plan fail to pass the legislative process, a third plan must be submitted. The third plan may be amended in the manner of any other piece of legislation (Cook 2007). In the four reapportionment cycles since the Legislative Services Agency was created, three have seen either the first or second map accepted by the legislature and governor (1991, 2001, 2011); one (1981) went to the third plan, but it was adopted without amendment (Cook 2007, 2).

When one examines the borders for Iowa's congressional districts in Figure 12.1, one sees what are essentially the four quadrants of the state following the existing political boundaries of the counties. If one were to compare this to any other state's congressional map (besides the seven smallest states with at-large representation), stark differences would be apparent as few other states keep counties whole. Furthermore, because only population and county boundaries can be considered, it is worth noting what criteria cannot be considered, especially because virtually every other state will consider at least some these factors. Partisan registrations, voting patterns, and incumbent residency are all factors that cannot be taken into account when drawing maps in Iowa. McDonald (2004) found that many bipartisan commissions used by some states produced plans that protected incumbents (which is a factor that cannot be considered in Iowa). In fact, it is not unusual for Iowa incumbents to feel the need to move after redistricting. In 2011 after the new Iowa map came out, Representative David Loebsack moved one county south to the new 2nd district to avoid being paired with fellow Democrat Bruce Braley in the new 1st district. Tom Latham moved to the new 3rd to avoid being paired with fellow Republican Steve King in the new 4th. Latham's move set up a battle in the general election with Democratic incumbent Leonard

272   *Chapter Twelve*

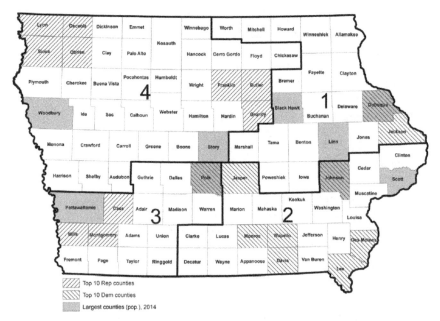

Figure 12.1. Iowa Political Geography. Source: Legislative Services Agency, 2011. Congressional boundary data from data.gov.

Boswell (Clayworth 2011), who himself had had to move to friendlier territory after the 2001 redistricting (Norman 2001). A similar pattern of moving and incumbency matchups occurs with more frequency for state legislative races. The point bears repeating that those drawing the lines are not partisan political actors.

Other states' redistricting processes involve partisan legislative actors and/or commissions (some of which will be partisan) in the actual drawing of congressional boundaries. Courts will also play a role in some states. Iowa's system is the only one where a neutral agency is involved in line composition, and it was one of only two states where the 2001–2002 redistricting outcome was judged as being a neutral plan (as opposed to partisan plans or plans protecting incumbents) (McDonald 2004).

Political scientists disagree over whether certain types of redistricting schemes make for more (or less) competitive elections.[9] Carson and Crespin (2004), classifying Iowa as a commission, found that courts and commissions make for more competitive districts than districts drawn by legislatures. Masket, Winburn, and Wright (2012) coded Iowa as a bipartisan commission, but found little effect for redistricting mechanisms in state legislative (not congressional) results on competition. Most recently, Lindgren and Southwell (2013) found evidence that independent commissions did produce districts that had closer House races. However, they have mis-classified Iowa as a state with a back-up commission (that acts when the legislature fails). What is clear is that Iowa should not be included as either a bipartisan or partisan commission in models that seek to determine the effect on district competitiveness because it has a unique structure not replicated in any other state. Because existing studies have differed on how they have classified the state and there is no agreement on whether different modes of redistricting affect competition significantly, we need to examine the outcomes of recent U.S. House races in the state to get a handle on their competitive nature.

There are different mechanisms for determining competitive districts. Political handicappers such as Charlie Cook (*The Cook Political Report*) engage in ex ante determinations of safe, likely, leaning, and toss-up districts. In 2014, each of Iowa's four districts was contained on Cook's House Race Ratings ranging from likely Democratic, to toss-up, to likely Republican (Cook 2014). Models in political science may rely on ex post margins of victory to determine district competitiveness (Lindgren and Southwell 2013; Masket, Winburn, and Wright 2012). Abramowitz, Alexander, and Gunning (2006a) determined competitive districts by using a normalized measure of the two-party presidential vote in districts. Others determine district electoral competitiveness by judging districts where the winner won less than 60 percent of the two-party House vote (Carson and Crespin 2004).[10] This approach is utilized in Table 12.2, which contains each winner's percent of the two-party vote in U.S. House districts in Iowa back to 2000. Of the 38 district contests that have been held since that time, 23 (60.5 percent) of them were competitive by this measure. Almost one-third (12) of the contests were won with 55 percent of the two-party vote or less. It is also worth considering how Iowa compares to other states in terms of competitiveness at this level. If one uses the average margin of victory in House races from 2002 to 2008, Iowa ranks as having the third most competitive races in the country (Ostermeier 2010a).

Table 12.2. **Winner's Percentage of Two-Party Vote in Iowa Congressional Districts, 2000–2014**

Districts	2000	2002	2004	2006	2008	2010	2012	2014
IA-01	63.2	57.3	56.0	56.0	64.6	51.0	57.8	51.1
IA-02	55.9	53.3	60.1	51.4	59.6	52.6	56.7	52.6
IA-03	65.1	54.3	55.3	52.7	57.2	52.2	54.5	55.5
IA-04	62.0	55.9	61.0	57.2	60.6	67.3	54.1	61.7
IA-05	70.2	62.2	63.3	62.2	61.6	67.0		

Source: Almanac of American Politics, various years. Data on 2014 from Iowa Secretary of State (http://sos.iowa.gov/elections/results/index.html#13).

Furthermore, during the same period, Iowa had both the 8th most competitive district in the country (IA-03), as well as the 19th most competitive district in the country (IA-02) (Ostermeier 2010b).

We cannot conclude that this competitiveness is due to the way that Iowa draws its districts, as the evidence is circumstantial. In addition, other factors such as partisan strength and distribution play roles, as well. But it is certainly the case that Iowa districts are not gerrymandered to result in partisan outcomes or incumbency protection. We can conclude that not only is Iowa a swing state in terms of presidential politics, but it also tends to have competitive House elections. Not only may redistricting contribute to this, but also the strong party organizations that the caucuses have fostered likely do, as well. Another factor that needs to be explored, however, is the partisan composition of voters in the state.

VOTERS OF "NO-PARTY"

Iowa is a closed state, where to participate in a partisan primary, one must be registered with the party. The party-run caucuses also require that participants be members of the party. Knowing this fact and subsequently examining the number of "no-party" registrants in the state can be quite surprising. The no-party element in Iowa is strong and has been for the last four presidential cycles as shown in Table 12.3. This table shows the proportion of active voters in the state registered as Democrat, Republican, and no-party from 2000–2014. As is readily apparent, the no-party bloc in Iowa consistently makes up more than a third of the electorate and is consistently the largest voting bloc in the state. Furthermore, pooled survey data from 1976–1982 showed 37.4 percent of Iowans self-identified as independent (Wright, Erikson, and McIver 1985). Data from McDonald (2010) enable us to put Iowa into perspective with other states, where it registers as the state with the eighth highest level of unaffiliated or minor party voters.[11]

Why are these numbers so high? In 2007, Iowa joined seven other states and began allowing same day registration for voters at the polls; four other states have since added this feature (National Conference of State Legislatures 2014). Prior to this law, Iowans had to be registered 10 days before the election. However, this change cannot be part of any explanation of high no-party levels we see in Table 12.3 before the 2008 election, when the change took effect. It is the case that prior to the adoption of this law, voters already registered could change their partisan affiliation at the polls (Norrander 1989). This has also been true at the party-run caucuses (Redlawsk, Tolbert, and Donovan 2010, 53). Few states allow this kind of freedom for

Table 12.3: Active registration by party, 2000–2014

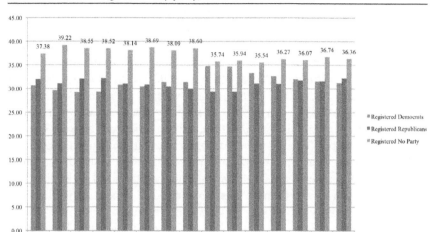

Note: Bars represent active party registration for each year for each party as a percentage of all active voters in the state measured in December of each year for 2000-2013. The bars shown for 2014 are taken from September of that year. The percentages displayed are for the proportion of active voters registered as No Party for each year.

Source: Iowa Secretary of State, (https://sos.iowa.gov/elections/voterreg/regstat.html).

voters within a closed primary system (Norrander 1989). This feature has long enabled Iowans to arrive at a caucus or primary event, and change their affiliation so that they may participate as a partisan, if they choose. In the state, one can choose to be an unaffiliated registered voter without suffering consequences in terms of not being able to participate in closed events, as long as one is willing to become a registered partisan, at least for a short period of time.

While some states have recently eliminated same-day registration laws, there has been no serious discussion of doing so in Iowa. Furthermore, there has been no discussion of eliminating the ability of registered voters (which pre-dates the adoption of same-day registration) to switch partisan affiliation at the polls. Thus, the proportion of no-party registrants in the state should continue to be an enduring feature of the political landscape.

Iowa having a closed system that functions more like an open one, where voters can arrive at the poll and choose which party's ballot they get, is a rare structural feature.[12] Furthermore, so many no-party registrants in the state cannot be ignored by campaigns.

Turning again to Table 12.3, we see that since 2000 the average differential between no-party voters and the next highest group of active registered voters is over 5 percentage points. Only during the hyped presidential election of 2008 did active Democrats get within 1 percentage point, in terms of size, of active no-party voters. To be sure, the extant political science research on so-called "independents" has shown that a very small portion of the electorate is truly independent, that is, undecided and capable of voting for either party in any given election (Bartels 2000; Keith et al. 1992). Assuming, however, the probability that a randomly selected no-party voter in Iowa leans Democratic (or Republican) is .50, we can expect this no-party bloc to break down evenly within both parties. And, in fact, if we rerun the numbers in Table 12.3, splitting the no-party bloc equally between Democrats and Republicans, the average difference between the two major parties since 2000, using the absolute value of the difference, is just 1.82 percentage points (and 1.79 in the four presidential election years during this time period). In short, no matter how once slices it, party registration in Iowa is competitive.

To this point we have examined competitiveness in the state by looking at three structural features. Two of these features, the first-in-the-nation caucuses and the redistricting process, are unique to the state. The third feature, the way Iowa does party registration is not unique to Iowa, but only one other state has this mechanism. Understanding the competitiveness in the state, however, is contingent upon considerations of political geography and recognizing the east versus west/rural versus urban divide. Iowa is often called a "purple" state in presidential politics. But being a purple state does not necessarily imply competition across the entire state uniformly. Rather, as we will illustrate, there are pockets in the state that are very red (Republican) and very blue (Democratic), and these patterns tend to follow a distinct rural-urban division.

GEOGRAPHICAL ASPECTS OF IOWA'S COMPETITIVENESS

To truly understand the impact of levels of partisanship on the state's competitiveness, one has to examine the political geography of the state. The western part of the state is dominated by Republicans, with Republicans in some counties comprising 60 to 70 percent of all active voters in the county. However, these areas tend to be sparsely populated, with between 15,000 and 20,000 votes cast county-wide in a presidential election. The eastern, more urban parts of the state are more Democratic, but not to the extent of the more Republican counties in the west. Moreover, since 2000, voters registered with no party have consistently represented the largest bloc of active voters in the state at close to 35 percent. The result of this mixing of partisan intensity with vote share is a deeply competitive state, with Republicans often campaigning in some of the more Democratic parts of the state. In short, while Republicans will continue to rack up big victories in the western part of the state, the vote share forces Republican candidates to visit and compete in the eastern, more populated, and more Democratic/no-party part of the state. The result of these dynamics is a state that has been and will continue to be competitive for any candidate seeking to capture the statewide vote.

Despite the statewide appearance of competitiveness, within Iowa there are very clear partisan patterns. According to the Iowa Secretary of State's website, as of September 2, 2014, there were 1,918,968 active voters spread across 99 counties in the state. However, just 9 of those counties contained more than 50,000 voters. Taken together, those 9 counties contain nearly half of the active voters in the state with 47 percent in total. Moreover, the three largest counties (Linn, Polk, and Scott) comprise over one-fourth of the active electorate in Iowa at 26.3 percent. Table 12.4 shows the nine dominant counties in Iowa, with the proportion of active votes in each county, the proportion of active voters in each county registered Democratic and no-party, and the percent two-party vote going to the Obama-Biden ticket in 2012. As Table 12.4 illustrates, despite having 99 counties, only a handful of counties are relevant for any statewide election in terms of vote share. Complicating the story even further, seven of the nine dominant counties are located in the central or eastern part of the state (see Figure 12.1). Only Pottawattamie and Woodbury Counties are in western Iowa, but the combined active voter total from both

Table 12.4.   Geography and political dominance of Iowa's nine largest counties

County	Active voters	% of total active voters	% Democrat	% No Party	% two-party for Obama-Biden in 2012
Black Hawk	81,249	4.23	35.79	38.57	60.28
Dubuque	62,589	3.26	39.10	35.96	57.48
Johnson	88,807	4.63	43.56	35.24	68.13
Linn	127,978	6.67	35.13	36.76	59.02
Polk	266,258	13.88	38.19	30.82	57.21
Pottawattamie	55,480	2.89	*27.98*	34.31	*47.33*
Scott	111,077	5.79	31.44	40.73	56.94
Story	52,612	2.74	30.11	39.48	57.11
Woodbury	55,840	2.91	*32.59*	33.38	50.52
Average	100,210	5.22	34.88	36.14	57.11

Note: The active votes, % of total active voters, % Democrat, and % No Party columns are based on party registration numbers obtained from Iowa Secretary of State's website as of September 2, 2014.

Source: Iowa Secretary of State, (https://sos.iowa.gov/elections/pdf/VRStatsArchive/2014/CongSept14.pdf

counties is just 111,320, just 243 voters more than in Scott County alone which is in far eastern Iowa, over 16,000 voters less than in Linn County, also eastern Iowa, and just 41.8 percent of the total in Polk County. As shown in Table 12.4, the average number of active voters in each of these nine counties is just over 100,000. This compares to an average of 11,301 active voters in the remaining 90 counties, indicating these nine counties contain almost nine times as many active voters as are in the remaining counties.

As expected, the larger, more urban counties, also have a distinct partisan tilt. The dominance of the three counties mentioned above (Linn, Polk, and Scott) should be evident in Table 12.4, but so too should be the Democratic leaning in seven of the nine counties. In only two of the nine counties is the proportion of active voters registered Democratic less than the proportion registered as Republican, and both are located in the far western parts of the state (Pottawattamie County in southwest Iowa and Woodbury County in northwest Iowa). Not surprisingly, these two counties are also the two counties where the Obama-Biden ticket received the least support. While the average support across the nine counties for the Obama-Biden ticket was 57 percent, in Pottawattamie County this dipped below 50 percent, and was just barely above this mark in Woodbury County (just 461 votes separated the Obama-Biden ticket from the Romney-Ryan ticket in this county). Pottawattamie stands out as the only one of the nine in which the proportion of active voters in the county registered Democratic is less than 30 percent and where Obama received less than 50 percent of the vote. Taken as a whole, President Obama received 52.90 percent of his total vote share in Iowa from these nine counties, whereas Mitt Romney garnered just 43.37 percent of his total vote received from these same counties.

The political geography analysis illustrated in Table 12.4 can be further dissected by analyzing Iowa's most Republican and Democratic counties. The top portion of Table 12.5 provides a list of the top ten most Republican counties in Iowa in terms of party identification since 2000. The rankings were determined as follows. Party registration numbers released in December of each year were used to calculate the proportion of active voters in each county registered as Republican. Data were then sorted to create a list of counties from highest to lowest in terms of the percent Republican. These rankings were then averaged across 13 years (December 2000– December 2012) to capture Iowa's most Republican counties across the last four presidential elections. The bottom portion of Table 12.5 shows the top ten most Democratic counties using the same formula. These are also illustrated in Figure 12.1.

As shown in Table 12.5, Sioux County in northwest Iowa is the most Republican county in the state; in fact it is the only county which averages above 70 percent GOP per year and is more than two standard deviations above the

Table 12.5. Top ten Republican and Democratic counties by location and political leanings, 2000–2012

TOP 10 REPUBLICAN COUNTIES				
County (years 2000–2012)	Avg. ranking	Avg, % GOP	Std. deviation	% 2-party vote for Romney 2012
Sioux	1.00	71.78	1.87	84.22
Lyon	2.00	62.84	1.57	77.77
Osceola	3.46	55.93	2.58	70.97
Montgomery	3.62	54.72	1.51	60.96
O'Brien	5.46	50.97	2.07	72.79
Grundy	7.38	47.92	2.31	61.53
Mills	7.62	46.83	0.71	59.68
Butler	8.31	47.17	1.67	55.23
Cass	8.46	47.09	2.57	59.60
Franklin	9.08	46.73	3.19	55.47
Top 10 average		53.20	2.00	65.82
Statewide average (N = 89)		32.37	1.69	50.65

TOP 10 DEMOCRATIC COUNTIES				
County (years 2000–2012)	Avg. ranking	Avg, % Dem.	Std. deviation	% 2-party vote for Obama (2012)
Wapello	1.38	48.40	2.37	56.06
Des Moines	2.08	46.72	1.32	59.37
Jackson	4.15	44.90	2.02	58.58
Lee	4.23	43.68	2.74	57.92
Davis	4.77	43.54	2.23	41.55
Johnson	6.23	42.28	3.20	68.13
Dubuque	6.31	41.24	1.17	57.48
Monroe	8.23	39.59	1.65	46.07
Jasper	9.62	38.38	1.31	53.61
Polk	9.77	38.86	1.99	57.21
Top 10 average		42.76	2.00	55.60
Statewide average (N = 89)		26.50	1.74	46.94

Source: Iowa Secretary of State, (https://sos.iowa.gov/elections/voterreg/regstat.html).

group mean. What is also striking from Figure 12.1 is the clear geographic pattern; seven of the top ten GOP counties are located in two clusters in the extreme northwest and southwest corners of the state. The other counties all border each other and are located in north central Iowa.

Looking at the counties in more depth, the third column shows the average proportion (since 2000) within each county registered as Republican. As shown in the last two rows of the third column, the average percent GOP for the top ten counties is over 20 percentage points, or 64 percent, higher than the average for the other 89 counties. For both the top ten GOP counties and the remaining 89 counties, there is remarkable stability in Republican party identification; the proportion of Republicans in each county deviates, on average, from the county mean by 2 percentage points or less for the 13 years examined.

The fifth column in Table 12.5 compares the percent of the two-party vote in each county (among the top ten and statewide) going to the Romney-Ryan ticket in the 2012 presidential election. The percent GOP vote in the ten counties is consistently Republican (almost 30 percent higher than the other 89 counties) and consistently higher than what is shown in the third column (this reflects the additional support of no-party and possibly Democratic voters in these counties). While this voting pattern represents a clear break from the rest of the state, the influence of these counties on the final outcome must be put into context. The average vote total coming out of these ten counties that went to the GOP in 2012 was 4,946, representing just 6.8 percent of the total vote cast for the Romney-Ryan ticket in Iowa.

The bottom portion of Table 12.5 shows the top ten Democratic counties in Iowa using the same formula and layout as was discussed for the top ten Republican counties. The geographic difference is once again apparent. All of the top Democratic counties are located in the eastern or central parts of the state (see Figure 12.1), including the urban centers of Polk, Dubuque, and Johnson Counties, compared to the predominantly western location for top Republican counties. The third column shows that the top ten Democratic counties differ significantly from the other 89 counties, with a difference of 16 percentage points or 61 percent. A simple difference of means test tells us that the likelihood of finding such a large difference due to random chance is less than one in one thousand ($p < .001$). As with the top ten Republican counties, the fourth column shows very little variation within counties, with standard deviations of two percentage points or less. Looking at the third column, what should be immediately noticeable is the fact that in none of the top ten counties does the average proportion of Democrats exceed 50 percent. Bear in mind that in the top ten Republican counties the average proportion of the county registered as Republican was 53 percent.

In other words, the top Republican counties are more Republican than the top Democratic counties are Democratic, but both groups of counties are uniquely located within the state.

The fifth column provides the two-party vote from each county going to the 2012 Obama-Biden ticket in Iowa. Two details immediately jump out. First, recall that the total number of votes from the top ten Republican counties represented just under 7 percent of the total vote share going to the Romney-Ryan ticket in Iowa. By contrast, the top ten Democratic counties constituted just over 31 percent of the total vote share for the Obama-Biden ticket in the state. Second, note that in two of the top ten Democratic counties (Davis and Monroe), a majority of the vote share in each county went to the Romney-Ryan ticket in 2012. The average proportion of Democrats in these two counties was 43 and 39 percent, but these are rural Democratic counties averaging less than 4,000 votes total in each county in the 2012 presidential election. It may be that these rural counties, while Democratic, vote differently than urban Democratic counties. Note also from the bottom portion of Table 12.5 that Polk County is among the top Democratic counties in the state; this reinforces the findings from Table 12.4 about the outsized influence this particular county can have on statewide elections.

To get a better sense of how sharp the partisan divide is across Iowa, we conducted bivariate correlations between the proportion of voters in each county registered as Republican, Democrat, and no-party for all counties for each year from 2000 to 2012. Although not shown, for every one of the thirteen years (2000–2012) the correlation between the percent Democrat and percent Republican was negative and significant ($r = -0.84$; $p < .01$). This is not surprising as it suggests it is rare to find a county with a high number of registered Democrats and a high number of registered Republicans. What is surprising is that we also found the correlation between the proportion of no-party voters in the county and the proportion of Republicans in the county to be significant and negative ($r = -0.54$; $p < .01$). By contrast, the correlation between the proportion of voters registered Democratic and the proportion of voters registered no-party in each county was not significant ($r = .01$). Put another way, it is not unusual to find counties with proportionally high numbers of registered Democrats and no-party people; what is unusual is finding a county in which the number of registered Republicans is roughly equal to the number of registered Democrats or registered no-party folks. While the state as a whole may be purple, individual counties are not. Counties that are strongly Republican tend to be strongly Republican and nothing else, and are predominantly located in western Iowa. Counties that are strongly Democratic counties may also have a strong no-party component and tend to be in central and eastern Iowa.

The interaction between vote share and political geography is critical to understanding why Iowa continues to serve as a swing state. Take, for example, the results of the 2012 presidential election in Iowa. The Romney-Ryan ticket received 84.2 percent of the vote in Sioux County, the most Republican County in the state according to Table 12.5, and a county with 17,107 active voters. This constitutes 14,407 votes compared to only 2,700 for the Obama-Biden ticket. However, in Dubuque County, the Obama-Biden ticket received 57.5 percent of the vote, but with a total of 50,048 votes cast in the county, this constituted 28,768 votes. In other words, while Republicans have huge victories in counties in northwest and southwest Iowa (the strongly conservative counties), these represent a small percentage of the total vote share. This begins to explain the increasing tendency of Republican candidates to visit the eastern part of the state with more regularity (Wiser 2013).

WHAT DOES THE FUTURE HOLD?

Given the structural and geographic features of Iowa's political landscape, what can one expect for the 2016 presidential contest? We expect Iowa's swing state status to continue unabated. The 2014 Senate election results support this conclusion. Though not a presidential election, the 2014 Senate election in Iowa was historic on multiple fronts. In terms of money, the Center for Responsive Politics (2015) estimates that approximately $83 million (candidate plus outside spending) was spent on the U.S. Senate race in the state between State Senator Joni Ernst and Congressman Bruce Braley, making it the third most expensive Senate race in the country. This equates to over $73 per vote cast in the election. For context, consider that this was the first open Senate seat in Iowa in 40 years, and the winner would replace Senator Tom Harkin, a Democrat and the 26th most liberal member of the U.S. Senate according to rankings compiled by *National Journal* (2013). Despite Harkin's status as a reliable Democrat, the race to replace him would not be one the Democratic Party could automatically assume would be in their win column. In fact, we would not have seen the amounts of money spent in this election if candidates, parties, and outside groups had not considered the race a tossup.

The Republican Joni Ernst won the election by over 8 percentage points, becoming the first woman to be elected to Congress from the state of Iowa. That a Republican could win a seat that had previously been held by a staunch Democrat for 30 years speaks to the competitiveness of statewide elections in Iowa, and the state's swing status. As we have discussed throughout this chapter, the institutional and geographic parameters of the state contribute to this characteristic. The results reinforce the extent to which candidates and parties firmly believe Iowa can swing to the Democrats or to the Republicans.

Turning to 2016, as we noted earlier in the chapter, potential presidential candidates had barely let the ink dry on the 2012 election results before visiting Iowa in anticipation of 2016. Potential presidential candidates from both parties spent time traversing the state in the lead up to the 2014 midterm elections, as they frequently campaigned for congressional candidates, state legislative candidates, and even some vying for local offices. After the midterms concluded, the pace of visits to the state picked up speed. New Jersey Governor Chris Christie attended the inauguration of Iowa Governor Terry Branstad in January 2015. A litany of Republican hopefuls attended the Iowa Freedom Summit in late January 2015, sponsored by Iowa Congressman Steve King and Citizens United. Attendees included former Arkansas Governor and 2008 Iowa Caucus winner Mike Huckabee, former Republican Vice Presidential nominee Sarah Palin, Governor Chris Christie, former Texas Governor Rick Perry, Governor Scott Walker, U.S. Senator Ted Cruz, former U.S. Senator and 2012 caucus winner Rick Santorum, Carly Fiorina, Donald Trump, former U.N. Ambassador John Bolton, and Dr. Ben Carson (Hayworth 2015; *Des Moines Register* 2015).

Much has been written on the divide within the Republican Party in terms of the turnout at the Iowa Caucuses, and the extent to which more socially conservative voters influence the outcome (Winebrenner and Goldford 2010). But it is clear from early activity in the state that less socially conservative candidates such as Governor Christie, U.S. Senator Rand Paul, and Governor Walker also view the state as a viable starting point for their respective campaigns. An October 2014 *Des Moines Register* Iowa Poll showed a close race among Republicans with Mitt Romney with 17 percent support among likely caucus goers, followed by Ben Carson (11 percent), Rand Paul (10 percent), and Mike Huckabee (9 percent). On the Democratic side, Hillary Clinton was the clear front runner in the same poll with the support of 53 percent of likely Democratic caucus goers; Senator Elizabeth Warren was second with 9 percent support.

What is clear is that candidates and parties continue to see Iowa as a swing state, one that is competitive in terms of party registration and has the potential to "swing" to either the Democrats or Republicans. As with any election, candidate quality matters, as do the atmospherics of the election, but in Iowa, the institutional structures regarding redistricting, voter registration, geographic distribution of voters, and the organizing function of the Iowa Caucuses serve to reinforce its position as a swing state. In addition, the lesson from the 2014 Senate race is that in the absence of an incumbent, as will be the case in the 2016 presidential contest, the race within and between the two parties will be highly competitive.

CONCLUSION

Investigating Iowa's swing state status reveals a unique combination of structural features and political geography that have intertwined to make it the battleground in presidential politics that it is today. The first-in-the-nation precinct caucuses, the run-up to which sees presidential hopefuls flocking to the state, has served to foster strong party organizations at the county level. In addition, it's not just every four years that Iowans caucus, but caucuses occur every two years and are important in the way the parties in the state govern themselves. Caucuses require organization at the county level and a measure of participation at the precinct level. In the competitive caucuses, presidential candidates have to successfully mobilize voters if they are to amass delegates for the nomination. The strong party organizations sustained by the caucus process have helped to foster competition and not just at the presidential nomination level. We also explained the unique way that Iowa redistricts after a decennial census. Congressional districts cannot be partisanly gerrymandered, nor can counties be divided. Lines are drawn by agency staff without taking into account incumbents' residency. Examining the results of U.S. House elections in the state indicate that there also tends to be a high degree of competition at this level when looking at the state as a whole. Finally, we examined the high numbers of voters in the state that choose to register with no party. While Iowa is a closed state, voters who are unaffiliated with the party may arrive at either a caucus or a primary and as long as they are willing to declare themselves a partisan for the day (as they can change their lack of affiliation back the next day), they can participate. Where these no-party voters live is also a critical feature of examining Iowa's swing state status.

Iowa's vote share is concentrated in just a handful of counties that will decide any statewide election, rendering the other 90 plus counties virtually irrelevant. These counties are located mostly in the eastern part of the state, and generally lean Democratic. Moderate Republicans can win statewide elections (as has been the case with U.S. Senator Charles Grassley and Governor Terry Branstad), but they have only been able to do so by minimizing losses in the more urban counties, or even winning Polk County as Grassley and Branstad both did in 2010. Vice versa, Democrats running statewide could conceivably focus on just a handful of counties in the eastern part of the state, virtually ignoring the western, more rural, half. Republicans such as Grassley and Branstad are incumbents who are known commodities in the state, with approval ratings in the high 50s (Branstad) or high 60s (Grassley). For Republican challengers, the political geography of the state presents a challenge. In 2012, Barack Obama won 38 of the 99 counties in Iowa, only one of which could be considered to be truly in western Iowa, but won the statewide two-party vote by nearly 6 percentage points.

As we peer into the future, it seems unlikely that any of the structural factors that we examined will change. While it is the case that there is quadrennial complaining about the outsized influence Iowa has in the presidential nomination system, the fact the other systemic players (states and parties) are unlikely to be able to agree on a different system in the near future seems to bode well for Iowa maintaining its first-in-the-nation caucuses. This means the health of the party organizations in the state should be sustained.[13] There also do not appear to be any reform movements on the horizon that would seek to change either the way redistricting is done in Iowa, or the same-day registration features that make it less costly for one to be unaffiliated. Finally, the patterns exhibited in Iowa's political geography seem likely to continue; as long as Republicans campaign and remain somewhat competitive in the eastern or blue part of the state, Iowa's swing state status will remain intact.

NOTES

1. We consider battleground states as determined by CNN, which are ex ante determinations. See Bergan et al. 2005; CNN politics 2008; and Stark and Roberts 2012. It is based on these kinds of determinations that campaigns decide where to place resources. The fact that Iowa is a swing state has made it a battleground.

2. The authors have fielded media inquiries about the caucuses from places such as Brazil, Japan, Greece, Italy, Finland, and Poland.

3. National Republican Party rules will require delegates in 2016 to be bound, but it remains to be seen exactly how this will affect the GOP's precinct caucuses' procedures (Jacobs 2014).

4. This is a very rough estimation as precincts may vary dramatically by both population and partisan composition due to whether they are urban/suburban or rural. Of course, all eligible partisans do not attend a caucus.

5. One may argue that the 2012 Republican caucuses in Iowa were not, in fact, successful. On the evening of the caucuses, Mitt Romney was declared the "winner" by eight votes. But, 16 days later Rick Santorum was declared to have prevailed by 34 votes (Fahrenthold and Wilgoren 2012). But, these results merely reflect the changing results of the razor-close preference poll (taken largely to satisfy the media's desire to declare a winner) that is hand tabulated on caucus night. The Republican caucuses *were* successful in electing delegates to the county convention, one of the main purposes. It is also instructive to note that 22 out of 28 Iowa delegates to the Republican

National Convention in August would end up casting their ballot for Ron Paul (who finished third in the caucus night preference poll) (Obradovich 2012).

6. We should note that even if a party does not have a contested nomination as Republicans in 2004 or Democrats in 2012, the Iowa parties still caucus and attend to their party business. Even without a competitive Republican caucus in 2004 (but a lively one on the Democratic side) and without a competitive Democratic caucus in 2012 (but a spirited one on the Republican side), the state was a battleground in the general election (and won by the incumbent).

7. Originally, this entity was called the Legislative Services Bureau, but it was folded into the Legislative Services Agency in 2003 (Cook 2007, 2).

8. For both the first and second plans, only corrective amendments are allowed. For both the second and third plans, public hearings are not required. In the case of the state legislative boundaries, counties do not have to be kept whole (Cook 2007).

9. For a sample of the debate that surrounds this area see the authors included in a 2006 issue of *PS: Political Science and Politics*. Abramowitz, Alexander, and Gunning (2006a; 2006b) and McDonald (2006a; 2006b).

10. The less-than-60 percent threshold is standard for determining "marginal" seats. See Jacobson 2013, 35–38 for a discussion.

11. Twenty-nine states and the District of Colombia register voters by partisan affiliation. States ranking above Iowa are: AK, MA, RI, NJ, CT, NH, ME.

12. As of February 2012, only one other state, Wyoming, had a closed system but allowed voters to change partisan affiliation on the day of the event (FairVote 2012). Norrander (1989) identified three states (IA, WY, and OH), but Ohio has since become an open state (FairVote 2012).

13. We would add that the extreme compression of nominating events brought on by frontloading in the nominating system (especially evident in 2008) has served to bolster Iowa. It becomes especially important to do well right off the bat if very shortly after the first event (Iowa), more than 20 states will be holding contests on the same day.

BIBLIOGRAPHY

Abramowitz, Alan, Brad Alexander, and Matthew Gunning. 2006a. "Don't Blame Redistricting for Uncompetitive Elections." *PS: Political Science and Politics* 39 (1): 87–90.
———. 2006b. "Drawing the Line on District Competition: A Rejoinder." *PS: Political Science and Politics* 39 (1): 95–98.
Bartels, Larry M. 2000. "Partisanship and Voting Behavior, 1952-1996." *American Journal of Political Science* 44 (1): 35–50.
Bergan, Daniel E., Alan S. Gerber, Donald P. Green, and Costas Panagopoulos. 2005. "Grassroots Mobilization and Voter Turnout in 2004." *Public Opinion Quarterly* 760–77.
Carson, Jamie L., and Michael H. Crespin. 2004. "The Effect of State Redistricting Methods on Electoral Competition in United States House of Representatives Races." *State Politics and Policy Quarterly* 4: 455–69.

Center for Responsive Politics. 2015. "Most Expensive Races." Open Secrets. https://www.opensecrets.org/overview/topraces.php?cycle=2014&display=currcandsout

Clayworth, Jason. 2011. "Redistricting Plan is Signed into Law." *Des Moines Register*, April 20.

CNN Politics. 2008. *Political ticker*. June 9. http://politicalticker.blogs.cnn.com/2008/06/09/cnn-projects-whos-ahead-in-the-fight-for-electoral-college-votes/.

Cook, Charles. E. 2014. *2014 House Race Ratings*. August 8. http://cookpolitical.com/house/charts/race-ratings/7661.

Cook, Ed. 2007. *Legislative Guide to Redistricting in Iowa*. Des Moines: Legislative Services Agency. https://www.legis.iowa.gov/DOCS/Central/Guides/redist.pdf.

———. 2011. *First Redistricting Plan*. Des Moines: Legislative Services Agency. https://www.legis.iowa.gov/docs/resources/redist/2011/2011-03-31/Plan1_Report.pdf.

Des Moines Register. 2012. "Iowa Republican Caucus County Totals." January 5: 5A.

———. 2015. "Iowa Freedom Summit."January 18: 11A.

Epstein, Reid J. 2014. "This Week in Would-Be 2016 Candidates." *Wall Street Journal*. July 23. (http://blogs.wsj.com/washwire/2014/07/23/this-week-in-would-be-2016-candidates-michele-bachmann-and-jay-nixon/.

Fahrenthold, David A., and Debbi Wilgoren. 2012. "Santorum finished 34 votes ahead of Romney in new Iowa tally; votes from 8 precincts missing." *Washington Post*, January 19. http://www.washingtonpost.com/politics/report-santorum-finished-34-votes-ahead-of-romney-in-new-iowa-tally-votes-from-8-precincts-missing/2012/01/19/gIQAJGuRAQ_story.html.

FairVote. 2012. *Congressional and Presidential Primaries: Open, Closed, Semi-Closed, and "Top Two."* February. http://www.fairvote.org/research-and-analysis/presidential-elections/congressional-and-presidential-primaries-open-closed-semi-closed-and-top-two/.

Fernandez, Manny. 2015. "Perry Exits Texas Stage Making a Case for His Past, and His Future." *New York Times* 16 January: A1.

Finkel, Steven E., and Howard A. Scarrow. 1985. "Party Identification and Party Enrollment: the Difference and the Consequences." *Journal of Politics* 620–42.

Fraga, Bernard, and Eitan Hersh. 2010. "Voting Costs and Voter Turnout in Competitive Elections." *Quarterly Journal of Political Science* 5: 339–56.

Gerber, Alan S., and Donald P. Green. 2000. "The Effects of Canvassing, Direct Mail, and Telephone Contact on Voter Turnout: A Field Experiment." *American Political Science Review* 94: 653–63.

Gerber, Alan S., Donald P. Green, and Ron Shachar. 2003. "Voting May be Habit-Forming. Evidence from a Randomized Field Experiment." *American Journal of Political Science* 47 (3): 540–50.

Green, Donald P., and Ron Shachar. 2000. "Habit Formation and Political Behaviour: Evidence of Consuetude in Voter Turnout." *British Journal of Political Science* 30: 561–73.

Hayworth, Bret. 2015. "King's conservative cavalcade coming Saturday." *The Courier* (Waterloo-Cedar Falls, IA), January 18: A4.

Iowa Secretary of State. 2012. *Monthly Voter Registration Totals.* January 3. https://sos.iowa.gov/elections/pdf/VRStatsArchive/2012/CongJan12.pdf.

Jacobs, Jennifer. 2012. "Political parties consider names, strategy for 2016." *Des Moines Register*, November 11. http://archive.desmoinesregister.com/article/20121111/NEWS09/311110095/Political-parties-consider-names-strategy-2016.

———. 2014. "GOP delegate rules to change." *Des Moines Register*, January 21. http://www.desmoinesregister.com/story/news/politics/2014/01/21/gop-delegate-rules-to-change/4693969/.

Jacobson, Gary C. 2013. *The Politics of Congressional Elections.* 8th. Boston: Pearson.

Keith, Bruce E., David B. Magleby, Candice J. Nelson, Elizabeth Orr, Mark C. Westlye, and Raymond E. Wolfinger. 1992. *The Myth of the Independent Voter.* Berkeley: University of California Press.

Lindgren, Eric, and Priscilla Southwell. 2013. "The Effect of Redistricting Commissions on Electoral Competitiveness in U.S. House Elections, 2002-2010." *Journal of Politics and Law* 6 (2): 13–18.

Masket, Seth E., Jonathan Winburn, and Gerald C. Wright. 2012. "The Gerrymanders Are Coming! Legislative Redistricting Won't Affect Competition or Polarization Much, No Matter Who Does It." *PS: Political Science and Politics* 46 (1): 39–43.

McDonald, Michael P. 2004. "A Comparative Analysis of Redistricting Institutions in the United States, 2001–02." *State Politics and Policy Quarterly* 4 (4): 371–95.

———. 2006a. "Drawing the Line on District Competition." *PS: Political Science and Politics* 39 (1): 91–94.

———. 2006b. "Re-drawing the Line on District Competition." *PS: Political Science and Politics* 39 (1): 99–102.

———. 2010. *Partisan Voter Registration Totals.* October 13. http://www.huffingtonpost.com/michael-p-mcdonald/partisan-voter-registrati_b_761713.html.

National Conference of State Legislatures. 2014. *Same Day Voter Registration.* May 6. http://www.ncsl.org/research/elections-and-campaigns/same-day-registration.aspx.

National Journal. 2013. "2013 Vote Ratings." http://www.nationaljournal.com/2013-vote ratings.

Norrander, Barbara. 1989. "Explaining Cross-State Variation in Independent Identification." *American Journal of Political Science* 33 (2): 516–36.

Norman, Jane. 2001. "Boswell's stand on trade draws flak from GOP candidate." *Des Moines Register*, December 16.

Obradovich, Kathie. 2012. "Yes, Ron Paul Won the Iowa Caucuses." August 28 *Des Moines Register*, http://blogs.desmoinesregister.com/dmr/index.php/2012/08/28/yes-ron-paulwon-the-iowa-caucuses/article.

Ostermeier, Eric. 2010a. "The Top 50 Most Competitive U.S. House Districts in the Nation, 2002-2008." March 16. Smart Politics. Humphrey School of Public Affairs http://blog.lib.umn.edu/cspg/smartpolitics/2010/03/the_top_50_most_competitive_us.php.

———. 2010b. *Which States Have the Most Competitive U.S. House Elections?* March 15. Smart Politics. Humphrey School of Public Affairs http://blog.lib.umn.edu/cspg/smartpolitics/2010/03/which_states_have_the_most_com.php.

Patterson, Samuel C., and Gregory A. Caldeira. 1984. "The Etiology of Partisan Competition." *American Political Science Review* 78 (3): 691–707.

Redlawsk, David P., Caroline J. Tolbert, and Todd Donovan. 2010. *Why Iowa?: How Caucuses and Sequential Elections Improve the Presidential Nominating Process.* Chicago: University of Chicago Press.

Stark, Caitlin, and Amy Roberts. 2012. "By the numbers: Swing states." October 26. CNN Politics http://www.cnn.com/2012/10/11/politics/btn-swing-states.

Stone, Walter J., Lonna Rae Atkeson, and Ronald B Rapoport. 1992. "Turning On or Turning Off? Mobilization and Demobilization Effects of Participation in Presidntial Nomination Campaigns." *American Journal of Political Science* 36 (3): 665–91.

Trish, Barbara. 1999. "Does Organization Matter? A Critical-Case Analysis from Recent Presidential Nomination Politics." *Presidential Studies Quarterly* 29 (4): 873–95.

Winebrenner, Hugh, and Dennis J. Goldford. 2010. *Iowa Precinct Caucuses: The Making of a Media Event.* 3rd ed. Iowa City: University of Iowa Press.

Wiser, Mike. 2013. "The political ground game begins in Iowa." *The Gazette*, July 14. http://thegazette.com/2013/07/14/the-political-ground-game-begins-in-iowa/.

Wright, Gerald C., Robert S. Erikson, and John P. McIver. 1985. "Measuring State Partisanship and Ideology with survey data." *Journal of Politics* 47: 469–89.

Chapter Thirteen

Indiana Politics at a Crossroad

Democrats Competing in a Conservative State

Matthew L. Bergbower

Indiana is the 16th largest state in the U.S. and provides 11 Electoral College votes to the victor of presidential contests. For many recent elections these 11 Electoral College votes are not highly contested because Indiana is frequently identified as a conservative state by politicians, journalists, and pundits.[1] Articles published by the *The Economist*, *The Wall Street Journal*, and *Associated Press*, as well as local media like the *Evansville Courier & Press*, *Journal Review*, and *The Courier-Journal*, call Indiana a conservative Midwestern state, with the *Indianapolis Business Journal* going as far as to characterize it as a "traditional dead-red state."

There is some sound reasoning behind this popular characterization. Since World War II, Indiana has supported only two Democratic candidates for President: Lyndon Johnson in 1964 and Barack Obama in 2008. More recently, George W. Bush did well in Indiana during his two presidential campaigns. In 2000, Bush garnered 56.7% of the Hoosier vote and that was followed by 59.9% in 2004. In 2008, Obama's close Indiana battle with McCain ultimately netted him just a 1% edge on Election Day. Four years later, the tables turned dramatically, and Mitt Romney won Indiana by 10%. While it may be easy to disregard Obama's 2008 victory as an anomaly in Indiana politics and ignore the potential Indiana has as a swing state in future presidential elections, such a dismissal would ignore recent trends in state politics. After all, neither McCain (48.8%) nor Romney (54%) was able to reach the same electoral returns seen in the Bush elections. Perhaps there is a slow movement towards more Democratic support during presidential elections occurring in Indiana.[2]

The assumption that Indiana is a conservative and Republican state based on presidential election outcomes is a fair one. Nonetheless, a closer examination of Indiana's rich past and unique political culture is necessary. The next few sections present evidence that indicates Indiana may not be red, but purple. This includes an examination of (1) down-state ballot results, (2) state public opinion on salient issues of the day, and (3) Democratic campaign strategies including expenditures and messages. These three reasons provide the best explanation for why Indiana is not a dead-red state. Downstate ballots demonstrate Democratic competitiveness and victories. This is not surprising because, in part, public opinion polls show Hoosiers as being moderate on many issues. The data presented in this chapter suggest that based on these two observations Indiana ought to be classified as a swing state. However, if these first two points are so self-evident, one must ask why we do not typically see presidential campaign intensity in Indiana? This answer leads to the third point, a lack of Democratic presidential campaign prioritization and investment in the state's 11 Electoral College votes. The future of Democrats competing in the state is largely conditioned on the party, and their candidates, investing in voters and changing the commonality of Hoosier conservativeness.

HOOSIER CONSERVATIVENESS

Indiana's political nature needs to be viewed in the context of its existence as a territory, while also considering its migration patterns, statehood transition, first constitution, and unfulfilled policy goals (Bodenhamer and Shepard 2006; Lovrich, Daynes, and Ginger 1980; Madison 1990). Surprisingly, some of the earliest decisions by Indiana politicians were in fact progressive. As a territory and state born out of the Northwest Ordinance of 1787, slavery was banned. The state's first constitution in 1816 included clear directions for a free public school system throughout the state.[3] This same Article established that libraries should be created in each newly established county.

Two major infrastructure acts passed by early Indiana general assemblies also provide evidence of the state's liberal goals. In 1821, the General Assembly passed "An Act Authorizing the Laying Of Certain State Roads in this State" which, through its appropriations, committed $100,000 to road construction.[4] The second major infrastructure project spearheaded by the state was expanding the Erie Canal through Indiana, a plan that was approved in 1832. This canal already connected the Atlantic Ocean, the ports of New York City, and the rivers and canals of the state of New York until they reached Lake Erie. The Indiana extension sought to connect Lake Erie with the rivers of Indiana[5] until they reached the Ohio and Mississippi rivers and, ultimately, the Gulf of Mexico. However, the natural rivers of Indiana do not succinctly link the northern part of the state (close to Lake Erie) to the southern part of the state (bordering the Ohio River). Like New York, Indiana had to dig canals for the connection.

These two projects were obviously motivated by economic goals, seeking to make Indiana a "crossroads" connecting the nation's East to its West, North to its South. Even still, the important ideological takeaway of these early projects is that these aggressive plans and goals were pursued by state government, not private interests. In fact, the state had to borrow money for some of the Erie Canal's start-up costs. Much of the funding for the canals was appropriated through a $10 million dollar loan charged with 5% interest in 1836 (Madison 1990).[6] Overall, Indiana spent large amounts of government funds to improve the economic well-being of its citizens and the reputation of the state. However, the Erie Canal expansion, along with economic recessions, depleted the state's budget. The result was that Indiana had to default on its loan.

The state's ambitious goals of widespread public education, established public libraries, expansive road system, plus an extension of the Erie Canal did not materialize as planned. Indiana's success was hampered by a lack of public funds dedicated to its projects. It was not until the mid-1800s that an organized effort to fulfill statewide education began. The state passed a series of laws empowering local governments to collect revenue from property and poll taxes to support schools. These laws then encountered legal challenges that stalled the state's education initiatives. Indiana's Erie Canal expansion was not completed until many years later than expected. The economic gains of the completed canal never materialized in the state either. By the mid-1800s, goods were increasingly being transported across the nation by train instead of waterways.

These unfilled policy commitments had consequences. First, they contributed to the 1851 passing of a new state constitution with a more traditional and conservative design, which remains today. Second, some scholars argue that these massive public disappointments affected the ideology of the state's citizens (Madison 1990). After all, a key component of ideology is how an individual views the role of government over societal problems and the goals it ought to pursue. In the face of such failures, the public moved to a more conservative perspective on proper governing. In other words, Hoosiers started to reject more progressive ideals and adopted the mantra of "good enough is good enough" (Bodenhamer and Shepard 2006, 3).

In addition to progressive policy failures, another early state characteristic that may also contribute to Indiana's conservative nature is the state's cultural makeup. Using Elazar's (1966) political culture typology, Lovrich, Daynes, and Ginger (1980) identified a strong presence of traditionalistic, individualistic, and moralistic cultures in Indiana. Traditionalistic cultures believe in

keeping the status quo of social order and class structure, while individualistic cultures stress individual economic well-being. Individualistic cultures
feel the government's only role in economy should be to encourage the success of the private sector. Conversely, moralistic cultures see government
as playing a necessary role in meeting societal needs and serving the public
good (Elazar 1966). Of the 92 Indiana counties, 35 can be described as traditionalistic, 38 can be described as individualistic, and 11 can be described as
moralistic. Although the state may be considered politically diverse based on
this classification, it is clear that the most liberal of the three cultures, moralistic, is seen the least in Indiana.

Although these migration patterns occurred well over 125 years ago,
Lovrich, Daynes, and Ginger (1980) argue that the cultural makeup of the
state, established by migration patterns, remains the same today. Indeed, the
important takeaway of these cultural foundations is that they affect future political behavior and public policy output. As Barone and McCutcheon (2011)
describe, Indiana still retains the old societal norms that were popularized in
the famous sociology studies of "Middletown," published in the early twentieth century. However, a closer look at the evidence suggests that more current
electoral behavior is not driven by these cultural patterns. Table 13.1 provides
an analysis of the political culture typologies per county, as well as electoral
support in the 2008 and 2012 presidential elections. While it is expected that
moralistic cultures are the most liberal, none of these counties supported
Obama in his two elections. Instead, a low number of counties identified as
having individualistic and traditionalistic cultures supported Obama. Overall,
the cross-tabulation has low predictive power and alternative explanations
need to be explored to determine why Indiana communities vote the way they
do. More recent political science literature does an excellent job of explaining
voting behavior, which includes race and income correlations to party preferences. In recent Indiana elections, the largest Democrat vote shares came
from urban areas like Indianapolis and Lake County, which house the largest
number of racial minorities.

Electorally, Indiana's history has been more diverse than its conservative
description would suggest. It can be described as a swing state for many
elections between the Civil War and World War II. In fact, between 1864
and 1936, Indiana supported 13 Republican and 6 Democratic presidential
candidates. Of these 19 electoral contests, 7 were decided with a vote margin
over 10%, but 10 were decided with a vote margin of under 4%. The take-
away from this historical record is that it is too simplistic to solely identify
Indiana as a culturally and ideologically conservative state. Its historical
record is complex and mixed. From the state's cultural diversity and early
policy proposals to its nineteenth- and twentieth-century party politics, what

Table 13.1   Political Culture Typology and Presidential Election County Results in Indiana (2008 & 2012)

	2008 Presidential Election		
	Republican County	*Democratic County*	*Total*
Individualistic	36	10	46
Moralistic	11	0	11
Traditionalistic	30	5	35
Total	77	15	92

Chi2 = 3.24 (p. = .20)

	2012 Presidential Election		
	Republican County	*Democratic County*	*Total*
Individualistic	40	6	46
Moralistic	11	0	11
Traditionalistic	32	3	35
Total	83	9	92

Chi2 = 1.81 (p. = .41)

emerges is a state that has been more politically balanced than preconceived notions may suggest. It is then worth explaining what happened to Indiana as the nation moved from the twentieth to the twenty-first century. Down-ballot elections suggest that there is still potential for swing state politics in Indiana, despite the fact that it has only supported one Democratic candidate out of the 12 contests for president from 1968 to 2012.

Indiana's Down-Ballot Elections and Presidential Contests

Republican Governor Mitch Daniels ended his two terms in 2013 with high approval ratings (around 58%). His Republican successor, Mike Pence, won the 2012 race, but it was not an easy contest. Despite the fact that Pence was able to outspend his opponent by over a two to one margin, Pence won the election by only 3%. Overall, Indiana Republicans had a good election year in 2012 not only because of Pence's victory, but also because they obtained super-majority status in their state House of Representatives and sustained super-majority status in the state Senate.

Aside from these Republican victories, Indiana Democrats were still able to procure a few successes in 2012. After some controversial education reforms were shepherded through the General Assembly, one of the state's Republican leaders, State Superintendent of Public Instruction Tony Bennett, was voted out of office. The Democratic challenger, Glenda Ritz, only had

$350,000 to spend during the campaign and relied on grassroots tactics and the support of the teachers union to defeat Bennett. U.S. Senator Richard Lugar was unopposed in the 2006 primary and general elections. Six years later, Lugar was seen as being too moderate for the state's Republicans and was defeated by State Treasurer and Tea Party supporter Richard Murdock in the GOP primary. Like many other Tea Party candidates, his momentum was unable to carry over to general election voters and Joe Donnelly defeated Murdock in 2012 for the U.S. Senate seat by 6% of the vote. This contest is a one signal that the Tea Party does not have a strong enough foothold on state politics to win general elections in Indiana.[7] If Republicans were to nominate a Tea Party candidate at the presidential level, Indiana would be likely to lean more Democratic in the election.

Table 13.2 lists election and campaign resource data for Indiana's gubernatorial and U.S. Senate races from 1996 to 2012.[8] Of the five races for governor, three were won by Republicans and two by Democrats. While only one gubernatorial race, 2012, demonstrates an election that was close, the average Democratic and Republican vote share for this time period is very similar.

Table 13.2. Indiana Governor and U.S. Senate Results and Campaign Money Raised (1996–2012)

Election	Democrat Candidate (%)	Republican Candidate (%)	Democrat Candidate Raised ($)	Republican Candidate Raised ($)
Governor				
2012	46.6	49.5	6,472,738	14,841,352
2008	40.0	57.8	5,275,797	17,580,040
2004	45.5	53.2	12,661,631	19,271,845
2000	56.6	41.7	8,234,484	7,957,140
1996	51.5	46.8	6,674,522	11,423,171
Average	48.0	49.8	7,863,834	14,214,709
Senate				
2012	50.0	44.3	5,661,997	8,834,849
2010	40.0	54.6	2,368,351	4,396,274
2006*	--	--	--	--
2004	61.7	37.2	7,638,591	2,265,166
2000	31.9	66.6	1,179,029	5,248,217
1998	63.7	34.8	4,158,990	645,270
Average	49.5	47.5	4,201,391	4,277,955

Source: Election returns and campaign money raised data compiled from the Federal Election Commission, OpenSecrets.org, and the National Institute on Money in State Politics.

*Richard Lugar (R) was not opposed by a Democratic candidate in 2006.

Gubernatorial campaign funding tells a different story, as Republicans outspent Democrats by large margins in four out of the five elections. Even despite a significantly lower amount of campaign funds at their disposal in 1996 and 2012, Democratic gubernatorial candidates competed well these years.

There are also no close races in Indiana's U.S. Senate contests, as none of the races from 1998 to 2012 ended with a margin of victory under 5%, and one was even unopposed. Nonetheless, the races demonstrate three Democratic and three Republican victories. Overall, there is parity in the average vote totals from both parties and the average amount of money raised by the candidates.

Presidential contests in Indiana offer a different perspective, despite the evidence of Republican and Democratic competitiveness in gubernatorial and Senate campaigns. Of the five presidential elections from 1996 to 2012 listed in Table 13.3, Republicans handily won four. On average, the five elections demonstrate a Republican vote share around 10 points higher than that of Democrats. Bill Clinton competed well in 1996, and Obama won the state in 2008. Both these years include a Democratic investment in campaigning for state voters. According to the campaign ad data, these two election years are the only of the five in which Democrats campaigned significantly in the state.

Table 13.3 Presidential Election Results and Campaign Money
Spent in Indiana (1996–2012)

Presidential Election	Democrat Candidate (%)	Republican Candidate (%)	Democrat Candidate Ad Spending in Indianapolis ($)	Republican Candidate Ad Spending in Indianapolis ($)
2012	43.9	54.0	0	300
2008	49.8	48.8	5,437,708	239,005
2004	39.3	59.9	0	0
2000	41.0	56.7	0	0
1996	41.6	47.1	163,236*	653,901*
Average	43.1	53.3	1,120,188	178,641

Source: Campaign ad money spent in Indianapolis from Andrews, Keating, and Yourish (2012), Scheinkman, G.V., McLean, and Weitberg (2012), the Wisconsin Advertising Project, and Shaw (2006).

Note: Data includes ads sponsored by the candidate and outside groups. Some other media districts that cover portions of Indiana are based in other states (i.e., Louisville, KY, Cincinnati, OH, and Chicago, IL). This makes it more difficult to get an accurate picture of ad spending, as a whole, that targeted Indiana. Thus, presidential ad spending in Indianapolis (which is a designated market for 32 counties in central Indiana and covers the largest population of Hoosiers) is to serve as an illustration for a level of overall presidential campaign intensity in Indiana.

*Ad spending in 1996 is an estimate based on the number of ads ran by Clinton and Dole multiplied by the average cost of running an ad in Indianapolis during one of the three major network nightly news programs.

In 1996, Clinton was outspent by Bob Dole, and in 2008 Obama prioritized the state, while McCain did not.

Local television advertising is only one way to campaign in competitive races. Candidates also decide, for example, to give stump speeches, open up field offices, advertise through different mediums (radio, internet, print, billboards, etc.), direct door to door canvassing, and send mailers to certain states. These are important decisions for campaigns, given the finite amount of resources available to them (Shaw 2006). This is why, for example, some presidential candidates elected not to invest in Indiana. An important lesson from the data demonstrated here is that Indiana leans Republican in recent presidential elections. However, salient down-ballot elections illustrate that the state is more diverse in its candidate preferences. The opportunity for Democratic gains is apparent if campaign resources are prioritized in Indiana.

Why Indiana Voted for Obama in 2008 but not in 2012

The Obama campaign fully invested in Indiana during the 2008 election. According to Barone and McCutcheon (2011), that year Obama's Indiana campaign "opened 44 offices, hired 210 paid staff, attracted 80,000 volunteers, and had 50,000 people going door to door and making phone calls in the final week" (574). These investments had real-world effects on turnout. In Indiana, over 140,000 more people voted in 2008 than in 2012. This trend did not occur at the national level, where over 10 million more people voted in 2012 than in 2008. This statewide decrease in the 2012 turnout rate is not randomly distributed, rather Democratic counties saw a disproportionate drop-off in voter turnout compared to all other counties. More specifically, those counties that supported McCain in 2008 saw a drop-off of around 796 votes per county in 2012. On the other hand, those counties that supported Obama in 2008 saw a drop-off of around 5,420 votes per county in 2012.[9] Calculating these results a bit further, if Republican and Democrat vote shares and vote totals per county were the same in 2012 as they were in 2008, Romney would have gained 34,847 votes, while Obama would have gained 45,568 votes. While this 10,721 vote difference does not produce a scenario in which Obama wins Indiana in 2012, the fact that voter turnout levels decreased in the state does help explain why Obama's support declined from 2008 to 2012.

Obama's 2012 campaign was also unique in that it did not receive the same level of support from the state's African American voters as expected. In fact, 92% of the Indiana African American vote went to John Kerry in 2004, 90% to Obama in 2008, and 89% to Obama in 2012. While the Indiana African American vote share for Democratic presidential candidates went down during the three election cycles, it has gone up nationally. African Americans supported John Kerry at around 88% in 2004, while Obama enjoyed their support at 95% and 93% in 2008 and 2012 respectively. Because Indiana's African American voter turnout level is relatively high—68.4% in 2012— Obama's vote total in Indiana would have increased by over 7,600 votes if he had received the national average of African American Democratic support in 2012.

Table 13.4 lists data from exit polls on key socio-demographic characteristics and support for Obama in 2008 and 2012. Amongst almost all groups considered, Obama lost support in his state effort to win reelection. Indiana voters demonstrate a gender gap, but women still supported Romney more than Obama in 2012. A 7 point decrease is observed for white voters, but African Americans remained consistent in their support of Obama in the two elections. The biggest decrease observed, a 17 point drop, is with young voters. Nationally, 66% of young voters (under 30) supported Obama in 2008— which is close to what is seen in Indiana. In 2012, around 60% of young voters supported Obama nationally (Pew Research Center 2012)—which is far

Table 13.4. Socio-Demographics and Obama Voter Support in Indiana (2008 & 2012)

	2008 Obama	2012 Obama	% Change
Sex			
Male	47	40	–7
Female	52	48	–4
Race			
White	45	38	–7
Black	90	89	–1
Age			
18–29	63	46	–17
30–44	47	48	–1
45–64	49	44	–5
65+	37	34	–3
Education			
No college	50	45	–5
Some college	49	46	–3
College graduate	44	39	–5
Postgraduate	55	50	–5
Income			
Under $30,000	66	60	–6
$30,000-$49,999	48	49	+1
$50,000-$99,999	46	42	–4
$100,000 or more	45	34	–9

Source: New York Times (2012); CNN (2012)

Note: Number of respondents for 2008 Indiana exit polls is 2,422 and for 2012 is 1,539.

more than the 46% reported in statewide exit polls. Senior citizens in Indiana are also 8–10% below the national average for support of Obama in 2008 and 2012 (Pew Research Center 2012). Small decreases are observed for the education groups and the breakdown for Obama support amongst different income brackets is theoretically expected—the wealthier one is, the less likely they are to support Democratic presidential candidates.

Looking at the Future: Public Opinion and Issue Attitudes in Indiana

Since support for Obama dropped off so much from 2008 to 2012 what evidence suggests that such losses in support could be regained for Democratic candidates in future presidential elections? One possible beacon of hope from Democrats in the state is from public attitudes on major issues of the day. A close examination of political attitudes in Indiana reveals a mixed record of preferences. For example, 2013 state polling found that over 32% of potential voters consider themselves Democrats, while only 21% consider themselves Republican (with Independent, party-leaners nearly evenly split). Political science literature provides robust evidence in support of the fact that party identification is a powerful predictor of voter choice. This 11 point Democratic edge in party identification makes the lack of Democratic victories in the state suspect. One contrary piece of evidence to this party identification gap is that this same survey found that over 32% of the state identifies as conservative, and only 17% as liberal.

In *Statehouse Democracy*, Erikson, Wright, and McIver (1993) examine public opinion polls from the 1970s and 1980s and find that party identification and political ideology are not correlated within states. Thus, Indiana may not be unique in its division between ideology and matching party identification. However, in an updated 2006 study using more recent polling, the authors find partisanship and political ideology to be sorting—or aligning themselves along ideological and partisan lines. The most commonplace illustration of this point is that during the mid-twentieth century, it can easily be observed that Southern states were ideologically conservative but solidly Democratic. Yet, as the twentieth century concluded, partisanship and political ideology started to "sort" in the South as conservative ideological tendencies remained stable and Republican victories dominated the South. This means partisanship and political ideology are more correlated today, but given the Indiana polling numbers on ideology and party identification, the state does not clearly demonstrate this trend.

Another important contribution from *Statehouse Democracy* is that elected leaders prioritize the public opinion of their constituencies. One implication of this finding is that public attitudes have an impact on election outcomes. With this logic, this section takes a closer look at the political attitudes of Hoosiers. These issue positions further characterize the state as moderate, with potential for Democratic candidates to capitalize on their current position stances. Table 13.5 considers some salient topics unique to the state and nation. First, gay marriage has been a prominent legal and legislative issue in Indiana. Since the mid-2000s, Republican leaders in the Indiana General Assembly have pushed for a state constitutional ban on gay marriage, but these efforts were thwarted in 2014 by a federal court. While public opinion has not always favored legalized gay marriage in the state, more recent surveys suggest strong opposition (57%) to constitutionally banning it.

Other polling results prove unconventional for a perceived conservative state. Legalized marijuana use, which may play a large role in presidential politics given the medical and recreational legalization efforts seen in some states, demonstrates a small edge towards support in Indiana. Gun control has also infamously made its way into national debate. This complex issue touches upon many areas, such as mental health services and reporting, school safety, background check processes, and the question of which guns can constitutionally be banned. Overall, for the gun related questions posed, Indiana citizens support federal efforts to curb gun violence.

Indiana is not a state at the forefront of the immigration debate. According to the Pew Research Center approximately 13% of the U.S. population is foreign born (Brown and Patten 2014). Only 4.6% of Indiana residents are foreign born, an average representing the lower third of states' foreign born populations. Nonetheless, the immigration debate remains a promising national issue to be considered by future presidential candidates. Using the DREAM Act as a proxy for overall immigration viewpoints, Indiana citizens appear supportive of nationalization policies for foreign-born populations.

Taken as a whole, the only salient issue reported in Table 13.5 that bodes well for the Republican party in Indiana is their opposition to Obamacare, which Hoosiers oppose at 53%. Taking a closer look at these political attitudes in the state is important because of the potential any one of these issues may have as a "wedge" issue in future presidential elections. Indeed, Hillygus and Shields (2006) find that presidential candidates target divisive issues with the expectation of pulling votes away from their opponent. Their theory proposes that a campaign can "help voters translate their predispositions into the candidate selection by increasing the salience of one consideration over another" (185). The polling numbers presented in Table 13.5 suggest Indiana is one state where persuadable voters can be primed for greater Democratic gains.

Table 13.5. Public Issue Attitudes in Indiana

Issue: Support for	Support (%)	Oppose (%)	Margin of error	Date	Source
Affordable Care Act	42	53	4.8	10/2013	WISH-TV/Ball State
Allowing gays and lesbians to legally marry	48	46	4.8	10/2013	WISH-TV/Ball State
Constitutional amendment banning gay marriage	38	57	4.8	10/2013	WISH-TV/Ball State
Reducing penalties for marijuana use	54	37	3.5	10/2012	Howey-DePauw
Legalizing marijuana	52	45	4.8	10/2013	WISH-TV/Ball State
All gun sales subject to background checks	83	15	3.5	04/2013	Howey-Gauge
Assault-weapons ban	54	44	4.8	10/2013	WISH-TV/Ball State
Federal government database tracking gun sales	64	35	4.8	10/2013	WISH-TV/Ball State
DREAM Act	54	32	4.8	10/2013	WISH-TV/Ball State
Tea Party Movement	24	34	4.0	11/2012	General Election Exit Polls

In previous presidential elections, one sees the dominance of national security and foreign wars (2004) or the economy (2008) in driving presidential debates, campaign messages, and voter priorities. While 2012 focused on health care and economic recovery efforts, it largely failed to prime many other salient issues. For example, the three 2012 presidential debates failed to address gun control, gay marriage, and climate change (Babington 2012). In future presidential elections, potential for gains in Indiana are apparent if Democrats are able to capitalize on their issue strengths. Polling completed in 2014 suggests that Democrats have a national edge on issues surrounding global warming, same-sex marriage, income inequality, and health care, while Republicans have an edge in the economy, foreign affairs, and the federal budget deficit (Newport 2014; Pew Research Center 2014).[10] The polling averages reported here suggests Democrats can campaign on their issue strengths, and do so creditably, in Indiana.

Concluding Remarks and Reservations

How likely is it for Indiana to serve as a swing state in future presidential elections? Based on the public opinion polls and downstate ballots it can be argued there is swing state potential in Indiana. The Democratic party has focused some of its attention on women's issues, and inroads can be made on Indiana women voters supporting Democrats. On the national stage, Democrats have coined the phrase "war on women" and accused Republicans of blocking measures that would benefit women. As one example, in 2012, Senate Republicans blocked the Paycheck Fairness Act which would, in part, help ensure women were given equal pay for equal work. On a more local front, Indiana Republicans' effort to block Medicaid funds to Planned Parenthood could resonate with some female Hoosiers as evidence of a war on women. Another local element to this war on women is the fact that Mike Pence, as a congressman, was the chief House sponsor of a failed attempt to ban federal funding for Planned Parenthood in 2011. The academic literature suggests such a message strategy can work (Schaffner 2005), and given the lower share of state female support for Obama in 2008 and 2012 (both under the national average by 4–7%) Indiana is a prime target for increased Democratic votes.

As for a wedge issue that could define the 2016 race in Indiana, one could easily look at the fight for LGBTQ civil rights. The state-level prominence of this issue came from Governor Pence signing the Religious Freedom Restoration Act on March 26, 2015. Many interpreted this act as legalizing discrimination against the LGBTQ population. Indiana infamously made national headlines in the days following the bill being signed into law. Thousands protested the act daily outside the Indiana Statehouse and opponents to the law could be seen on national television, online media websites, newspapers, magazines, and social media. In addition to these pressures, many Indiana businesses threatened to de-invest in the state because of the law's discriminatory interpretation. Despite state Republican efforts to defend the act's intentions, they reluctantly "fixed" the law just seven days after the bill was signed. In this clarification effort, new language was inserted into the act which specified that the law could not be interpreted as a denial of services based on, among many other populations, one's gender identity or sexual orientation. As a consequence of these events unfolding, the debate over civil rights protections for the Indiana LGBTQ community was brought to widespread attention. The possibility of future socially conservative Republican presidential candidates may likely re-open these wounds in the state, with electoral consequences.

Campaign stump speeches, local media interviews, and targeted regional advertising allows for presidential nominees to get more local. Democratic presidential nominees should take notice of these opportunities. Small Democratic investments early on may quickly see Indiana emerge as a battleground state in future presidential elections. For this to happen, investments are needed, as there are payoffs to presidential campaign state spending. Despite being typically outspent in down-ballot elections, Democrats compete and win statewide elections in Indiana. If Indiana is to become a swing state in future presidential elections, Democrats' resources must be utilized to gain persuadable independent voters (Hillygus and Shields 2006) and mobilize the party base. They can do this by targeting Northwest Indiana (Chicago suburbs) and Indianapolis. These two counties, Lake and Marion, represent around 21% of the voting population in Indiana and they supported Obama in 2012 by over 60%. In the case of Indianapolis, this city's population is growing faster than most other areas of the state.

In October of 2000, Bush decided to target Tennessee with a share of his campaign resources. Al Gore's campaign failed to respond in a timely manner, and Bush taking the state is attributed to this aggressive campaign tactic (Shaw 2006). Similar stories can be found in other campaigns, such as Obama's commitment to Indiana in 2008. The important lesson of these examples is that when campaign resources are invested in a state, its voters respond. Recent Indiana history tells us that early presidential polling forecasts are likely to continue favoring Republican presidential candidates. Thus, the first move in campaign investments to Indiana will likely need to come from Democrats if the state is to move to the battleground category.

We know that down-ballot races foster competitive Democratic candidates. As discussed above, Donnelly won his 2012 race for U.S. Senate, while John Gregg lost his 2012 race for governor by around 3%. Of those who supported

Donnelly at the ballot box, exit polls show that around 84% also supported Obama. Similarly, of those who supported Gregg, around 83% also supported Obama. On the contrary, Mourdock and Pence voters also supported Romney at 96% and 92% respectively. To put this in other terms, around 16–17% of Indiana voters were willing to support Gregg and/or Donnelly but not Obama, while only 4–8% were willing to support Mourdock and/or Pence but not Romney in 2012. This split-ticket voting suggests that Obama did not maximize his support amongst independent minded voters in Indiana.[11] Arguably, as an incumbent president running for reelection, which equates to a slight edge in winning, Obama could have made Indiana more competitive in 2012 if his campaign decided to invest in the state.

Nonetheless, recognition of state Republican successes is needed. Despite some Democratic victories in statewide elections, Republicans have a strong record of holding majority or super-majority status in their state legislative chambers. This, in part, is largely due to their strong state party origination and fundraising ability. Furthermore, the "time-for-a-change" theory in presidential election forecasting (Abramowitz, 2008) does not lend itself to Indiana becoming a swing state in 2016. Ultimately, while a two-term penalty may be a phenomenon Democrats cannot ultimately overcome in 2016, the opportunity for competitiveness in Indiana is strong for future elections. There are a few scenarios in which Democrats could compete in Indiana in 2016. For example, Republicans selecting a Tea Party candidate could reduce their electoral chances. Or, if the Indiana Democrats select popular candidates for their governor and U.S. Senate races in 2016, then campaign investments in the Democratic party brand may be high that year and benefit that party's slate of candidates in the state.

NOTES

1. To name a few, such comments can be found from former U.S. Senator Evan Bayh, U.S. Senator Joe Donnelly, Larry Sabato, *ABC News'* Christiane Amanpour, and U.S. Representative Todd Rokita.

2. This relationship is found when examining the average county support for Bush in 2000 and 2004, with the average county support for McCain and Romney in 2008 and 2012. Paired group t-test = 8.005 (p. < .00).

3. Article IX, Section 2, of this constitution states that the General Assembly shall provide by law "a general system of education, ascending in a regular graduation, from township schools to a state university, wherein tuition shall be gratis, and equally open to all."

4. Other road construction projects were also passed at this time. See Indiana General Assembly (1831).

5. Indiana does not border Lake Erie. The plan connected the state with Lake Erie through the Maumee River, which also flows through Ohio.

6. Calculating for inflation, $10 million equals over $208 million by today's standards.

7. From a public opinion standpoint, a January 2013 *NBC News/Wall Street Journal* poll has the Tea Party unfavorability rating at 47% nationwide, which is similar to a December 2012 *WISH-TV*/Ball State University Hoosier Survey that found the state holding a 44% unfavorable view of the Tea Party (see also Table 13.5).

8. There was no Indiana U.S. Senate race in 1996.

9. Independent group t-test = -6.452 (p. < .00).

10. The economy, a top concern in nearly every election year, is not traditionally a Republican-owned issue. Rather, the parties fluctuate frequently on public perceptions of who is "better able to handle" the economy.

11. Or, conversely, that Donnelly and Gregg were both able to maximize independent minded voters.

BIBLIOGRAPHY

Abramowitz, Alan I. 2008. "Forcecasting the 2008 Presidential Election with the Time-for-Change Model." *PS: Political Science & Politics* 41: 691-95.

Andrews, Wilson, Dan Keating, and Karen Yourish. 2012. "Mad money: TV Ads in the 2012 Presidential Campaign." *Washington Post*, November 14. Accessed April 22, 2014. http://www. washingtonpost.com/wp-srv/special/politics/track-presidential-campaign-ads-2012/.

Babington, Charles 2012. "Obama, Mitt Romney Largely Leave Guns, Gay Rights, Climate Change on Election Sidelines." *The Associated Press*, October 25. Accessed June 15, 2014. http://www.huffingtonpost.com/2012/10/25/obama-election_n_2015586.html.

Barone, Michael and Chuck McCutcheon. 2011. *The Almanac of American Politics 2012*. Chicago: University of Chicago Press.

Bodenhamer, David J. and Hon. Randall T. Shepard. 2006. "The Narratives and Counternarratives of Indiana Legal History." In *The History of Indiana Law*, edited by David J. Bodenhamer and Hon. Randall T. Shepard, 3–20. Athens, OH: Ohio University Press.

Brown, Anna and Eileen Patten. 2014. "Statistical Portrait of the Foreign-Born Population in the United States, 2012." *PewResearch Hispanic Trends Project*, April 29. Accessed April 4, 2014. http://www.pewhispanic.org/2014/04/29/statistical-portrait-of-the-foreign-born-population-in-the-united-states-2012/.

CNN. 2012. "Election Center." *CNN*. December 10. Accessed April 23, 2014. http://www2.cnn.com/election/2012/results/state/IN#president.

Elazar. David J. 1966. *American Federalism: A View From the States*. New York: Crowell.

Erikson, Robert S., Gerald C. Wright, and John P. McIver. 1993. *Statehouse Democracy: Public Opinion and Policy in the American States*. New York: Cambridge University Press.

Erikson, Robert S., Gerald C. Wright, and John P. McIver. 2006. "Public Opinion in the States: A Quarter Century of Change and Stability." In *Public Opinion in State Politics*, edited by Jeffrey E. Cohen, 229–53. Stanford, CA: Stanford University Press.

Hillygus, Sunshine D. and Todd G. Shields. 2008. *The Persuadable Voter: Wedge Issues in Presidential Campaigns*. Princeton, NJ: Princeton University Press.

Indiana General Assembly. 1831. *The Revised Laws of Indiana*. Indianapolis, IN: Douglass and Maguire.

Lovrich, Nicholas P., Jr., Byron W. Daynes, and Laura Ginger. 1980. "Public Policy and the Effects of Historical-Cultural Phenomena: The Case of Indiana." *Publius* 10: 111–25.

Madison, James H. 1990. *The Indiana Way*. Bloomington, IN: Indiana University Press.

New York Times. 2012. "Presidential Exit Polls." *The New York Times*. November 29. Accessed May 27, 2014. http://elections.nytimes.com/2012/results/president/exit-polls.

Newport, Frank. 2014. "Republicans have Edge on Top Election Issue: The Economy." *Gallup Politics*, May 19. Accessed June 25, 2014. http://www.gallup.com/poll/169352/republicans-edge-top-election-issue-economy.aspx#1.

Pew Research Center. 2012. "Young Voters Supported Obama Less, but may have Mattered More." *PewResearch Center for the People & the Press*, November 26. Accessed May 28, 2014. http://www.people-press.org/2012/11/26/young-voters-supported-obama-less-but-may-have-mattered-more/.

Pew Research Center. 2014. "Deficit Reduction Declines as Policy Priority." *PewResearch Center for the People & the Press*, January 27. Accessed June 25, 2014. http://www.people-press.org/2014/01/27/deficit-reduction-declines-as-policy-priority/.

Schaffner, Brian F. 2005. "Priming Gender: Campaigning on Women's Issues in U.S. Senate Elections." *American Journal of Political Science* 49: 803-17.

Scheinkman, Andrei, Xaquin G.V., Alan McLean, and Stephan Weitberg. 2012. "The Ads Wars." *New York Times*, May 23. Accessed May 12, 2014. http://elections.nytimes.com/2008/president/advertisin/index.html?hp.

Shaw, Daron R. 2006. *The Race to 270*. Chicago: University of Chicago Press.

Conclusion

Why States Swing in
American Presidential Elections

Stacey Hunter Hecht and David Schultz

The reality of recent United States presidential elections is that there are only about ten states which are the object of attention for candidates and campaigns. It is in this handful of states where presidential candidates spend most if not all of their general election campaign time and resources. It is these states where the elections are close, where there is a history of either a Republican or Democratic Party candidate having actually won or been competitive in winning it since 1988, and where victory in that state seems a harbinger of who will eventually win the presidential electoral vote in that election. These are the swing states.

The goal of this book has been to identify and explain the swing state phenomena. Swing state has become the preferred term in recent elections among journalists and political analysts to describe those states which are the focus of campaign activity for the major presidential candidates. Swing state as used by journalists and political analysts is often interchanged with other terms such as battleground, competitive, or purple states. Each of these terms may denote some meaning and may or may not be appropriately used inter-changeably. However, swing state as the preferred *nom de jour* lacks precise meaning and it has not been subject to rigorous political science analysis. Is being a swing state simply a label or does it signify a real and meaningful political phenomena? Explaining the swing state phenomena was the goal of this book.

The methodology of this book has been to identify those states which display four characteristics, as described in the introduction, in presidential elections from and inclusive of 1988–2012. First, they are ones which are competitive in the sense that the margin of victory between the winning and second place candidate was five percent or less. The second characteristic is being a bellwether; by that, in how many elections have the results (who won that state) predicted or followed who eventually won the Electoral College. A third characteristic is that of actual swinging—how many times has a state actually flipped from supporting one of the major party candidates to another? Finally, the methodology looked to whether a state was a battleground, specifically how many times major presidential candidates held post-convention 2012 events in that state. Applying these four criteria, ten states were identified as those which qualify as swing-states.

These ten states were the subject of separate cases studies in their respective chapters, along with Missouri and Indiana. The latter two were included to provide additional information regarding the factors that may determine why some states swing. Missouri was included as a state that historically was a reliable bellwether, battleground, and often competitive state whereas Indiana was included as a state that may possibly be a swinger given that in 2008 it flipped for the first time in recent history. Altogether, examination of these 12 states was meant to explain why they are *sui generis*. By that, why are they less predictable in terms of their presidential voting in comparison to the other 40 plus the District of Columbia? Second, what conditions bring about an end to swinger status. Finally, is the phenomena of being a swing state something that is objectively new or real or is it in the end, simply something that is a trendy term to apply to something that has already existed?

First, the concept of being a swing state is something that is distinct. There are a cohort of states—ten as identified in this book and by a methodology—that standout as different from all the other states and District of Columbia. They are the states that embody the four characteristics of being bellwether, competitive, flipable, and battleground. These ten states among themselves embody these four characteristics to varying degrees and they also are distinct from the other states in terms of displaying these four traits. While this book did not publish a comprehensive 51 jurisdictional or case study analysis to show this, the methodology to arrive at the core ten states chosen are the ones that bore these characteristics in ways that distinguished them from the remaining 41 cases. Thus, states that display more of these four characteristics as described in this book are those which would be more firmly defined as swing states. Among the ten states here, some such as Ohio and Florida display more of these traits than do others such as Wisconsin, for example. In effect, some states are better swingers than others. Others, such as New Mexico, seem to be exiting the camp as a swing state because of a growing Latino population that make it an outsized model of what is happening in the United States as a whole.

Is the swing state phenomena a recent trait or characteristic of American presidential elections? That is a difficult question to answer. On the one hand there have always been a group of states that have been highly contestable or the center of candidate attention. But as discussed in the introduction, the exact number of states, for example, decided by five percent or less—the competitive criteria—has varied even since the 1960s. What would one find if the four criteria articulated here were applied across time? Would one find other states in other periods fitting the bill of being a swing state? Perhaps, and that may be a question for further research. But in defense of arguing that being a swing state is a recent or new phenomena, several claims can be made. First, as noted in the introduction, the number of competitive states does seem lower now (1988–2012) than in previous time periods. Second, there does seem to be fewer and few states candidates invest time in. Three, it does appear that the number of flipable states is smaller than at other times. Finally, there is a stability in the last seven presidential election cycles that seems to endorse the idea that there may be something unique when it comes to the states under examination.

A combination of factors seem to explain the uniqueness of swing states. As the 12 case studies disclose, there are clearly a host of unique or *sui generis* factors accounting for why a specific state is prone to swing. New Hampshire, for one is in part unique because of its brand of libertarian conservatism that distinguishes it from the evangelical national Republican party. This means that Republican as well as independent voters in that state are not as conservative or differently conservative from elsewhere in the United States, therefore contributing to an independent streak. Iowa's nonpartisan redistricting agency and process fosters competitive congressional districts. New Hampshire and Iowa uniquely have the first presidential primary and caucus and both provide the impetus for significant partisan political mobilization. Nevada is unique because of the powerful gambling interests that detach local party interests from those nationally. The other states in this book also display unique characteristics that have made them swing states for reasons that are not shared or could not be replicated elsewhere. Such a conclusion that it is all basically unique factors in a state that render it a swinger would mean that the cases studies here are simply a collection of discrete histories and no more. Yes, simply writing a book explaining why these 12 states are, were, or could be swingers may be valuable in itself. But even better is seeing if the stories of these 12 states reveal some broader trends or common characteristics that provide insights into what constitutes or makes for a swing state. In fact, the 12 case studies here do reveal a cluster of factors that contribute to making a swing state. The chapters reveal a pattern of repeated characteristics.

First, swing states are those where there is an even balance or percentage of individuals who identify or affiliate as either a Republican or Democrat. This is what one sees in Colorado. Additionally, in terms of affiliation, there is no one party that dominates the other. These two traits go together. There are no states here where 50% of the population equally identifies with one of these two parties. Instead, a repeated pattern is where no party enjoys major- ity status. While one may have a plurality of support, one characteristic of a swing state is where no party enjoys majority status and where the gap be- tween Republican and Democratic Party affiliation is narrow. How narrow? Many of these states found, based on exit polls or other surveys, that the gap between the two parties in terms of voter identification was simply a matter of no more than five percentage points. But even in cases where there were gaps, there was also evidence across the chapters that partisan attachments in swing states may be weaker than those in other states.

A second factor contributing to being a swing state is the percentage of the population which identifies as independent or with no affiliation. If swing states are ones where no party has achieved majority status, there also seems to be a pattern where in these states there is a large percentage of the voters who are independent. In places such as Colorado or Florida for example, the percentage of the population which considers itself independent or unaffili- ated either rivals that of those who identify with one of the majority parties or it is the fastest growing segment of the electorate. In Wisconsin 40% of the population identifies without an affiliation. North Carolina has a history of weak partisan attachments, and Nevada too has a high percentage of those not expressing a political affiliation. As Scott McLean noted in his chapter, and as described in several others, swing states seem to have a high percentage of swing voters. These are voters who do not have strong partisan attachments; they often include young voters or Millennial generation voters. Thus states such as Colorado display this. These are individuals who do not consistently vote or, if they do, seem less attached to traditional party labels than others.

A third characteristic is demographics. Repeatedly the authors of these chapters noted how changing demographics seem to be key to why states were, are, or will be swing states. States with many young people, highly- educated populations, changes in racial composition, or significant migration patterns seem to be swinging. Demographics are important because there is a connection between demographics and voting. Several chapters noted how states such as Missouri once and Ohio now have demographic patterns—ra- cial, gender, religious, party, and ideology for example—that are microcosms of the nation. There is an argument that Indiana's changing demographics set it up to be a future swing state. Demographic changes in Colorado, Virginia, and North Carolina have made those state swing, and such changes may also be transforming or moving New Mexico out of that category. The same may be true in Indiana in terms of how demographics are changing the state. De- mographics, such as rapidly growing urban populations in Colorado, Nevada, and Virginia, seem particularly important to understanding these states. In summary, if presidential elections, at least in terms of popular vote, are close, then a state that mirrors national demographics will similarly be close.

A fourth characteristic has to do with specific ideology in the state and how voters compare to the country as a whole. Here there are a couple of issues. The first are patterns found in several states that the ideology, political orientations, or policy preferences of the median voter in a state mirror that of the median voter nationwide. This is still essentially an argument suggesting a demographic microcosm among independent voters within a state. But second, there is also the ideology of the median Republican or Democratic voter in a state compared to the nation. In states where the national party or candidate is further to the right or left than the state party, there is less partisan attachment of party voters to the national candidate. This mismatch between national and state party political orientations or preferences seems to weaken the strength of state partisan voters to national presidential candidates, thereby setting the stage for voters to change normal patterns at the polls. This is part of the reason why Missouri seems to be moving away from being a swing state and becoming Republican and why there is a drift from Republicanism to swing state status in New Hampshire. Policy issues seem particularly salient in Colorado and Florida, where voters are mobilized or activated around them.

A fifth characteristic of swing states appears to be that they have many distinct political regions. Florida, Ohio, Nevada, Virginia, North Carolina, just to name a few, are really several states in one. They each have multiple and distinct political regions in the state. This is important because these regions create power centers where the two major parties have strengths. Iowa is split down the middle with the Democrats stronger in the eastern half and Republicans in the western. These distinct regions create situations where some parts of the state favor one set of interests. The presence of distinct regions leads to a sixth and seventh characteristic. Having many political regions in the state means that there may overall be competitive state elections. That control of the state legislatures may swing from party to party or the geographic distribution of party strength across the state may mean that there are only a few swing districts or regions in it. These swings control the balance of power within a state. This balance of power means, seventh, that the ability of the two parties to mobilize their bases in their safe districts and in the competitive ones. Swing states seem to be ones where mobilization of the parties are roughly equal, or, in cases where one party has an advantage, better mobilization by one party may account for why a state remains competitive (the case of Florida) or why one has become less competitive (Missouri). In both of these cases, Republicans have out-mobilized Democrats, thereby changing the balance of power in the state, moving one out of the swing state category (Missouri) and ensuring that the other stay in it.

These seven traits may not be the only reasons why some states are swingers. They seem to be commonalities that many of the swing states share, but there may be other factors at play too. There is need for additional research into what factors across swing and non-swing states seem critical in determining why some are more likely to be bellwethers, competitive, flipable, and battleground. Of course one question is whether campaign activity has made some states swingers? By that, does persistent interest or campaign activity in states such as New Hampshire or Colorado induce or cause them to be swingers or are they swing states independent of what candidates and campaigns do? This is an important question because it gets to the root of asking what the recent and continued focus on some states means and will they remain contestable and swing?

Conversely, does this mean that the other 40 states could not become swing states? This too is an important question both for political scientists and campaigners because they lead to questions about whether effectively a ten-state strategy makes sense or whether a 50-state approach might make more sense. In the case of Indiana and North Carolina in 2008, Obama's decision to campaign in them paid off. Similarly, Democrats now believe, as pointed out in the introduction, that states such as Texas and Georgia are at tipping points. Howard Dean, former governor of Vermont and presidential candidate, was famous for advocating a 50-state strategy for Democrats and not conceding any to the Republicans. Depending on how one views the nature and causes of swing states, a 50-state strategy may make sense or it might be a foolish waste of resources and time.

One final curious feature about swing states is what appears to be the relative stability of them in the last few years. Yes, Ohio and at one time Missouri were states that had long histories displaying many of the swing state traits, but at least over the last seven presidential races there seems to be relative stability in terms of the number of states that are swingers. There is perhaps an unwarranted or ill-advised caution against assuming that voting patterns that persist for now will remain permanent.

It was barely a generation ago that some claimed Republicans had a permanent lock on the Electoral College, much in the same way that many assume that for Democrats now. Those who claim "demographics is destiny" may or may not be correct. Demographics may change voting patterns, but they do not guarantee votes. They do not guarantee turnout; they do not ensure against parties nominating bad candidates or running bad campaigns. There is also no promise that some major economic or political crisis will not force some type of critical or electoral realignment of the political system. It is also possible that states may change the way they allocate electoral votes or that a constitutional amendment might alter the political landscape. All of this is a reminder that while for now American politics is dominated by a campaign focus on only a handful of swing states, conditions can change, thereby altering or even eliminating this phenomena as a defining feature of contemporary American presidential campaigns.

Index

abortion, 236, 238
Abramowitz, Alan, 157
ACA. *See* Affordable Care Act
Adams, John Quincy, x
Adelson, Sheldon, 193
advertising spending: between 1988–2012, *73*; in Florida, *74*, 102; in Indiana, *297*, 298; of Kerry, 74; measurement of, 72–73; in North Carolina, 126n2; Obama, 8; in Ohio, 74; in Pennsylvania, *74*; Romney, 8; in Virginia, 252
Affordable Care Act (ACA), 156, 158; controversy over, 251; in Indiana, 301, *302*; in New Hampshire, 234; repeal of, 159. *See also* health care
African American population: in Colorado, 171; in Nevada, *210*, 212; in New Hampshire, 237; in New Mexico, 149; in North Carolina, 113–114, 126; in Wisconsin, 134
AGOs. *See* Attorney General Opinions
agriculture, unionization and, 134
Alaska, Native American population of, 146
Albuquerque, role of, 151, 153–154
American National Election Studies (ANES), xxiii

ANES. *See* American National Election Studies
Angle, Sharron, 193
Arizona, as swing state, xxix
Asian population: in Nevada, 210; in Wisconsin, 134
Attorney General Opinions (AGOs), 204

Baby Boomers, xl
Baldwin, Tammy, 133
ballot design, x
Balz, Dan, 157
Barrett, Tom, spending by, 138–139
battleground states: bellwether states compared to, xiii; Colorado as, 166–167; definition of, xxix, 310; determining factors of, 6; electoral votes and, 7; Florida as, 165; Iowa as, 265; Missouri as, xxix, 310; Nevada as, 265; New Hampshire as, 265; New Mexico as, 148; Ohio as, 265; Pennsylvania as, xxix, xxxiii; selection of, 12–14; swing states compared to, xiv, xvii; Virginia as, 262; voting laws in, xxvii. *See also* competitive states; states; swing states

312–313; swing voters in, xxi–xxii;
turnout in, 249; 2008 presidential
election and, 248–251; 2012
presidential election and, 251–254;
2016 presidential election role of,
254; urbanization of, xli, 246, 254,
255; white population of, 262–263
voter choice, xx; party identification
and, 114–117
voter eligibility laws, x
voter fraud, x
voter identification laws, x; in North
Carolina, 126
voter registration: in Nevada, *207*; in
New Hampshire, 230; same day,
274–275
voter suppression, x
vote share, political geography and, 282,
284–285
voting: as habit forming, 270;
polarization in, xi, xv
voting age population (VAP), 176
voting behavior, xx; Catholic, xxiv;
demographics and, 314–315
voting laws, in battleground states,
xxvii
Voting Rights Act (1965), 114
voting studies, competitive states and,
xx–xxi

Walker, Scott: campaign themes,
138–139; controversy of, 139;
future implications of, 139; in Iowa,
283; presidential run of, 132, 142;
reelection of, 132; on right-to-work
law, 143–144; spending of, 138–139.
See also Wisconsin
Wallace, George, 224
Warner, Mark, 249, 253–254, 262
Washington, PVI of, *11*
Washoe County, NV, 201, *202*
Washtenaw County, MI, 155
Wasserman-Schultz, Debbie, 104
Watergate Scandal, 119–120; Nevada
and, 198, 200

Weaver, James, 197
Whitehouse, Sheldon, 239
white population: Clinton, B., and,
158; as declining percentage,
148–149; Democratic Party and,
158; educational status in, 150; of
Hawaii, 146; McCain and, 151; of
Nevada, 209, 212, 218n10; of New
Hampshire, 237; of New Mexico,
146; Obama and, *54*, 158; in
Virginia, 262–263; voting patterns
of, 149–151
Wisconsin: African American
population, 134; Asian population
in, 134; Biden in, 141; campaign
spending in, 141; changing economy
in, 134–135; as competitive state,
xxxi; Dane County, 155, 160n9;
Democratic Party in, 138, *139*;
demographics in, 134–135; divided
electorate in, 133; Electoral College
votes of, 139; ethnic settlement of,
131; exit poll data, 133; future of,
141, 142; gubernatorial elections in,
138, 138–139; history of, 132, 142;
Latino population in, 134; moralistic
political culture of, 131–132;
national elections in, 139–141;
Obama in, 141–143; political history
of, 135–137; political ideology in,
133; as political oddity, xxxviii–
xxxix; political order in, 131–132;
presidential elections in, 139–141;
Progressive Party of, 136–137;
Republican dominance in, 132, 135,
138; Romney in, 141, 142; Roosevelt
in, 135–136; Ryan in, 141; as swing
state, xiv, xxx–xxxii, 12, *13*, 131,
143; third-party politics in, 136; two-
party competition in, 136–141; union
membership rate in, 134, 143–144.
See also Walker, Scott
Wofford, Harris, xii
Worthington, Henry Gaither, 216n2
Wyoming, xi

About the Editors and Contributors

Donald W. Beachler (PhD, Cornell) is associate professor of politics at Ithaca College. He has co-authored the books *Winning the White House 2004* and *Winning the White House 2008*, both published by Palgrave-Macmillan. Beachler published several studies of electoral politics in various states including articles on elections in Pennsylvania, Florida, and Mississippi. He also published an article in the special issue on Barack Obama in the British journal *Patterns of Prejudice* titled "Barack Obama and the South." This article analyzed Obama's victories in Florida, North Carolina, and Virginia in the 2008 presidential election and compared demographic changes in these three states to population shifts in other southern states.

Matthew L. Bergbower (PhD, Southern Illinois University) is assistant professor of political science at Indiana State University. His research focuses on state politics, campaign information, and voting behavior, and can be seen in the *Journal of Elections, Public Opinion, & Parties, Social Science Quarterly*, the *Indiana Journal of Political Science*, and *The Oxford Companion to American Politics*. Bergbower teaches classes on American politics, state politics, and research methods. Prior to coming to Indiana State University, Bergbower served as a James H. Dunn, Jr. Memorial Fellow from 2009 to 2010 for Illinois Governor Pat Quinn.

Christopher A. Cooper is professor and department head of political science and public affairs at Western Carolina University. He is the coeditor of *The New Politics of North Carolina* (UNC Press) and has published articles and book chapters on state politics, political behavior, political communication, and political psychology. He is a frequent source for news media seeking commentary on North Carolina politics and has been quoted in the *New York*

Times, Washington Post, USA Today, Christian Science Monitor, and many other news outlets.

David F. Damore is associate professor of political science at the University of Nevada, Las Vegas, and a senior nonresident fellow in the Brookings Institution's Governance Studies program. Damore has written a number of book chapters and scholarly articles examining campaigns and elections in Nevada, and is presently working on two book projects relevant to Nevada politics. The first, co-authored with John Tuman, assesses the contours of Nevada's Latino community, and the second examines how Nevada's geography has shaped its political economy since the state's founding in 1864.

Sean D. Foreman is associate professor of political science at Barry University and was president of the Florida Political Science Association in 2012–2013. He coedited *The Roads to Congress 2010*, writing about Marco Rubio's election to the U.S. Senate, and *The Roads to Congress 2012*, writing about the Florida D-26 campaign. His article, "Top 10 reasons why Barack Obama Won the Presidency in 2008 and what it means in the 2012 Election," was published in the *Florida Political Chronicle*.

Rebecca D. Gill is associate professor of political science at the University of Nevada, Las Vegas. She is the co-author of *Judicialization of Politics: The Interplay of Institutional Structure, Legal Doctrine, and Politics on the High Court of Australia* (Carolina Academic Press, 2012). She is currently working on a multi-year National Science Foundation grant to study judicial elections and performance evaluations. Her work has appeared in a number of scholarly journals, including the *Law & Society Review*, the *Ohio State Law Journal*, and *Judicature*.

Henriët Hendriks (PhD, University of Minnesota, 2009) is a fiscal analyst with the Minnesota House of Representatives, and has served as visiting assistant professor in the Department of Political Science at St. Olaf College in Northfield, Minnesota, and as assistant professor at Susquehanna University. Hendriks's research focuses on the interplay between electoral institutions and political behavior, in particular the Electoral College's effects on both candidates' campaign strategies and mass attitudes.

Donna R. Hoffman is associate professor and head of the Department of Political Science at the University of Northern Iowa. She is the co-author of *Addressing the State of the Union: The Evolution and Impact of the President's Big Speech* (Lynne Rienner, 2006). Her research has been published in such outlets as *Social Science Quarterly*, *Political Research Quarterly*, and *PS: Political Science and Politics*. Hoffman regularly contributes political commentary as a guest on Iowa Public Radio's River to River and is frequently called upon to explain the Iowa caucuses and other intricacies of Iowa politics to the national and international media.

Stacey Hunter Hecht is associate professor of political science and chair of the political science department at Bethel University. She routinely teaches courses in American politics, public policy, and political theory, teaches as part of an interdisciplinary team in a Western civilization course, and has collaborated on courses in anthropology and history. She is the author of articles and book chapters on religion and politics, social policy, and state politics. Hecht is a regular commentator for the local media in the Twin Cities metropolitan area.

Rafael Jacob is a doctoral candidate in political science at Temple University. He has taught in the United States and Canada, most recently at the University of Ottawa's School of Policical Studies, while also serving as a fellow at the Raoul-Dandurand Chair's Center for U.S. Studies. His research interests mainly center on elections, political communication, public opinion, and voter behavior.

H. Gibbs Knotts is professor and department chair of political science at the College of Charleston. From 2000 to 2012, Knotts taught at North Carolina's Western Carolina University. The coeditor of *The New Politics of North Carolina* (UNC Press), Knotts has published numerous articles and book chapters on topics related to state politics, political behavior, and Southern politics. He is a frequent source for news media seeking commentary on Southern politics and has been quoted in major media outlets, including the *Los Angeles Times*, *Washington Post*, *USA Today*, and the *Raleigh News and Observer*. He has also written dozens of op-eds about Southern politics in newspapers across the Southeast.

Neil Kraus is professor of political science at the University of Wisconsin, River Falls. His research has focused on urban politics and policies, including two books: *Majoritarian Cities: Policy Making and Inequality in Urban Politics* (University of Michigan Press, 2013) and *Race, Neighborhoods, and Community Power: Buffalo Politics, 1934–1997* (State University of New York Press, 2000). He has also written several articles and book chapters on topics such as minority mayors, race and urban politics, local government collaboration, and urban education policy.

Chris Larimer is associate professor of political science at the University of Northern Iowa. He is the co-author of *The Public Policy Theory Primer, The Public Administration Theory Primer* (2nd and 3rd editions), and has authored or co-authored articles that have appeared in such outlets as the *American Political Science Review, Political Behavior,* and *Journal of Politics.* Larimer is a past president of the Iowa Association of Political Scientists and teaches a class every spring on Iowa politics. He is a regular guest on Iowa Public Radio's River to River and a frequent commentator on Iowa politics to a wide variety of media outlets. He also serves as the political analyst for KWWL television news and writes a blog, Politics in Iowa, for the station.

John J. McGlennon, PhD, is professor of government at the College of William & Mary and chair of the Department of Government. A specialist in American politics and government at the subnational level, he has published widely on political party activists and on Southern politics. His co-edited book, *The Life of the Parties: Activists in Presidential Nominations* (University Press of Kentucky, 1986), analyzed the attitudes of more than 17,000 state party convention delegates, and his research has been published in the *Journal of Politics, Australian Political Science Review, International Political Science Review,* and *American Politics Review,* as well as multiple edited volumes.

Scott L. McLean is professor of political science at Quinnipiac University. He is also director of the Presidential Public Service program at the university, and serves as a political analyst with the Quinnipiac University Polling Institute. McLean is active in local and Connecticut state politics on issues of food and nutrition policy. His courses and many articles focus on public opinion, political thought, political parties, and campaigns. His *Social Capital* (2002) was coedited with David Schultz and Manfred Steger. His commentary on elections most frequently appears in major national and international media such as *The Washington Post, New York Times, Wall Street Journal, The Guardian,* NPR, and CNN.

Niall J. A. Palmer gained a PhD in political science from Bristol University in 1989. His published work includes *The New Hampshire Primary and the American Electoral Process* (Praeger, 1997), *The Twenties in America* (Edinburgh University Press, 2006), and *Calvin Coolidge: Conservative Icon* (NovaScience, 2013). He has published articles in *Presidential Studies Quarterly* and the *Journal of American Studies,* and is currently working on a biography of President Warren Harding, scheduled for publication with Kansas University Press in 2018. Palmer has been lecturer in American government and political history at Brunel University since 1998.

Robert R. Preuhs (PhD) is associate professor of political science at Metropolitan State University of Denver (MSU Denver), specializing in state politics, racial and ethnic politics, and public policy. His work has been published in *The American Journal of Political Science, The Journal of Politics*, and *Political Research Quarterly*, among others, and he is the co-author of *Black-Latino Relations in U.S. National Politics: Beyond Conflict and Cooperation* (Cambridge, 2013). In 2012, Preuhs served as a consultant for a leading polling firm specializing in Latino voters, and has contributed commentary on Colorado politics to major media outlets such as the *New York Times, NPR, PBS*, and *The Financial Times*.

Norman W. Provizer (PhD, University of Pennsylvania) is a professor of political science and the director of the Golda Meir Center for Political Leadership at Metropolitan State University of Denver. He is the coeditor of three books on the Supreme Court and the author of numerous articles and book chapters on leadership.

David Schultz is a Hamline University professor of political science who teaches a wide range of American politics classes, including public policy and administration, campaigns and elections, and government ethics. Schultz is also professor at the University of Minnesota Schools of Law where he teaches election law. He is the author of thirty books and more than one hundred articles on various aspects of American politics, election law, and the media and politics, and he is regularly interviewed and quoted in the local, national, and international media on these subjects including the *New York Times, Wall Street Journal, Washington Post*, the *Economist*, and National Public Radio. His most recent book is *American Politics in the Age of Ignorance: Why Lawmakers Choose Belief Over Research*, and he is the author of the forthcoming *Election Law and Democratic Theory*. A three-time Fulbright scholar who has taught extensively in Europe, Schultz is the 2013 Leslie A. Whittington national award winner for excellence in public affairs teaching.

Andy Thangasamy (PhD) is assistant professor of political science at MSU Denver. His research areas include American politics and public policy, focusing on state policy making. He is the author of *State Policies for Undocumented Immigrants: Policy Making and Outcomes in the U.S., 1998–2005* (LFB Scholarly Publishing, 2010), and in 2012, he published his research examining state-level immigrant policy making in the *California Journal of Politics and Policy*. Thangasamy has also worked at the National Conference of State Legislatures (NCSL) in Denver where he co-authored online and print reports on state level policy making addressing health care issues.

Bas van Doorn (PhD, University of Minnesota, 2008) is associate professor in the Department of Political Science at the College of Wooster in Ohio, where he has taught since 2007. He is generally interested in the interactions between politicians, media, and citizens, and he has published on topics in media and politics, public opinion, and presidential debates.

Kenneth Warren is professor of political science and public policy at Saint Louis University. He teaches and conducts research in the area of American politics. President of *The Warren Poll* for over three decades, he has conducted numerous polls for the media, government, private clients, and politicians, including former House Majority Leader Richard Gephardt. Warren has actively studied and written about Missouri politics for decades. He is the author of many works, including *In Defense of Public Opinion Polling* (2001), *Administrative Law in the Political System*, now in its 5th edition (2011), and served as chief editor and contributor to the *Encyclopedia of U.S. Campaigns, Elections, and Electoral Behavior*, Volumes 1 and 2 (2008). His most recent work, "Regulators Throughout American History Have Been Reluctant to Regulate Cigars and the FDA Is Today, But Why?" was published in 2014 in the *Pittsburgh Journal of Environmental and Health Law*. He serves as a frequent political analyst for the local, national, and international media.

Aaron Weinschenk is assistant professor of political science at the University of Wisconsin-Green Bay in the Department of Political Science. His research focuses on campaigns and elections, voting behavior, and political engagement. To date, his research has appeared in *Political Research Quarterly*, *American Politics Research*, *Political Behavior*, and a variety of other outlets. His co-authored book, *A Citizen's Guide to U.S. Elections: Empowering Democracy in America*, will be published by Routledge Press in 2015.